AUTH N CAPTURE

Revised Edition

AN INTRODUCTION TO INDIA'S
DIGITAL PAYMENTS ECOSYSTEM

ADITYA KULKARNI

INDIA • SINGAPORE • MALAYSIA

ISBN

Hardcase 979-8-89519-514-7
Paperback 979-8-89475-613-4

AUTH N CAPTURE *(first book)*

Drawn by my daughter, Anagha

Ganga

Wonderful partner in my life's journey

Table of Contents

Foreword

The digital revolution has transformed many aspects of our lives, and nowhere is this more evident than in the realm of digital payments. India's journey towards digital payments has been both remarkable and inspiring. It is not just a technological advancement but a narrative of profound societal change. India has witnessed a paradigm shift in how people, merchants, and governments (both central & state) conduct financial transactions. The adoption of digital payments is helped by a myriad of payment products/platforms such as cards, digital wallets, UPI, BBPS, AEPS, recurring payments and cross-border payments. This transformation is the result of regulatory policies, government initiatives, innovation by payment networks and the entrepreneurial spirit of Indian startups. Digital payments industry continues to be shaped by the regulator, NPCI, banks, UPI apps, merchants, and consumers.

The world of payments is diverse, complex, and constantly evolving. In this book, Aditya provides a simplified but comprehensive explainer of various payment technologies that paved the way for this revolution. The book covers the various payment products & platforms, processes, protocols, systems, and policies providing an in-depth explanation that offers the readers a clear picture of how these complex systems work. The book offers deep and yet practical explanation to very complex concepts thereby making it easy for both novices and experts in this field. This book will be a very valuable guide for a variety of professionals such as product managers, salespersons, software engineers and payment operations persons.

As India embraces digital further, the importance of digital payments in fostering economic growth, financial inclusion and transparency in governance cannot be overstated. This book will help you understand the challenges facing today's payment systems and their future possibilities.

India's success in digital payments will be a story that will be told for several decades. It is a testament to innovation and perseverance. It is a shining example of leveraging technology to challenge the status quo and creating value for all. As you read this book, I hope you find valuable knowledge, inspiration, and a deeper appreciation of the transformative power of digital payments.

Welcome to the fascinating world of digital payments in India.

– Ramanathan RV
(Co-founder - Hyperface, Juspay)

Recommendations

"Auth N Capture: Introduction to India's Digital Payments Ecosystem" by Aditya Kulkarni offers a clear and engaging overview of India's diverse digital payments landscape. It simplifies complex topics for beginners, making it an essential read for FinTech professionals, bankers and enthusiasts who want to understand the regulatory, technological, and business aspects shaping the industry. It is a fantastic guidebook…. you will keep coming back to it.

– Kashinath Hariharan
MD & CEO, Jio Payment Solutions Ltd

Auth N Capture clearly illustrates the evolution of payments in India and details of its current features. I recommend Aditya Kulkarni's book (and blog!) for anybody interested to learn payments in India and develop product strategy more broadly.

– Matt Watts
Head of Payments BD, Plaid *(Ex-Coinbase, Payoneer, PayPal)*

India's digital payments space is vast and difficult to understand the complexity of this space. Aditya has explained the complex topics of payments in simple words. This book is a great contribution to the FinTech community.

A must read for every Digital Payments enthusiast and professional.

– Anand Dutta
Partner, Nexus Venture Partners

"Auth N Capture is an essential and comprehensive encyclopedia for Fintech professionals and students. This book serves as a one-stop destination for newcomers to the industry and empowers seasoned professionals to delve deeply into diverse topics. The rapidly evolving Fintech industry in India is well-captured in this new edition. I particularly enjoyed the in-depth exploration of UPI's transformation from a payment mode to payment rails, the landscape evolution into B2B areas, and its internationalization."

– Ravindra Govindani
Merchant Payments Product Head, AmazonPay

As someone new to the payments industry, "Auth and Capture" offers a fantastic overview of the Indian payments landscape. It helped me connect the dots and contribute significantly to my company's success.

The updated version, "Auth N Capture 2.0," delves into new payment options and other crucial details. I highly recommend this book for product managers, business managers, developers, and architects.

– Sudhindra Magadi
CTO, Wibmo

Aditya's book is a must-read for anyone venturing into the payment industry, particularly product managers. It offers a comprehensive look at the history and evolution of payments in India, making it equally valuable for those already in the field. The book stands out for its simplicity and engaging style, allowing readers to grasp complex concepts effortlessly. One of its key features is that it's designed in small, manageable chapters, making it easy to read in any order. Aditya's profound knowledge of the payment industry shines through, and his use of witty analogies makes the Payment journey not only informative but also entertaining.

– Udaykiran Joshi
SVP, Sharekhan

"With a background in technology, strategy and business development, Aditya is empowered with the right knowledge and tools to guide any professional on subject matter expertise. I see this book as a philanthropic attempt to share his knowledge of Payments 101 for the Indian landscape with budding professionals and give them deep insights into a complex ecosystem. Aditya does this with ease and simplicity, making it a learner's go to guide. I would recommend this book to working professionals, students aspiring to work in Digital India, as it would broaden their horizon and perspective immensely.!"

– Shubhra Saxena Ved
Vice President Product Management, PayU

Acknowledgements

This book is the culmination of the experiences and learnings of many people I met in my personal and professional life. A few of them taught me payments, a few guided me to excel in my job, a few showed me how to have fun, and a few helped me to be a better person.

Thank you - Rahul Mahapatra, Michael Chozhaa, Aravind Ashok, Nijesh Prakash, Shweta Mohan and Shreya Sharma for your unconditional support and friendship.

Friends and colleagues from the industry - Without you, this journey would have been boring and dull. Thank you, Madhavi Sharma, Ishan Sharma, Dhinesh Radhakrishnan, Pragya Chaturvedi, Vincent Lucas, Raunak Chaudhary, Gunjan Kaur Jabbal, Deepak Chandel, Harsha Chandra, Sparsh Jain, Shubhra Saxena Ved, Nitin Jai Singh, Naveen Borawar, Sanoop Sreedharan, Animesh Lahiri, Pratyush Ravi, Roshan Prabhakar, and Celine Wee.

In a way, I was fortunate that my post-MBA career coincided with the rise of payments in India. I worked at amazing companies, TechProcess *(now Worldline)*, Juspay, PayU, Cashfree, and Coinbase. I would like to thank the leadership of these companies - Kumar Karpe, Milind Kamat, Vimal Kumar, Ramanathan RV, Sheetal Lalwani, Reeju Datta, Akash Sinha, Manas Mishra, and Matt Watts.

I have led and nurtured teams, and I did my best to be a good leader and friend. Without my teams *(from various companies)*, my journey and learnings are incomplete. Thank you all.

Writing is difficult, writing consistently is more difficult, and writing about payments consistently is much more difficult. I would not have started the blog that paved the path for the book (and this upgraded book) without the encouragement from my wife (Ganga), Michael Chozhaa, Sagar Gubbi, and Amit Nayak. Thank you all - you are awesome!

Aravind Ashok - Thank you for reviewing the content, pushing me to complete the 2.0 version (which took me more than a year), and constantly reminding me 'why this is important'.

Special thanks to Sarthak Singh for designing an amazing cover page for the book, and for proofreading and editing.

I would like to thank the thousands of people across the world *(Yes… across the world)* who read and appreciated the blog and the book. Without your encouragement, I would not have been able to write the revised version.

Whatever little I have achieved in my life and career is because of the support and encouragement from my family. Loads of love :)

– Aditya Kulkarni

Preface

The first lesson of car driving is to remember 'A-B-C' i.e., Accelerator - Brake - Clutch.

That is how I learned driving and have been driving based on the same lesson for years. I am sure most of you did or are doing the same.

Now, we have an automatic (transmission) car. So suddenly it became only 'A-B,' and 'C' was gone.

That doesn't mean my driving lessons or experience were futile or wrong. Although there is a big change in how I drive now, the fundamentals of driving remain the same.

It has been 3 years since I published my first book. In fact, '**AUTH N CAPTURE**' was **the first book** ever published on fundamentals of India's digital payments ecosystem.

Why did I write a book on digital payments, which is dynamic and ever changing?

I have given different answers depending on who is asking and when. But the simple truth is, I just wanted to write one, as no one else did. The book was always meant to be a primer to give the basic understanding of payments in a structured manner. It helped many in doing their jobs and helped many to get the job in the payments space.

So the book did serve its intent.

Three years is a long time, especially in the payment domain and especially in India. Although the fundamentals of payments remain the same, i.e., money will move from point A to point B in the most secure, efficient, and economical way, but a lot of things have changed in terms of products, processes, and policies.

So here is the revised/updated version.

In this book, apart from the basics, I have added new topics on UPI, regulations, tokenization, CBDC, new payment flows, and many more interesting updates.

The book also covers other value-added products such as offer engine, reconciliation module, and fraud & risk management modules. Also, I have covered working of payments in more industries/sectors.

This book will also take you outside India with topics on the internationalization of Indian payment products and platforms, and I have touched upon the international payments landscape.

Payments will keep evolving, so will I be writing book 3.0 in a couple of years?

No!

I believe that only Jason Bourne deserves to have a trilogy, not a book on payments.

So, I will stop at 2.0.

If not many, a few things will change in the coming months or years. But that doesn't mean that book will become obsolete. It will be very much relevant, as fundamentals will remain the same.

The reader has to be a little flexible while reading this book and be aware that few things may change - transaction limits of products/platforms, authentication methods, payment flows, regulations, processes, and international expansion.

Even in this dynamic and evolving landscape, the book will always be a good reference for someone who wants to learn the basics of the Payments domain.

Enjoy Reading!

Chapter 1

Jargons

To understand the payments domain, one has to know certain jargons and abbreviations. Throughout this book, you will come across many jargons, so keep an eye on those. Here is a small set of jargons to start with:

Word	Explanation
2FA or AFA	Two-Factor Authentication or Additional Factor Authentication is Way to authenticate a transaction based on what the user has and what user knows. Example: With Cards - Card number and expiry date are what user has and OTP/PIN is what user knows
3DS	3 Domain Secure - is a protocol that is used to authenticate a transaction among three domains (Acquirer, issuer, and interoperability). 3DS is managed by EMVCo (Euro Pay, MasterCard, Visa). 3DS 2.0 is upgraded version that can enable issuers to do better risk-based authentication
Acquiring Bank	An acquiring bank is a bank that processes various types of payment instruments such as cards and UPI and does settlement to Payment Aggregators (PAs) or merchants. For Card Transactions: Acquiring banks uses PG to process various types of cards. For UPI Transactions: Acquiring bank uses TSP to process UPI transactions
ACS (Access Control Server)	Entity that implements 3D secure solution for the issuing bank. Basically, these entities send and validate the OTP for the issuing bank.

Word	Explanation
Alternate Credit Products	Unsecured credit products that are not based on conventional credit cards. Example: BNPL (Buy Now Pay Later) and Cardless EMIs of NBFCs
API (Application Programming Interface)	A set of functions and procedures that allow the creation of applications which access the features or data of an operating system, application, or other service.
Authentication and Authorization	Main steps of card transactions (a) Authentication: card is authenticated with OTP validation (b) Authorization: Transaction is authorized based on balance & risks (c) Capture: Transaction is captured, and the settlement process begins.
BBPS	Bharat Bill Payment System - Platform that connects billers and customers via Operating Units and Control Units. BBPS is managed by NBBL. COU: Customer Operating Units (integrates Agents and its customers to BBPS) BOU: Biller Operating Units (integrate billers to BBPS platform)
BIN	Bank Identification Number is assigned by a card scheme to each of its member financial institutions, banks, and processors. Usually the first 6 digits of the card number. Visa is upgrading BIN to 8 and 9 digits.
BNPL	Buy Now Pay Later are alternate credit products; a user gets a credit line which can use to make purchases and user has to repay the utilized amount
Card Association / Card scheme / Card Network	Payment networks linked to cards. By becoming a member of the scheme, the member (e.g., banks) can issue or acquire cards operating on the network of that card scheme Example: Visa, MasterCard, RuPay, Amex
Card Details	Attributes of the card that includes card number, expiry date and CVV2. Cardholder name (optional) Card number may vary: Visa, MasterCard, RuPay: 16 digits Amex: 15 digits

Word	Explanation
Card Not Present (CNP)	Transactions where the card is not physically present (e.g., online shopping) CNP transactions are deemed more riskier than CP (Card Present) transactions so the MDR for CNP transactions is higher compared to CP transactions
Card Present (CP)	During the payment the card is present at the Point of Sale (e.g., Card swipe done at grocery store). Usually, MDR of CP cases are lower than CNP cases
Card Tokenization	Process of replacing the card number with a unique coded string (token). Types of tokenization: Device (on mobile or other devices), Card on File (online) Token issuers: Card Issuing Bank or Card network
Card Verification Value (CVV) **Card Verification Code - CVC** **Card Security Code - CSC**	String of digits on card for the purpose of establishing the owner's identity CVV1: Part of magnetic stripe or EMV CVV2: 3 or 4 digits on back side of the card Visa, MasterCard, RuPay: 3 digits Amex: 4 digits (Card Identification Number) CVV is not mandatory for tokenized card transactions
CBDC	Central Bank Digital Currency - is digital currency issued by the central bank of a country (e.g., eRupee is CBDC issued by RBI) Variants: Wholesale (for financial institutions), Retail (for consumers & businesses)
Chargeback	A dispute raised by a credit cardholder with an issuing bank. Merchant has to provide proof to defend the chargeback and if proof is not adequate then chargeback will be in favor of customer and amount is reversed to customer
Co-branded cards	Credit or prepaid cards that are issued by a bank along with a card network and also have the company branding. Example: Amazon-ICICI-Visa Credit Card
COD (Cash on Delivery)	Customer pays in cash upon delivery of the product or service

Word	Explanation
Credit Cards	Cards that work on credit line. Spend amount is limited to the credit line and the cardholder is obliged to repay the used credit line before the due date.
Debit Cards	The cards that are linked to the customer's bank account. Purchase or ATM withdrawal is limited to available balance in the linked account.
EMI	Equated Monthly Instalments - a user can split the large purchase amount into equal parts and repay on monthly basis
Escrow Account	Special purpose non-interest earning accounts that are used as a pass-through account (e.g., used by payment aggregators to get settlement from bank and then settle to merchants) or hold customer's funds (e.g., wallet balance).
GTV or GMV	Gross Transaction Value or Gross Merchandise value is the value of transaction processed; usually measured in INR for a specific period (Rs.1 Crore per month)
IMPS	Immediate Payment Service (IMPS) is a 24x7 and real time interbank transfer platform that is managed by NPCI
Issuing Bank	A financial institution that issues cards (or payment instruments) to customers
KYC	Know Your Customer - Set documents establish a business entity or person's credentials. Example: PAN Card, Aadhar, Certificate of Incorporation, GST
MDR	Merchant Discount Rate is the fee charged by acquiring a bank to a merchant. Also called as TDR (transaction Discount Rate)
Merchant	The business entity that sells goods or services to customers or businesses. Example: eCommerce merchants, Electricity Board, Insurer, Education Institute
Merchant Category Code (MCC)	Codes assigned by network/scheme for a particular sector (E.g., Airline, retail, Education etc.). Based on the MCC, acquiring banks offers differential MDR
MID	Merchant Identification - An identification number assigned to a merchant by an acquiring bank. MID is used for managing merchant's payment life cycle - transaction, settlement, refund, chargeback.

Word	Explanation
	At times, MID is referred as Terminal Identification Number (TID)
Mobile Wallet	Digital prepaid payment instruments where consumers can load the funds and utilize them for purchases where the wallet is accepted.
NACH	National Automated Clearing House - Recurring payment solutions that enable a customer to set-up a mandate on his/her bank account. NACH has both paper and digital variants.
NEFT	National Electronics Fund Transfer is an inter-bank fund transfer system managed by RBI. NEFT is available 24x7 and works in batches of 30mins
NFC	Near Field Communication - protocol that works in proximity. Users can make transactions by holding card closer to the acceptance terminal (or POS)
Nodal Account	Special purpose non-interest earning accounts created for coordinating a special type of transaction. Nodal accounts are regulated by the RBI.
NPCI	National Payments Corporation of India is an umbrella entity set-up by RBI and Indian Banks' Association (IBA) to build and manage retail payments products and infrastructure. NPCI manages CTS, UPI, IMPS, NACH, AePS, FASTag NPCI has two subsidiaries. 1. NIPL (NPCI International Payments Ltd) for international expansion 2. NBBL (NPCI Bharat Bill Pay Ltd) to promote BBPS
On-Us, Off-Us	On-us flow: acquiring and issuing banks are the same. Off-us flow: acquiring and issuing banks are different.
P2M	Person to Merchant payments (e.g., Aravind paying his Airtel Bill)
P2P	Peer to peer / person to person transfer (e.g., Ishan transferring money to Nijesh)
P2PM	Payments done on small merchants or unorganized retail sector merchants (e.g., Aditya paying in tea shop)

Word	Explanation
PA-DSS	Payment Application Data Security Standard - Set of compliance standards and processes to be followed by the companies that intend to manage payment data
Payee	Payee or beneficiary is the person or entity that receives the funds.
Payer	Payer or remitter is the person or entity that transfers the funds to payee
Payment Aggregator (PA)	Entity that aggregates various payment modes by integrating with acquiring banks, PSPs, and banks on a single platform (e.g., BillDesk, Cashfree) Also, referred as PA-O (PA-Online)
PA - CB	Payment Aggregator Cross Border - Entities that facilitate export and import related cross-border payments
PA-P	Offline Payment Aggregator - PAs that operate in offline space or Point of Sale
Payment Gateway (PG)	Software module that is used for processing of cards. Acquiring banks use PG to process card transactions (e.g., CyberSource, MPGS)
PCI-DSS	Payment Card Industry Data Security Standard (PCI-DSS) is set of security standard for organizations that manage (access, process) cards
POS (Point of Sales)	Point of Sales (POS) is machine used to process cards at stores
Prepaid Cards	Prepaid cards are issued by PPI (Prepaid Payment Instrument) licensed entities. Depending on acceptance, prepaid cards can be closed & open loop. Variants of Prepaid cards: Gift cards, General Purpose Reloadable cards Forex cards are prepaid cards that can be loaded with non-INR currencies.
PSP	Payment Service Provider - An entity that is involved in payment processing (e.g., wallets, Payment Aggregators, Payment Gateway)

Word	Explanation
QR Code	Quick Response (CR) code is a two-dimensional code which is machine or mobile readable. QR can be embedded with beneficiary's Virtual Payment Address
RBI	Reserve Bank of India (RBI) is India's central bank and regulatory body responsible for regulating Indian banking and financial systems.
Recurring Payment Solutions	Solutions that enable customers to set-up a mandate on payment instruments to make periodic payments. Example: Utility bill, insurance premiums Solution: NACH, Standing Instruction on Cards, UPI AutoPay
Refund	A request posted by the merchant (for customer) for returning the transaction amount to the customer's source account or card.
RTGS	Real Time Gross Settlement is an inter-bank fund transfer system managed by the RBI. RTGS works 24x7 and allows transfer amounts more than Rs.2,00,000. RTGS works in gross settlement where each transfer is settled separately.
Settlement	Funds that a merchant receives from its PA or acquiring banks towards the successfully processed transactions. PA/Banks will settle funds to merchant's current, nodal or escrow a/c
SI on Cards	Standing Instruction on cards is recurring payment solution on cards where user can set recurring payment mandate
TPAP	Third Party Apps are certified Apps that provide UPI facility to users. Example: PhonePe, Cred.
TSP	Technology Service Provider - entities that provide software/technology services to banks, merchants without being part of fund movement/settlement
Unified Payments Interface (UPI)	UPI is an interoperable digital payments platform managed by NPCI. UPI allows customers to make P2P and P2M payments. User can link bank account, PPI wallet, credit card and credit line to UPI ID
UPI AutoPay	AutoPay is recurring payment solution on UPI infrastructure where user can set-up recurring payment mandate

Chapter 2

Shaping the Payments Ecosystem

Just like how our planet is constantly getting shaped by shifting of tectonic plates, the payments space is getting shaped by various forces. On the surface, things may appear normal, but those in the Payments space know how fast things move. This space is complex and dynamic.

The Payments landscape has been evolving for decades, the initial phase was slow but in the last decade the pace has increased.

Many things gave momentum to the digital payments space:

1. Smart phones and data - Most of the western countries started with desktop and then moved to mobile whereas India jumped directly to mobile revolution, and that is clubbed with data *(not the cheapest in the world but it is cheap)*.

2. National Id i.e., Aadhar Number *(Made the KYC process easier and efficient)*.

3. Jan Dhan Accounts - Government promoted opening of bank accounts.

And the most important one is the increase in economic activities and higher disposable income. With its large population, India has a huge domestic market which boosted digital commerce.

In this chapter, we will cover some of the key entities and events that have shaped and continue to shape India's payments ecosystem.

- Reserve Bank of India (RBI)
- National Payments Corporation of India (NPCI)

- Card Networks / Card Schemes
- Banks
- Payment Instrument Issuers
- Payment Service Providers / Payment Processors
- Governments (Central and State Govts)
- Other Regulators (IRDAI, SEBI)
- Mobile Platforms - Android and iOS
- Courts
- Merchants
- Customers
- Black Swan Events

2.A   Reserve Bank of India

RBI (Reserve Bank of India) is India's central bank *(Do not confuse it with the Central Bank of India, a Public Sector Bank)*. Everyone knows about the RBI as it is printed on our currency notes.

RBI does more than just printing currency notes.

The Preamble of the RBI describes the basic function of RBI as,

"To regulate the issue of Bank notes and keeping of reserves with a view to securing monetary stability in India and generally to operate the currency and credit system of the country to its advantage; to have a modern monetary policy framework to meet the challenge of an increasingly complex economy, to maintain price stability while keeping in mind the objective of growth."

That is quite a mouthful... isn't it?

Below are the primary responsibilities of RBI:

- Monetary policy
- Regulation and supervision of the banking, NBFC, and credit information companies

- Regulation of money, forex, govt securities markets, and certain financial derivatives
- Debt and cash management for Central and State Governments
- Management of foreign exchange reserves
- Foreign exchange management—current and capital account management
- Banker to banks and Banker to the Central & State Governments
- Currency management
- Developmental role
- Research and statistics
- Oversight of the payment and settlement systems

The last one is of our interest. RBI does many things for the payments space:

1. **Setting the Vision:** RBI's vision is "*To ensure that all the payment and settlement systems operating in the country are safe, secure, sound, efficient, accessible and authorized*".

   To achieve this vision, RBI sets a time bound vision *(literally publishes vision documents)* and implements policies/guidelines to achieve that vision.

   RBI has published vision documents for the following time frames: 2001-03, 2005-08, 2009-12, 2012-15, 2018 and 2019-21.

   The recent vision document was published in 2022 for the duration till 2025.

   Whatever we see today in the payments landscape is done as part of these vision documents or RBI's vision.

2. **Guidelines:** RBI issues guidelines and periodically updates these guidelines. Below are some of the important guidelines related to payments.

- Payments and Settlement Act
- PA/PG Guidelines - Domestic, Cross-border, Offline
- Prepaid Payment Instruments (PPI)
- Master KYC guidelines
- BBPS
- Card issuance, tokenization, and SI on Cards guidelines

We will talk about these guidelines in detail in **Chapter 5 - Guidelines**

3. **Licenses:**

RBI issues licenses for various entities to operate the banking, financial market, and payment related services.

Few of the licenses:

Banks (Various types)	NBFC (Non-Banking Financial Company)
Retail payment Organization	Financial Market Infrastructure
Central Counterparties	BBPS Operating Units
Card Networks	ATM Networks
White label ATM operators	Cross-Border Money Transfer (Inbound)
Prepaid Payment Instruments	Instant Money Transfers
Trade Receivables Discounting Systems	Payment Aggregators

Interesting Point: Online Payment Aggregator licensed entities can not only operate domestic online payments but also can operate **cross-border (import-export)** payments and become **BBPS Operating Units**. *(of course, with approval from RBI).*

Offline aggregators will be licensed under PA-P.

4. **Products and innovation:** RBI manages two key payment platforms - NEFT and RTGS

   Also, RBI is in forefront in launching innovative products such as:

   - Cross border trade settlement in Indian Rupees
   - eRupee - Central Bank Digital Currency (CBDC)

   RBI has set up a subsidiary 'Reserve Bank Innovation Hub' (RBIH) to promote and facilitate innovation across the financial sector.

5. **Regulatory Sandbox:** One of the biggest challenges with respect to innovation in financial services is: Regulation & Compliance. But without innovation, we cannot solve the larger problems. So, RBI provides a sandbox, which is a controlled environment where regulators and financial service providers can build solutions for certain problems. Such sandboxes help all the stakeholders to identify the risks and thus come up with processes, frameworks and solutions that can be rolled out for larger audiences.

   So far, RBI has announced 5 themes for Regulatory Sandboxes

   - 1st Cohort (Nov'19): Feature phone payments, offline payments, contactless payments
   - 2nd Cohort (Nov'20): Cross-border payments
   - 3rd Cohort (Sep'21): Micro Small Medium enterprise (MSME) lending
   - 4th Cohort (Jun'22): Prevention and mitigation of financial frauds
   - 5th Cohort (Sep'22): Neutral - Innovative products, services, and technologies cutting across various functions in the RBI's regulatory framework

6. **Statistics and Reporting**: RBI publishes data on various modes of payments including bank accounts, ATMs, debit & credit card.

7. **Measurement:** We know that digital payments are growing but, have you ever wondered- How big is it? Is the 'big', 'really big' enough? Is it growing 'big' uniformly?

To answer these questions RBI has come up with the **Digital Payments Index (DPI)** to measure the extent of digitization of payments and RBI will publish DPI data on semi-annual basis

The RBI-DPI comprises five parameters with different weightage (As shown below)

Payment Enablers	Payment Infrastructure – Demand Side	Payment Infrastructure – Supply Side	Payment Performance	Consumer Centricity
Internet	Debit Cards	Bank Branches	Digital Payment Systems - Volume	Awareness and Education
Mobile	Credit Cards	Business Correspondents	Digital Payment Systems - Value	Declines
Aadhar	Prepaid Payment Instruments	ATMs	Unique Users	Complaints
Bank Accounts	Customer Registered – Mobile & internet Banking	POS Terminals	Paper Clearing	Frauds
Participants		Intermediaries	Currency in Circulation	System Downtime
Merchants	FASTags	QR Codes	Cash Withdrawals	
25%	**10%**	**15%**	**45%**	**5%**

Source: https://rbidocs.rbi.org.in/rdocs/content/pdfs/PR87401012021.pdf

DPI from Mar'18 (base period) till Sep'23

Mar'18	Mar'19	Sep'19	Mar'20	Sep'20	Mar'21	Sep'21	Mar'22	Sep'22	Mar'23	Sep'23
100	153.47	173.49	207.84	217.74	270.59	304.06	349.30	377.46	395.57	418.77

2.B   NPCI

National Payments Corporation of India (NPCI) is an umbrella organization for retail payments in India. NPCI was set up with the guidance and support of RBI and Indian Banks Association (IBA). NPCI has launched many payments platforms that changed India's payments landscape.

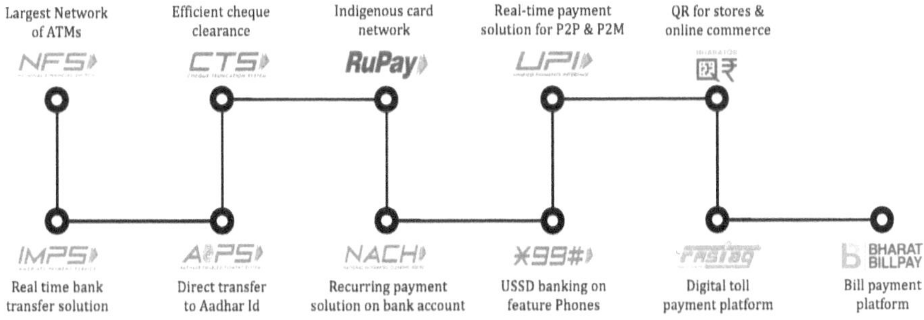

NPCI has floated two subsidiaries:

a.   NPCI International payments Limited (NIPL) to promote these payment products globally.

b.   NPCI Bharat BillPay Limited (NBBL) to manage BBPS

NPCI manages >70% of retail payments on its platforms, so imagine the impact if NPCI goes down for a couple of hours or even for a few minutes!

Has NPCI become too big to fail? - That is what RBI thought and to reduce the dependency on NPCI, RBI called for the formation of NUE (New Umbrella Entities).

An NUE is a consortium of various companies that are experienced in the payments space in various capacities. The selected NUE(s) are expected to build infrastructure, platforms, or products to drive growth of digital payments.

Below is the list of NUE groups *(Looks like an IPL tournament among companies!)*

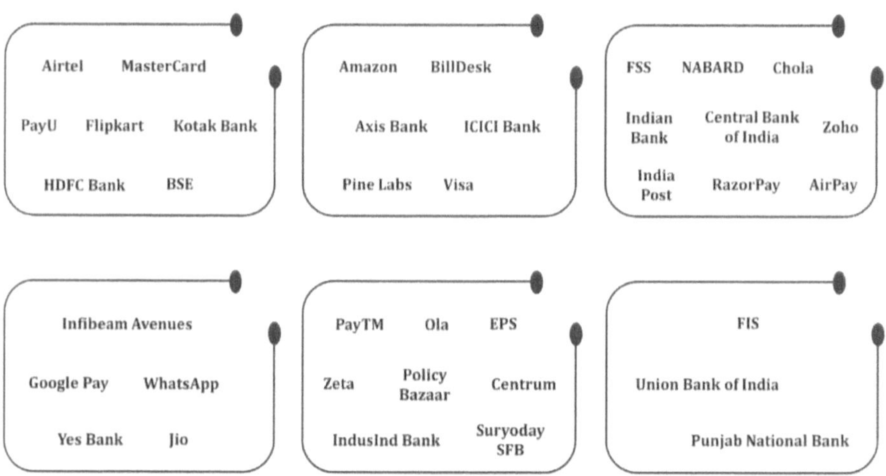

NUE discussion created a lot of buzz as everyone was expecting something big. The big surprise was SBI and HDFC were kept away from participating in NUE.

In Jan '23, the RBI put NUE licensing on hold as none of the participants proposed anything groundbreaking and not sure if NUE discussion will take shape any time soon.

2.C   Card Networks

Card networks or schemes are the entities that facilitate card issuance, security (2FA, tokenization), processing, settlement, dispute management framework, and card acceptance.

Card schemes earn different types of fees for facilitating these services: (1) BIN fees (2) Certification fees (3) Interchange fee, which is typically a percentage (%) of transaction value.

Visa, MasterCard, RuPay, Diners and Amex are the leading card schemes in India. 'Diners' doesn't have a direct presence in India and is operated by HDFC bank. Other big card schemes such as JCB, Discover, Union Pay are yet to make a splash in the Indian market.

Few ways the card schemes influence the payments ecosystems: card issuance *(including co-branded cards)*, issuance capabilities *(e.g., NFC capability)*, platform features *(e.g., tokenization)*, security *(e.g., 3DS 2.0)*, commercials *(plays a role in setting interchange for different merchant categories)* and merchant acceptance *(type of merchants that are allowed)*.

Other services offered by Visa and MasterCard:

- Disbursement: Visa Direct and Master Money Send are disbursement solutions where funds can be moved from account to the card or from one card to another card. The solution is used for instant refunds and credit card bill payments.

- Checkout: mVisa and Masterpass are checkout services of these schemes *(imagine them as card wallets for easier checkout experience)*.

2.D Banks

Banks are the most important stakeholders in the Payments Ecosystem. They are the ones who provide APIs for various services such as Payment Gateway, Recurring Payments and Payouts, and banks are quintessential in money movement.

Every bank operates with different levels of compliance processes. Although they adhere to the guidelines of RBI, Govt of India, and card networks, they also decide on what type of merchants they would like to work with or want their partner Payment Service Providers / Payment Aggregators to work with.

E.g.: SBI doesn't allow wallet loading, HDFC doesn't allow skill-based gaming.

Banks are consolidated either on their *own (e.g., ING Vysya merger with Kotak, Citi sold its retail business to Axis Bank)* or mandate from the

Govt. of India *(e.g., All State Banks are consolidated under State Bank of India)*. Whenever such consolidation happens, the integration needs to be upgraded and customers need to be transitioned. Considering such mergers are rolled over a period of 1-2 years, there is enough time for everyone to get adjusted.

One of the biggest jolts the payments ecosystem had was in March 2020 when Yes Bank was put under moratorium. This move affected all services such as UPI, card PG, payout and NACH of the bank that are used by various Payment Aggregators (PAs), merchants, and customers. The impact of the moratorium was highest on PhonePe as it didn't have a backup or secondary bank to process UPI, so PhonePe was blacked-out for a couple of days till they went live with ICICI Bank.

Bank and payment players share unique relationships - They cooperate, co-create, co-sell while competing with each other.

2.E   Payment Instrument Issuers

Apart from banks, there are other entities that issue payment instruments such as digital wallets (e.g., Mobikwik), pay later products (e.g., Simpl), and cardless EMI products (e.g., Bajaj Finance) etc.

Such products cannibalize the share of traditional payment instruments such as net-banking or credit cards but also increase the pie *(convert cash orders to online)*.

These companies are not immune to changing customer behavior, regulatory frameworks, and intense competition. Example: Prepaid card issuers and many of the mobile wallets took a severe hit over a period due to competition from UPI and mandatory KYC guidelines.

But that doesn't mean the new payment instruments issuers won't arrive at the 'great Indian Payments Party' - Expect more credit/EMI products in the coming days which will keep adding diversity to our payments landscape.

2.F   Payment Service Providers and Payment Aggregators

Payments is a super competitive space with multiple players, with a high possibility of commoditization of services. So, companies keep innovating, build value added services or go aggressive on commercials *(and start price wars)*.

Also, the industry is not new to mergers, acquisitions, or strategic investments.

- Ingenico initially acquired EBS (e-Billing Systems) and then acquired TechProcess Payment Services Ltd. And then Worldline acquired Ingenico.

- Cashfree acquired Zecpe (one-click checkout company) and invested in Telr (UAE)

- RazorPay acquired EzeTap (mobile POS) and acquired Curlec (Malaysia)

- Pine Labs acquired Setu (APIs for BBPS)

- PayU has acquired Citrus (PA), Wibmo (ACS solution) and PaySense (Lending)

Innovations, acquisitions, and price wars make this space interesting, dynamic, and messy.

2.G   Merchants

From neighborhood small shops to large eCommerce companies, from government utility companies to education institutes, all types of businesses adopted digital payments.

Various payment modes played their own role in popularizing digital payments among merchants (e.g., PayTM wallet during demonetization (2016)).

UPI turned out to be the real game changer because it is simple to use *(for customers)* and cheapest *(for the merchant)*. Millions of QRs enabled the smallest of small merchants to accept digital payments in the most economical way.

Even the enterprise merchants started promoting UPI by showing it more prominently on their checkout pages *(and hiding net-banking options)*.

Whenever something changes in the ecosystem (regulation, new product/feature, or process), merchants have to adopt. Few examples:

- Card Tokenization: Merchants have to redo integration and encourage/nudge users to tokenize their cards.
- Digital lending Guidelines: Merchants have to comply with new guidelines and change their payout/loan disbursement model *(apart from hundred other things)*

In nutshell, businesses or merchants are as dynamic as the payment ecosystem itself. So, merchants also keep adjusting to both internal and external factors.

2.H Mobile Platforms

As mobiles have become an important channel of payments, mobile platforms such as Android (Google) and iOS (Apple) wield bigger power in the overall ecosystem.

In 2018, Google banned auto-reading of OTPs unless the companies followed a prescribed SMS format. This had a significant impact on FinTechs, merchants who had SDKs to auto-read OTP. Eventually, Google relaxed the rule to read bank OTPs (only after whitelisting of Apps) but for other use cases, the Apps had to implement Google's policies.

Google and Apple enforce gaming Apps to use in-house payment infrastructure and charge up to 30% fees for digital goods. To avoid it, the gaming merchants do not distribute their Apps through Play Store or App Store. Only in 2022, Google Play Store allowed Fantasy Sports gaming merchants to use their own payment providers.

2.I Government

Both State and Central Governments are important stakeholders in boosting digital payments as well as shaping the industry with policies.

One of the biggest of such policies was 'demonetization' on 8-Nov-2016. Government of India nullified Rs.1000 and Rs.500 currency notes. People and businesses had no other option but to use digital payments until new currency notes were available.

Although digital payments have increased manifold since then, so has the cash. Irrespective of that, demonization forced people to change their payments behavior.

GOI's role is huge in the growth of UPI and RuPay cards by enforcing zero MDR. Also, earmarked budgets to subsidize UPI and RuPay small value transactions. For Financial Year 2023-24, Govt of India has kept a budget of Rs.1500 Crore.

Under 269SU of Income Tax Act, all businesses with turnover of more than Rs.50 Crore are mandated to provide RuPay, UPI and QR as collection options.

GOI has also taken decisions related to certain sectors such as banning e-cigarettes (2019), Chinese lending and gaming Apps (ongoing since 2020), Forex trading Apps (2022).

State Governments also have shaped the domain by either promoting FinTech companies or banning certain sectors *(e.g.: Ban on skill-based gaming by Andhra, Telangana, Orissa, Sikkim etc.)*

2.J Courts

India's independent judiciary system *(High Courts and the Supreme Court)* have issued judgements for certain sectors that have indirectly impacted the payments domain.

E.g.: Allowing skill-based games *(e.g., Rummy and Fantasy Sports)*

2.K   Industry Specific Regulators

There are regulators who govern specific sectors.

IRDA *(Insurance Regulatory and Development Authority of India)* for the insurance sector and SEBI *(The Securities and Exchange Board of India)* for the regulated investments sector.

These regulators also have guidelines that impact the payments related to these specific sectors.

E.g.: As per SEBI guidelines, regulated investment can be done only (1) by the registered bank account of the user (2) no credit products or wallets to be used for investment (3) investor's funds for Mutual Fund purchases shouldn't go through Mutual Fund Distributors' account (4) UPI One time mandate *(Single block multiple debit)* for secondary market investment.

2.L   Customers

Yes, we are the most important stakeholder in the payment ecosystem. What if we decide not to pay online? What if we prefer cash over UPI?

India has come a long way in digital payments because of users. As users, we started trusting these online payments systems, we started trusting online businesses.

All these regulations, innovations and price wars are for us. To provide us a secure, reliable, and economical way to transfer funds to our family or friends, buy products online, book flight tickets, pay our bills or play only rummy.

No doubt digital payments make our lives better but also, there is a 'dark side to digital payments'. There are bad actors who exploit the users and defraud them. It is extremely important that customers should safeguard themselves.

Few basic things: (1) do not share OTP or PIN (2) do not click on unknown links (3) do not share your PAN or Aadhar and most importantly, if something goes wrong then DO NOT PANIC! Just reach out to your bank or PA or Cybercrime Police immediately to find the remedy.

2.M Black Swan Events

These are unprecedented events that no one could have anticipated, and no one would have factored in their business models. Couple of recent Black Swan events

- Demonetization (8-Nov-2016): It was a positive boon to payments companies especially for PayTM wallet *(Remember, UPI was still not matured at that time)*. But all and all, demonetization boosted digital payments in India.

- Covid-19 pandemic: The entire world changed within weeks in March 2020. The pandemic boosted digital payments and changed our payments behavior to a large extent. Pandemic affected few sectors positively such as OTT, Gaming, hyperlocal (grocery), and EdTech, while few sectors came to grinding halt such as Travel & Hospitality.

Closing Remarks:

We are still at the beginning of the payments journey. The payment ecosystem will keep changing as business models keep evolving, many payment players compete to gain the market share, and RBI and NPCI will keep envisioning new products and new guidelines that will impact *(positively and/or negatively)* FinTechs/Payment Companies.

We are in the most interesting times of the Great Indian Payments Journey!

Chapter 3

Payment Players

Let's start with the fundamental meaning of 'Payments'.

At one end there is a payee *(one who receives the money)* and on the other end there is payer *(one who is paying)*. Payee and payer can be a person, business (merchant), or Government entity.

In simple words, 'online payment' is all about moving money from payer to payee.

Not just that, this movement of money has to be done securely, efficiently, and economically!

There are companies who are in the business of this money movement, and they make money to perform these activities. To make a payment, a customer needs a 'Payment Instrument' that is issued by 'Payment Instrument Issuer' and to process those instruments, merchants would need 'Payment Service Providers/Processors'.

3.A   Payment Instrument Issuers

As the name suggests, these are the entities that issue payment instruments that a user or a company can use to make payments.

Here are a few of the payment instruments:

- Cards (Credit Card, Debit card, prepaid card)
- Bank accounts
- UPI
- Wallets
- Alternate credit product (cardless EMI and pay later products)
- Cash (*Yes, it is also payment instrument*)
- Crypto Currencies
- Central Bank Digital Currencies (CBDC)
- Cheque / Demand Draft
- Reward Points

Banks *(Cards, bank account)*, NBFCs *(Alt credit products)*, and PPIs *(wallets)* are the important payment instrument issuers.

Read details about various payment instruments in ***Chapter 4***.

3.B   Payment Service Providers (PSPs)

The acceptance mechanism to process or accept a payment instrument is provided by Payment Service Providers

A set of APIs that are integrated among '**merchant <> Payment Service provider <> Payment Instrument Issuer**' to facilitate the transactions, settlements, and refunds.

There are various types of PSPs depending on their integration with merchant:

1. Payment Instrument Issuer = Payment Service Provider

ONLY the payment instrument issuer can process that payment instrument. That means, merchant needs to have direct integration with these entities.

Example: Wallets, Net-banking, BNPL, Cardless EMI, Amex cards.

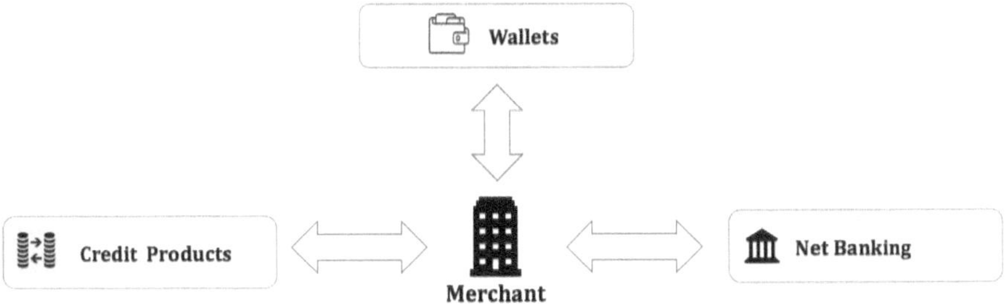

Example: To process a BNPL (Example: Simpl), the merchant will have to do direct integration with the BNPL issuer (i.e., Simpl) or to facilitate SBI net-banking, an integration with SBI is required.

As per NPCI Circular of Mar-2023, PPI wallets (e.g., PayTM, Mobikwik) can be linked to UPI and users can make payment via PPI wallet balance. So, UPI is bringing interoperability and removing the constraint of direct integration.

2. Acquiring Banks

These entities process certain types of payment instruments. These are intermediaries who connect merchants with issuing entities.

Example: Card Acquiring Banks (that use PG-Payment Gateway) process certain types of credit & debit cards, or UPI Acquiring Banks processes UPI transactions.

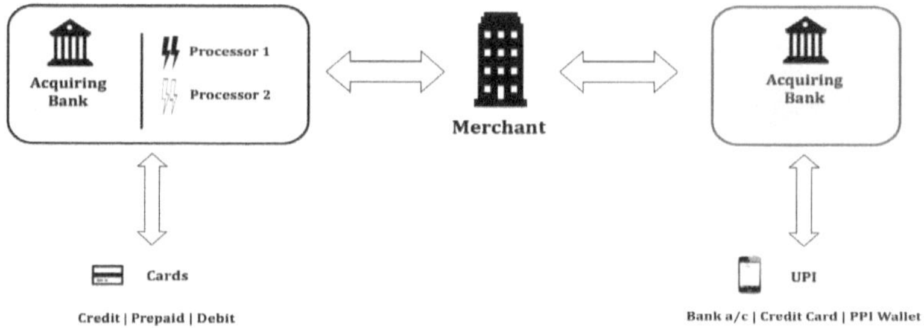

Example: To process Visa and MasterCard credit & debit cards, a merchant has to integrate with *(at least)* one acquiring bank (e.g., HDFC, Axis, ICICI etc.) which in turn will use PG (Payment Gateways - FSS, ISG, MPGS or CyberSource) for processing.

NOTE: There are few disadvantages with the above two methods. If merchant wants to increase payment coverage (support multiple payment instruments/payment modes),

- Merchant has to do multiple integrations that means extra effort.
- Operation effort increases due to multiple settlement from each entity.

To address these issues, Payment Aggregators (PAs) were born.

3. Payment Aggregators (PA)

As the name suggests, a Payment Aggregator (PA) aggregates multiple payment processing entities *(acquiring banks - for cards & UPI, net-banking, wallets, and alternate credit products - BNPL, Cardless EMIs)* on a single platform and offers bundled solution/platform to merchants that increases payment coverage and reduces integration effort while doing single settlement for all payment instruments.

Also, PAs bundle recurring payment solutions *(NACH, UPI AutoPay and SI on cards)* by partnering with acquiring bank(s) and sponsor bank(s).

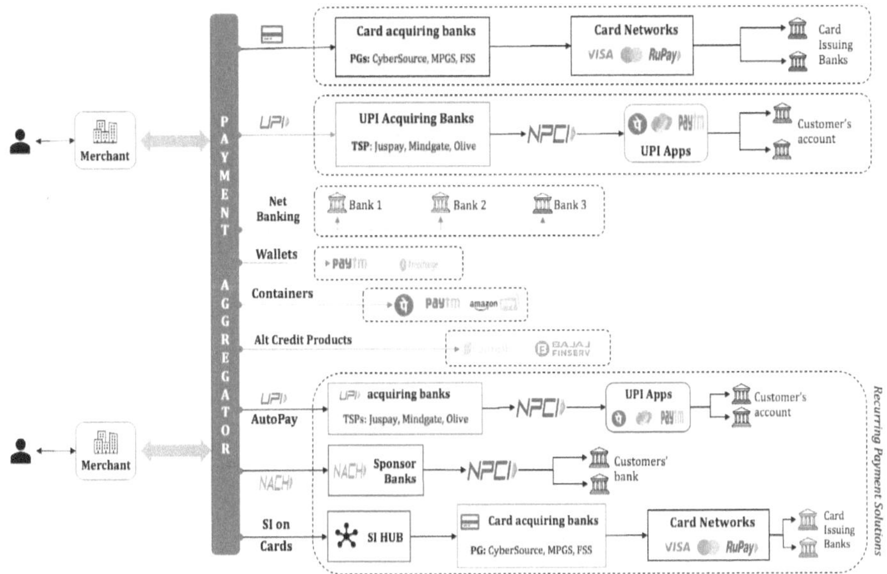

Only RBI licensed entities are allowed to operate Payment Aggregation business.

Few of the PAs are BillDesk, Cashfree, RazorPay, Worldline, CC Avenue (50+ more)

Note: People refer Payment Aggregators (PA) as Payment Gateway (PG), but they are not the same. No harm in referring but keep in mind that PG is card processing software (e.g., CyberSource, MPGS etc.) and PA is a platform that bundles multiple processing entities to perform various payment modes and does settlement (e.g., BillDesk, Cashfree etc.)

Payment Aggregators that support online merchants are called online payment aggregators (PA-O) and PAs that facilitate payments for offline payments/POS are called offline or physical payment aggregators i.e., PA-P.

Note: I will refer to Online Payment Aggregators as Payment Aggregators, PA, or PA-O.

4. Payment Containers

These can be considered as 'lite-payment aggregators'; they also partner with acquiring banks, PAs acquiring PSP and wallets on a single platform. A container can enable users to create VPA, tokenize cards (device token), have a wallet and even BNPL products.

A user can make P2P (person to person) or P2M (person to merchant) transactions. *(Subject to capabilities and restrictions)*

Examples: PhonePe, AmazonPay, Google Pay, Cred Pay

For some strange reasons, payment containers are clubbed under *'Wallets'*. Doesn't matter as long as you know the difference.

The primary difference between a Payment Aggregator and Payment Container is that the user has to create an account with the Payment Container and login to that account every time before accessing the payment instrument to make the payment.

A merchant can integrate directly with the Payment Container or through PA.

Impact of Card on File Tokenization: Containers used to allow users to '**Save Cards**' and saved cards can be used on any merchant where the payment container is enabled. This was one of the USPs of a payment container as the user doesn't have a vault card on every merchant site/App.

As per tokenization guidelines, cards should be tokenized specific to a merchant. So, containers cannot tokenize cards that will work for all merchants.

Interestingly, all the payment containers (PhonePe, Cred, AmazonPay, Google Pay) have applied for PA (Payment Aggregator) license.

5. **TSP (Technology Service Provider)/Wrapper/Orchestrator**

These entities provide a platform for merchants to integrate with multiple online Payment Aggregators, Payment Containers, Wallets, and other types of payment processors along with features such as unified 'card token vault', unified dashboard, routing engines etc.

TSPs are not involved in fund settlements or managing disputes/chargebacks.

Orchestration or TSP service providers: Juspay, Nimbbl, Cashfree, RazorPay, PayTM

Read more about wrappers/TSPs/orchestrator in *Chapter 18*

6. **TPAPs / UPI Apps**

The payments landscape is incomplete without the mention of TPAPs (Third Party Applications) and UPI Apps as they play an important role.

TPAPs/UPI Apps are used by consumers to make P2P transfers, P2PM payments *(QR scan & pay at brick-and-mortar stores)* and P2M payments *(payments on merchants' websites and Apps)*

TPAPs are managed by FinTechs and any consumer facing entities. TPAPs work in partnership with sponsor bank(s) and are certified by NPCI.

Example: PhonePe, Google Pay, Amazon Pay, Cred, Flipkart, Groww etc.

Banks also have their own UPI Apps. Example: HDFC PayZapp, iMobile Pay by ICICI

A user can create VPA/UPI ID and can link various payment sources such as bank a/c, credit card, PPI wallet, credit line, UPI Lite wallet.

Read more about UPI in ***Chapter 4.E, 8.C, 10.D, 13.C***

Closing Remarks:

Merchants can have integration with any of the above Payment Service Providers or a combination of Service Providers to process payment instruments.

- A wallet can be integrated directly or through a Payment Aggregator
- Cards can be processed by direct integration with the Acquiring Bank or by Payment Aggregator who uses the Acquiring bank.

All this may sound a bit confusing, but it is not.

I would say the payments ecosystem can be likened to Matryoshka Dolls (Russian Nesting Dolls), one payments entity within another one (and so on) but operating with the aim of moving money from point A to point B.

Chapter 4

Payment Instruments

Payment Instruments are the means/methods that are available with customers to make payment. These instruments are issued by various banks and non-banking entities (PPIs, FinTechs etc.).

Few of the Payment Instruments:

- Cards: Credit, Debit and Prepaid
- Wallets
- Online Banking account
- UPI
- Alternate credit products (e.g., Buy now Pay later, Cardless EMI)
- Cash *(Yes, still an important payment instrument)*
- Crypto currencies *(Not of great relevance especially in India but will cover this)*
- Central Bank Digital Currency (CBDC)
- Cheque
- Reward Points

These Payment instruments are linked to a source.

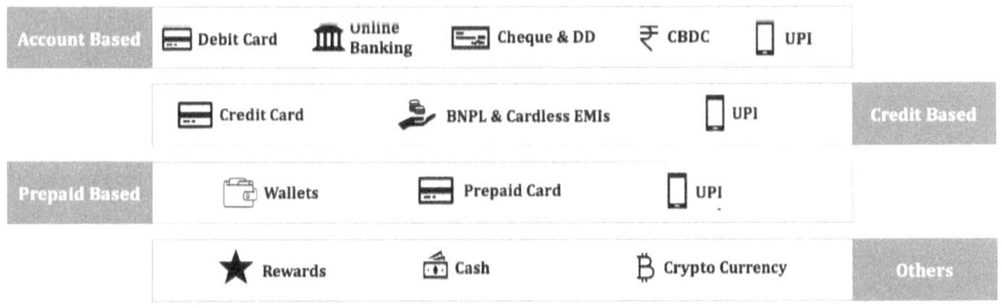

- **Bank Account**: Customer's spend amount is limited to available balance in the account.

- **Prepaid**: The amount to be loaded to the instrument and then the user can spend within the available balance.

- **Credit Line**: Customers will have an approved credit line and can spend within that credit limit. And customers are obliged to pay back the credit amount that he/she has availed. Any delay in repayment will attract interest fees.

- **Others**: Instruments that are not based on the above three traditional sources. Example: cash, reward points, and crypto currencies

Note: UPI is omni-present as it can be linked to bank a/c, credit card, credit line, and PPI wallet

In the next few chapters, we will cover various payment instruments and their workings.

4.A   Credit Cards and Debit Cards

There are three types of cards: Credit Cards, Debit Cards, and Prepaid cards.

In this chapter, I will cover credit and debit cards.

a.   Credit Cards

Credit cards are issued by scheduled banks, selected non-banks (Amex) or NBFCs *(SBI Cards and BOB Cards)* along with card networks (Visa, MasterCard, RuPay, Amex, Diners).

Based on the card issuing entity's criteria, qualified customers receive a credit line (or credit limit). The credit limit can be used for purchases at merchant terminals (both in-store and online) and for cash withdrawals at ATMs.

Here are a few features of credit cards:

- Credit limit: Customers get credit limit which depends on their profile (income, profession, and credit score etc.)

- Spending Rules: There can be limits on spend across various channels (in store, online and cash withdrawal). Also, cards can have restrictions on international payments.

- Credit Period: Customer is obliged to repay the spent amount on or before the due date *(billing is done once a month)*. Delayed repayment or non-repayment attracts charges *(interest on credit)* and will impact the customer's credit score.

Types of Credit Cards: Consumer Credit cards (issued to customers) and Corporate Credit Cards.

Also, there are co-branded credit cards that are launched by a bank for a brand (company) along with the card network *(e.g.: Swiggy-HDFC-MasterCard, Amazon-ICICI-Visa)*

In Apr-2022, RBI issued new regulations for credit card issuance that focuses on consumer safety, transparency, and data privacy.

Read *Chapter 5.B* – Regulations for details.

Cardholders have an option to convert the transaction amount into EMI (Equated Monthly Instalments) for specific tenure. EMI conversation can be done during transactions *(supported by all major card issuing banks)* or offline *(by contacting the bank or on the bank's portal).*

Note: NPCI is wants to provide EMI conversion feature for credit cards that are linked to UPI

b. Debit Cards

Debit cards are issued by banks along with the card network. The debit card is linked to the customer's bank account. Customer's spending *(purchases and cash withdrawals)* is limited to the balance in the account. Even debit cards have a few rules with respect to the limit on daily cash withdrawal or spends on online purchase or usage territory that are dictated by the bank or user can configure those.

Cardholders can convert the transaction amount into EMIs for specific tenure. EMI conversation can be done during transactions; debit card EMI is supported by few banks.

Know Your Card:

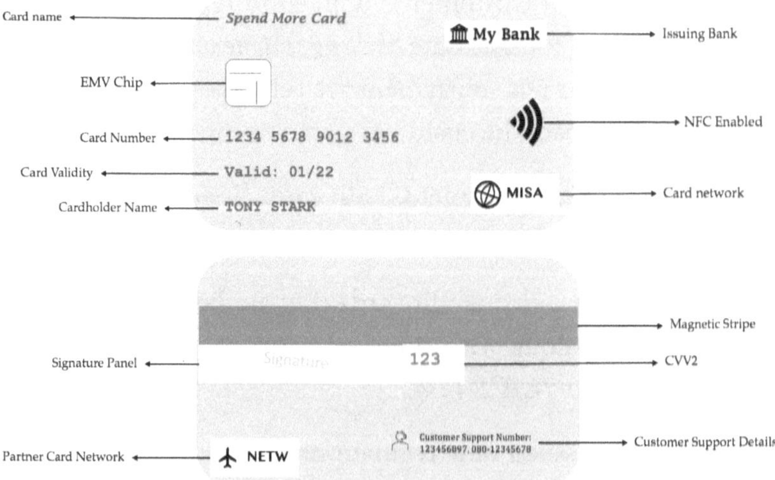

1. Card Name: Specifies some sort of branding (Regalia, Super Saver etc.)

2. Issuing Bank: Bank that has issued the card (e.g., ICICI, HDFC)

3. Card network: Entities *(e.g., Visa, RuPay)* that define the issuance, acceptance, operational, security protocols, integrations, and dispute management framework.

4. Partner card network: Few cards have a partner network. Such cards are accepted on the partner network(s). Example: RuPay' s partner network is 'Discover'. That means a RuPay card can be accepted on terminals that accept Discover. Such partnerships increase the acceptance network especially in different geographies/countries.

5. Card Number: This is the unique number of the card. Length of card number can vary from 13 to 19 digits depending on the card network. Example: Visa Credit card that I have has 16 digits and Amex has 15 digits

   - First digit is MII (Major Industry Identifier). Amex: 3, Visa: 4, MasterCard: 5

   - 1–6 digits are BIN (Bank Identification Number) or IIN (Issuer Identifier Number) and these numbers identify the issuing bank.

   - 7th to the last but 1 digit are unique card account number.

   - Last digit is the checksum digit that validates the correctness of the card number. Checksum is calculated basis the Luhn's algorithm or Mod10 algorithm.

   Note: Few of the card schemes are issuing 8-to-11-digit BINs

6. Expiry date: Validity period of the card for usage, and beyond that period the plastic card will turn into ONLY PLASTIC

7. Cardholder name: Name of the cardholder printed on the card. Sometimes there won't be any name (E.g., Debit card that is part of the welcome kit when you open a new bank a/c)

8. EMV Chip: EMV (Euro Pay-MasterCard-Visa) is a global standard to provide better security through chip-based transactions. The card is inserted in the POS machine to process the transaction.

9. Magnetic Stripe: The stripe behind the card that has encoded card details and can be swiped in a POS machine to process the transaction.

10. NFC: The symbol shows that the card is enabled for transaction on NFC (Near Field Communication) technology. A user can Tap on NFC enabled POS and make the transaction. User doesn't need to enter the PIN for a transaction amount up to Rs.5000.

11. CVV2/CVC2: Card Verification Code (CVC) or Card Verification Value (CVV) is 3 digits (for Visa, MasterCard, RuPay - printed on back of the card) or 4 digits (for Amex - printed on the front of card) CVV2 is not mandatory for tokenized or saved cards.

    Note: CVV1/CVC1 is encoded on EMV Chip and magnetic stripe; It is validated during POS transactions

12. Signature Panel: The cardholder can sign on this panel. Earlier days when 2FA (PIN prompt) was not mandatory the cashier could cross-check the signature on the reverse of the card with signature on receipt. But now it has no value.

13. Customer support details - For cardholders to reach out to those numbers for support.

Note: Cards can be virtual or physical; Physical cards can be of plastic, metal, or wood!

Entities that play role in card processing:

a. Card Management System (CMS) platform:

   • Lifecycle management: issuance, activation, hot listing, blocking, issuance of add-on card, reissuance of card and cancellation of card

- Risk Management: Velocity Checks and risk checks

- Usage Rules: Spend controls, spend channel control and geographic control.

b. Card Switch: Piece of software that connects the issuing bank (CMS) to the card network.

c. Authentication system: Mechanisms deployed to validate the transaction. PIN for POS transactions and OTP/password for online transactions. ACS (access control server) companies (e.g., Wibmo) provide this authentication service for online transactions.

d. Acquiring Bank: Banks that use PG *(Payment Gateway)* to process the card transaction when the customer uses the card on the merchant terminal (Physical and online)

2nd Factor Authentication and 3D Secure

We all are familiar with the OTP that we receive during card transactions. Entering and validating OTP is part of 2nd Factor Authentication (2FA) or Additional Factor Authentication (AFA).

All card networks *(Visa, MasterCard, Amex, RuPay etc.)* have their own protocol/process for 2FA which pretty much does the same thing. So, let's focus the oldest of those i.e., 3 D Secure

Visa and MasterCard implemented 2FA on 3DS (3 Domains Secure) protocol.

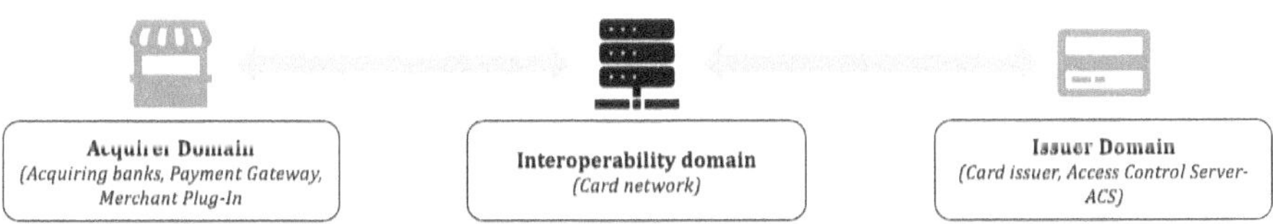

In simple words, 3DS protocol establishes authentication among these three domains.

Little bit of history:

- 3DS was conceptualized in 1999.

- In 2001, Arcot System *(later acquired by CA Technologies)* implemented it for Visa *(Verified by Visa and later renamed as Visa Secure)*. Then MasterCard rolled out Secure Code.

- 3DS standard is managed by ***EMV Co*** (Euro Pay-MasterCard-Visa).

- On 1ˢᵗ May 2012, 2FA became mandatory for card payments in India.

3DS 1.0 did its job as sufficiently as any protocol was expected to do!

But things have changed — we have moved from desktop browsers to mobile Apps, tabs and other IoT devices. Fraudsters have also become smarter so the 'risks' in payments systems have increased. It is important to provide a seamless and yet, highly secure payment experience.

So naturally, in 2016, EMVCo, launched the next variant i.e., 3DS 2.0.

- 3DS 1 is already phased out globally (except in India and Nepal).

- In Dec-2022, international card transactions *(customers outside India using their home country cards to buy things on Indian merchants)* migrated to 3DS 2.0.

- The gradual roll out of 3DS 2.0 for domestic cards started from the last quarter of 2023.

Special about 3DS 2.0

- Provides capabilities to pass more data pointers *(e.g., device info, customer info, merchant info etc.)* to the issuing banks which can be used to make decisions to reduce the risks.

- Allows banks to implement various methods for 2FA such as biometric based (face Id, retina scan, voice based, thumb print etc.) *(basically… payments in James Bond style!)*

Note: In many countries, 2FA is not mandatory but used only as a step-up challenge for 'high risk' transactions. With 3DS 2.0, banks will be able to profile the risks in a much better way and impose step-up challenges more effectively.

Changes in card transaction flow:

3DS 1.0 has only authentication and authorization legs whereas 3DS 2.0 has an additional leg i.e., Device Data collection *(along with Authentication and Authorization legs)*

Impact on participants:

- Acquiring banks and issuing banks have to implement 3DS 2.0.

- Customers: No changes *(You will continue to get the OTP that you are used to, and we are still far away from enjoying silent authentication methods)*

- Merchant — Nothing much

  Note: Merchants who have Direct OTP *(where OTP is entered on the merchant's page)* will be impacted. Either merchant has to use new APIs or implement EMVCo certified SDK.

The onus of pushing banks to migrate to 3DS 2.0 is on Visa and MasterCard. They may talk about penalties if banks do not meet the deadline *(but not sure if they can impose it)*.

RBI is not involved in rolling out 3DS 2.0 — RBI doesn't care whether it is 3DS 2.0 or 3DS 3.142 as long as the transactions follow a safe and secure 2FA or AFA.

Closing Remarks:

Every bank account is connected to a debit card. So, debit card numbers will continue to grow and there is a shift from Visa/MasterCard to RuPay network.

Along with a 30–45-day credit period, conversions to EMI for large ticket purchases, revolving credit *(move the due amount to next cycle)* and reward programs continue to fuel growth of credit card numbers *(count and volume)*.

In the light of the latest credit card issuance guidelines of RBI, card issuing banks are forbidden to have exclusive issuance contracts with card networks and users should be given the option to select card networks. This may fuel the growth of RuPay credit cards.

In the online payments space, UPI is cannibalizing the share of debit cards.

Now, a user can link a credit card to UPI and use it on the UPI acceptance network. At present, the feature is available on RuPay credit cards. Definitely, this model will continue to grow as more card issuing banks are added and more features such as EMI conversion and reward points are supported. Just one problem i.e., unlike UPI on bank account, UPI on credit card is not free and this MDR of UPI + Credit card *(which is same as regular credit card MDR)* may be a small hiccup for merchants who are used to 'zero MDR UPI'.

It will be interesting to see how long Visa and MasterCard will stay away from the UPI infrastructure.

Also, a user can link the **credit line** to the UP Id/VPA. That means, no need for a plastic card. This model is in its early stage. So, only time will tell whether UPI will cannibalize the credit cards and whether UPI and RuPay will further reduce the share of Visa and MasterCard.

4.B   Prepaid Cards and Wallets

In this chapter, we will talk about prepaid cards and wallets as both share many common traits:

- Issued under PPI (Prepaid Payment Instruments) License of RBI

- Spend is limited to the load or balance available on the instrument.

- Neither customer nor the PPI issuer earns interest on the balance amount as funds are parked in a non-interest earning nodal account

- Can be issued after completion of KYC (Minimum KYC: allows balance up to Rs. 10,000 and Full KYC allows balance up to Rs. 2,00,000)

Refer to *Chapter 5.B* for PPI guidelines.

There are few differences:

- Form factor - prepaid cards can be physical or virtual, whereas wallets are virtual.

- Acceptance method - wallet can't be used on a POS machine, but card can be swiped.

- Cards come with Expiry Date, but wallets don't (technically)

    Note: If the wallet is not used for a year or so then the wallet issuer may deactivate the wallet, but it can be reactivated by following the issuer's process.

Types and Variants:

There are two main types of prepaid payment instruments:

- **Non-reloadable**: Funds can be added ONLY ONCE but can be used multiple times before the expiry date till the balance amount is exhausted (E.g., Gift Cards)

- **Reloadable**: Funds can be added multiple times and can be used multiple times before the expiry date (E.g., PayTM wallet, Meal card, Forex card)

Then there are different variants depending on their acceptance network

- Closed loop: Acceptance is limited to single merchant or small merchant group.
- Open loop: Accepted by a wider network of merchants.

	Closed Loop	**Open Loop**
Non-Reloadable	Levi's Gift Card that is accepted only at Levi's shop/ site	Bank's Visa Gift cards that is accepted in all stores/sites
Reloadable	Cafeteria Card	Bank's Visa Forex Card

Few other rules for prepaid payment instruments:

a. Limit on the amount that can be loaded.

- Gift Cards: One time loading
- Reloadable Instruments: Rs. 10,000 *(Minimum KYC)* and Rs.2,00,000 *(Full KYC)*
- Forex Cards: $2,50,000 per year (max amount of $10,000 per loading)

b. Currency that can be loaded

- Domestic PPI wallet/card — INR only
- Forex card — Other currencies

c. Restriction on cash withdrawal through ATM or transfer to bank a/c

- Gift Cards are not allowed for cash withdrawal as well as transfer to bank a/c

- General Purpose Reloadable prepaid cards and Forex cards are allowed for cash withdrawal at ATM and balance amount can be transferred back to bank a/c

Note: There will be restriction on the withdrawal amount

d. Restriction on acceptance based on

- MCC (merchant category code): card is accepted only with certain category merchants (e.g., Sodexo card at grocery merchants)

- MID (Merchant Id)/TID (Terminal Id): Card is accepted on specific merchant or terminals (e.g., Health card that works at partner hospitals)

- Territory: Forex cards issued in India are not accepted in India, Nepal, Bhutan.

Story of Prepaid Payment Instruments:

Prepaid cards have existed for quite some time and have promised great potential, as the industry thought that prepaid cards are ideal solutions for financial inclusion, direct benefit transfers etc. Apart from banks, there were quite a few prepaid card companies (ItzCash, Beam cash etc.). However, the business model had hurdles of stringent KYC and logistics costs.

Then came the wave of *'Mobile Wallets'*. After the first wave of wallets (PayTM, Mobikwik, Freecharge). Later, telcos entered the game - Vodafone M-Pesa, Airtel Money, Idea Money, Tata mRupee and Jio Money.

Then, arrived the biggest challenger to wallet - i.e., UPI. And the wallets started becoming more and more irrelevant and less interesting to merchants and users. The mobile wallets are struggling and trying to pivot into consumer FinTechs. And the fate of 'telco company' wallets was no different. A few wallets died (Idea money, Tata mRupee), and few are breathing because of their patrons' deep pockets (Airtel, Jio).

My heart weeps silently for Vodafone M-Pesa, the company that built an amazing financial inclusion story in Kenya but sadly had to shut down its operations in India.

Prepaid Card + Lending:

Out of the blue prepaid cards became popular in 2020-22 as NBFCs and Digital Lending companies started issuing prepaid cards to lend money with *Just-In-Time* funding to the card. These entities not only earned revenue from the lending business but also revenue from the interchange *(prepaid card MDR is similar to that of credit card)*.

It was a clever model but still in a regulatory '*Gray Area*'.

In June-2022, RBI issued guidelines that prepaid cards shouldn't not be funded with credit line. With this one line, lending companies had to shut down the prepaid card-based lending model.

New kid on the block - UPI Lite:

As you know, UPI crumbled the wallet story. Now, UPI has its own wallet - *UPI Lite* *(kind of what goes around… comes around!)*

In 2022, NPCI came up with the concept of a wallet on UPI Apps - UPI Lite.

It is an on-device wallet where users can load up to Rs.2000 and make payments up to Rs.500 *(changed from earlier Rs.200)* without 2nd Factor Authentication (i.e., without entering MPIN).

Remember, UPI Lite is conceptualized not as competition to wallets but to reduce the load on UPI/banks as around 50% of UPI transactions are small ticket purchases (i.e., of less than Rs.200).

Usage of UPI Lite is limited to the P2PM category *(static QRs at small stores)*.

During the Global FinTech Festival of 2023, NPCI announced an upgrade to UPI Lite. UPI Lite will have **Tap and Pay** feature where users can tap the mobile on NFC *(Near Field Communication)* tag or Smart QR and complete the payment without entering PIN. Wonderful. Isn't it?

New Ray of hope: PPI + UPI

One of the challenges for any payment instrument is building a large acceptance infrastructure, and wallets are no exception. On one end, wallets have to onboard users; on the other, they have to onboard merchants. This is a catch 22 situation - Wallet issuers have to focus on both areas, which means they have to spend a lot of resources (money, human resources).

But now, PPI wallet can be linked to UPI. So, the wallets can ride UPI's infrastructure.

- Step 1: A user can link PPI wallet on TPAP/UPI App.

- Step 2: While doing UPI payment on a merchant site/App or QR, users will be shown the option of a bank account, PPI Wallet *(Apart from UPI Lite and Credit card, if linked)*.

- Step 3: Select the PPI wallet and complete 2FA to complete the payment.

Although the merchant has to bear MDR for transactions above Rs.2000 for Off-Us flow *(where PPI issuer and TPAP are different e.g., Using PhonePe to pay using AmazonPay wallet)* but, considering the majority of our transactions are less than Rs.2000, so MDR may not be a major hurdle or NPCI may come up with favorable MDR model to create win-win situation for PPI issuers, TPAPs, banks, merchants and consumers.

Co-branding of PPI:

There are clear guidelines for co-branding of prepaid cards, but there was no clarity on co-branding of digital wallets. Many consumer brands partnered with PPI licensed entities to launch co-branded wallets.

In July 2023, RBI clarified that digital wallet cannot be co-branded and instructed PPI companies to have the wallet within their own App.

Closing Remarks:

Merchants continue to have their closed-loop wallets as it is the simplest way to manage refunds, add reward points, and thus create customer stickiness. Many eCommerce, gaming, and travel merchants have such wallets.

Closed loop wallet doesn't require any license from the regulator except the funds need to be parked in non-interest earning special purpose account (i.e., nodal/escrow account).

That seems a bit open... Isn't it? - So, we can expect some guidelines for closed loop wallets.

Freebies such as cashback and discounts boosted growth of digital wallets. As these offers have reduced, users as well as merchants are not seeing great value in these wallets.

A few types of prepaid cards still have 'some' value: Gift Cards (*lazy person's gifting choice*), Forex cards (*for overseas trips*), and specialized cards (*Sodexo Meal Cards*).

We are still far away from 'writing PPIs off'. It will be interesting to see how the industry will come up with new use cases for PPI and how UPI+PPI linking will change the landscape!

4.C Net-Banking

During the dawn of online payments, when card penetration was low *(and, of course, there were not many wallets and UPI)*, net-banking was quite popular.

Apart from online payments and regular banking activities (managing Fixed/Recurring Deposits), a net-banking account can be used for transferring funds to other bank accounts (via RTGS, NEFT, IMPS, FT) and bill payments (credit card, utility).

Let's start with different types of banks *(and we have a bunch of those)*

1. **Commercial Banks**: For-profit banks that are regulated by Banking Regulation Act of 1949

    *   Public Sector banks: Majority shares owned by the Govt. of India or RBI. After multiple mergers, now we have 12 PSU banks (e.g., SBI, PNB, Canara etc.)

    *   Private sector banks: Owned by the private shareholders. There are 21 such banks (e.g., HDFC, ICICI, Axis, Yes Bank, Kotak etc.)

    *   Foreign Banks: As the name suggests, these are foreign origin banks. At present, there are 45 foreign banks in India (e.g., JP Morgan, HSBC, DBS etc.)

    *   Regional Rural banks: Formed to provide credit to marginal farmers and small businesses. There are 43 RRBs operating in various parts of India.

2. **Co-operative Banks**: These banks are registered under Co-operative Societies Act (1912). These banks are classified as State or Urban Co-operative banks based on the type of business they do.

3. **Small Finance Banks (SFB)**: Niche banks that are formed with the objective of providing financial inclusion. We have 12 SFBs (e.g., AU SFB, Equitas, Ujjivan, Jana, etc.)

4. **Payments Banks**: These banks can only take deposits up to Rs.1,00,000 but cannot do 'lending'. Initially there are around 8-9 banks but now we have fewer payments banks (India Post, Airtel, Fino, Jio)

5. **Specialized Banks**: Introduced for specific purpose (e.g., NABARD, EXIM, SIDBI)

Note: All banks do not offer online payment or net-banking facility

Net-Banking Details:

Net-banking is a payment mode where customers can make payment using a bank account enabled for online commerce or eCommerce payments.

- The user's spending is limited to balance in the account (the balance earns interest)

- During the transaction, the user is redirected to bank's website to complete the validation *(Note: Some banks may pose additional authentication steps such as OTP, security question or grid challenge)*

Types of bank accounts

- **Retail accounts:** Operated by individual users. Retail transactions go through a standard validation process.

- **Corporate Accounts:** Belong to businesses/companies and are operated by more than one user. The corporate net-banking transaction may have **maker-checker process** (The maker initiates the transaction, and the checker approves the transaction)

Integration

Net-banking is one of the value propositions offered by Payment Aggregators (PAs).

50+ banks allow online net-banking transactions, but it is not practical for a merchant to have integration with all banks. Moreover, many of these banks do not even have capability, resources, or interest to do direct integration with merchants.

So, PAs integrate all these banks and offer them to merchants on a single platform. It is possible that few PAs have direct integration with a few large banks (HDFC, SBI, ICICI, Kotak, Axis) and for other banks they use another PA's platform.

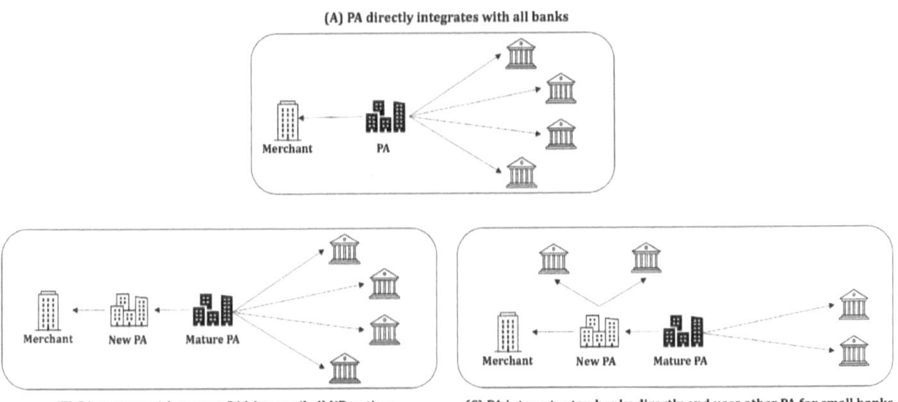

Didn't I tell you... the payments ecosystem is like Russian Nesting Dolls... One payment player inside another, and so on!

Net-banking Trend:

Net-banking used to be an important payment method because of lower credit card penetration and the fear of using cards for online transactions.

Over a period, net-banking users started moving to debit cards (*as every bank account has a debit card*), but the rise of UPI drastically affected net-banking transactions.

Erosion of net-banking can be attributed to both merchants and customers alike:

- Customer: Multiple steps to complete the transaction, non-optimized mobile pages, and remembering password. *In summary: Not user-friendly*

- Merchant: Success rate is inconsistent and lower, and higher commercials compared to debit cards and UPI *(for majority of sectors)*

Few years ago, net-banking options were prominently displayed on merchant's checkout pages.

But now, net-banking options are at the bottom of the page or hidden as the merchants still want to have it but don't want users to pay using them.

Exceptions

Net-banking is still a dominant payment method in investment, lending, B2B and education sectors because of,

- Commercials: Flat fee model. So, whether the merchant bears the charges or passes to the customer, it is economical for high ticket transactions.

- Features: Net-banking provides TPV (Third party Validation) feature which is important for regulated investment sector / capital market *(Mutual Fund or Stock brokerage)*

- Transaction limit: Useful for high ticket transactions *(whereas UPI has upper limits)*

- B2B Payments: Supported by corporate net-banking flow (i.e., maker-checker process)

Over the period, limits on UPI have increased for various sectors – Rs.2,00,000 for capital market, loan repayment, Credit Card Bill payment, and Rs.5,00,000 for Education, healthcare, IPO, Government Securities purchase. *(Note: These limits may change in future.)*

Combined with the **_TPV feature_** and variants of **_one-time mandate_** (single block - single debit and single block - multiple debit), UPI fits well for the capital market use cases.

NPCI is in planning to launch maker-checker flow for UPI; this feature can be used by businesses, and they can link current a/c to VPA/UPI ID.

Plus, UPI still has the most minimal commercials compared to cards.

So, UPI is and will continue to gain a share of net-banking.

The future of Net-Banking:

Net-banking is extremely complex and full of challenges; here are few:

- Integration: Varies from bank to bank (in nutshell 50-55 different integrations)

- Commercial: Just like other modes, even NBs have sector specific pricing which can be % of transaction value or flat fee per transaction. But every bank may have different commercial (_e.g., few banks will offer 1.5%, a few at 1.2% and others at 1%_)

- Commercials to PA: Few banks work on fixed fee (_e.g., 1.5%, 1.1%_) and few banks work in revenue sharing model (_e.g., 60:40, 50:50_), few bank will have revenue sharing model with minimum value (_e.g., 60:40 for bank and PA but the bank should get 0.50%_)

- Settlement time: Varies for each bank. At times, banks may miss giving settlement to PAs.

- Performance: Not consistent - Varies drastically from bank to bank

- Authentication Methods: Customer ID + Password, OTP, Security question, grid challenge (_worst of them is Remembering password... horrible... who does that?_)

- Refunds: No definite Turn Around Time (TAT) or tracking mechanism

- Dispute Management: No framework for handling disputes or chargebacks

In a way, NB was not liked by customers, merchants, or most of the PAs *(Except the one who has direct integration with all banks and making good revenue).*

So, everyone knew net-banking would die in a few years until, out of the blue, RBI mentioned, *'create payment system for processing online merchant payments using internet/mobile banking',* in **'the Payments Vision 2025 document'** (released in 2022).

And in Feb-2024, the RBI Governor announced **interoperability for Net-banking.**

Interoperable system:

Interoperable platforms are not new - Cards, NACH, BBPS, UPI - All are interoperable.

It is possible that the Net-banking interoperable model will be similar to either BBPS or NACH or UPI.

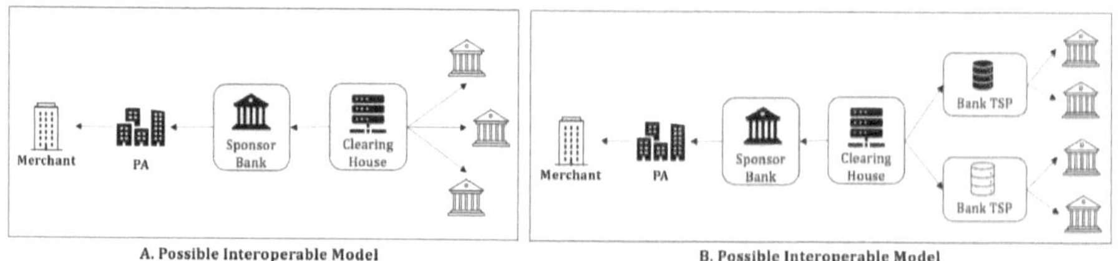

A. Possible Interoperable Model   B. Possible Interoperable Model

Irrespective of the model, NB interoperable model will standardize, Settlement time

- Uniform commercials *(Note: Commercials may reduce).*
- Dispute management framework and TAT *(Turn Around Time)*
- TAT and tracking of refunds.
- Harmonize the reversal of failed transaction and penalties.

Impact on participants:

- Customers: might experience better payment flows

- Old PAs *(who have all net-banking options)*: May lose direct revenue *(from merchants)* and indirect revenue *(from other PAs who use old PA's net-banking stack)*

- New PAs *(who do not have all net-banking options)*: Do not have to wait on banks to extend their APIs or partner with old PAs on higher commercials.

- Merchants: Better commercials, experience, processes, and frameworks

- Banks: Integration effort to get onboarded on the new platform. Possible loss of revenue if the commercials are reduced.

Closing Remarks:

A few years back, one of the biggest advantages of online Payment Aggregator was that it could offer multiple net-banking options, and net-banking used to be an important payment mode.

With consolidation of banks and declining usage of net-banking, merchant payments will be skewed towards UPI and cards. And these modes can be offered by acquiring banks.

So, I wonder what 'the value' of PA will be?

Sadly, the net-banking space didn't see many innovations. Few payment companies have built mobile SDK-based features such as bank page optimizer or 1-click payment experience on a couple of banks to smoothen the payment experiences, but nothing big or game-changing.

The recent announcement by the RBI on developing an interoperable net-banking platform is great news. It may impact few participants negatively, but overall interoperable model may fix the problems of net-banking *(non-standard commercials, products, and processes)*.

I wonder if this new interoperable model will change the fate of net-banking or will net-banking continue to be less and less relevant in the coming years.

They say, 'the more the merrier' and that holds true for payments as well. So, I hope Net-Banking stays around in this 'Payments Party'.

4.D Alternate Credit Products - BNPL, Cardless EMIs

In this chapter, we will cover ***Alternate Credit Products (ACPs)*** - Buy Now Pay Later (BNPL) and Cardless EMIs.

Although I am covering both products in the same chapter, they vary in their operations and value proposition to users and use cases. So, keep an eye on those points!

Why do such Alternate Credit Products (ACPs) exist when we have credit cards?

Everyone cannot get credit cards due to the stringent credit check process. But people need credit for various reasons such as small purchases, aspirational purchases, and emergencies. BNPL and cardless EMI products fill that gap to some extent.

Let's start with basics of each product and followed by generic details:

A. BNPL

BNPL issuers give a 'small credit line' to users for a short period *(a couple of weeks)*. Users can make purchases on the partner merchant network using 'the available' credit line and repay the utilized amount.

BNPL issuers: FinTechs (Simpl, LazyPay), Merchants (Ola, Amazon, Flipkart), Banks (HDFC, ICICI)

BNPL products are not designed to meet the big credit requirements. The idea behind BNPL is very different - Most of our spends are on small tickets e.g., Food order, medicine, mobile bill, or bus ticket booking. So, BNPL companies are targeting these use cases and trying to replace credit cards and/or other payment instruments by providing a faster payment experience.

Value for participants:

Participants	Benefits	Drawbacks
Issuers	• Revenue (and profits) • Cross-sell other credit products	• Cost of capital, NPAs • Acquisition cost (users, merchants) • Operation cost
Customers	• Credit line • Seamless payment experience	• One more payment product to manage. • Limited acceptability
PAs/TSPs	• Additional payment mode • Additional revenue (and margin)	• Integration and ops effort
Merchants	• Additional payment mode • Access to user base	• Additional effort of integration & Ops • Higher MDR

B.   Cardless EMIs:

Users get 'a bigger' credit line that can be used on the partner merchant network for purchase of big-ticket items such as mobile, home appliances, air tickets etc. The utilized credit or the spend amount is paid back in EMIs *(Equated Monthly Instalments)*.

Issuers: Bajaj Finance, Kredit Bee, banks (e.g., HDFC, IDFC)

Value for participants:

Participants	Benefits	Drawbacks
Issuers	• Revenue (and profit) • Cross-sell other credit products	• Cost of capital, NPAs • Acquisition cost (users, merchants) • Operations cost
Customers	• Higher Credit line • Ease of repayment (EMIs)	• One more payment instrument • Limited acceptability
PAs/TSPs	• One more payment mode • Additional revenue (and margin)	• Integration and ops effort
Merchants	• Additional payment mode • Access to user base • Increase in order value	• Additional effort (integration, Ops) • Higher MDR

C.   Generic Details - BNPL and Cardless EMI

I will keep it as much generic as possible and highlight the differences when applicable.

1.   Participants:

- **Customers**: People who avail credit line from the BNPL or cardless EMI issuers

- **Issuers**: Entities (FinTechs, banks, NBFCs) that issue these ACPs *(Alternate Credit Products)* to customers in partnership with banks/NBFCs.

- **Merchants**: Merchants (online or offline) where users can pay using these ACPs

- **PAs/TSPs**: Extend these ACPs as payment modes to their merchants.

2. User onboarding:

Users must register with the issuing entity to get credit lines for BNPL or Cardless EMI products. For issuers, a simpler way to give a credit line is to check users' credit score, but millions of potential users do not have a credit score or are new to credit (NTC). So, the issuers have their own logic or alternate data *(e.g., salary, postpaid bill etc.)* to give credit.

BNPL issuers may do minimum KYC to extend a small credit line (Rs.1,000 - Rs.2000), and then, based on user's spending and repayment behavior, issuers will increase the credit limit.

BNPL issuers may give higher credit line basis full KYC and credit score check.

Cardless EMI issuers may check the user's credit score, considering the credit line is higher.

3. Acceptance Network

Alternate Credit Products (ACPs) such as BNPL and Cardless EMIs can be processed by the same issuers (*'payment issuer = payment processor' model*).

There are mainly two ways a merchant can integrate ACPs as payment mode:

- **Direct**: Integrate with merchants directly Advantages: Direct engagement with merchants and enable better/customized flows Disadvantages: Sales effort, integration effort, and operation support

- **PA and TSP/Orchestrator**: Integrate with PAs and TSPs, and those PAs and TSPs will offer it to their merchants.

  Advantages: Wider reach, faster Go-to-market

  Disadvantages: No direct engagement with merchants, standard flows

Note: ACP issuers deploy hybrid approach - They do direct integration with large or enterprise merchants, and partner with PAs to capture smaller merchants

BNPL's tryst with UPI:

Success of any payment mode depends on a wider acceptance network. BNPL companies tried to ride the UPI network by designing clever work-around solutions.

- Read the payee VPA from static QR *(when user scans the QR using BNPL issuer's App)* and do UPI payout to that payee VPA using a common escrow/current account.

For a brief period, things looked positive, and many FinTechs jumped on to build BNPL products using UPI rails, but NPCI stopped this.

4. **Transactions**

   a. **BNPL:**

   - First time: Merchant calls eligibility check API (*check whether the user is an existing BNPL user and what is the available credit*). Then, the user needs to complete the authentication leg (OTP validation) to complete the transaction.

   - Subsequent flow: Eligibility check is done, and then user just approves the transaction (*no authentication required as token is stored after first transaction*)

   Note: Such seamless payment experience is possible only when the issuer is willing to enable such flow either directly (to the merchant) or via TSP.

   b. **Cardless EMI:**

   - Merchant calls eligibility check API (*check whether customer is an existing user and what is the available credit*). Then, the user will select the EMI tenure (3 months, 6 months, etc.) and then needs to complete the authentication leg (OTP validation) to complete the transaction.

Note: Merchants/PAs show the interest rates and/or EMI calculations

5. **Operations:**

   a. **Settlement:**

   - **BNPL**: Every purchase/transaction is settled to the merchant (directly or through PA) on T+1 or T+2 days (*after adjusting MDR, refunds etc.*)

   - **Cardless EMI**: Irrespective of the tenure of EMI, the merchant receives the full settlement (directly or through PA) on T+1 or T+2 days (*as per agreement – after adjusting MDR, refunds etc.*).

   Example: Customer does transaction for Rs.6000 and opted for 3-month EMI. Merchant will receive Rs.6000 (-) MDR on T+1/T+2 days. The customer will pay Rs.6000 (+charges) over period of 3 months (*say, Rs.2100 per month*)

   Note: Merchant is not involved in repayment; Customer will repay the amount + charges to the issuer directly over the tenure in EMIs

   b. **Refunds**: Any refund marked by the merchant is adjusted from the next settlement amount. And the issuer will adjust the refund amount against the outstanding credit line of the customer.

6. **Repayment Flow:**

   a. **BNPL**: Typically, the credit period is a couple of weeks. Post that, the user has to repay the utilized amount. Users can repay using debit card, net-banking, or UPI on BNPL issuer's website/App.

Users can set-up mandates (NACH, UPI AutoPay) where the BNPL issuer will debit the user's payment instrument as per mandate parameters.

b. **Cardless EMI**: The user will make the monthly repayment towards the outstanding amount + charges. Users can repay using debit card, net-banking, or UPI on the cardless EMI issuer's website/App.

Users can set-up mandates (NACH, UPI AutoPay) where the cardless EMI issuer will debit the user's payment instrument as per mandate parameters.

7. Non-repayment

a. **BNPL:** Users will be charged a fee for delayed repayments. If the user is on minimum KYC, then non-repayments may not be reported to the credit bureau. If the user is on full KYC, then delayed or non-repayment will impact the credit score.

b. **Cardless EMI**: Users will be charged a fee for delayed repayments. Non-repayment will be reported back to the credit bureau and will impact the user's credit score.

D. Bonus Read - Maths behind BNPL

Borrowing Rate (per Year) [A]	15%
Borrowing Rate (per day) [B]	0.041%
Charges for merchant [C]	1.50%
Repayment Rate (PG) [D]	1%

Pattern of Usage	Day 0	Day 1	Day 8	Day 12	Day 18
Available Credit [E - F + G]	5000	4000	2000	1000	5000
Credit usage [F]		1000	2000	1000	
Credit Repayment [G]					4000

TDR Charged to Merchant [H = F * C]			15	30	15

Interest Charged	
On amount used on Day 1 [I]	6.99 [17 days * B * 1000]
On amount used on Day 8 [J]	8.22 [10 days * B * 2000]
On amount used on Day 13 [K]	2.47 [6 days * B * 1000]

Revenue [M]	60
Merchant charges [G * C]	60
Costs [N]	57.68
Cost of Capital [I + J + K]	17.68
Repayment Fee [G * D]	40
NPA	0

P&L [M - N]	2.32

- BNPL issuers do not charge interest to customers but charge late repayment fees.
- Merchant is charged MDR - percentage (%) of the transaction value. *(Reason: Merchants are familiar with the MDR model.)*

MDR and penalty fees are cleverly arrived after factoring cost of funds, risk costs, and write-off to be done for Non-Performing Assets (NPAs - amount that users do not pay back).

In summary, to be profitable, the issuing entity should get the lowest interest rate from banks/NBFCs *(i.e., cost of capital)*, reduce repayment costs *(i.e., PA's charges)*, have a large number of active users, control customer acquisition cost, and charge higher MDR to merchants but most importantly, reduce NPAs.

Yes, I am stating the obvious. Yes, it sounds simple, but extremely difficult to 'nail it' correctly.

Closing Remarks:

BNPL is a global phenomenon - but getting the model right is not simple.

Issuers have to battle on two fronts - build an extensive merchant acceptance network and, at the same time, build a large user base. While doing all this, keep NPA in control.

In 2022, the global BNPL companies saw erosion of their valuation, and many BNPLs shut down.

The Indian landscape looks 'little' optimistic, as many are doing 'just fine' and new BNPL products are being launched.

Even the cardless EMIs are going through a similar struggle. These companies have to struggle with growth while keeping the cost of capital and NPA in control. On top of that, they compete with credit cards, which are well ahead in the credit as well as EMI game. In 2023, we witnessed the fall of Zestmoney (one of the earliest online cardless EMI issuers).

The digital lending guidelines tightened the fund flows, FLDG and collection processes. It is quite possible that BNPL may be brought under some regulation/guidelines by the RBI.

In 2023, NPCI announced linking of the credit line to UPI and it is quite possible that a cardless EMI variant may come on UPI. As you all know UPI has the largest acceptance network. It will be interesting to see how things unfold in this space.

India is credit hungry; customers have aspirations, emergencies and seek instant gratification (*want to buy that iPhone today or want to go Goa this weekend*). So, I presume such alternate credit products will have 'some role' to play in digital commerce and payments space. The issuing entities may prosper as long as they give the 'right amount' to the 'right users' while balancing cost (capital, acquisition, operations) and NPAs.

So, I would say, "Credit is fun, until it stops being"!

4.E   UPI

We do various types of transactions: P2P (C2C), P2M (C2B), B2C (P2M), B2B, G2C and C2G *(P=Person, C=Consumer, M=Merchant, B=Business, G=Government).*

We started with cash, cheque, and demand drafts, and then we moved online with RBI's NEFT and RTGS. Then came NPCI's IMPS which works in real time and 24x7.

Then came the most disruptive payment mode — **UPI (Unified Payments Interface)**

UPI is simple to use, mobile friendly, and works in real-time and 24x7 for P2P *(person-to-person)*, P2PM *(payment at small stores or unorganized sector)*, and P2M *(person-to-merchant)* payments.

UPI was launched in 2016, and in a very short span of time, UPI has evolved and has become a dominant solution for various payment use cases.

UPI has become omnipresent and omnipotent.

Products and Usage:

P2P Transfer	Online Payment (P2M)	In-Store Payment (P2PM)
User can transfer money to other bank account	To purchase products or services on merchant's website/App	Users can scan the QR and make the payment.
UPI Lite User can load up to Rs.2000 and make payment up to Rs.500 without 2FA (or MPIN)	**UPI AutoPay** User can set-up mandate on merchant to make recurring payments	**One-time Mandate** One-time mandate where funds can be blocked once and debited one-time or multiple times
UPI Payout Merchants can do payout to users account	**Virtual VPA solution** Virtual VPA based solution for seamless payment collection	**UPI 123Pay** Designed for facilitating UPI payments on feature phones

e-RUPI	UPI for NRIs	For Indians Visiting Abroad
e-RUPI Govt or companies can issue vouchers to users that can be redeemed on partner merchants	UPI for NRIs NRIs can use their residence country mobile number to connect NRE account to UPI	For Indians Visiting Abroad Indian Travelers can use UPI in more than 20 countries in Asia, Middle East, and Europe
UPI One World Foreign tourists can exchange currency to load INR on PPI and pay from UPI	Cross-border Remittance UPI can be used for last mile connectivity for inward remittances	UPI <> Other RTP Linking UPI is linked to other country's real-time payment rails for cross border transfers
ATM Withdrawal UPI can be used for cash withdrawal at NFS ATM	Coin Vending Machines UPI+QR based model to disburse coins at banks' vending machines	UPI Tap and Pay User can tap mobile on NFC tag or Smart QR to pay via UPI Lite
Conversational UPI Users can talk and pay *(UPI PIN needs to be entered manually)*	UPI Lite X Offline payment using UPI Lite; useful in low network areas	

The journey of UPI started with linking of **savings bank accounts,** and today, a user can link Overdraft (OD) Account, Credit Card, Credit line, PPI Wallet, NRE account, UPI Lite (wallet).

To keep it simple, let's start with the UPI on the bank account and then we will cover other solutions, features.

A. Basics of UPI

a. Participants:

- Issuer PSP: Bank/PSP that creates the VPA.
- Acquirer PSP: Bank/PSP that processes UPI transactions
- Issuer and acquirer talk to each other via NPCI switch.
- Payee: Person/entity which is receiving the money in 'beneficiary bank'

- Payer: Person who is paying the money from 'remitter bank'

This is familiar... Doesn't it feel like a card ecosystem?

Yes... A unique card issued by the issuing bank and transactions processed by the acquiring bank via card network.

But UPI comes with some twists, some smoothness, and a whole lot of awesomeness!

b. **Virtual Payment Address (VPA) or UPI ID and UPI Number**

Anyone on the UPI platform requires VPA or UPI ID to pay. VPAs look similar to email id (tony.stark@okhdfc or 1234567890@ybl)

- A VPA can be linked to multiple banks *(but one bank will be 'primary'; user can select the bank during transaction but receive money in primary bank a/c)*

- A bank account can be added or deleted *(Always one bank account should be there)*

- Multiple VPAs can be created on a single bank a/c on different TPAPs/UPI Apps

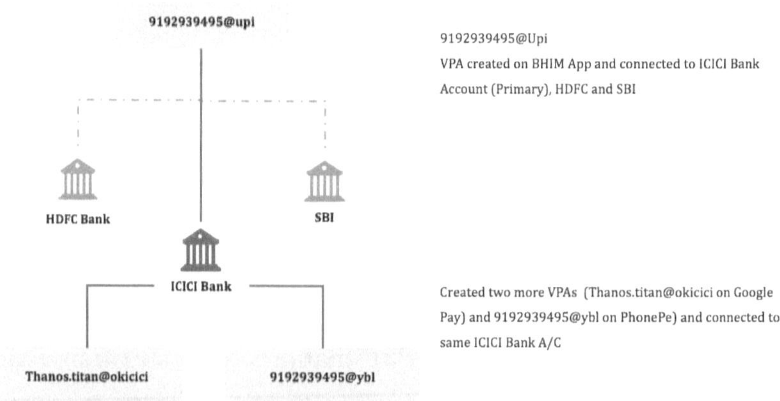

Note: RBI/NPCI mandates TPAPs/UPI Apps to delete VPAs which are inactive for a year

UPI Number mapper:

Users can also have an 8-11 Digit UPI Number. Users can select their mobile number as UPI number or choose a unique number. This number in turn is linked to VPA.

c. **UPI + Sources:**

A user can link various payment sources to UPI ID

Bank Account	Overdraft Account	Credit Card	PPI Wallet
NRE Account	UPI Lite wallet	Credit Line	

Note: We can expect linking of current a/c to UPI ID

Savings account is the most dominant source of UPI Payment.

A user can register for UPI (bank account based) in two different ways: (1) Using debit card credentials (2) Aadhar OTP based.

d. **Security Device & PIN**

Didn't I say that UPI is mobile friendly? That is great but it's not sufficient unless it is 'super' secure. Security is achieved by device binding and SIM binding combined with PIN or biometric to open the UPI App and another MPIN *(as 2nd Factor Authentication)* to validate the transaction.

*Note: MPIN is mandatory for all UPI transactions with exception of **UPI Lite** transactions up to Rs.500 and subsequent transactions of **UPI AutoPay** within prescribed limits*

e. **UPI Apps / TPAPs**

Two types of entities can have UPI Apps

- Banks (ICICI, HDFC etc.)

- Non-Bank - FinTechs or merchants (PhonePe, Google Pay, Cred, Flipkart etc.) - *Called TPAP (Third Party Application Provider)*

TSPs build/run UPI stack for the banks (examples: Juspay, Olive, Mindgate, Sarvatra)

Only a bank can connect with NPCI. So TPAPs tie up with bank(s).

Examples: PhonePe (Yes, ICICI, Axis), Google Pay (Axis, HDFC, ICICI, SBI), Cred (Axis)

Users can perform various activities on TPAPs / UPI Apps:

- Manage bank - add bank(s), change primary bank, remove bank.

- Add or remove supported payment sources - credit card, PPI Wallet, NRE account, credit line *(if TPAP and the bank support)*

- Manage UPI Lite wallet (enable, disable, loading and usage)

- Make payments: P2P transfers *(To other VPA & bank account)*, P2PM *(Small stores - QR scanning)*, P2M payments *(Merchant's website/app or QR)*

- Manage AutoPay and One-time mandates *(approve or revoke)*

- Check balance and view transaction details.

- Raise disputes.

Note: Becoming TPAP is a mammoth undertaking, but merchants can become partial-TPAP by using **UPI Plug-in** *SDK of banks. We will cover this in a later part of this Chapter.*

B. Payment Flows (of UPI on Bank Account)

Ishan and Nijesh went out for dinner at Nando's. Nijesh owes Rs.750 to Ishan. Both have UPI Apps, so either Nijesh can transfer funds to Ishan or Ishan can request Nijesh to transfer the money via a UPI App. Here is how the transaction is done.

There are two types of Transactions:

- Pull / Collect Payment: Payee (Ishan) sends collect request to Payer (Nijesh)
- Push / Intent Payment: Payer (Nijesh) initiates the transfer to Payee (Ishan)

Also, the flow varies depending on the number of entities involved. Here are few combinations:

a. Two party model:

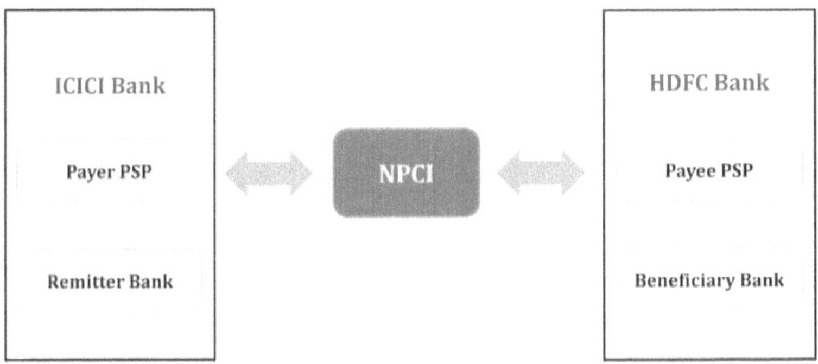

Payer PSP and remitter Bank are one entity, and Payee PSP and beneficiary bank are one entity

b. **Three Party model:**

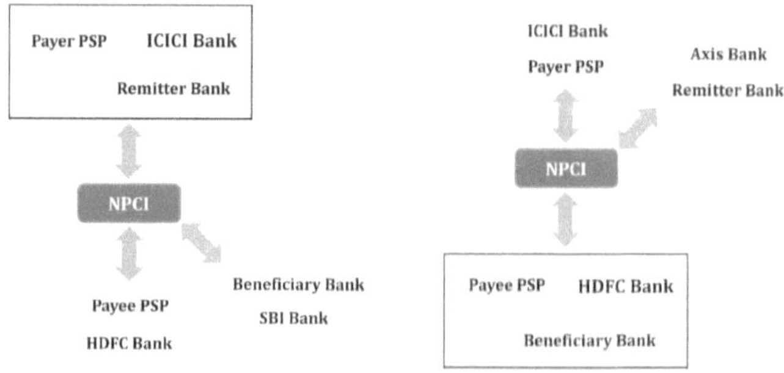

c. **Four Party model:**

Payer PSP, remitter bank, payee PSP and beneficiary bank are different entities.

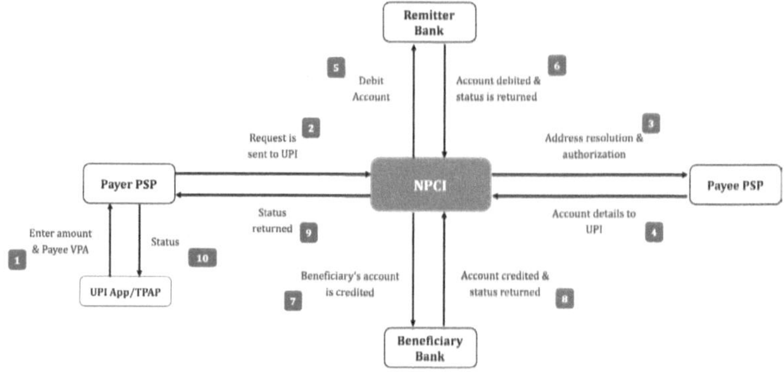

Illustration: Payer initiated P2P transfer (Push Method)

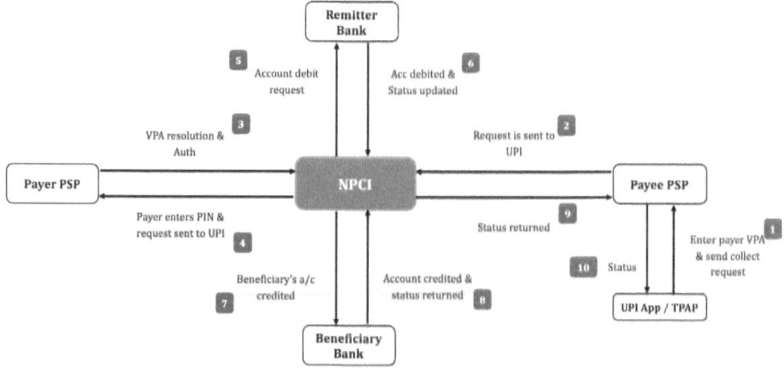

Illustration: Payee Initiated (Collect) P2P transfer (Pull Method)

UPI + Sources and Payment use case:

	UPI + Bank A/C	UPI + Credit Card	UPI + PPI Wallet	UPI Lite
P2P	Allowed	Not Allowed	Not Allowed	Not Allowed
P2PM	Allowed	Allowed	Allowed	Allowed
P2M	Allowed	Allowed (Except: Lending, Investment)	Allowed (Except: Lending, Investment)	Not Allowed (At present)

Transaction limits:

Rs.1,00,000 (for P2P, P2PM, P2M) - All categories *(with following exceptions)*

- Rs.2,00,000 (Capital markets, loan repayment, credit card bill payment, insurance)
- Rs.5,00,000 (IOP, Govt Securities, Education, Healthcare)
- Rs.2,000 (shared intent and shared QR)
- UPI Lite: Rs.500 (without MPIN), and up to Rs.2000

Customer's banks enforce limits on per transaction, 1st transaction to new beneficiary, and daily, weekly, or monthly transaction limits.

Note: Transaction limits (banks and NPCI enforced) may change from time-to-time.

Merchant Transactions

A merchant who wishes to collect funds via UPI would require a VPA. Acquiring banks create payee/collection VPA for the merchant.

Merchants can enable UPI acceptance by integrating with

- UPI Acquiring bank(s)

- Online or offline Payment Aggregator(s) *(who in turn uses UPI acquiring bank(s))*

Refer *Chapter 9. A (Transactions)* to read more about different types of UPI flows.

C.   Other UPI Products and Features:

1.   QR Code

A QR code is nothing but payee's (beneficiary's) VPA in QR format.

There are two types of QR Codes and with their own utilities/use cases.

QR Type	Description	Use case
Static QR	The amount needs to be entered by the payer	Fits better in payer-initiated flows (brick-and-mortar stores)
Dynamic QR	The amount is embedded in the QR and dynamic QR will expire after certain time *(configurable)*	Works better in merchant-initiated transactions as checkout page of website, delivery package, POS, or Kiosk.

2.   Virtual VPA based collection

A merchant can create and assign unique customized VPAs for each of the payers, and the payer will make payment to the assigned Virtual VPA.

The solution enables merchants to reconcile payer-initiated transactions efficiently.

Use cases: lending merchants (create virtual VPA for each borrower and borrower will transfer funds to assigned VPA from his TPAP) and wallet top-up cases.

For details refer to **Chapter 14** (Virtual Account Number / Virtual VPA)

3.   One time Mandate (OTM)

The OTM feature was rolled out as part of UPI 2.0 (in 2017), where a user can set-up an OTM for a certain amount. The merchant can debit or void the mandate, or the mandate will expire automatically.

As OTM works only once, it has very few practical use cases such as IPO subscription and security deposit refund.

In 2022, NPCI announced a variant of OTM where users can set-up a mandate for a certain amount and the merchant can do multiple debits as long as the sum of multiple debits is less than or equal to the mandate amount.

This variant can cater to few new use cases, such as radio cabs (*A user can set a mandate for Rs.2000 and take multiple rides till the Rs.2000 is exhausted*). Even grocery, quick commerce or food delivery merchants can use it (*User will set a mandate on Swiggy for Rs.1000 and keep ordering till the mandate amount is exhausted*).

The most interesting use case *(for single block – multiple debits)* is for secondary market trading (i.e., stock purchase), where an investor can block the amount, and whenever shares are purchased, the amount is debited.

For details refer to ***Chapter 13.E** (One Time Mandates)*

4.   UPI AutoPay

In Aug '20, UPI Autopay was launched. Recurring payment solution wherein a user can register a mandate on UPI and the merchant can debit the user's bank account as per mandate parameters.

For details refer to ***Chapter 13.D** (UPI AutoPay)*

5. UPI Lite

UPI Lite is an on-device wallet - a user can load up to Rs.2000 and make purchases for amounts up to Rs.500 *(increased from Rs.200)* without entering MPIN and with a daily limit of Rs.4000.

UPI Lite is available on all major TPAPs/UPI Apps.

The UPI Lite idea was conceptualized because UPI puts a heavy load on banks' infrastructure, and nearly half of UPI transactions are less than Rs.200. So, a wallet can address a bank's infrastructure concerns.

Features:

- One TPAP will have one wallet on a single bank.
- User can enable or disable wallet any time.
- User can load wallet from linked bank a/c (loading requires 2FA i.e., MPIN)
- User can disable wallet - balance is credited to linked bank a/c *(without MPIN)*
- User won't earn 'interest' on wallet balance.
- Wallet transactions are shown separately in TPAP and not shown in bank statements; only wallet loading and withdrawal to a/c are shown in statements.

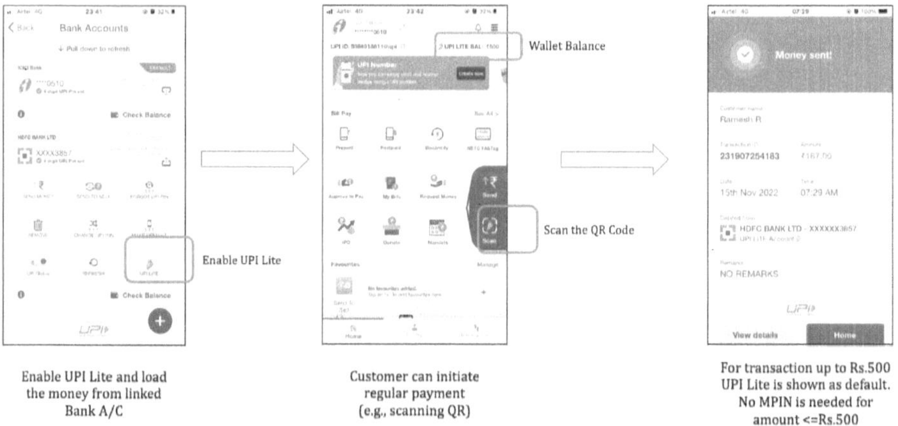

Enable UPI Lite and load the money from linked Bank A/C	Customer can initiate regular payment (e.g., scanning QR)	For transaction up to Rs.500 UPI Lite is shown as default. No MPIN is needed for amount <=Rs.500

6. UPI Tap and Pay

In 2023, NPCI announced the Tap and Pay feature for UPI which will be rolled out in 2024.

- User can tap the mobile on an NFC Tag or a Smart QR and

- Amount is deducted from **UPI Lite** wallet.

- Maximum amount per debit is Rs.500 *(without entering MPIN)*

7. UPI Lite X

Users can send and receive funds offline (without internet or poor internet connectivity)!

This could be good, considering many places (even in big cities) have poor data network.

8. UPI 123 Pay

Smartphones with data connectivity were one of the limitations of UPI. To include the feature phone users, in Mar '22, NPCI launched UPI 123.

UPI 123 Pay works on different models

- **IVR (Interactive Voice Response) Based**: Customer calls a specific number and is prompted to link bank account and set-up UPI over IVR.

  For payments, customers can select the given options (Press 1 for bank transfer, press 2 for bill payment etc.) and complete the transaction.

  IVR functionality is available in many Indian languages.

- **Missed call based**: During the billing, the merchant will create a token with the amount and customer's mobile number.

The customer gives a missed call to a specific number shown on the merchant's site/location.

The customer will receive an incoming call from 08071 800 800 and will be prompted to enter UPI PIN to complete the payment.

- **Sound Based**: User to call IVR number 6366 200 200 and select 'Pay to Merchant' option. User to tap the phone on merchant's device, and device will emit a unique tone, and user to press # key and UPI PIN to complete the payment. Once POS accepts the payment, the user will receive confirmation through IVR.

- **App Based**: The solution provider to partner with mobile manufacturers and embed the App on the feature phones *(with camera)*. Then the App can be used for Scan & Pay.

9. e-RUPI

It's a one-time usage prepaid instrument *(like a voucher or gift card)* built on UPI rail.

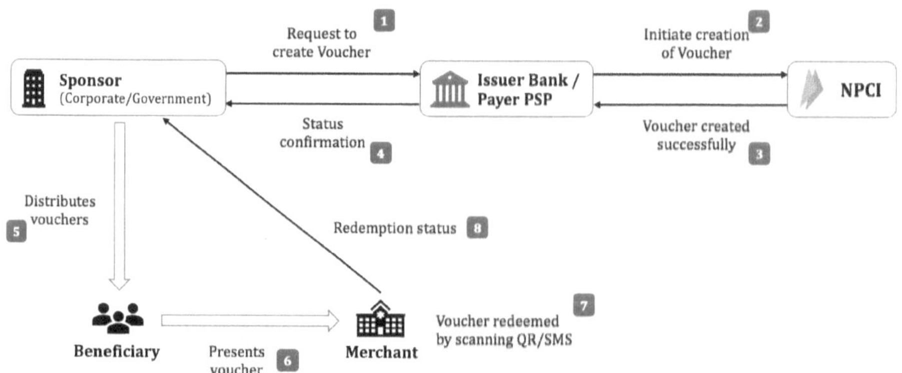

- A sponsor entity (Government or Corporate) can issue e-RUPI to beneficiaries for a fixed amount (Up to Rs.1,00,000).

- Beneficiaries can redeem it on the selected merchant network without the internet *(SMS string for redemption)* or with the internet *(by scanning QR)*.

- e-RUPI is an ideal solution for Government's direct benefit transfers.

10. Hello! UPI

'Conversational payment' is the next frontier of payments where users can make payments by inputting voice commands. UPI is stepping into this frontier and exploring various use cases and methods for conversational payments in English and other regional languages.

Hello UPI on IVR or IoT devices will work on UPI 123Pay model (i.e., server-side common library). We are yet to see any substantial usage or implementation of this feature.

11. UPI Payout

UPI is a perfect solution for many B2C disbursement use cases such as incentive payout, disbursing winnings of skill-based games, and COD refunds.

UPI payout is real time and works 24x7.

A merchant would need to set-up a source account *(from where funds will be debited)*, UPI rail *(through one of the banks)* and require beneficiary's UPI ID/VPA or UPI Number to transfer funds.

A merchant can also make payouts to the account numbers (+IFSC) of the beneficiary.

Read more about UPI payout in ***Chapter 15*** *(Payout or Disbursement Solutions)*

12. UPI Plug-in

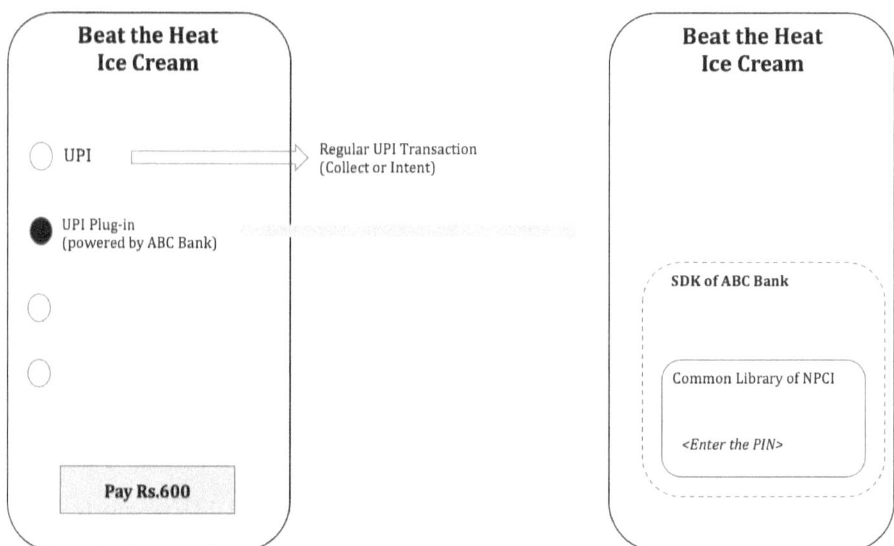

UPI Plug-in allows a merchant to facilitate UPI transactions within its own App by integrating it with the sponsor bank's SDK. Considering transactions are happening within the merchant's app *(no redirection or App-to-App switch)*, the transaction is done faster, and the performance or success rate will be higher.

With UPI Plug-in, in a way, merchants will become 'Partial-TPAP'.

- User can create VPA/UPI ID, link bank account and set UPI PIN
- If the user has VPA on sponsor bank, then that can be fetched on UPI Plug-in
- Merchant App can be used only for facilitating P2M transactions.
- Plug-in will not provide all TPAP features such as Scan QR and P2P transfer.
- UPI ID/ VPA can be used on any merchant App.
- Data exchange for transaction must happen between bank PSP and bank server.

- Merchant SDK will not have access to customer sensitive data *(personal data)*

- Merchants allowed to share transaction data with 3rd parties only with the approval from the bank and NPCI.

- Sponsor Bank is responsible for KYC adherence, due diligence of merchant, compliance including data localization, and is fully liable to merchant's actions and activities.

Merchants who have a large customer base want to become a TPAP so that they can engage the customers beyond their core product/services. However, they may not have time or resources to become a TPAP. So, such merchants can implement UPI Plug-in and provide better experience to their users and achieve higher success rate.

13. UPI for NRIs and Foreign Tourists

- **UPI for NRIs:**

  NRIs *(Non-Resident Indians)* of 10 countries can link their international mobile numbers to their NRE/NRO accounts and make payments using UPI.

  As of Jan '24, this feature is available for Singapore, Australia, Canada, Hong Kong, Oman, Qatar, Saudi Arabia, UAE, and the UK *(and in future more countries may be added)*

  This feature will be useful for NRIs when they visit India and, to make purchases on Indian websites.

  Member banks are expected to follow FEMA guidelines and are responsible for adhering to Anti-Money Laundering (AML) and Combating of Financing of Terrorism (CFT) checks. As per guideline, all member banks should be ready by 30th Apr 2023.

- **UPI One World:**

  UPI is made available to tourists visiting India, so they do not have to carry India Rupees *(after converting their home currencies)* or have to their credit/debit cards of their home countries *(and incur forex charges)*.

  UPI One World is launched in partnership between ***FFMC*** (Full Fledged Money Changers) and **PPI** (Prepaid Payment Instrument) issuers on UPI infrastructure.

  As on Mar-2024, a few PPI issuers (ICICI Bank, IDFC First Bank, Pine Labs and Transcorp) and FFMCs (EBIX CASH, Thomas Cook) are supporting this feature.

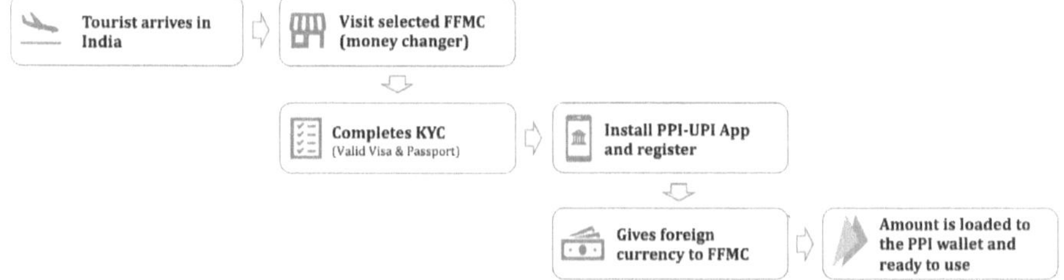

  At present, only tourists from G20 Countries can avail UPI One World at selected port of entries (Bangalore, Mumbai, and Delhi).

  This is just the beginning and UPI One World may be extended to all inbound visitors across all entry ports in India.

14. Internationalization of UPI

- **Last mile for inward remittance:**

  Users outside India can transfer money to VPA in India. This is a standard cross-border inward remittance case where last mile payout is done to Indian beneficiary's VPA.

- **UPI <> RTPs of other countries**

  UPI is linked to Singapore's RTP *(Real-time Payment)* Rail **'PayNow'**. With this linking now users can do cross-border remittance from UPI to PayNow and vice versa.

  NIPL (NPCI International Payments Ltd) is working on increasing coverage and is already in discussion with Thailand, UAE, and Sri Lanka.

  Such RTP rail linkages *(sort of cross-border express highways)* will make cross-border remittance convenient, efficient, and economical.

- **UPI outside India**:

  Indian travelers can pay using UPI in 20 countries (as on Mar '24): Bhutan, Cambodia, Hong Kong, Japan, Malaysia, Nepal, Philippines, Singapore, South Korea, Taiwan, Thailand, Vietnam, Oman, UAE, Belgium, France, Luxemburg, Netherlands, Switzerland, United Kingdom.

  The solution has a major drawback that users have to bear the forex charges which may fluctuate. That is the reason people use Forex cards.

  However, NPCI may amalgamate UPI with the Forex card/ wallet. Of course, there are challenges in terms of KYC, compliance, limits, usage, and acceptance network.... But when there is a will there's a way *(in this case UPI)*

Closing Remarks:

In a short period, UPI gained tremendous popularity among customers as well as merchants. Customers appreciate the convenience, and merchants are thrilled about the performance and cost *(the most economical payment mode)*.

It feels that UPI is omnipresent and omnipotent, with a wide range of products and features that can effectively solve a variety of use cases.

Not just domestic, UPI has now gone international and is increasing its footprint across the globe. In April 2020, NPCI floated wholly owned Subsidiary, NIPL to promote RuPay and UPI outside India. And as you see NIPL is doing a great job.

This is where I am going to end this chapter on UPI, but there is more (a lot more) when you read along, as I have covered UPI transactions, UPI recurring payment, UPI OTM, and UPI payout in future chapters.

4.F Cash

"Cash is the king and digital is divine", that's what RBI said.

We can debate about the second half of the sentence, but the first half is indisputable.

A lot of people 'like' cash... It is easy to understand, it is tangible, it is anonymous, it can be hidden from 'the taxman' and if you have plenty of 'it', then you can swim in that like Uncle Scrooge (*From Disney's Duck Tales*).

India's cash landscape and its workings are quite broad and complex so I will narrow the scope to online commerce.

'Is cash acting as a catalyst for eCommerce growth or creating a hindrance? Or who will win the race, cash, or online payments?'

Let's see!

Despite all the talks about digital payments, cash remains an important mode of payment. Even in online eCommerce, more than half of the transactions are still cash (COD - Cash on Delivery).

Many users who have the means to pay online still prefer cash. Because:

- Lack of trust in the merchant *(whether my dress or food will be delivered)*
- Fear of paying online *(oh... what if they steal my money?)*
- Lack of knowledge about how to use a payment instrument.
- Simply random stubborn reason, "I prefer cash" *(let us not ignore the ignorant people)*

How 'cash' helped eCommerce grow?

Cash on Delivery (COD) helped merchants to build trust. After successful order fulfillment *(maybe multiple orders)*, a skeptical customer would start paying online *(FYI - I am one of those skeptics)*. eCommerce merchants do not mind cash *(although it has its own problems)* as long as they are selling.

Having said that, merchants do enforce certain restrictions on COD orders based on the products, ticket size, delivery location, and user's cancellation history.

How 'Cash' is a hindrance to eCommerce?

a. Cash management costs: Either the merchant's delivery person or 3rd party delivery company will collect cash from the customer.

   If cash is collected by the 3rd party delivery company, the company will charge additional 'cash handling fees' apart from delivery charges from the merchant.

   If the merchant's delivery person collects cash, then the bank charges 'cash management charges' to handle cash. The point is ***cash is not free!***

b. Delivery person may lose collected cash.

c. Refunding cash transactions is a bigger problem. Merchants cannot send a person to a customer's home to return the money. Can they?

How do you deal with cash?

Companies tried and are still trying various ways to convert COD (Cash on delivery) orders to POD (Payment on Delivery) through various means:

a. Mobile POS machines to swipe cards

b. ePOS or Soft POS: Mobile App for delivery person that can generate dynamic QR code, or send payment links, or even facilitate NFC based card payment.

c. QR codes: Send static QR Code (*amount needs to be entered after scanning*) with the delivery person or stick dynamic QR code (*amount is embedded in the QR*) on the package so the customer can pay using UPI App

d. Send payment link to customer, and customer will open the link (that opens checkout page) and pay using cards, net-banking, wallet, or UPI.

There is '***no silver bullet***' to the COD problem. Each of the above methods has one or other issues, such as data connectivity, limited payment options, or commercials. After doing all this, if the customer still wants to pay in cash, the merchants can't say 'no' to her.

Refunding 'Cash of delivery (COD)' orders

Cash on delivery creates bigger problems when it comes to refunds. When a cash order is canceled/returned, how do you return the refund amount to the user?

Reverse logistics person who collects the product from the customer is not responsible for returning the money.

So, how do you deal with this situation?

There are multiple options:

a. Put that refund amount in the merchant's closed-loop wallet and thus avoid hassles of refund. Plus, feel happy that you have increased 'customer stickiness' *(the customer has to buy something on your website as funds are stuck in that closed-loop wallet)*

b. Collect the customer's bank account details and push the money to that account via IMPS or NEFT

   Note: Merchant should be sure that account details are correct by (1) collecting the canceled cheque (2) verify the beneficiary details *(by doing penny drop)*

   c. Collect the VPA/UPI ID and push the refund amount to that VPA or initiate UPI transfer to customer's mobile number *(after checking if mobile number is linked to VPA)*

Note: Make sure to validate the VPA and beneficiary name before initiating refund

Problems start cascading when you have to do these processes (mentioned in b and c) at scale with efficiency. Plus, all of this involves additional cost and effort.

Closing Remarks

Flipkart is one of the first companies which promoted COD (Cash on Delivery) and look where it is now *(just to clarify… it is in a very good position)*.

Uber added **'cash'** as payment option for the first time, only for Indian users.

Every merchant wants every customer to pay digitally, but cash is inevitable.

India is well advanced when it comes to digital payments.

The government and RBI have a great vision for digital payments. Reducing MDR on payment modes *(UPI and RuPay Debit Cards)*, innovative platforms *(UPI, BBPS, etc.)*, penalties or charges for cash handling, regulations & frameworks for safeguarding customers - Many such actions were taken to boost the digital economy, but still, there is more cash in circulation than ever.

A complete (100%) digital economy is a dream and a very big dream. India is progressing one step at a time towards that. But for now, we have to live with **'cash'** and have to figure out better ways *(solutions, processes, awareness)* to reduce the usage of cash.

4.G   Cryptocurrencies

Cryptocurrencies are everything that you don't understand about money combined with everything that you don't understand about computers — John Oliver

Before we get into details of Cryptocurrencies, let's start with the basic question.

What is money/currency?

That is a simple question - we all know 'what is money', right? Are you sure?

Investopedia defines money as *"liquid asset used to facilitate **transactions of value**. It is used as a **medium of exchange** between individuals and entities. It's also a **store of value** and a **unit of account** that can measure the value of other goods"*.

Wow… heavy definition. Don't worry, we will get there in few paragraphs.

We started with an exchange of barley and goats *(barter system)*, then precious metals *(gold, silver)*, and now reached currencies *(coins and banknotes)*

Currency issued by RBI

Currency issued by Bantu (My Daughter)

There is not much difference between the currency note issued by the RBI and the one designed by my daughter... 'as long as you *"**believe**"* that 'these papers' have '**value**'.

A currency note is nothing but a *'promise'* - a promise that the person holding it can exchange it for goods/services worth that amount.

And that promise is 'literally' printed on every currency note along with the signature of RBI's Governor.

"I PROMISE TO PAY THE BEARER THE SUM OF FIFTY RUPEES"

With RBI issued Rs.50 currency note, I can buy anything worth Rs.50 in a grocery store.

Come to think of it, **'Bantu Money'** also has a value; in exchange for her money, she allows me to watch any NEWS channel of my choice for 1 hour.

The only difference is that the entire country believes in RBI's currency, and only the 3 people in my family believe in Bantu's currency.

So, if enough people believe **'something'** *(peanuts or Pokémon card or Bitcoin)* has a value, then yes, those items can become currency for them.

How are Cryptocurrencies min(t)ed?

In the non-crypto world, the central bank will print currency notes based on various macroeconomic conditions *(earlier, it used to be against gold reserves)*. A currency note is nothing but a loan, and it's expected that all currencies issued will return to the bank.

Expectedly, there is a limit to how much money you can print. It is just standard supply-demand - more the supply, lesser demand, and the currency loses value. If you print more, then you will push the economy to hyperinflation *('Rapid, excessive and out-of-control general price increases in an economy' - Investopedia)*, and that is what happened in Argentina and Zimbabwe.

In the Crypto world, these virtual currencies are created by a process called **'mining'** - the process of verifying the validity of crypto transactions added to the blockchain. The fastest node that performs this task accurately will be awarded with new cryptocurrencies.

Although cryptocurrencies are generated 'out of thin air' (*technically, hardware and software*) that doesn't mean there is an infinite supply of virtual currencies, as excess supply will drop the value (*standard supply-demand logic*). Hence, there is a limit to how much virtual money you can create *(Example: There can be only 21 million Bitcoins)*.

If creation has no such limit, then some currencies have the logic of destroying currencies to keep a check on the number of virtual currencies (*tokens*) in circulation.

Ledger & Verification

For government issued money, the central bank keeps track of it — how much is printed, how much is with the banks, and how much is in circulation. As cryptocurrencies are mined *(issued)* by not one single authority or entity, everyone (*called 'nodes'*) will keep the ledger. In this distributed ledger model, every node will update the ledgers for every transaction.

Considering the central banks' money is printed and managed by one entity, that entity has to provide platforms/rails and clearing services to transfer the money among entities and users. In India, we have NEFT, UPI, IMPS, and more.

In cryptocurrencies, there is no such barrier or central clearing house. Anyone can transfer money to anyone, but every time the transfer happens, the nodes are required to update the ledgers. So basically, everyone (node) is keeping count of everything.

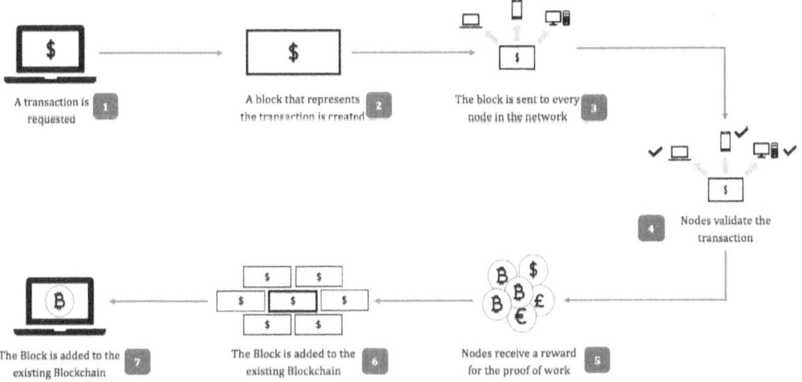

Let's summarize these points:

- Money has value if people believe in it.
- Money can be created out of thin air.
- Limit the supply so currency's value won't drop.
- Have ledger to keep the count.
- Have mechanism to exchange it.

When these points are brought together, cryptocurrencies are born. Today, we have thousands of cryptocurrencies with notable ones such as Bitcoin, Ether, and Dogecoin.

Users can buy or sell crypto currencies on crypto exchanges such as Binance, Coinbase etc.

Utilities of Crypto:

- Transfer: Considering it is just wallet to wallet transfer, so it is faster

- Purchase: One can buy things using cryptocurrencies *(if merchants are ready to accept crypto as currency)*. Cryptocurrencies are extremely volatile so 'crypto people' came up with 'stablecoins' that are pegged to USD, so volatility is predictable.

- Investment: As cryptocurrencies are volatile, one can buy them at low price and sell them at high (*sort of get rich or become poor fast scheme*)

Cryptocurrencies in India:

Only a couple of countries have accepted cryptocurrencies as '**legal tender**' (*same status as sovereign currency*), and many countries treat cryptocurrencies as 'virtual assets' rather than currency, few countries have banned crypto currency related activities, and many countries have regulated crypto exchanges.

The most important concern with cryptocurrencies is, they are not issued by the Government or central bank of the country. Also, there is no clear end-to-end tracking of fund movement (*who owns it and whom it is being transferred to*).

In India, the crypto sector went through ups and downs (*more downs than ups*). As of today, RBI is against crypto mainly because (1) Cryptocurrencies doesn't come under any regulatory oversight (2) these currencies are volatile and speculative (3) they are opaque, so they can be exploited by bad actors for money laundering and terror financing.

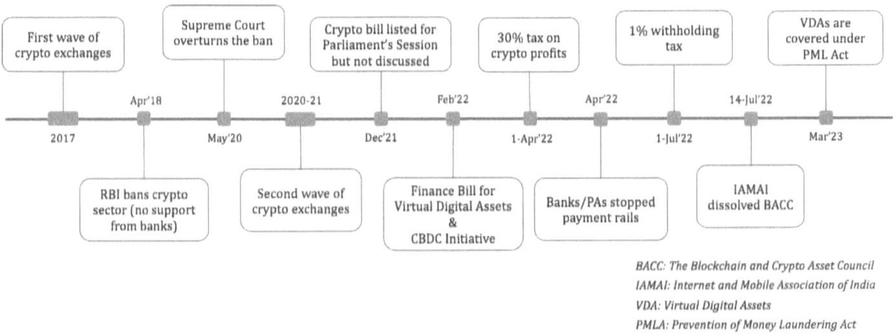

At present, the crypto sector in India is in trouble - High taxation, withholding tax, unavailability of payment rails, and *(most importantly)* an uncertain regulatory environment.

If you think that one day you will be able to order food on Swiggy using Bitcoin, then forget it; that day may not come in the foreseeable future.

If you are a real fan of blockchain and digital currencies, and your interest is beyond making some quick money, then cheer up, everything is not that gloomy.

RBI has launched ***eRupee*** - CBDC (Central Bank Digital Currency).

Read the next chapter.

4.H CBDC - Central Bank Digital Currency

100+ countries are researching, piloting, and launching CBDCs to achieve various goals:

- Reduce usage of paper cash
- Reduce cost of printing, distribution, and cash management.
- Provide something similar to 'cash' but in the digital form.
- Make cross-border transfers faster and cheaper.
- Counter private virtual currencies (aka cryptocurrencies); provide something similar to cryptocurrencies without the risks that come with those.

In the last quarter of 2022, RBI launched India's own CBDC named **eRupee**.

(do not confuse it with e-RUPI, UPI based voucher product)

*"**CBDC is a legal tender issued by the RBI in a digital form. It is same as sovereign currency and is exchangeable 1:1 with fiat currency.**"*

- CBDC is a liability in RBI's books whereas our existing money is liability on banks' books.
- Digital Form factor
- CBDC holder doesn't earn interest on the CBDC amount.
- To some extent, retail CBDC will be anonymous *(similar to cash)*

A bit confusing… isn't it?

Understandable… we will have three types of money: cash, digital money *(the one that we see in our bank accounts)*, and eRupee.

Here is the comparison:

	Cash	Digital Money	eRupee (CBDC)
Liability of	Banks	Banks	RBI
Form Factor	Paper	Digital	Digital
Earn Interest?	No	Yes	No
Fungible#	Yes	No	Yes
Anonymity	Yes	No	Not Fully

#Fungible: No need of a bank account to hold

Types of CBDCs:

We will have two types of CBDCs:

1. **Wholesale eRupee** for financial institutions
2. **Retail eRupee** for users and businesses

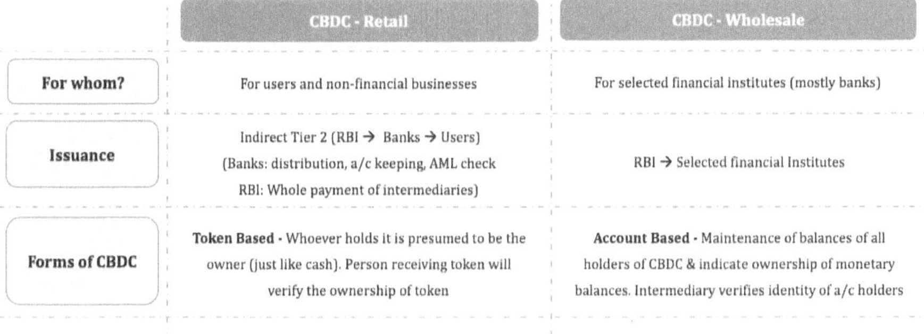

Understanding eRupee:

eRupee is similar to a digital wallet where the user doesn't earn interest on the balance amount, but eRupee is different from a wallet as a digital wallet works on homogenous amounts, whereas eRupee works on tokens.

In a digital wallet, Rs.203 is just Rs.203, whereas in CBDC eRupee, Rs.203 is made of different denominations (e.g., Rs.200 note and two coins of Rs.1 and Rs.2)

Let's say if you spend Rs.50 from each of the wallets.

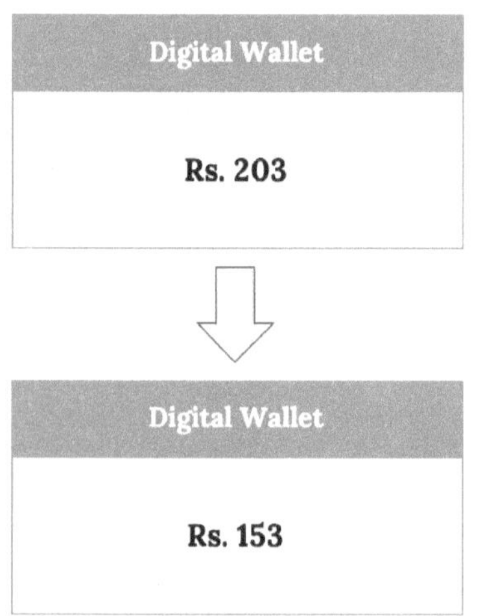

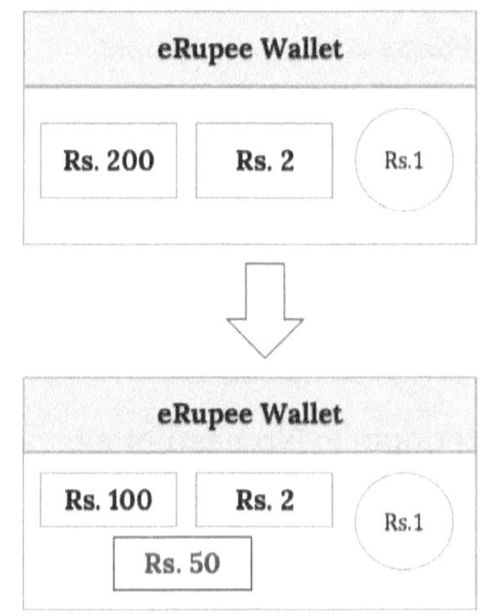

In a digital wallet, the balance is reduced by Rs.50, and the new balance will become Rs.153.

Whereas in the eRupee, Rs.200 note is removed and new notes of Rs.100 and Rs.50 are introduced and still the balance (after spending) will be Rs.153

Fascinating… isn't it?

Little more on working:

Each of the eRupee currency coins and notes will have a 15-digit unique serial number *(just like our regular currency notes)*.

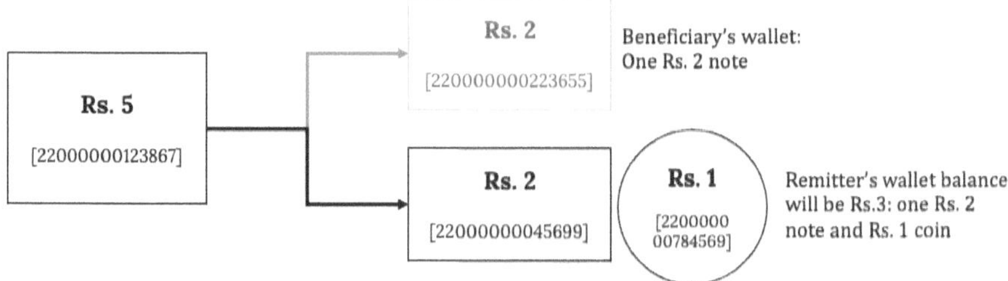

Remitter had one note of Rs.5 and transferred Rs. 2 to Beneficiary.

Beneficiary received one note of Rs.2

The remitter's new balance is Rs.3, which is made up of one note of Rs.2 and one coin of Rs.1

[Each of these new notes and coin will have unique serial numbers]

What happened to that Rs.5 note?

It was removed from the system *(even from bank's ledgers)* to avoid double counting *(if that original Rs.5 note is not removed, then we will have Rs.10 in the system)*

Working of CBDC for users

- A user has to install the bank's App *(that are live with eRupee)*
- Convert the INR to eRupee by loading eRupee wallet *(few banks allow loading via UPI)*
- eRupee balance can be withdrawn to bank account (eRupee → INR)
- eRupee balance doesn't earn any interest *(just like cash or wallet)*
- User can make P2P transfer and pay at stores by scanning QR.
- eRupee will be shown as separate payment mode *(as it is different money)*
- User can deregister the eRupee App (of bank) and the balance amount is credited to the linked bank account.

Path to success for eRupee

- Curiosity and interest of retail customers, businesses, and banks
- *(We get excited to visit the new Panipuri stall... why not for CBDC? :))*

- Cheaper processing cost: UPI is free for customers but not for the banks as the banks do incur infrastructure and operational costs. If the cost of eRupee transactions is lower than UPI, then… Yes, then banks will promote it.

- eRupee will ride on UPI's acceptance infrastructure.

- RBI intends to allow non-bank entities to participate in the eRupee ecosystem.

- *(UPI's huge success is because of TPAPs like PhonePe, Google Pay, PayTM etc.)*

- eRupee has strong use cases in cross-border payments and inter-bank transactions.

Challenges ahead for eRupee:

- **Will it beat UPI?**

  We have UPI and IMPS that work in real-time and are cost efficient. So, what is that eRupee will do extra?

- **Education:** Users will have to learn a new thing (*not just a thing but a new type of 'money'*), and it takes a lot of effort to educate the masses.

- **Plenty is a problem:** RBI/banks will not issue '*a lot of eRupee*' because it may lead to loss of deposits to banks; and that will hamper their credit-creating capacity.

- **No Interest:** This could be a buzzkill… If one has to hold digital money without earning interest, then there are PPI digital wallets and UPI Lite wallet.

- **Acceptance:** It is not easy to build acceptance infrastructure. eRupee did try on its own, but then it eventually will ride on UPI acceptance network of QRs. Nonetheless there will be changes in product and process that ecosystem participants have to work on.

Can CBDC be an alternative to cryptocurrencies?

We are assuming that people are interested in cryptocurrencies because of their utility.

But is it the case? - I think mostly, people were into 'crypto' to make easy money.

But can they make similar money in eRupee? - **NO**

Then will they be interested in this boring virtual currency (eRupee) that won't even earn interest, let alone make them rich overnight?

Can CBDC be an alternative to Cash?

People prefer cash for various reasons such as convenience (*cash is easy to understand*), to avoid taxes, and to hide it from authorities (e.g., *bribes*).

So, I assume a few will move to eRupee *(mostly the ones who are already comfortable with digital money)*, but the cash hoarders will continue to hoard it in physical form because it is completely anonymous.

Can CBDC solve problems of Cross Border payments?

Popular opinion is that CBDC will make cross-border transfers cheaper and more efficient.

- **Expensive**: Cross-border payments are expensive *'by design'*. Banks make big margins. Although CBDC may lower the cost of transfers, will banks let go of their margins?

- **Compliance**: Cross-border payments have higher compliance. Those compliances add to cost and time. And these compliances will not go away for CBDCs.

- How do you connect 100 CBDCs *(of 100 countries)* that work on different protocols and technologies? We would need a common protocol *(something similar to SWIFT)*.

Note: SWIFT is developing a protocol for CBDCs (New money, same problem, same solution)

Maybe it is possible that inter-country CBDCs will work bilaterally among groups of countries. Already, a few countries have formed groups to build private cross-border payment channels. (Example: Project Jasper - Canada, UK, Singapore)

Read the details in Chapter 25.A

Closing Remarks

India is in the early stages of CBDC. In fact, the entire world is in the early stages. Curiosity and excitement around CBDC are high.

Wholesale CBDCs may play an important role in fund transfer between inter-financial institutions within a country and beyond borders, whereas retail CBDCs are yet to establish their utility, especially in India, where we have UPI.

India's CBDC, **eRupee,** is still evolving, after allowing scan and pay at UPI QRs, RBI is allowing 3rd party Apps (likes of PhonePe, Cred etc.) be part of eRupee ecosystem.

There is work happening around '*programmable CBDC*' wherein eRupee can be used only at selected places. Programmable eRupee can be used for Government subsidies or direct benefit transfer schemes.

Example: A farmer can use subsidies *(which is issued as eRupee)* only at fertilizer stores. Sounds exciting, but RBI has to remove dependency on smartphones and data connectivity.

Interesting but too early to conclude that CBDC will be a successful story.

In due time, we will know whether CBDC will be a great success and solve the problems that it is meant to solve, or it will be reduced to 'just another money'.

4.1 Cheque

Long ago, very long ago... before UPI, before cards, before internet... There was only cash and Cheque... the first one is thriving and the latter one is still surviving.

Cheques do not have the glamor of UPI, so we don't get to hear about them, but even today, Cheques are relevant.

In 2022, 722 million Cheques worth $862 Billion were processed. That is like roughly 23 Cheques per second... wow! (*It is kind of fun to measure everything in 'per second'*)

What is Cheque?

It is a document issued by the bank that can be used by the payer to make payment of a specific amount to the payee or the bearer.

Benefits of Cheque	Drawbacks of Cheque
• Preferred for large value transactions. • For future payments (*postdated cheque*) • Covered under negotiable instruments act (*Cheque bounce is a punishable crime*) • Can be used for all types of transactions (C2C, C2B, B2C, B2B, C2G, G2C) • No need to ask for beneficiary's account details or adding details to net-banking	• Delays due to physical movement: Payer to give cheque to Payee which payee has to deposit in her bank. • Not instant (*Physical movement + clearance time after cheque deposit*) • Cheque clearance happens only on weekdays

C = Customer, B = Business, G = Government

Cheque - Layout, Paper, and Security

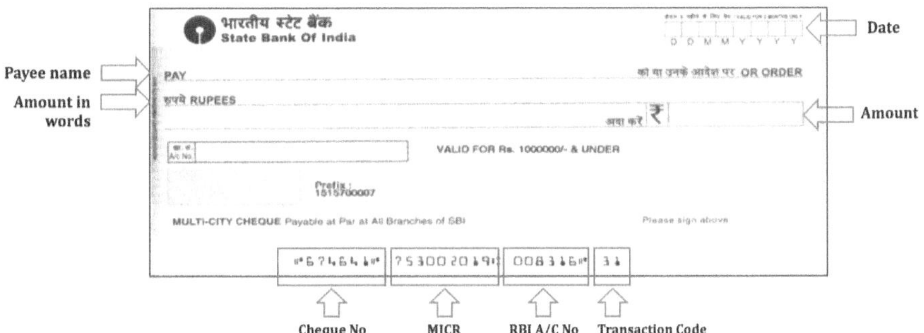

MICR Code *(Magnetic Ink Character Recognition):* 9 Digit number that represent <3 digits-city>, <3 digits-bank>, <3 digits-Branch>

Cheques come in standard size: 202mm length, 92mm width, 220mm diagonal length, 13mm width for white space at the bottom. The Cheque is printed on 94 GSM paper with a thickness of 110 micrometers. The paper should be carbon and UV free.

To make it tamper proof, a bunch of security features such as watermarks, UV features, microscopic features, and photographic images are added.

Few things to remember while writing a cheque:

- Write 'a/c payee' on top left corner.
- Add '/-' after you write the amount *(e.g., Rs. 10,000/-)*
- Do not write on the bottom white space.
- Signature as per your bank's records.
- Do not scratch and/or re-write.

Types of Cheques:

There are nine types of Cheques… Yes, nine different types of Cheques. *(No kidding)*

(1) bearer cheque (2) order cheque (3) crossed cheque (4) open cheque (5) post-dated cheque (6) stale cheque (7) Traveler's cheque (8) self cheque (9) banker's cheque

Post-dated Cheque is the most interesting one; The post-dated cheque will have a future date, and it can be encashed after that date, not before.

Example: If I give you a Cheque on 4-Feb-2024 with the date 14-Feb-2024, then that Cheque can be encashed only on or after 14-Feb-2024, even if you deposit it on 5-Feb-2024.

Post-dated cheques are valid for three months. So, the cheque will be valid till 13-May -2024

Note: Three months as per calendar days irrespective of days in those months

Post-dated cheques are used for all types of future payments, including installment payments.

Cheque Processing:

Cheques are processed using CTS (Cheque Truncation System) - A platform managed by NPCI.

Example: The Payer gives a Cheque drawn from ICICI, and the payee deposits it in HDFC bank.

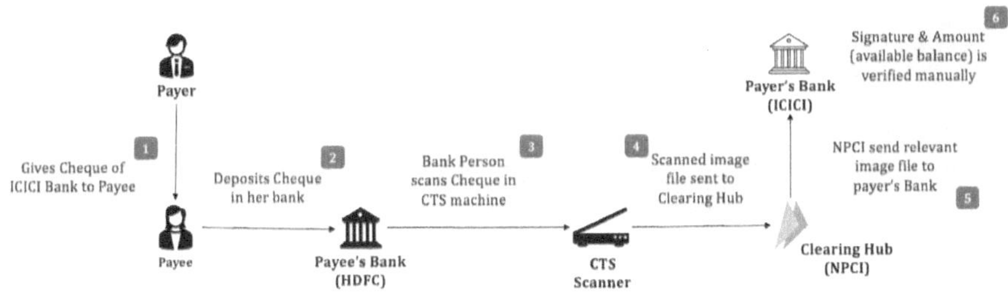

CTS processing is done in three grids.

- **Southern (Chennai)**: Andhra, Telangana, Karnataka, Tamil Nadu, Odisha, West Bengal, Sikkim, Tripura, Mizoram, Arunachal Pradesh, Nagaland, Assam, Meghalaya, Puducherry

- **Western (Mumbai)**: Maharashtra, Goa, Gujarat, Madhya Pradesh, Chhattisgarh

- **Northern (Delhi)**: NCR of New Delhi, Haryana, Punjab, Uttar Pradesh, Bihar, Jharkhand, Rajasthan, Chandigarh

To improve overall efficiency (fund management, infrastructure, faster TAT), RBI has implemented a national grid - **"One Nation One Grid"**.

TAT for Clearance:

1 day if the payer and payee bank are the same, 2-3 days if the payer and payee banks are different. CTS operates only on RBI/Bank working days.

Fund Movement:

Once the Cheque is cleared, the payer's account (ICICI bank) is debited, and the payee's account (HDFC Bank) will be credited through RBI *(clearing house for the interbank money movement)*.

CTS Failure Reasons:

There are more than 90 reasons for failure that can be classified into business *(user related)* and technical *(CTS process or bank related)*.

Few of the top failure reasons: (1) Insufficient funds, (2) Signature mismatch, (3) Stale cheque *(older than 3 months)*, (4) Stop payment.

Cheque Bounce/Dishonor:

This means that the Cheque is not cleared *(the payee didn't receive money)* due to insufficient balance or account is closed by the payee.

To qualify as 'dishonor/bounce', the transaction should involve some sort of liability from the payer to payee (e.g., loan repayment or payment towards product/service availed)

Cheque bounce is a criminal offense under Section 138 of the Negotiable Instruments Act of 1881. The offender may get a jail term up to 1 year or penalty equal to twice the cheque amount or both.

The original Negotiable Instrument Act needed a physical Cheque to be presented to the payer's bank. In 2002, the Act was amended to include digital images of the cheque.

Note: To upgrade legacy products, not only tech; even related regulations need to be amended

Positive Pay System:

To prevent fraud *(e.g., Cheque tampering)*, RBI rolled out 'Positive Pay System'. Think of it like the Additional Factor Authentication (AFA) of the CTS process.

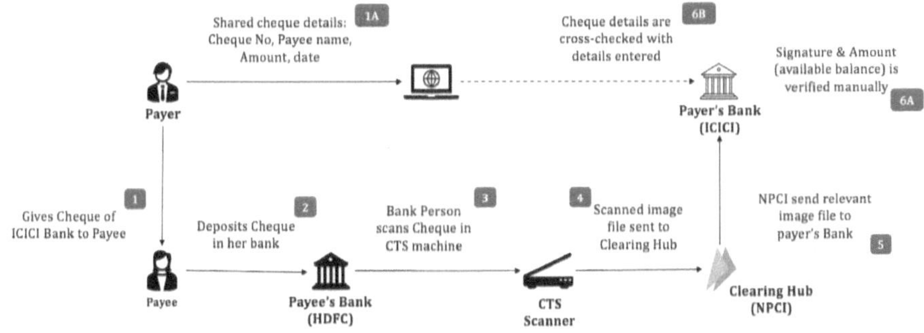

1. After issuing the cheque, the Payer should provide the cheque details (*Cheque No, payee name, amount, date*) to his/her bank (*at the branch, by mail or in internet banking*) at least 24 hours before payee deposits the Cheque.

2. During the cheque clearance, these details are cross-checked and cleared.

Note: Positive Pay process is optional for the amount >Rs.50,000 and <=Rs.5 Lakh; Positive Pay is mandatory for the amount > Rs.5 Lakh.

Closing Remarks:

RBI's vision document 2025 (released in 2022) sets a target of reducing Cheque-based payments to less than 0.25% of the total retail payments.

Banks have taken few steps to reduce Cheque usage: (a) Promote NEFT, RTGS, IMPS, and UPI transfers (b) Charge fees for issuance of new

Cheque books (c) Make Cheques expensive for payee, so a payee will insist on online transfer *(Not sure if it is done)*

There is no doubt that overall Cheque usage is reducing as the numbers are halved in last 15-20 years. However, cheques are still popular among certain users and businesses. So, cheques will survive for a few more years.

Chapter 5

Guidelines

When I was a teenager... I asked my close friend, "What do we need to ride a bike?".

Without a second thought, he said, "We need a bike... just a bike".

The answer made perfect sense at that moment, but later, I realized that we needed a license, bike insurance, knowledge of traffic rules, and most importantly, money to buy a bike.

What did I learn?

There are guidelines that apply in all spectrums of life – a few are mandated by governing or regulatory bodies, and a few are self- imposed.

'Red light' at a traffic signal means that we should stop the bike — that's by regulation. But if there is no cop at the signal & no traffic, but you still stop at the red light, that's self-regulation.

Payment space cannot operate on self-regulation. So, RBI enforces regulations and guidelines.

I will touch upon relevant regulations or policies when I cover various products and platforms. So, keep an eye on those.

In the next two sub-chapters, I will cover a few of the important guidelines and master directions related to various payment entities, platforms, and products.

5.A Payment Aggregator Related

Payment Aggregators (PAs) are very important entities in the Payments Ecosystem. In this subchapter, we will cover guidelines related to PAs.

Payments and Settlement Systems Act (2007)

This was the main guideline that is followed by the online payments industry. This is not one single document but rather multiple notifications that were issued over a period. One needs to read all notifications and related guidelines to get the complete view.

A few of the notable points of these directives are:

Intermediaries *(Payment Aggregators, acquiring bank or payment service provider)* should move money via nodal account *(collect money from acquiring banks and other payment service providers to nodal account and then settle to merchants)*. Also, do not keep funds in the nodal account for more than 3 working days without justification.

Follow the Master KYC (Know Your Customer) guidelines while on-boarding merchants. That means conducting due diligence about the merchant (business model) and collect KYC documents of the merchant and its director(s) and/or authorized signatories.

These are not stringent guidelines. A financial intermediary doesn't have to get a license or anything to report back to the regulator unless you appear on RBI's radar.

However, it so happened that, along with the growth of digital payments, even the frauds increased. So, RBI came up with comprehensive PA/PG guidelines in March 2020 for online Payment Aggregators and Payment Gateways.

I. PA/PG Guidelines

1. **Authorization**: Get an authorization from RBI to run a PA or PG business

2. **Capital requirement**: Do you want to move the money for merchants? Then first, show the money. That is a minimum of Rs. 25Cr net-worth

3. **Governance**: Bring in corporate governance in the company; Active participation of the board and senior management in PA's policies. Also, appoint various Officers *(Nodal, Grievance, Service Assurance, Principal)* and committees *(IT strategy, IT steering, vendor outsourcing etc.)*

4. **Merchant Due Diligence**: Conduct due diligence of merchants and follow Master KYC (Know Your Customer) and AML (Anti Money Laundering) guidelines.

   - Classify the merchants into various risk categories (Low, medium, high)

   - Based on the risk profile of the merchant, PAs should do enhanced due diligence and periodic re-KYC of the merchants.

5. **Security & fraud prevention**: Follow highest level of security, data protection, and data localization practices along with PCI-DSS. Conduct audits periodic as per guidelines, including annual PA-System Audit Report (PA-SAR) audit by CERT-in empaneled auditor.

6. **Customer Grievance**: Customer is important; safeguard them and address all customer complaints/grievances.

7. **Escrow Accounts:** PAs can have two escrow accounts.

   - Higher flexibility in terms of holding the funds in escrow accounts (depending on payment confirmation, shipment date, delivery date, or refund date).

   - The cherry on top is an opportunity to earn 'interest' on a 'core portion'. PA guidelines define the calculation of core portion.

   - Merchant and PA can pre-fund the escrow accounts

       – Guidelines advise to avoid fund movement between two escrow accounts.

8. **Permissible credits/debits:** Only permissible credits and debits are allowed.

   - Permissible credits to escrow: payments from customers (i.e., acquiring banks), prefunding by merchants/PAs, transfers related to refunds, disputes etc., and payments received toward promotional activities, incentives, cashbacks.

   - Permissible debits to escrow: Payments to merchants and service providers, transfers related to refunds for failed/disputed transactions, payment commission (at predetermined rates), payment amount received under promotional activities, incentives, cashbacks.

9. **Reports**: Different types of reports *(transaction, escrow balance etc.)* to be submitted to RBI on annual, quarterly, monthly, and based on events.

10. **Monitoring and reporting:** Monitor transaction patterns of merchants and report suspicious transactions and merchants to FIU-IND *(Financial Intelligence Unit – India)*

Here are few other important points:

- ATM PIN cannot be used as 2FA for card-not-present (online) transactions.

- PAs cannot enforce transaction limits, but only bank/issuing entity are allowed.

- Refunds can go to a different source based on customer's consent.

   Note: That means, PAs can use payout rails (IMPS, NEFT, UPI, Visa Direct, MasterCard Money Send) to process refunds directly to the customer's account or card. Also, merchant can take customer consent and move refund to merchant's own closed loop wallet.

- Only card networks or card issuers are allowed to issue the card tokens and card number is not stored by the PA or its merchants.

Hold on… why are we rushing to licenses… We are not done with guidelines yet.

On 16-Apr-2024, RBI issued a draft circular for comment:

- PAs to perform CPV (Contact Point Verification), Bank a/c verification and/or verify OVD (Officially Valid Document) for small and medium merchants.

  Note: Based on turn over, merchants are classified into small and medium.

- PAs can appoint agents to perform Video based Customer Identification process (V-CIP)

- A PA can use another PA for the transaction processing and both PAs are expected to do merchant due diligence - This is specifically meant for PAs who use another PA for net-banking *(That's relief until the Net-banking interoperable model is rolled out)*

Licensing Process:

PA/PG guideline was issued in March-2020 and entities were expected to apply for the license by end of Sep-2021. Later allowed, entities to apply for license by end of Sep-2022.

RBI started issuing in-principle approval from July-2022 and started giving final approval *(Certificate of Authorization)* in Dec-2023.

An entity which is new to PA business is expected to commence the business only after receiving final authorization, and existing PAs *(who already operate PA business)* are allowed to operate unless RBI had put them under embargo *(i.e., not to onboard new merchants)*.

Entire licensing process was long… a very long journey. Few entities were asked to re-apply *(PayU, PayTM)*, many entities got rejected, few were put under embargo for more than a year *(Cashfree, RazorPay, PayU)*.

Even after 75+ entities got rejected, 60+ entities are in various stages of approval process *(under review, in-principle authorization, final authorization)*.

So, the PA space will continue to be crowded, but hopefully, it will be much cleaner.

II. PA - CB Guidelines

There are different types of cross border payments **(Read Chapter 13)**

Here we will cover the guidelines of cross-border Export and Import.

Past Guidelines:

Earlier such cross-border transfers were covered under ***OPGSP (Online Payment Gateway Service Providers)*** guidelines.

In April '2022, RBI issued draft ***OEIF (Online Export-Import Facilitators)*** guideline with the intention to replace OPGSP guideline but didn't implement it.

On 31st Oct 2023, RBI issued the new guidelines to regulate companies that operate cross-border payments. i.e., **PA-CB guidelines**

PA-CB guidelines define three distinct licenses for entities.

- **PA-CB-E (Export)** - To move funds inside India against export of goods or services.
- **PA-CB-I (Import)** - To move funds outside India against import of goods or services.
- **PA-CB-E&I (Export and Import)**: To do both activities.

Note: Irrespective of the model, the entities would need AD (Authorized Dealer) -I bank to move the funds

Also, the guidelines clearly defined different application timelines and net-worth requirements for existing and new entities.

- **Existing PA-CB**s are the ones presently operating cross-border services (under OPGSP). These companies include Payment Aggregators (E.g., Cashfree, BillDesk) and non-PAs (e.g., Skydo, EximPe).

- **New PA-CBs** are the ones who do not have cross-border remittance business.

Note: Authorized Dealer Category I banks do not need separate authorization to operate PA-CB

Timelines: Existing PA-CBs to inform RBI by 31st Dec 2023 to seek approval, and new PA-CBs to take approval before commencing business

Summary of PA-CB guidelines:

a. PA/PG guidelines is applicable to PA-CB as well; everything that is expected of online PA in terms of process, security, compliance etc. is applicable.

b. Registration with FIU-IND (Financial Intelligence Unit - India) and expected to monitor the transactions, beneficiaries, and remitters, and report suspicious cases.

c. Net-Worth:

    - Existing PA-CBs to have Rs.15Cr during application and Rs.25Cr by 31-3-2026.

    - New PA-CBs to have Rs. 15Cr during application and Rs. 25Cr by end of 3rd Financial Year after receiving license.

d. Accounts: PA-CBs to have accounts with Category-I scheduled banks.

    - PA-CB-I to have Import Collection Account(s) (ICA)

- • PA-CB-E to have Export Collection Account(s) (ECA), a non-INR account.

  Separate ECA accounts for each of non-INR currencies.

- – Domestic PA escrow account to be separate from ECA and ICA

e. Transaction Limits:

- • Rs. 25,00,000 per unit of goods or service.

- • For import transactions, if the amount exceeds more than Rs.2,50,000 per unit then PA-CB-I to conduct due diligence on beneficiary (importer)

f. Authorized PA-CB wants to change activity (in import or export) then seek approval from RBI before starting new business.

III. Offline – Payment Aggregator (PA-P)

On 16-Apr-2024, RBI issued a draft circular for comments; and most likely the final guidelines/circular will be issued in a few months.

a. The guidelines on governance, net-worth requirement, merchant onboarding, security, monitoring, and reporting that are applicable to online PA (PA-O) *(refer to Section I)* are applicable to Offline PAs (i.e., PA-P) as well.

b. The card tokenization is applicable to PA-Os; card number is not allowed to be stored by any entity except card issuers or networks.

c. Existing offline payment aggregators are expected to seek approval from RBI within 60 days from the issuance of the circular and PA-Os who wish to start the offline payment business should seek approval from RBI.

d. PA-P can have two escrows for collection and settlement of funds and in case, the PA-O that wants to operate PA-P has to use the PA-Os two escrow accounts. (i.e., no additional escrow accounts to operate offline payments business)

e. Banks have to shut down any escrow/nodal accounts of offline payment aggregators who do not apply for PA-P license or with from application process or fail to receive authorization.

Closing Remarks:

An online Payment Aggregator (PA-O) licensed entity can operate Cross-border remittance (import and/or export) as PA-CB-Export and/or Import, can operate as COU and/or BOU in BBPS *(Read Chapter 17),* and operate Offline payment aggregation (PA-P).

So, the online PA license is similar to The ONE RING from JRR Tolkien's The Lord of Rings.

So, you can say, "The One License to rule them all" :)

In a way, PA license is the most important license in India, apart from banking license.

"Great power comes with great responsibility" - *Ben Parker (The Spiderman's Uncle)*

A PA license comes with great responsibility, compliance and hundred other reporting and auditing requirements. So, it is not necessary that all online PAs become PA-CB, COU/BOU, and PA-P. And many PA-CBs or COUs or PA-Ps will not operate Online Payment Aggregation business as each of these licenses will require a lot of effort or resources to manage the compliance apart from product development and business development.

But all these efforts are worth it, if the entity wants to play a significant role in this Payments Ecosystem.

5.B Other Guidelines

In this subchapter we will cover PPI and card specific guidelines

I. Prepaid Payment Instrument (PPI) Guidelines

Prepaid Payment Instruments (PPIs) work on pre-loaded amount, i.e., the amount has to be loaded on the instrument (Card or wallet), and then the available balance can be used for purchases (in-store and online) or cash withdrawal at ATMs (*Depending on the type of PPI*)

PPI guidelines:

- Banks and non-bank entities can apply for PPI license.

- Capital requirement is Rs.15 Cr positive net worth.

- PPI licensed entities to procure separate approval from RBI for co-branded prepaid cards.

- *Note: Co-branded card is launched among a company, PPI issuer and card network*

- RBI doesn't allow co-branding of PPI wallets.

- Funds of prepaid balance are parked in non-interest-bearing special purpose account *(e.g., Nodal Account)*

- Prepaid instruments can be issued to customers only after completion of KYC process.

- Limit of loading depends on the type of KYC. Rs.10,000 with minimum KYC (*only mobile OTP verification*) and Rs.2,00,000 with full KYC (*user's id validation*)

- PPIs are allowed for cash withdrawal at ATM or POS (*depends on type of PPI*)

- PPI licensed entities can avail NEFT/RTGS facility by directly setting up accounts with RBI *(Note: RBI is yet to share clear guidelines on this)*

- PPI entities to allow interoperability among payment instruments *(This is achieved by allowing linking of PPI wallet to UPI)*

- PPI can be loaded using credit card, debit card, bank account, or UPI.

- PPIs cannot be loaded with credit-line *(Just in time funding model)*

There are certain specific guidelines for different types of PPIs.

1. Expiry Date:

   - Gift Cards: 1 Year

   - General Purpose Reloadable Cards: 3 years.

   - Wallets don't expire *(Deactivated if the wallet is inactive for more than year)*

2. Limit on the PPI balance

   - Gift Cards: One time loading

   - Reloadable open loop PPIs: Rs.10,000 (min. KYC) and Rs.2,00,000 (Full KYC)

   - Forex Cards: $2,50,000 per year (with one-time max amount of $10,000)

3. Currency that can be loaded

   - Domestic PPIs — INR only

   - Forex Cards — Non-INR currencies only

4. Restriction on cash withdrawal through ATM or transfer to bank a/c

   - Gift Cards are not allowed for cash withdrawal as well as transfer to bank account.

   - Reloadable cards and Forex cards can be allowed for ATM withdrawal. Balance amount can be transferred to bank account.

5. Restriction on acceptance based on

   - MCC (merchant category code): card is accepted only with type of merchants (e.g., Sodexo card at Grocery merchants)

- Merchant ID/Terminal ID: Health card that works at partner hospitals.
- Territory: Forex card is not accepted in India, Nepal, and Bhutan)

II.   Guidelines for Cards

A. Credit Card issuance Guidelines:

In April 2022, RBI issued new guidelines for issuance of credit cards.

- **Card issuing**: With RBI's approval, Scheduled Commercials Banks, Regional Rural Banks, Urban Cooperative Banks, and NBFCS with net worth of Rs.100 Crore can issue credit cards.

- **Issuance**: Decision to issue credit card to a customer is with card-issuer; Inform applicant of the rejection reason; Issuance of unsolicited card or card upgrade will attract penalties.

- **Charges**: Transparency in communicating rate of interest, EMI conversion charges; MITC *(Most Important Terms & Conditions);* no hidden charges

- Card issuer to give **one month's notice** if there are any changes to charges and allow customer to cancel the card without levying additional charges.

- Card issuers to get **customer's consent** for card activation (OTP based), insurance, upgrades, replacement card, add-on card or any other products.

- **Calls to customer**: Tele-calling hours between 10AM–7PM; strictly not to mis-sell cards, upgrades, or no-cost EMIs

- **Billing:** One time option to change the billing cycle; send correct bill on time and provide at least fortnight for customer to repay

- **Bill Dispute**: Customer raised disputes to be resolved within 30 days; No charges to be levied on 'fraud' transaction until dispute is resolved.

- **Recovery:** Adhere to 'fair practices' - recovery agents shouldn't damage integrity and reputation of customers; maintain customer confidentiality

- **Card Blocking:** Should block card immediately in case of complaint; formalities can be done later; Provide 24x7 channel to block cards.

- **Card Closure:** Provide multiple channels (IVR, email, website, App etc.) to raise card closure request; Request for closure to be honored in 7 days and communicate closure information to customer via SMS, mail etc.

- **No default enablement for online payments:** Customer to enable card for online transactions.

- **Deactivate:** Initiate closure of card that is inactive for one year

Co-branded Credit Cards:

- Prior approval of RBI is not required; only to be approved by the card issuer's board and issuer should conduct proper due diligence of the co-branding partner.

- The co-branding partner should always promote it as co-branded card and mention 'issuer' name in all marketing materials.

- The co-branding partner shall not have access to card transaction data and will not be involved in any process or control of the card program.

Option to choose Card Network: In 2023, RBI updated the guidelines, and instructed credit card issuing banks to provide at least 2 options to customers to choose the card network (Visa, MasterCard, RuPay etc.) and also prohibited card issuers from having exclusive partnership with one card network.

B. 2nd Factor Authentication (2FA)

2FA is a process of establishing the authenticity of the payment instrument holder.

2 Factors - **What you have** *(e.g., Card number, customer id, VPA etc.)* and **what you know** *(e.g., OTP, password, MPIN etc.)*.

2FA is also called AFA (Additional Factor Authentication)

- Since May 2012, RBI has made 2FA mandatory for both card present (CP), card not present (CNP) and IVR *(Interactive Voice Response)* based transactions.

- All card networks have standard protocol to implement the 2FA process.

- 2FA / AFA is applicable for all payment modes *(cards, UPI, Net-banking, wallets etc.)* with exception MOTO (Mail Order Telephone Order) transactions; NFC payments up to Rs.5000, subsequent transactions of recurring payment solutions (NACH, SI on Cards, UPI AutoPay – within permissible debit amount), and UPI Lite wallet (up to Rs.500).

Innovation in 2FA:

SMS-based OTP is a synonym for 2FA because it is easier to implement. Back in 2012, when 2FA became mandatory, SMS based OTP was a natural choice, but now, with technological advancement, many things can be done. *(this feature is up for disruption)*

In February 2024, RBI proposed to adopt a principle-based framework for 2FA to promote alternatives to SMS based OTP.

This initiative can open scope for innovation; we can have voice-based, fingerprint-based, face recognition-based 2FA *(or anything fancy that we have seen in James Bond movies)*, and also, the frauds will reduce *(Eliminate the cases fraudsters get OTPs from innocent customers and cheat)*.

C. Card on File (CoF) Tokenization Guidelines

- **Coverage:** Applicable to all domestic cards *(credit, debit & prepaid)* and networks *(Visa, MasterCard, RuPay, Amex and Diners)*; not applicable to international cards

- **Flows:** Applicable on all types of flows - Standard, direct OTP, SI on cards; exception of MOTO (Mail Order Telephone Order)

- **Entities:**

  - Token Service Providers can be card issuing bank or card network.

  - Token requesters can be merchants, PAs or TSPs

  - Token processor can be PA or acquiring bank.

- **Uniqueness:** Token is unique to the card, PA/TSP, and merchant combination

- **Processing:** Token can be created and processed by the same PA; Transactions should be always initiated from merchant, and then the token requestor

- **Migration:** Tokens created for a merchant with a PA cannot be migrated to another PA

- **Consent:** Merchant to take consent from the customer for the tokenization

- **Token Deletion:** Card issuing bank to make provision for the cardholder to view tokenized card across merchant and provide provision to delete tokens for specific merchant(s)

- **For customer:** Customer can tokenize any number of cards on a merchant.

- **Display:** On checkout page, card network, bank name and last 4 digits of the card can be shown; first 6 digits (i.e., BIN) cannot be shown

- **Charges**: No additional charge for tokenization
- Merchants/PAs were expected to purge/delete all 'saved cards' by 30th Sep 2022.

After multiple extensions to deadline, tokenization is live since 1st Oct 2022.

For guest checkout cases (where the user doesn't opt for tokenization)

The plain card number is available/accessible to PAs/merchants for T+2 days *(changed from earlier T+4 days)* and to acquiring banks for T+90 days *(changed from earlier 180 days)*.

RBI wants to stop non-token flows of cards and implement a one-time usage token *(or Alt Id)* for guest checkout by 31-Oct-2023, but later, the deadline was extended. It is clear that 'Alt Id' will become mandatory, so the payment ecosystem participants are working towards readiness.

Token through Issuing Bank / Push Provisioning:

On 20-Dec-2023, RBI issued a circular on enabling tokenization through card issuing bank (aka push provisioning)

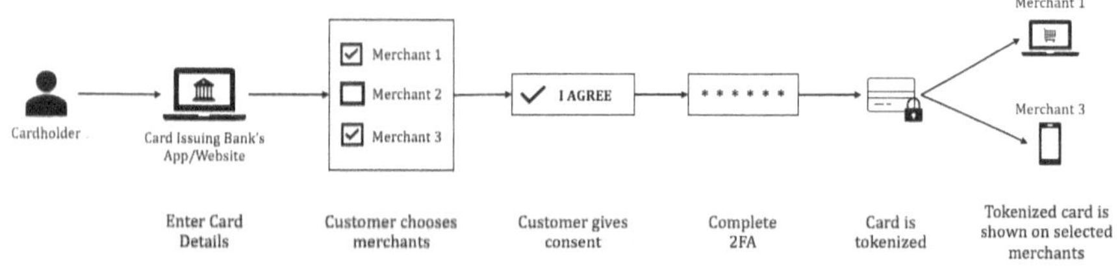

Customer can tokenize the card through her card issuing bank either during card issuance or any time later.

Once the customer selects the merchants, then the tokenized card will be available on the selected merchant's website/App for transaction. Cool… isn't it?

D. SI on Cards (Mandate on Cards)

- **Coverage**: All domestic cards *(Credit, Debit, Prepaid)*, card networks *(Visa, MasterCard, RuPay, Amex etc.)*

- **Debit limit**: Maximum of Rs.15000 per debit (as of Apr'24)

- **Registration & Debit:** First transaction done for the mandate registration should adhere to 2nd Factor Authentication; subsequent transaction doesn't require 2FA.

- **Card storage**: Card to be tokenized.

- **Pre-debit Notification**: Card issuing banks should send pre-debit notification to the cardholder at least 24 hours before the debit. Also, issuing banks should provide an option for the customer to opt-out of debit.

- **Post-debit notification**: Card issuing Bank should send post-debit notification to the cardholder.

- **Cancellation**: Card issuing bank to provide an online facility for the cardholder to cancel the mandate *(Customers can either opt only out from a specific debit or can opt entirely out of the mandate)*. Cancellation of mandate should follow 2FA.

- **Dispute Management**: Separate dispute management process for recurring payments from the regular chargeback process related to card payments.

More to come…?

Various types of entities have been regulated or require license or authorization to operate - Banks, card networks, NBFCs, PPIs, and BBPOUs.

Now, online PAs and PA-CB (Cross Border) have started receiving licenses, and soon, RBI will regulate offline payment aggregators.

With Digital Lending Guidelines, RBI has defined the way Digital Lending Apps, LSPs, and NBFCs should operate.

It is quite possible that other types of entities or business models such as payout and TSPs may come under regulations, authorization, or certification.

Closing Remarks

RBI has power to enforce these guidelines. From time-to-time RBI has imposed penalties, put embargoes, and even cancelled licenses of companies who violated these guidelines.

Few instances:

- In 2014, Uber was asked to adhere to 2FA on cards *(eventually Uber stopped using international PG and moved to PayTM wallet)*
- Embargo on MasterCard and Amex for not adhering to data localization guidelines.
- HDFC Bank and Kotak Mahindra Bank were stopped from issuing new credit cards.
- PayU, RazorPay and Cashfree were put under embargo *(not allowed to onboard new merchants)* for more than a year.
- PayTM Payments Bank was asked to stop bank account, wallet, and FASTag business.

Overall theme of all regulations is simple to interpret:

- Do not move/hold money of customers or merchants without authorization.
- Follow highest level of securities for payments system or infrastructure.
- Safeguard customers by providing secure payments systems; address complaints on time.

- Perform proper due diligence of merchants.

- Monitor suspicious transactions & merchants and report them to relevant authorities.

At times, regulations are not clear and leaves room for interpretation, and entities operate in that *'gray area' (fancy word – Regulatory Arbitrage)*. But eventually, RBI has plugged those gaps and stopped such models.

Example: Lending through prepaid cards was a big business; a single line update in RBI guideline, *'prepaid card cannot be loaded using credit line'*, brought that business model to a grinding halt.

Although we say that change is constant, frankly, nobody likes it when things change. At times, the guidelines feel a bit troublesome as the ecosystem has to undertake additional efforts to ensure adherence/compliance. But in the long run, these guidelines will help build a safe and secure payments ecosystem that both customers and businesses can rely on.

We will end this chapter here, but throughout this book, there will be references to various guidelines/regulations/circulars of RBI, other relevant regulators, and authorities. Keep an eye!

Reference sites to all guidelines are listed in *'the Reference'* section at the end of the book.

Chapter 6

Payment Aggregator (PA / PA-O)

Online Payment Aggregators (PA / PA-O) are the prominent players in the payment ecosystem.

Many times, people confuse Payment Aggregator with Payment Gateway (PG).

Payment Gateway (PG) is a piece of software that is used by acquiring banks to process card transactions. That's it. CyberSource, FSS, MIGS, ISG are some of the PGs in India.

Whereas Payment Aggregator (PA) brings multiple payment modes *(cards, net-banking, UPI, Wallets, BNPL etc.)* on a single platform by integrating with various acquiring banks, banks, issuers, and payment processing entities, and do the settlement to merchants.

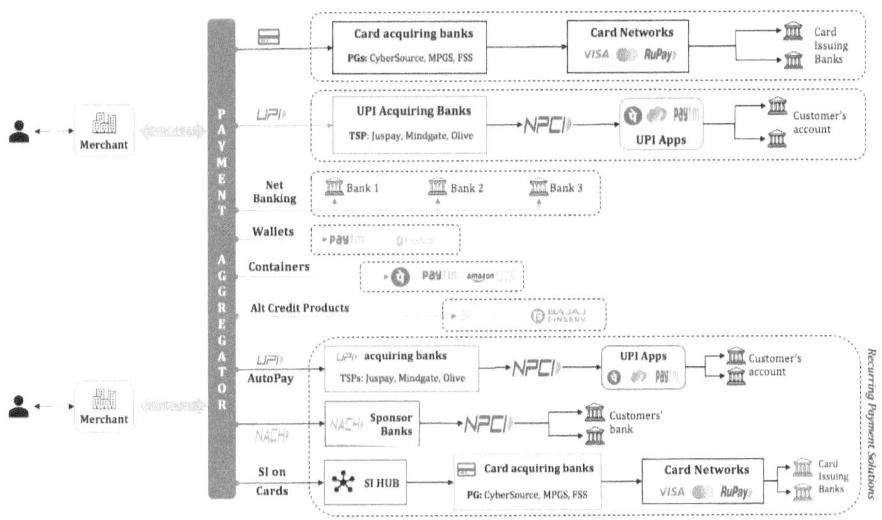

BillDesk is the 'official' pioneer of payment aggregation business in India and there are many PAs operating for a very long time.

In March 2020, RBI issues PA/PG guidelines, and companies who wish to operate the online PA business are required to receive approval from RBI.

Refer *Chapter 5.A* for PA/PG guidelines.

In the next few chapters, we will talk about integration, performance, settlement, and operations related to online Payment Aggregators.

6.A Merchant Onboarding

'Risk' is the underlying theme of payments; all processes, including technology, product features, guidelines, and merchant on-boarding process, are designed to reduce the risk.

MDR (Merchant Discount Rate) is the barometer of that risk in the payments ecosystem.

An e-commerce company may get MDR of 1.80% on credit cards, but an education institute will enjoy 1%. Reason for this differential rate is 'the risk' associated with these two different sectors.

Similarly, differential rates apply on POS *(point of sale)* and online transactions. In case of POS *(i.e., CP-Card Present scenario)*, the transaction charges are much lower compared to online payments *(i.e., CNP-Card Not Present scenario)*.

"Think of it like an insurance premium of a term policy. The premium amount for a 28-year-old non-smoker will be much lower than that for a same age person who smokes. Insurance companies perceive the second person 'riskier', so the premium goes high".

Risks in the Payments Ecosystem

There are two main types of risks: Financial Risk *(entities can lose money)* and Reputational Risk *(entities can lose credibility)*. These risks can be attributed to fraudulent transactions and excessive chargebacks.

The risks are mitigated by various participants of the ecosystem in various ways.

- **RBI**: Regulations and guidelines (e.g., mandatory 2FA, data localization, tokenization, PCI-DSS, PA-DSS, Master KYC guidelines, PA license)
- **Acquiring Banks**: Risk checks during transactions, issuing MID to 'good merchants'
- **Issuing Bank**: Risk check and velocity checks

- **Payment Aggregator (PA)**: Onboarding 'Good merchant', risk checks during transaction, certifications *(PCI-DSS)*, licenses *(PA/PG)*, and adhering to guidelines *(tokenization)*

One of the ways to reduce risks in the payments business is on-boarding "*good merchants*".

Good Merchant

- PA should on-board merchants/sectors which are allowed by Government, Courts, RBI, Card Networks, and partner banks.

- Understand merchant's business model: Sector, MCC *(Merchant Category Code)* product/service offering, mode of delivery *(physical or digital)*, business cycle *(regular, seasonal)*, vintage of merchant, founders/directors background, terms of service, privacy policies, and refund/cancellation policies - watch out for red flags.

  You will come across versatile business models: An e-commerce company delivers goods in a day and another one may take 15 days. A merchant may deliver service online (e.g., Gaming) but others may do physical delivery (e.g., Food Delivery). A merchant may allow refunds (e.g., Travel Booking) and another one may not allow refunds (e.g., Exam fee).

  So, PAs should understand the merchant's business model, processes, policies, and information available on customer touch points to 'underwrite' the merchant.

- A PA can ask for additional information such as licenses *(e.g., if a merchant is a regulated entity such as NBFC)*, or proof of partnerships.

- Collect and verify merchants' KYC documents (as per Master KYC guidelines)

  – Articles of Association, Memorandum of Association, Certificate of Incorporation

- Merchant's PAN and GST certificate
- Merchant's Address proof
- Board Resolution of appointing authorized signatory
- KYC of authorized signatory / directors (Id and address proofs)
- Merchant's financials *(only for enhanced due diligence)*
- Bank account details (canceled cheque, bank letter)

Note: PAs to do periodic re-KYC for the merchants as per PA's merchant onboarding policy

- Apart from the KYC, PA will perform other due diligence such as PEP *(Politically Exposed Person)* check, adverse media check *(any objectionable news)*, credit check, ultimate beneficial owner *(UBO)* check, and checks against various sanctions lists.

- A PA may conduct enhanced due diligence such as physical visit to merchant's location, proof of delivery checks and/or mystery shopping.

- A PA can also collect undertaking letters and/or take security deposits *(to safeguard from any financial losses)*

- PAs are mandated to follow PA/PG guidelines and Master KYC guidelines. At times, PA's acquiring banks may seek additional information/proofs of the merchants.

Note: Time-to-time RBI updates these guidelines. PAs are mandated to follow.

Reason for conducting merchant due diligence:

PA is just a facilitator of payments; the banks are the ones who issue MID *(Merchant ID)* or TID *(Terminal ID)*, process payments, and move funds. So, the PA is underwriting *(taking guarantee of)* the merchant to use the bank's payments system.

PA have to be careful while on-boarding the merchant and conduct proper due diligence to make sure the 'good merchant' with 'reasonable' business model is on-boarded.

PAs are regulated entities (REs), so they are expected to follow the norms as per regulations to avoid penalty, embargo, and cancellation of license.

Also, a PA must manage/safeguard its own reputational and financial risks. The cost of doing business with 'bad merchants' is very high.

Example: PG Charge: 2%, back-to-back cost = 1.90%

PA has to process 2000 transactions of Rs.500 each to make a profit of Rs.1,000 and only one valid chargeback of Rs. 1000 due to a bad merchant will wipe out that entire profit.

Imagine if there was a fraudulent transaction of Rs.20,000. You can calculate how many transactions the PA has to process to make up for that loss.

Closing Remarks

Merchants are growing and new business models are coming to light every day. Similar to merchants, even PAs want to grow fast.

Growth, revenue, profit - aren't these the reasons for being in any business?

Nothing wrong in that but in this fast-paced environment, bad actors try to exploit the payments systems. At times, the customers have suffered financially and, in extreme cases, have lost lives. So, PAs should onboard 'good' merchants.

6.B   MID and Live ID

Banks are the one who process the payments and a Payment Aggregator (PA) is just a layer above those banks. To process transactions, the PA needs to procure MID (Merchant ID) or Terminal ID (TID) from the banks and then link those MIDs to the Live ID of the merchant.

Note: Live ID and MIDs are used interchangeably, but I hope you know the difference.

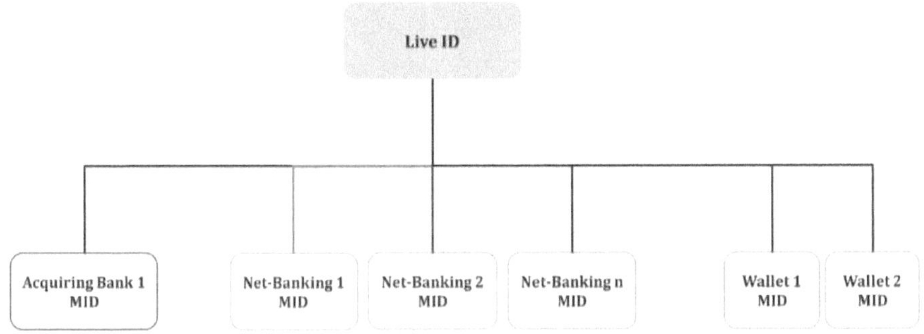

MID Procurement

To procure MIDs/TIDs from banks or other PSPs, the PA will share business details and/or KYC documents of the merchants in bank/PSPs in specified formats.

Partner Banks and PSPs reserve the right to issue the MID for the merchant. Sometimes, banks may seek additional documents or clarifications related to the merchant's business model.

Note: Banks usually refer to Terms of service, privacy policies, about us, customer support, and refund or cancellation policies that are written on the merchant's website.

MID/TID issuance policies followed by banks are a combination of:

- Guidelines of card networks (Visa, MasterCard, NPCI) *(e.g., do not onboard adult sites)*
- Policies/regulations by RBI and the Government *(e.g., ban on e-cigarettes)*

- Bank's internal compliance or risk policies *(e.g., SBI doesn't issue MID for wallet loading, HDFC doesn't onboard online rummy merchants)*

MID issuance Time

The MID approval process varies from bank to bank, and the TAT *(Turn Around Time)* may vary from 2 days to a couple of weeks.

PAs can have better SLA *(Service Level Agreement)* with the banks for issuance of MID. It may not always work as banks work with multiple PAs, and banks take time to do merchant due diligence.

Procuring MIDs from a bank takes time. So, PAs can wait till the bank issues MID *(merchant cannot start transactions)* or take an alternate route i.e., start transactions on Master MIDs.

Master MID

Few acquiring banks issue MID to PAs. A PA is a bank's merchant and PA's merchants are sub-merchants to the bank. The PA can configure those generic MIDs *(or Master MIDs)* for the merchant and start the transaction *(as a stop gap arrangement)* and eventually replace master MID with bank approved MIDs.

Challenges in using Master MID:

Master MIDs are issued at standard pricing so it may not be possible for a PA to run the show without making losses.

(e.g.: Credit Card rate of generic MID is 1.85% but PA's commercials with merchants is 1.80%. So, if master MID is enabled then the PA will lose 0.05% of value for every transaction). Solution: Procure Master MIDs with different pricing from different acquiring banks and configure them intelligently to reduce the loss.

Slippery Slope with Master MID:

Banks do not approve certain types of merchants. A PA can onboard such merchants on Master MID.

But that is wrong, and eventually, when the bank catches such practices, then PA will face either a penalty or get black-listed. So, beware!

Approval for net-banking:

Except 9-10 banks, all other banks work on carpet approval wherein PA issues MID based on its discretion and then shares merchant's details with banks (if needed). So, PA can enable 25–30 banks without any approval or delay.

Most of these long-tail banks do not have process or tech capability to issue individual MIDs for the merchant. These banks didn't develop it because they are not big in acquiring business. So, these banks give carpet approval to PAs and have a revenue sharing model.

Few of the banks that provide explicit approval are Axis, Bank of India, City Union, Corporation Bank, DCB, Deutsche, HDFC, ICICI, IDBI, IndusInd, Kotak Mahindra, SBI, Yes Bank.

Merchant Specific Vs. Master MID: Have you ever checked the narration in your card statement or bank account statement when you do an online transaction?

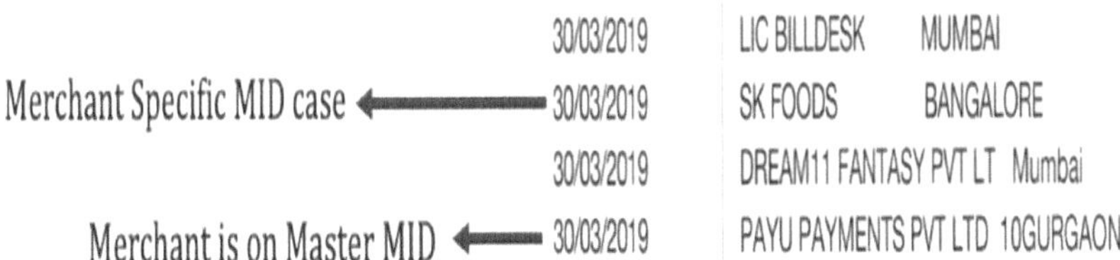

If a merchant is configured on its own MID, then the merchant's name would appear in the statement. In case a merchant is on generic/master MID, or a transaction is done on one of 'carpet approved' banks then PA's name will be shown.

Live ID (issued by PA)

Live ID is a unique identifier issued by a PA to a merchant (*sometimes they call it MID but to keep it simple, we will call it Live ID*).

As mentioned earlier, MIDs issued by the banks & wallets are linked to this Live Id. Transactions, refunds, settlements, chargebacks, and card vault of a merchant are linked to this unique Live ID.

Some of the attributes of Live Id are:

- Settlement Account: Each Live ID can be configured with one settlement account.

  Note: If a merchant requires settlement to different bank accounts, then then use split settlement solution or issue multiple live Ids for the merchant

- Acquiring bank: Multiple acquiring banks can be configured for one Live Id (*helps in configuring performance-based routing for cards or UPI*).

- Commercials: One set of rates (MDR) can be configured for one Live ID.

- Fee Model: One type of fee model (*upfront deduction, Surcharge, or Invoicing*) can be configured for one Live ID.

  Note: If you want to configure net-banking in upfront deduction model and debit cards in surcharge model then issue two Live Ids for the merchant

- Card Token Vault: Card vault is linked to the Live Id (ideal case). Multiple Live Ids of a merchant can be merged to provide a unified card token vault for the merchant.

- Number of Live Ids: PA can issue multiple Live IDs for a merchant without additional approval from banks.

Chapter 7

Payment Aggregator – Commercials

The fundamental objective of a business is making money. This becomes more interesting in the payments business as PAs make money while moving money.

In the next three chapters, I will cover commercials and commercials models in online payment business. Also, I will cover how Payment Aggregators (PAs) make or lose money.

7.A   PA Charges or MDR

When various entities move the funds from Point A to Point B, they charge certain fees.

PA will charge MDR (Merchant Discount Rate), which merchant can choose to absorb or pass it on to the customer.

Typical charges will be:

- Percentage (%) of successful transaction value (E.g., 1.80% of transaction value)
- Flat fee per successful transaction (Rs.10 per transaction)
- Hybrid model: Percentage (%) of value + Fixed Fee (E.g., 1.80% + Rs.1) – *very rare*

Note: GST is applicable on these charges

Factors that influence MDR

1. Merchant category code (whether e-commerce, utility, or insurance)

2. B2B or B2C business

3. Domestic or international card transaction

4. Payment Mode *(whether credit card, debit card, UPI, BNPL etc.)*

5. RBI guidelines *(E.g., Capping of MDR on Visa and MasterCard debit cards)*

6. Government guidelines *(E.g., Zero MDR on UPI linked to bank a/c and RuPay Debit cards)*

Also, the MDR depends on the PA's back-to-back commercial arrangement with banks and other Payment Service Providers, such as wallets and BNPL products.

Let's not forget that a PA will offer MDR to the merchant based on the merchant's volume, merchant's brand, and, of course, PA's loss absorbing capacity.

A start-up or small merchant may get a different MDR than a large enterprise.

Typical commercial structure for different merchant types (sectors):

	eCom / Travel/ Gaming	Insurance	Investment	NBFC	Government	Education
Credit Cards (Visa, MC, RuPay)	1.75% - 1.85% (Amex: 2.45% - 2.75%)	0.80% - 1.00%	-	-	0.80% - 1.00%	0.80% - 1.00%
Debit Cards (Except RuPay) Slab 1: Upto Rs.2000 Slab 2: Above Rs.2000)	Slab 1: 0.30% - 0.40% Slab 2: 0.80% - 0.90%	Slab 1: 0.30% - 0.40% Slab 2: 0.80% - 0.90%	Slab 1: 0.30% - 0.40% Slab 2: 0.80% - 0.90% (or flat rate: Rs.5 - 15)	Slab 1: 0.30% - 0.40% Slab 2: 0.80% - 0.90% (or flat rate: Rs.5 - 15)	Slab 1: 0.30% - 0.40% Slab 2: 0.80% - 0.90%	Slab 1: 0.30% - 0.40% Slab 2: 0.80% - 0.90%
Debit Cards (Rupay)	Nil	Nil	Nil	Nil	Nil	Nil
UPI (on Bank a/c)	Nil	Nil	Nil	Nil	Nil	Nil
UPI (on Credit Card)	1.75% - 1.95%	0.80% - 1.00%	-	-	0.80% - 1.00%	0.80% - 1.00%
Corporate Cards	2.00% - 2.30%	2.00% - 2.30%	-	-	2.00% - 2.30%	-
Prepaid Cards (Visa, MC, RuPay)	1.80% - 1.85%	0.80% - 1.00%	-	-	0.80% - 1.00%	0.80% - 1.00%
Net-banking	0.90% - 1.55%	Rs. 5 - Rs.15	Rs. 5 - Rs.15	Rs. 5 - Rs.15	Rs. 5 - Rs.15	Rs. 5 - Rs.15
International PG	2.40% - 2.75%	2.4% - 2.75%	-	-	-	2.4% - 2.75%
Wallets	1.70% - 1.90%	1.70% - 1.90%	-	-	1.70% - 1.90%	1.70% - 1.90%
BNPL	1.70% - 1.90%	1.70% - 1.90%	-	-	1.70% - 1.90%	1.70% - 1.90%
Cardless EMIs	1.50% - 2.50%	1.50% - 2.50%	-	-	1.50% - 2.50%	1.50% - 2.50%

Important Notes:

- MDR is exempted for UPI *(linked to bank a/c)* and RuPay Debit cards (since 1-Jan-2020) *Note: PAs charge fee wherever possible but call it by different names such as TSP fee, infrastructure fee, platform fee, API fee etc.*

- UPI *(bank a/c based)* and RuPay Debit Card MDR cannot be surcharged i.e., passed on to the customer *(as long as officially the MDR is zero)*

- UPI (on Credit Card), UPI (on PPI), and UPI (Credit line) have MDR *(or fees)*

- UPI on Credit Card rates will be same as regular credit card rates.

- UPI Lite do not have commercials (Free for users and merchants)

- Certain sub-sectors such as grocery, housing society fee payments have lower rate on Credit Cards compared to eCommerce, travel, or gaming sectors.

- Amex and Diners can have higher MDR compared to Visa and MasterCard *(Recently, Amex trying to normalize the MDR in par with Visa and MasterCard)*

- EMI on Credit Cards will have same rate as Credit cards *(but PA's add big margins)*

- Prepaid cards *(Visa, MasterCard, RuPay)* have similar MDR as credit cards.

- Payment Containers offer bundled rate irrespective of the payment mode *(E.g., 1.25% irrespective whether user pays using UPI or wallet)*

- B2B companies enjoy flat fee on net-banking *(Except few banks)*

External control of MDR:

- Wallets, BNPL, cardless EMIs, and Prepaid cards *(excluding Visa, MasterCard, RuPay)* issuers have complete say in their pricing.

- Net-Banking is a bilateral arrangement between the PA and bank.

- Few banks *(e.g., HDFC, ICICI, Axis, Kotak, Yes Bank, SBI)* work on a fixed cost model (e.g., 1.50% for eCommerce or Rs.15 per transaction for education sector)

- Few banks work on a revenue sharing model *(e.g., 50:50 or 60:40).*

  Note: To stop aggressive pricing by PAs, the banks that work on a revenue-sharing model set a floor price. Example: 50:50 revenue sharing with minimum 0.40% of transaction value. This forces the PAs to give a rate of 0.80% and above.

- Credit card rates are decided by interchange arrangement dictated by card networks for different Merchant Categories

- Debit cards and UPI (on bank a/c) rates are dictated by the Government of India/RBI with the purpose to boost digital payments.

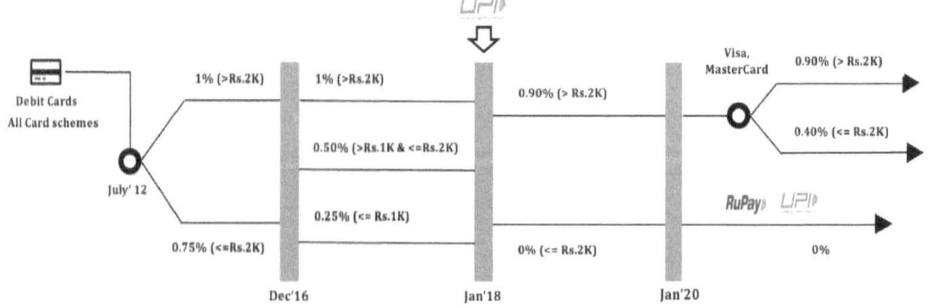

Subsidy for UPI and RuPay Debit Cards

Since Jan 2020, Govt. of India has exempted MDR on UPI *(bank a/c linked)* and RuPay debit cards.

However, banks, PAs, TPAPs do incur costs *(infrastructure, people etc.)* to operate UPI and RuPay.

So, the Govt. of India is providing a subsidy to banks, and banks may choose to share it with their TSP and TPAP partners. In Financial Year 2022-23, GOI spent Rs.1044 Crore and budgeted Rs.1500 crore for FY 2023-24.

Also, the banks do not have to pay GST on this incentive.

Settlement from partner banks and PSPs to Payment Aggregator.

So far, we covered the MDR or charges of banks and PSPs to a PA. Now, let's talk about how a bank/PSP recovers these charges from a PA.

- Invoicing Model: Bank or PSP will invoice the charges to a PA on a monthly basis. In this model, PA receives gross settlement (full amount)
  E.g., Net-banking for most of the banks, UPI acquiring banks.

- Upfront deduction model: Charges are deducted from the transaction amount and then settled to PA. In this model, PA receives net-settlement.
  e.g., Card acquiring banks.

In the next chapter, we will cover different commercial models of PA (to its merchants).

7.B Commercial Models

There are three commercial models in practice:

- Upfront Deduction
- Surcharge
- Invoicing

Let's assume: PG Charge or MDR = 1%, GST = 18%, Transaction Amount = Rs.100

1. Upfront Deduction

PA deducts the charges and GST amount before settling the transaction amount to the merchant.

This model is followed in eCommerce, Gaming, Travel, BFSI sectors.

Customer Pays = Rs. 100, PA deducts = Rs. 1.18 and merchant gets = Rs. 98.82

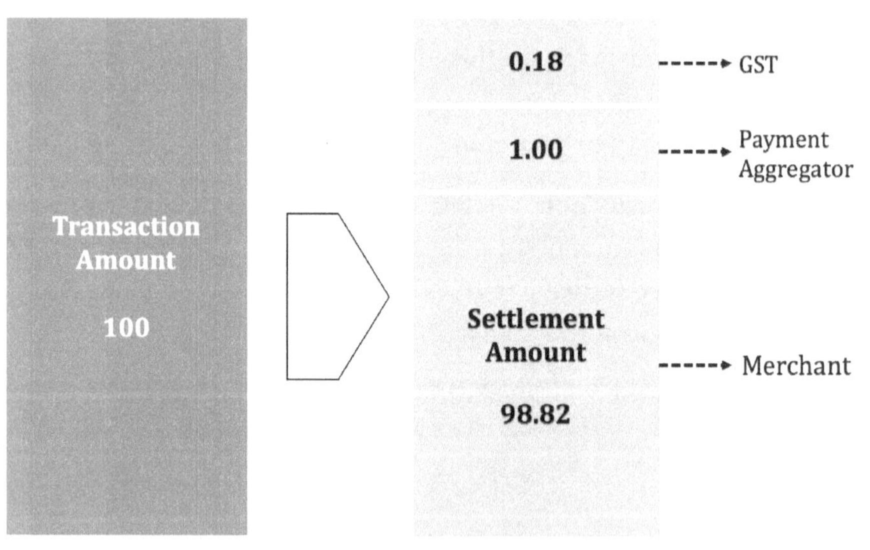

2. **Surcharge**

PG Charges + GST amount is passed to the user, and merchant receives gross settlement.

This model is followed in Utility, Government, Education sectors.

Customer pays = Rs. 101.18, PA keeps = Rs. 1.18 and merchant gets = Rs. 100

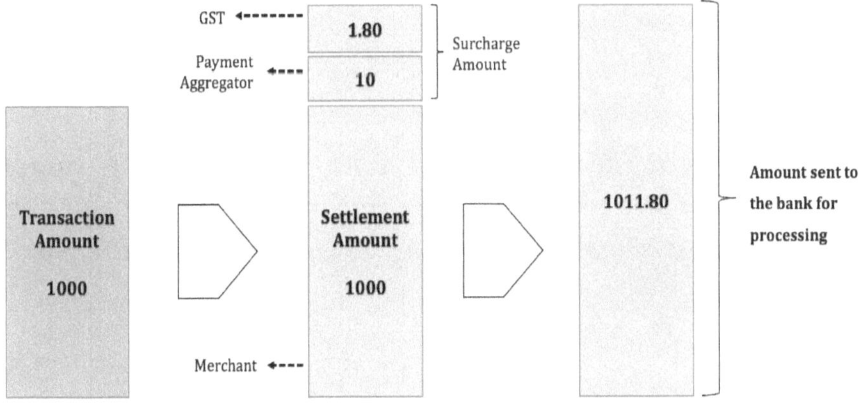

3. **Invoicing**

Sometimes, either merchant or merchant's business model doesn't allow to either deduct money upfront or apply surcharge to the user. In such cases, the PA will raise a monthly invoice to the merchant.

This model is followed in Mutual Fund Sector and (few) wallet top-up cases.

Customer Pays: Rs. 100, Merchant Received = Rs. 100 and PA will invoice amount = Rs. 1.18

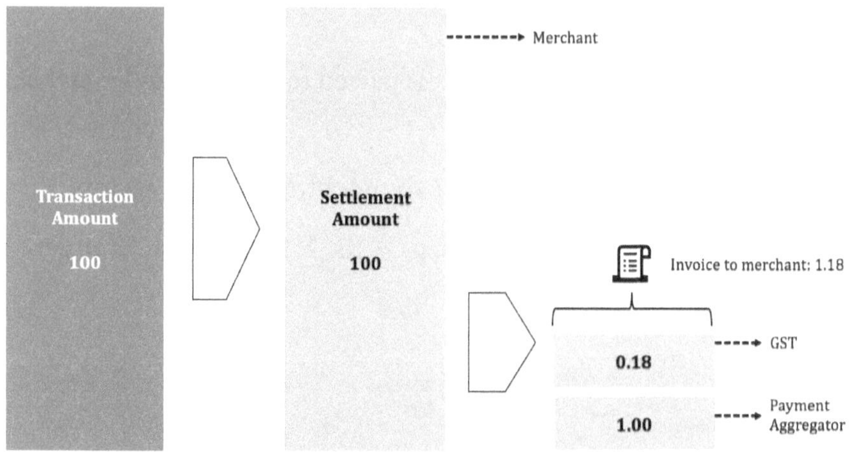

PAs avoid invoicing models *(as much as possible)* for obvious reasons: (a) It is always a pain to collect money from others (b) an opportunity cost *(more than a month delay in getting the money from the merchants).*

7.C How Payment Aggregators Make money?

The main purpose of a business is to make money. Not just revenue but also profit. Payment Aggregators (PAs) are not an exception to that.

A PA relies on partner banks, wallets, or other payment processors to enable payment services to its merchants, so the PA will have to pay those entities. The top line and bottom line of a PA depends on how it manages commercials with merchants and costs with the partners *(banks and other payment issuers)*.

Pricing Principle

- If cost is fixed, charges should be higher than cost *(Example: If fixed cost is 1.50% then MDR to merchant should be 1.50% or more)*.

- If there is revenue sharing arrangement, don't worry about making a loss but try to keep the top line intact *(Example: In 50:50 revenue sharing model if you close fees at 0.50% instead of 1%, then you won't make a loss, but your revenue will be reduced to half)*

Impact of pricing on the P&L

- **Example A: Standard commercials with healthy margin**

Average Ticket (Rs.) [A]	1,000
Number of Transactions per day [B]	1,000
GMV per day (Rs.) [C = A * B]	1,000,000

Payment Modes	GMV Split [D]	GMV [E = D * C]	Cost (from PSP) [F]	Total Cost [G = E * F]	MDR [H]	Revenue [I = E * H]
Credit Cards	25%	250,000	1.80%	4,500	1.85%	4,625
Debit Card (Visa, MC)	20%	200,000	0.40%	800	0.45%	900
Debit Card (Rupay)	10%	100,000	0%	0	0%	0
UPI	25%	250,000	0%	0	0%	0
Net-banking	10%	100,000	1.30%	1,300	1.35%	1,350
Wallets	10%	100,000	1.80%	1,800	1.85%	1,850
Total (Rs.)				8,400		8,725

Profit Per Day (Rs.)	325	(Total Cost - Revenue)
Profit Per Year (Rs.)	118,625	

On processing Rs. 10,00,000 per day, PA will make a profit of Rs. 325. i.e., Rs. 1.18 Lakh profit in a year.

Imagine the profit if the PA processes Rs.10 Crore per day… Awesome… isn't it!

- **Example B: <u>Super competitive pricing (Say… to win the merchant)</u>**

Average Ticket (Rs.) [A]	1,000
Number of Transactions per day [B]	1,000
GMV per day (Rs.) [C = A * B]	1,000,000

Payment Modes	GMV Split [D]	GMV [E = D * C]	Cost (from PSP) [F]	Total Cost [G = E * F]	MDR [H]	Revenue [I = E * H]
Credit Cards	25%	250,000	1.80%	4,500	1.65%	4,125
Debit Card (Visa, MC)	20%	200,000	0.40%	800	0.45%	900
Debit Card (Rupay)	10%	100,000	0%	0	0%	0
UPI	25%	250,000	0%	0	0%	0
Net-banking	10%	100,000	1.30%	1,300	1.35%	1,350
Wallets	10%	100,000	1.80%	1,800	1.85%	1,850
Total (Rs.)				8,400		8,225

Profit Per Day (Rs.)	-175	(Total Cost - Revenue)
Profit Per Year (Rs.)	-63,875	

I dropped the commercials on credit cards below the bank cost and ended up making a loss of Rs. 175 per day, which translates into a loss of Rs.63,875 for a year.

Now let's do what we did in the last example but in the opposite.

Calculate the loss on processing Rs.10 crore per day.

From awesome suddenly the situation becomes gruesome… right?

This is the beauty of the 'volume game': A small margin translates into huge profits over a period, but with a small mispricing, PAs will end up losing huge amounts of money.

A simple way to make profit!

The MDR offered by PA to a merchant should be higher than the cost. However, it is next to impossible to follow this rule, for all merchants on all payment instruments. So, the optimal approach is to try to make profit at the merchant level rather than on each payment instrument.

If you get correct details of total GTV, transaction count for a period (month or year), and transaction split across various payment modes *(Credit cards, debit cards, net-banking, UPI etc.)*, then you can provide optimal pricing for different payment modes and still make a profit at the merchant level.

Other channels of revenue or profit:

1. **Configure Cheapest Acquiring Bank + PG.**

   PA will have different cost with different Acquiring banks (HDFC, Axis etc.) also, acquiring banks may provide differential pricing basis the PG they use.
   (E.g.: HDFC + CyberSource will be costlier than HDFC+FSS)

   PA can simply configure the cheapest acquiring bank + PG combinations.

   But do remember that you may increase profit but may have to sacrifice success rate or performance, as the cheapest acquiring bank + PG may not always be good.

2. **On-Us rates**: Say PA has differential rate for **On-Us** *(acquiring bank and card issuing bank are same)* and **Off-Us** *(acquiring bank and card issuing banks are different)* from multiple acquiring banks then process On-Us transactions for respective issuers, and thus PA can optimize the cost.

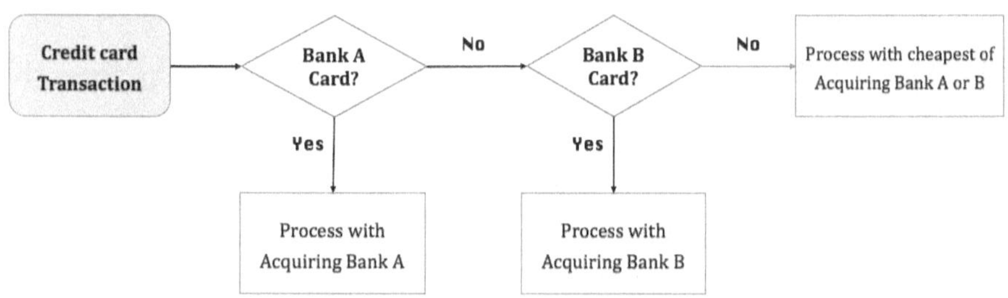

Here is an example of how On-Us routing optimizes the cost of processing.

Average Ticket (Rs.) [A]	5000
Number of Transactions per day [B]	1000
GMV per day (Rs.) [C = A * B]	5,000,000

Cost with Banks	On-Us	Off-Us
Bank A	1.75%	1.80%
Bank B	1.78%	1.80%

MDR (for merchant) [D]	1.80%

Issuing Banks	GMV Split [E]	GMV [F = E * C]	Revenue [G = F * D]	Using Bank A [H]	Using Bank B [I]	Using On-Us logic [J]
Bank A	15%	750,000	13,500	13,125	13,500	13,125
Bank B	20%	1,000,000	18,000	18,000	17,800	17,800
Others	65%	3,250,000	58,500	58,500	58,500	58,500
Total		5,000,000	90,000	89,625	89,800	89,425

				[G - H]	[G - I]	[G - J]
Profit (Per Day)				375	200	575
Profit (Per Year)				136,875	73,000	209,875

In the above example, the profit margin is maximum if the PA uses two acquiring banks and takes advantage of differential pricing offered by different acquiring banks.

Note: On-US/Off-Us routing is not possible with Card on File Tokenization.

3. **Subvention**: Banks enjoy the 'float' (money in a/c). Acquiring Banks often give subvention of a few basis points (bps) against volume commitment.

Banks don't work on this model all the time with all the PAs.

Example: Bank A has given subvention to **PA <ABC>** for merchant <MNO>. The same bank will not give subvention deals to **PA<PQR>** for the same merchant as there is no additional gain for the bank.

Also, the flipside is that the PA who availed a lucrative rate basis volume commitment may have to put money from their own pocket if the volume commitments are not met.

4. **Account Benefits**: PA's Escrow account is quite lucrative for any bank as a huge amount moves through the account.

    As per the RBI's PA/PG guidelines, the online PA is allowed to earn interest on 'core portion' amounts of the escrow account balance.

    If the PA has opened an escrow account with the acquiring bank, then acquiring bank may provide better rates on cards or UPI or give priority to the PA in partnership deals.

5. **Promote payment modes with higher margins:** Few payment modes have higher margins *(e.g., Credit cards, Card EMI, International card processing)*. PAs promote such payment modes to maximize profit.

6. **Banking Products**: A PA can offer other banking products to its merchants at healthy margins.

    A PA can offer lending to its merchants by partnering with banks or NBFCs. PA can bake the lending product in its core offering *(e.g., early settlement)*.

    PAs can also issue co-branded credit cards to its merchants.

    I have covered many such products in ***Chapter 23 (Banking as a Service)***

7. **Complimentary payment Products:** Offer complimentary products such as payout, bank account validation or PA-Cross Border *(Import and/or Export)*.

   Few of these products fetch better margins.

8. **Vertical Integration:** Payment processing involves multiple systems that are managed by various entities. PAs can do vertical integration *(e.g., Build ACS or Payment Gateway for the banks)* and use it in card transactions and thus reduce the cost or create additional revenue channels.

9. **Value Added Services**: PAs can provide value-added services and products to merchants and earn additional revenue.

   A few of the VAS products: Offer engine, reconciliation module, SDK for auto-reading OTP, risk engine, chargeback management module etc.

   Please refer to **Chapter 23 (Value Added Services / Products)** *for more details.*

10. **Acquisitions**: Yes, a company can grow in terms of revenue/ profit by acquiring another company. A PA can acquire another PA *(e.g., Worldline acquired Ingenico)* or a PA can acquire a company that provides complementary or tertiary services that can strengthen overall offerings *(e.g., RazorPay <> EzeTap, Pine Labs <> Qwikcilver)*.

Where does a PA lose money?

a. **Auto-refunded cases**: Merchants who need instant gratification would want PA to configure auto-refunds if transaction status is not definite (Success/failed) within specified time.

   When the transaction is successful, the PA will mark the refund and won't give settlement to the merchant. However, the acquiring bank has marked the status 'successful', so it will deduct the charges from the PA's settlement. As there is no merchant settlement for that transaction, the PA ends up losing that amount.

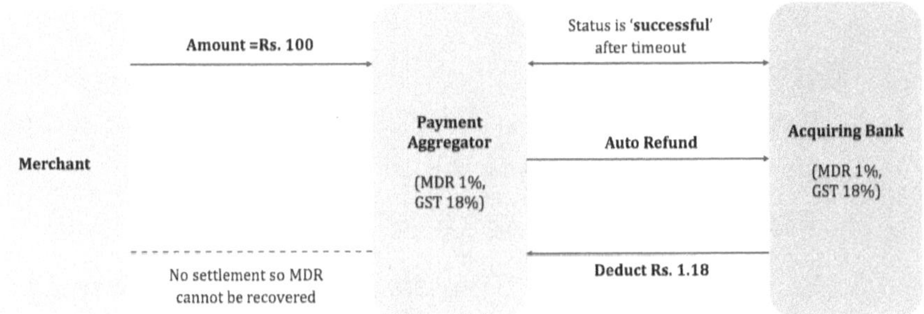

Example: Transaction Amount = Rs. 100, MDR: 1% + GST. Then PA ends up losing Rs. 1.18 for the auto-refunded case.

b. **Surcharge (bad configuration)**: In the surcharge model, MDR (+ GST Amount) is passed on to the customer. This model is typically used by merchants from the Utility, Government, Education and B2B sectors.

However, banks do not distinguish between transaction amount and surcharge amount. From the bank's point of view, it is one single amount. So, the bank applies its rate on the total amount, not just the transaction amount.

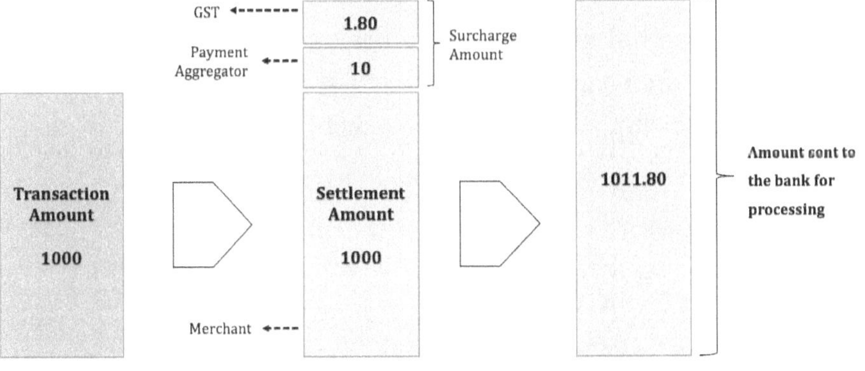

PA collects = Rs. 11.80 (i.e., 1% of Rs. 1000 + GST) But Acquiring bank deducts = Rs. 11.94 (i.e., 1% of Rs.1011.18 + GST) So, PA's loss = Rs. 0.14

And as payments is a volume game so more the transactions, more the loss.

c. **Bad chargeback cases:** A mismanaged chargeback will wipe out large profits as PAs work on razor thin margins.

   Example: PG Charge: 2%, back-to-back cost = 1.90%

   So, the PA will have to process Rs.10,00,000 to make a profit of Rs. 1,000. And one mismanaged chargeback of Rs. 1000 will wipe out the entire profit.

d. **Fraudulent Transaction**: PAs will have to compensate banks or merchants if the responsibility of a fraudulent transaction is attributed to PA, and such cases hurt PA's revenue and profits badly.

e. **'Price War'**: Pricing is a major differentiator and entry point for new PAs to get transaction share from large merchants. A PA will have to beat not only other PAs but also acquiring banks, wallets, and PSPs *(who also can directly integrate with merchants)*.

   Banks do not give subvention deals every time, so the PA will have to undercut competitors' rates and when the rates go lower than the cost, PAs start losing money.

f. **Operational Cost:** Running a PA is not simple - it is operations heavy business. Apart from processing the transaction, A PA has to manage many operations *(merchant due diligence, financial operations, dispute management, merchant* *support, customer support etc.)*. If the PA doesn't automate these functions, then it has to hire more and more human resources to do manual work.

g. **Compliance Cost:** After PA/PG guidelines, payment aggregation has become a compliance heavy business. A PA has to follow many guidelines related to the payments system, vendor onboarding, merchant due diligence, transaction monitoring, and fund movement etc. A PA has to conduct various audits *(internal and external)* and share different types of reports with RBI on a regular basis *(monthly, quarterly, bi-annually, annually, and as and when)*. That means, a PA has to deploy resources to manage the compliance related activities. These costs will eat into PA's profits.

Closing Remarks:

In the last decade, we have seen constant erosion of overall MDR or take rate of PAs.

Few of the reasons are change in the volume mix as UPI gained prominence *(and UPI is at zero MDR or lowest possible MDR)* and capping of rates *(e.g., debit card)*

But the main reason is 'competition' - never ending price war among players. It is a *'(price) war of attrition'*. For a decade, I have been seeing the trend - when one PA stops playing the price game, another PA will start the same game to gain market share.

It is a known fact that majority of PAs do not make profit. That doesn't mean being PA is a bad business. PAs are deploying various strategies to maximize their revenue and profit.

And off lately, the investors are not impressed with the GTV (Gross Transaction Value), i.e., the amount a PA is processing, but more interested about net-revenue *(after removing bank charges)* and/or profits or, at least, path to profitability. I am sure PAs will re-think about their pricing or, more precisely, their *'price war'* strategy.

Finishing this chapter with one of my favorite quotes:

"Best Results will come when everyone in the group does what is the best for themselves AND THE GROUP" - John Nash

Chapter 8

Payment Aggregator – Integration

In this chapter, I will cover two important aspects of online payments - payment page (checkout page) and card tokenization (save card).

8.A   Payment Pages

The Payment page or the checkout page is the page where the customer selects the payment method *(cards, net-banking, wallet, UPI, BNPL etc.)* to start the transaction.

Below are the various possibilities in payment pages.

A.   PA hosted page (non-seamless or redirection flow):

The payment page is hosted by a PA. When the customer clicks on the 'pay' button, the customer is redirected to PA's page to select the payment method and proceed with the transaction.

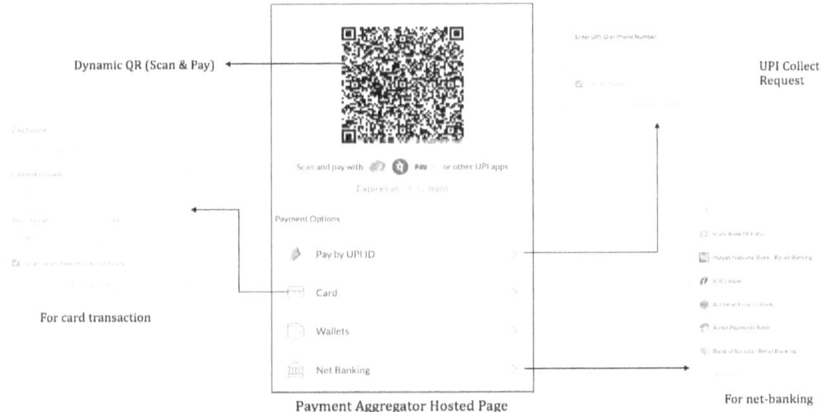

Advantages	Disadvantages
• Simple to integrate - Less effort • PA will manage the compliances related to card tokenization	• Limited control on the page design • Lock-in with the payment aggregator • Limited to payment modes and features offered by that particular PA

Note: If a merchant wants to add multiple PAs but does not want to create own payment page or use TSP/wrapper, then the merchant can simply add radio buttons for each PA. Once the user selects the PA, then, the user is redirected to the PA hosted payment page for the payment selection and transaction.

B. iFrame in merchant's site:

Merchants can embed the PA's checkout page into the merchant's website as an iFrame. The overall look of the page is in the merchant's control, except for the iFrame part.

Pros: Slightly better control on page look

Cons: Cannot add multiple PAs *(alternative, add radio button for each PA)*

C. Merchant hosted page (Seamless):

The payment page is hosted by a merchant, and the merchant is in complete control.

Note: TSPs/wrapper/orchestrator also can provide a payment page.

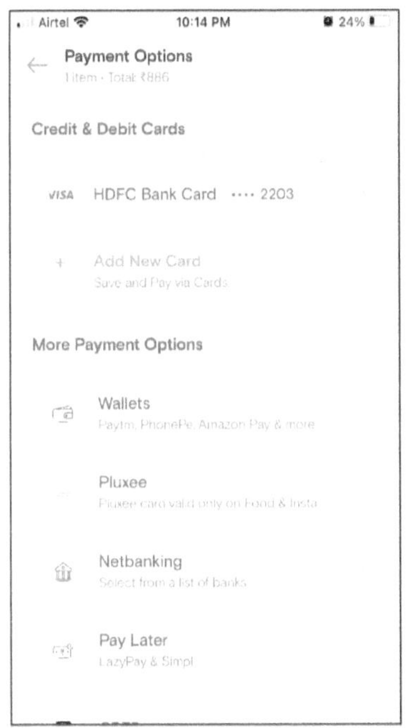

| Merchant hosted page | Merchant hosted page (Surcharge Fee) |

Advantages	Disadvantages
• Better control on page design • Flexibility to add multiple PAs, Banks, other PSPs • With routing logics, merchant can optimize performance & commercials	• Effort to maintain the page and mange routing logics • Integration effort when new PA or PSP is added • Need to have unified card tokenization strategy

Working of 'Seamless Flow'

Each PA, wallet, and banks issue a unique MID for merchants. Each bank, wallet, or PA also has unique code *(e.g., bank code or payment instrument code)*. So, with a combination of Live Id and bank code, merchants can route transactions.

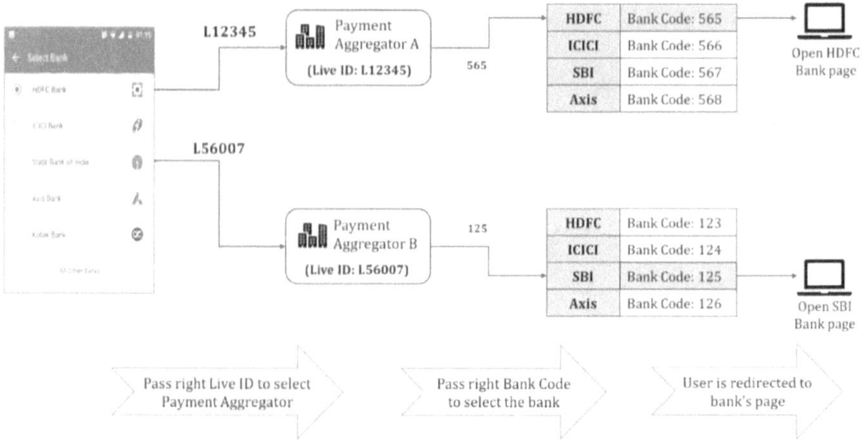

Capturing card details in Seamless Flow

Card number, CVV2, and expiry date can be entered on page of PCI-DSS compliant entities.

- If merchant is using non-seamless (redirection) page or iFrame page of PA/TSP, then anyway cards are entered on PA or TSP's pages which are PCI-DSS compliant.

- A PCI-DSS compliant merchant can allow customers to enter the card details on its page.

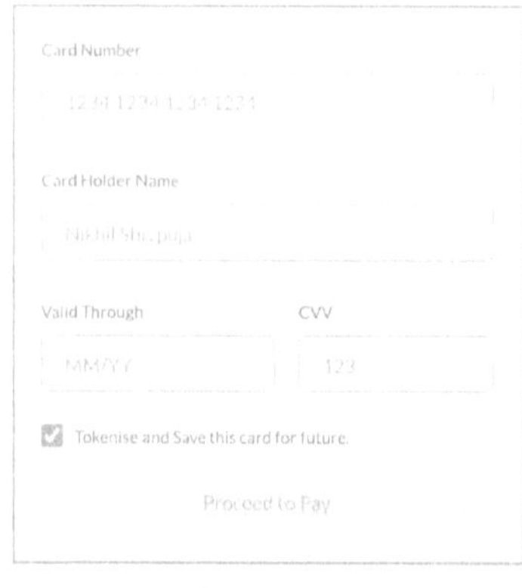

PA hosted Page

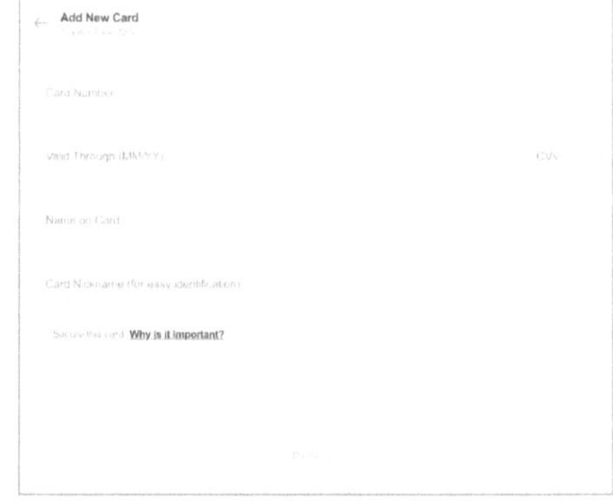

Merchant hosted Page

If the merchant is not PCI-DSS compliant and using seamless flow, then card details shouldn't hit the merchant's website or App. So, in this case, the PA or TSP provides iFrame elements that can be embedded in the merchant's page to capture card details.

Note: Cards can be saved or tokenized only by the token requestor as per tokenization guidelines. Read the details in **Chapter 8.B** [Save Card or Card Tokenization]

Points to be considered while developing card capture page (merchant or PA)

- Do not allow non-numbers in card number, expiry date, CVV2 field.

- Check card number length based on card type *(Visa, MasterCard, RuPay: 16, Amex: 15)*

- Implement Luhn's algorithm (Mod 10) check the correctness of the card number.

- Expiry date checks (months should be 1 to 12, and expiry date should not be older than present month)

- Length of CVV2/CVC2 *(Visa, MasterCard, RuPay: 3 and Amex: 4)*

- If enabling CVV less flow, then modify the CVV field accordingly *(Read in **Chapter 8.B**)*

Smart Payment Pages:

Saving card (tokenization) and saving VPA is quite normal. Now, merchants/PAs are working on 'smart payment pages' where payment modes are not just displayed, but customers will have recommendations such as,

- Showing the preferred or frequently used payment instrument on top

- Displaying relevant offers that are applicable to the customer.

- Display warning message if a payment mode is down or not performing well.

- Show the wallet balance or BNPL's available credit.

- Smart Retry: If debit card transaction fails then nudge user to do UPI transaction.

- Show relevant payment mode basis ticket size *(e.g., do not show wallet option for amount more than 2 Lakh)*

Closing Remarks

The best payment pages that you see *(e.g., Swiggy, Zomato, CRED etc.)* took years of effort. So, payment pages are not static or can be done with one-time effort, but they need to be refined and upgraded from time to time.

8.B Save Card or Card Tokenization

You might have noticed that many merchants show the option to *'save the card for future purchase'*. I am sure many of you have 'saved' card(s) on your favorite merchant's site.

Card vault or 'save card' feature is important because:

- Provides faster checkout experience.

- Success rate of transaction done with tokenized cards is higher than regular transactions.

I. Past and Present

The Past:

Any PCI-DSS *(Payment Card Industry Data Security Standard)* certified entity could save the card. It can be a PA, TSP, payment container, or merchant.

There were a few drawbacks with this model:

Entities could build any type of flow *(e.g., common card vault across all merchants)*

Users didn't have visibility on where all cards have been saved/vaulted, and there was no provision to delete the saved card *(only handful of merchants provided this facility)*

The Present Guidelines:

As part of PA/PG guidelines, RBI rolled out clear rules for card tokenization.

- **Coverage:** Applicable to all domestic cards and networks - Visa, MasterCard, RuPay, Amex and Diners; not applicable to international cards

- Card to be tokenized for all solutions involving cards (regular PG, SI on cards)

- **Entities:** Token Service Providers can be card issuing bank *(Issuer tokenization)* or card network *(Network Tokenization)*; **Token requesters** can be merchant, PA or TSPs

- **Uniqueness**: Token is unique to the card, PA/TSP **(TR)** and merchant combination

- **Processing:** Transactions should be always initiated from merchant and then token requestor to process the tokens

- **Migration**: Tokens created for a merchant with a PA cannot be migrated to other PA/TSP

- **Consent:** Merchant to take consent from the customer for the tokenization

- **For customer**: Customer can tokenize any number of cards on a merchant; Issuing bank to make provision for the cardholder to view and delete tokenized cards.

- **Display**: On checkout page, card network, bank name and last 4 digits of the card can be shown; first 6 digits (i.e., BIN) cannot be shown

- All entities who have saved cards are mandated to purge/delete cards by 30-Sep-2022

- The new guidelines came into effect on 1-Oct-2022.

Guest Checkout / Plain Card / Alt ID:

Initially, there were no specific guidelines for managing guest checkout or plain cards *(meaning: cards which are not tokenized as users did transactions without tokenizing/saving cards).*

In May 2023, RBI issued guidelines for managing plain cards.

- PAs/merchants can have access to card number for T+2 days *(changed from earlier T+4 days)* and Acquiring banks can have access for T+90 days *(changed from earlier 180 days)*

- Implement *one-time usage token* for plain card transaction by 31-October-2023 *(The given deadline was extended)*

Note: It's clear that RBI wants to restrict the access to sensitive data such as card number, and Tokenization is a well thought process to achieve it.

Network and Issuer Tokenization

There are two types of tokenization:

- **Network Tokenization** - card networks *(Visa, MasterCard, RuPay, Amex)* will be the token service providers *(meaning, create the tokens)*.

- **Issuer Tokenization**: The card issuing bank acts as token service provider and manages token *(creation and processing)*

  ***Note**: Issuer tokenization will help PA/Merchant to do direct integration with issuing banks and process On-Us transactions (skipping card networks) which can be economical.*

Journey and impact:

The journey from 'save card' to 'tokenization' was not simple, as the entire ecosystem *(card issuers, acquiring banks, PGs, PAs, merchants)* had to make significant changes. So, RBI gave few extensions, and finally, the tokenization came into effect from October 1, 2022.

Impact on various entities:

- New integration for Issuing banks, Acquiring banks, PAs, and merchants.

- Entities to delete 'saved cards' by 30-Sep-2022 *(PAs/merchant have to start from scratch)*

- No common vault across all merchants - this impacted PA's own checkout vaults and payment containers such as PhonePe

- Cannot support On-Us flows on network tokenization.

- PA or merchant cannot view a plain card once the card is tokenized.

- Without card numbers, merchants couldn't use services such as credit card repayment or instant refund solutions *(where funds are pushed to card number using IMPS, NEFT)*.

  To address this case:

  - Merchants moved to Visa Direct and Master Money Send solutions.

  - In Q1 of 2023, NPCI came up with concept of virtual card number where virtual card number is created using (<91><Mobile number><last 4 digits of card>), and IMPS rail can be used to push funds to virtual card number.

  *Read details in **Chapter 15** - Payout or Disbursement Solutions*

II. Tokenization Working:

In this section, we will cover the Card on File (CoF) tokenization.

1. Participants:

- Token Issuance Platform: Card networks work with issuing banks to provide platform.

- Token Requestor: Entities that are PCI-DSS certified to integrate with Token Issuance Platform. These entities can be Acquiring Banks, PAs, Payment Containers, TSPs, and merchants.

2. User Flow:

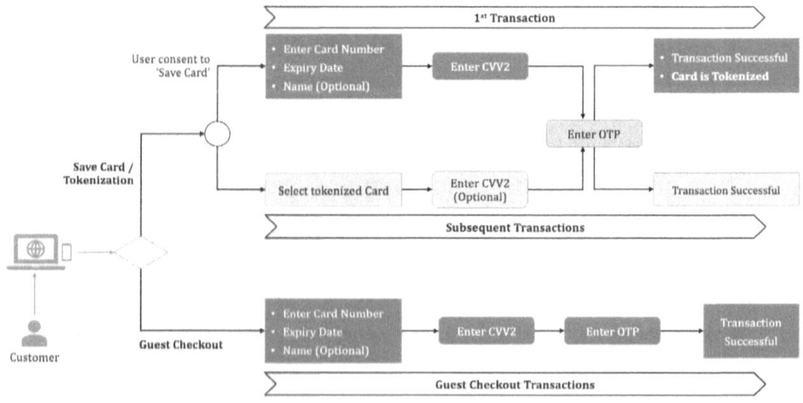

User experience remains the same as the earlier model.

First transaction: Customer to enter card number, CVV, and OTP *(card is tokenized when transaction is successful)*.

Customer can select tokenized card and enter OTP (2FA) to complete the payment. *(Note: CVV is not mandatory)*

3. CVV less Transactions:

CVV is not part of 2FA, so it is 'okay' to skip CVV validation.

CVV-less/skip-CVV flow existed for quite some time but was not popular as neither banks nor card networks promoted it.

Post tokenization, major card networks announced that they support CVV-less flow.

- **Value**: Skip-CVV flow will eliminate failures related to wrong CVV and thus increase the success rate. Also, skip-CVV flow provides faster checkout experience.

- **Working**: If CVV is passed to card issuer, then it is validated, but if CVV is not passed, then it is not validated

- **Coverage**: Tokenized (CoF) cards of Visa, MasterCard, RuPay and Amex

- *Limitations:* Skep-CVV flow can be processed by a few PGs (e.g., CyberSource, MPGS etc.) and few card issuing banks may not support.

  Note: Eventually, every PG and bank may support this feature

- **Challenges**:

  - All banks and PGs do not support this flow, so a PA or merchant has to incorporate all those limitations while building flows.

- For years/ages, users are used to entering CVV and know that CVV is validated. So, a merchant has to educate users about the new flow so as to avoid unnecessary panic among customers!

III.   Card Tokenization Strategy:

A merchant can tokenize cards with various entities, each with certain pros and cons.

1. **Merchant**:

   Advantages: No dependency on PA - merchant can use any PA for card processing

   Disadvantages: Costs and efforts related to PCI-DSS and token requestor process

2. **Payment Aggregator**:

   Advantages: Off-the-shelf solution - less effort

   Disadvantages: Lock-in with one PA - cannot use other PA for tokenized cards

3. **TSP/Orchestrator**:

   Advantages: PA neutral - no dependency on any PA, off the shelf solution - less effort

   Disadvantages: Additional cost of TSP and lock-in with TSP

More on Card Tokenization Strategy:

A merchant should consider a few points before using 'card tokenization' feature.

- **Frequency of purchase**: An insurance merchant has repeat payments, but that is once a year, so it really doesn't make sense to tokenize a user's card, but it is important for a food delivery App where users order frequently.

- **Mobile App is dominant channel**: Entering 16 digits card number every time on a mobile App is cumbersome, so the 'tokenization' will provide faster checkout experience.

- **Lock-in with one PA**: Cards tokenized with a PA will be locked-in with that PA. So, the merchant cannot remove that PA in the future *(without losing all those tokenized cards)*.

IV.   Push Provisioning of Token:

In December 2023, RBI issued a circular on enabling tokenization through card issuing banks. It is called '**push provisioning**'.

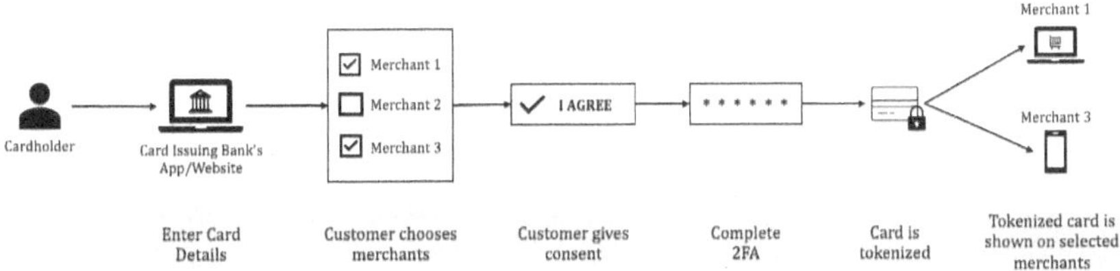

Customers can tokenize the card on her bank's website/App either during card issuance or later (any point of time)

The feature will be applicable for all cards *(As long as the issuer bank has implemented it)*

Cardholders can tokenize the card on the bank's app/site for choice of their merchants, and the tokenized card will be shown when the cardholder visits the selected merchant's website/App.

This feature will be special for co-branded credit cards as the cardholder can be nudged to select the co-branding partner brand.

V.   Device Tokenization:

In this chapter, my focus was on Card on File tokenization as it was the most dominant use case.

But let's quickly cover another type of tokenization i.e., Device Tokenization

RBI issued first guidelines on device tokenization in Jan 2019. The guidelines were focused on mobiles, and later, the guidelines were extended to other devices - laptops, wearable *(e.g., watches or rings)* and IoT devices.

In device tokenization, the card token is bonded with the device *(e.g., mobile phone)*, and the device can be used to make payment across merchants. The merchant or App that wants to do device tokenization would require a certified SDK from the network or token requestor.

As you noticed, Card on File tokenization is linked to a specific merchant, whereas device tokenization is merchant agnostic.

You can experience device tokenization on Google Pay App, Samsung Pay App, SBI + Titan Watch, Transcorp + RuPay Ring

Closing Remarks:

Tokenization is an important strategy as it improves user experience *(faster checkout)* and performance *(Success Rate)* and, most importantly, safeguards card data.

Merchants should think of a long-term strategy whether they need to tokenize customer's cards and with whom. Merchants can take off-the-shelf solutions from a PA but get locked in with that PA. A TSP/orchestrator can provide a PA-neutral tokenization solution but will incur additional costs and still be stuck with that TSP/orchestrator/wrapper. If a merchant wants to be truly independent, then the merchant should become a token requestor, but that is expensive.

Even customers should think about whether they want to 'save the card' on every website/app they transact on. If you rarely buy from a merchant, then you can avoid 'saving' your cards.

Chapter 9

Payment Aggregator – Transaction Related

In this chapter, I will cover different types of transactions of payment instruments and various types of transaction routing.

9.A   Transactions

This is where the payments start. Different payment methods have different transaction flows, and some of the payment methods can have different flavors of flows.

A.   Cards (Credit, Debit and Prepaid)

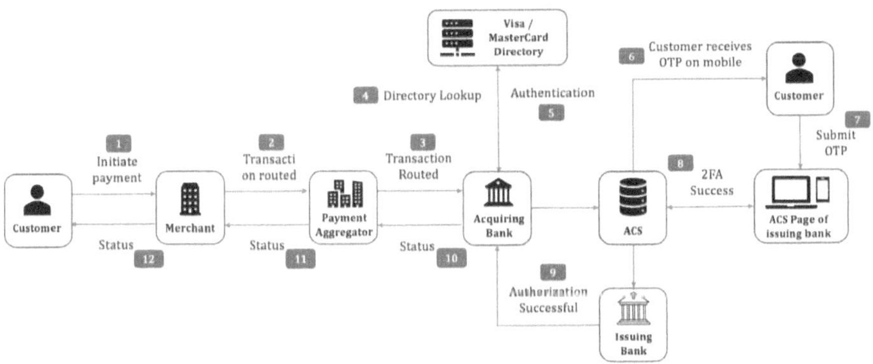

Do not get overwhelmed by the complexities of the above flow diagram. Trust me, it is super simplified than the actual flow!

Below is the summary of main steps:

1. Customer enters card details - Card number, expiry, CVV2 and name on card *(optional)* and initiates the payments *(through acquiring bank or Payment Aggregator)*

2. Device Data Collection: As per 3DS 2.0 protocol, device data is passed in payload data.

3. Directory Lookup: Card network will check the card and identify the issuing bank and ACS *(Access Control Server)* page of issuing bank is opened.

4. Authentication: In this leg, ACS of the issuing bank will trigger OTP to the user via SMS and/or email. User to submit the OTP on the ACS page.

5. Authorization: Once the authentication is successful, the issuing bank validates expiry date, CVV2, available credit or balance on card, and risk checks on the card

6. Once both legs are completed, the status is communicated to the acquiring bank → PA → Merchant → Customer. Also, the transaction is 'captured' by the bank, and fund movement *(settlement process)* will commence.

Flavors of card transaction:

1. Saved card / COF / Tokenized card flow

- Token registration flow: Based on the user's consent, the card is tokenized *(with card network)* once the transaction is successful.

  Note: Tokenization can be done during the transaction or on 'token amount' of Rs.2

- Repeat flow: Customer will select the CoF/tokenized card and enter the CVV *(optional)* and OTP to complete the transaction.

We covered this topic in detail in the previous chapter **(i.e., 8.B.)**

2. Skip-CVV / CVV-less Transaction:

Tokenized cards can be processed without CVV. This flow will reduce/remove CVV-related errors *(e.g., wrong CVV)* and increase the Success Rate.

We covered this topic in detail in the previous chapter **(i.e., 8.B.)**

3. On-Us and Off-Us

- On-Us transaction: The acquiring bank and card issuing Bank are same
  (e.g., HDFC Credit card processed by HDFC acquiring bank)

- Off-Us transaction: The acquiring bank and issuing bank are different.
  (e.g., ICICI credit card processed by HDFC acquiring bank)

Note: On-Us flow is not possible with CoF tokenization, but doable with issuer tokenization.

4. Direct OTP:

The transaction is done without redirection to the ACS *(Access Control Server)* page of the card issuing bank, and OTP is entered/captured on the merchant's or PA's page.

The transaction has two legs:

a. Triggering OTP:

- Merchant (Via PA or acquiring bank) triggers API to ACS of issuing bank to generate OTP.

- Customer receives the OTP on registered mobile number.

- Customer enters OTP on merchant's or PA's website or App.

Note: The same API can be used to re-send OTP (in case, user didn't receive OTP).

b. Validating OTP:

- Merchant triggers API to validate the OTP.

Once the OTP is validated by ACS successfully, the authorization leg is completed, and transaction status is communicated to PA → Merchant → Customer.

Important Note: Direct OTP is supported on both 3DS 1 and 3DS 2.0. For 3DS 2.0, apart from APIs, merchant *(via PA/TSP)* can integrate EMVCo certified SDK.

5. Decoupled Flow:

As you know there are two main stages in card transactions - Authentication and Authorization. Typically, a single processor (PA or acquiring bank) performs both the stages.

It is possible to decouple authentication and authorization - meaning, authentication is done by one processor and authorization by another.

This is a bit of an advanced type, but it boosts the success rate.

Note: 3DS 2.0 allows transactions to break into Device Data Collection (DDC), authentication and authorization stages.

6. Auth and Capture (Pre-Authorization):

There is another leg of transaction processing i.e., capture.

Basically, post authentication and authorization, the transaction is 'captured', and then fund movement *(from issuing bank to acquiring bank)* will start.

In Auth and Capture (pre-authorization), only authentication and authorization are completed, but the transaction is ***not captured***. The transaction is kept on hold, and the amount is blocked for a certain time (5-7 days).

Then merchant can take two actions:

- **Capture**: The card is debited, and MDR is charged
- **Void**: Transaction is canceled, blocked amount is released, MDR is not charged

If the merchant doesn't take any 'action' within the time frame, then the transaction is automatically nullified *(same as 'void')*.

This feature is limited to only Visa, MasterCard, and Amex cards. And doesn't work consistently for many issuing banks. *(Note: NPCI may add this capability to RuPay cards)*

Interesting point: MDR is not charged for 'void transactions' *(cost savings for merchants)*, and the block on the amount is released immediately *(kind of instant refund)*, so merchants will have lesser refund-related escalation.

Isn't it elegant? Now you not only understand pre–auth flow but also, you know why this book's name is Auth N Capture :)

7. EMI Transactions:

Credit Cards and a few debit cards allow the user to convert the amount to an EMIs *(Equated Monthly Instalments)*, and this can be done while doing the transaction, or the customer can do it on the bank's internet banking website/App.

During online card transactions, the user is shown the interest rates (fees) for various tenures *(3 months, 6 months etc.)* and prompted to select the tenure and then complete the card transactions.

Although the customer will make the repayment in installments, the merchant will receive the full amount in the next settlement cycle.

Working:

- **Credit Card**: EMI transactions are not unique; these are regular card transactions and EMI conversion happens offline wherein PA sends a file to the card issuer for EMI conversion. There is a slight possibility that the transaction may not get converted to EMI. The customer will come to know about it later.

  HDFC bank issues tenure wise Terminal IDs to identify EMI transactions. So HDFC EMI can be processed only by HDFC acquiring bank.

- **Debit Card**: A PA or merchant requires direct integration with the debit card issuing bank to provide the EMI feature.

An issuer would have imposed a limit on the minimum transaction amount and card types or card BINs that are eligible for EMI conversion. EMI Eligibility check APIs allow a PA/merchant to check whether a customer's card and transaction amount is eligible for the EMI. However, these APIs do not guarantee 100% accuracy, so few EMI transactions may not get converted to EMI.

8. MOTO Transaction:

In MOTO (Money Order Telephone Order) transactions, the merchant can debit the credit card without the need for 2FA/AFA.

This is used in the travel and hospitality segment where the user will give the card details *(during the booking)*, and the merchant will debit the card once the service is consumed.

This is an exotic flow and thus requires special approval from the acquiring banks. Any merchant who is getting this flow has to agree to absorb all chargebacks without any questions. That makes sense… isn't it!

9. International Card Transaction:

Merchants (with support of PA + Acquiring Bank + Payment Gateway) can enable international card processing for customers who are paying non-Indian cards.

Visa, MasterCard, and Amex cards are supported for such transactions.

There are two variants:

- Standard model where customer makes payment in merchant's currency (equivalent amount in card's base currency)
- Dynamic currency convertor where customer makes payment in base currency of the card.

Please read **Chapter 16.C** for details about International Card acceptance

Let's cover couple of flows that are stopped:

1. **Debit Card + ATM PIN**:

   For Debit cards of selected banks, instead of OTP or 3DS password, customers could use ATM PIN to complete the transaction. This flow was supported only by FSS. As per PA/ PG guidelines of RBI, this flow is stopped *(due to high risk)*

2. **Visa Safe Click (VSC) and MasterCard IDCx (Identity Check Express)**

   It is a SDK based 1-click payment solution from Visa and MasterCard wherein credit card transactions up to Rs.2000 don't require 2nd Factor Authentication.

   These were promising solutions to provide a frictionless payment experience, but VSC and MasterCard IDCx didn't 'make the cut' as the adoption was very low.

   In Jan '23, RBI stopped these solutions. Visa and MasterCard may still want to revive this solution by addressing 'risk' related concerns that were raised by the regulator.

Special Note:

1. **Auto Reading of OTP**

   In card transactions, entering OTP is a cumbersome step. So many PAs and TSPs have built an SDK that can read the OTP (from issuing bank's SMS) and then submit it.

   I am sure you would have seen it on many merchants' Android Apps.

   Although this is not a transaction flow, it is worthy of mention as it provides superior experience *(faster checkout)* and improves Success Rate *(no OTP input-related errors)*.

2. **Innovation in 2FA:**

   SMS-based OTP is a synonym for 2FA because it is easier to implement.

   Back in 2012, when 2FA became mandatory, SMS based OTP was a natural choice, but now, with technological advancement, many things can be done.

   In Feb-2024, RBI proposed to adopt a principle-based framework for 2FA to promote alternatives to SMS-based OTP.

   This can open up scope for innovation; we can have voice, face or fingerprint-based 2FA *(or anything fancy that we have seen in James Bond movies)* and also reduce frauds that happen where fraudsters get OTPs from innocent customers.

B. Net-Banking

Customer is redirected to the bank's online net-banking page to authenticate herself and complete the transaction.

Different banks have different ways of validating the transaction. Along with Customer Id and password, customers may be posed with additional steps such as entering grid number that is on back of the debit card, entering OTP, or answering security question.

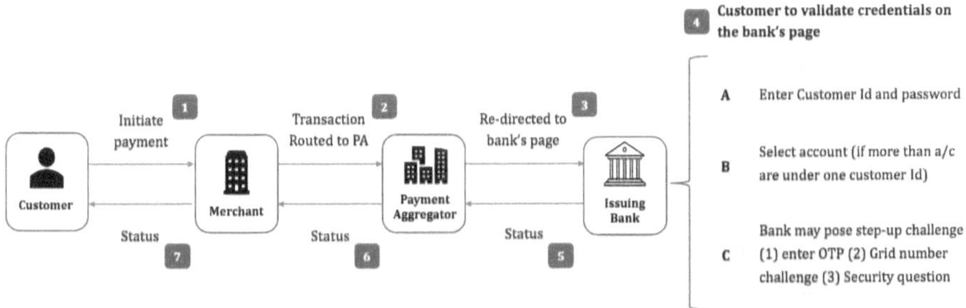

1. TPV (Third Party Validation) Flow

In this flow, the customer's bank account number is validated against the one that is registered with the merchant. TPV flow is mandatory for regulated investment (MF, stocks) use cases.

TPV flow is supported by 35+ banks through various Payment Aggregators.

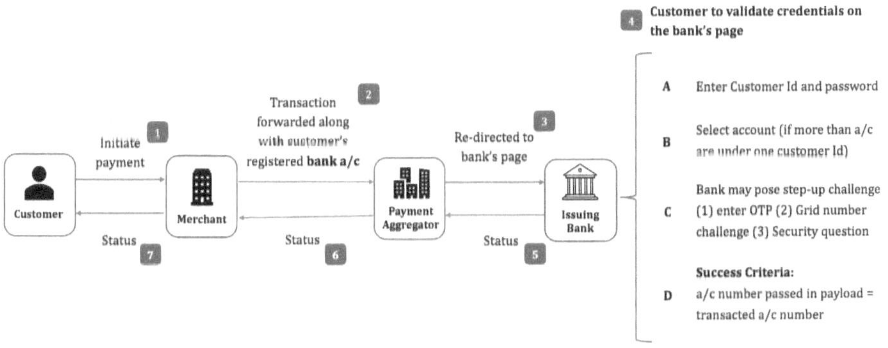

- Step 0: Merchant to collects customer's a/c number *(during onboarding/registration)*

- Step 1: Merchant to pass the customer's a/c number as part of payload data.

- Step 2: Customer is redirected to bank's page and customer to complete the transaction.

- Step 3: The account number that was passed in payload data is checked against the one that is used for the transaction. If there is a match then the transaction is marked as successful else, it is marked as failed.

2. Corporate Net-banking:

In case of corporate net-banking flow, there will be a maker-checker process where the maker initiates the transaction, and the checker approves it.

3. Special points in Net-banking:

Net-banking space didn't see many innovations. Here are couple of those innovations:

- **1-Click**: Couple of banks (e.g., ICICI, Axis) and FinTechs provide mobile SDK-based 1-click solutions for net-banking. In short, it is App to App switching.

  - **Learning step**: When a user selects the bank, user is switched to the bank's SDK/App where customer can set a PIN (4 digit) or 'train' fingerprint.

  - **Subsequent**: For subsequent transactions, the user is redirected to the banks' App, where the user can enter 4-digit PIN or 'scan' finger to complete the transaction

Note: There is a dependency of customers having the bank's App on mobile. But it looks like FinTechs are working on removing that dependency. Irrespective of the limitation, the flow is much better than remembering customer id and password.

- **Optimizing bank pages:**

  Majority of the banks' net-banking pages are not optimized for mobile devices. This means that if you open a net-banking page on a mobile, then fonts will be too small, content is not in a single screen, so users have to expand the screen or align content to type.

  Few PAs/TSPs have built SDK that can render the bank pages in the most optimal way, and users can complete the transaction comfortably. With better or mobile form factor optimized pages, the success rate will increase.

Future:

In 2024, RBI announced an interoperable model for Net-banking **(Read Chapter 4.C)**.

We can expect some change to transaction flow and/or settlement process.

C. Wallets

A customer is redirected to the wallet's page, where the customer validates the credentials *(enters mobile number and OTP)* and completes the transaction.

(a) Start with selecting the wallet on merchant's site   (b) Redirected to wallet's page

Illustration: Wallet Redirection Flow

Wallets also provide link and pay flow, where users can link the wallet with a one-time validation, and then wallet balance will be shown on the merchant's page and the wallet can be debited with a single click.

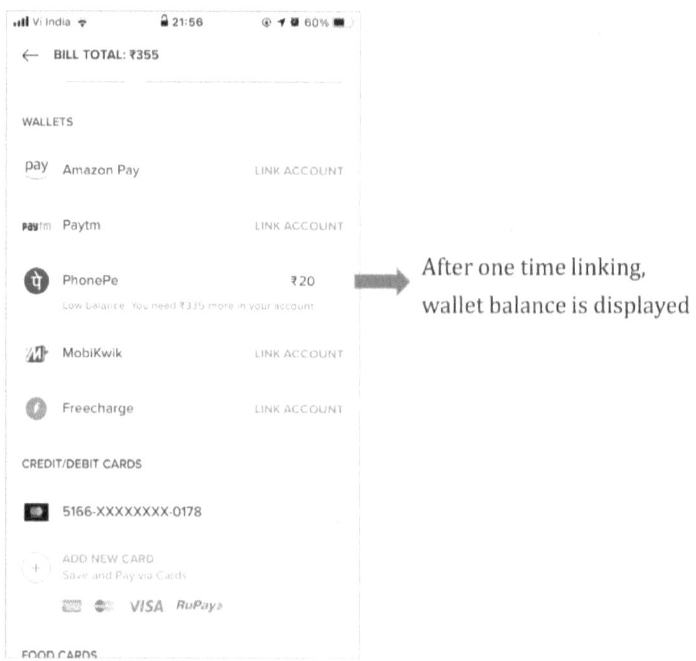

Illustration: Wallet Link + Pay Flow

D. Payment Containers

Containers (PhonePe, AmazonPay) are something which combine wallet and UPI under one user account.

Customers can select the preferred payment method to complete the transaction.

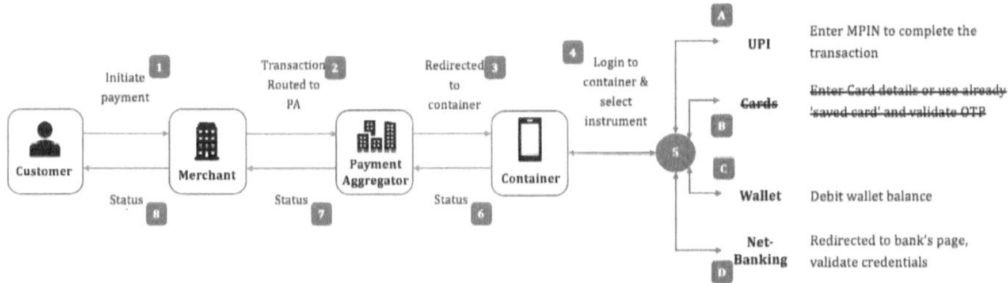

Illustration: Payment Container Transaction Process

Containers (e.g., PhonePe) also have intent flow where if the user select the PhonePe option on merchant's mobile App, then user is switched to PhonePe App *(if it is available on user's phone)*, and user can complete the transaction, and she will be switched back to merchant's App.

Note: Containers used to provide merchant agnostic card vault *(i.e., Cards saved on PhonePe will be available across all merchants where PhonePe is integrated/available).* As CoF tokenization guidelines enforce merchant-specific tokenization/card vault, so payment containers cannot save/tokenize cards on their App and use it on all merchants.

Many PAs club these containers under wallets. That is fine but I hope you know the difference between wallet and container.

E. UPI

UPI supports P2P (person-to-person), P2PM (payment at small stores or unorganized sector), and P2M (person-to-merchant) transactions.

We have covered the basics of UPI in ***Chapter 4.E (UPI)***. In this section, we will cover P2M flows.

1. Collect Request Flow:

1.a. VPA / UPI ID based

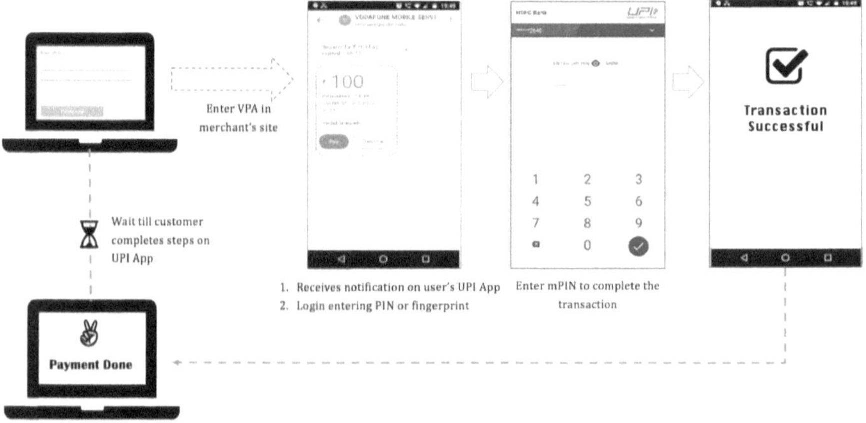

Advantages	• Works on all platforms (website, android, iOS, mobile web) • No lock-in with PA or TSP *(as there is no SDK)*
Disadvantages	• User needs to enter VPA. • Merchant has to validate VPA before processing *(additional API call)* • Broken flow: User enters VPA on merchant's website/App and then open TPAP to complete the next steps. • Merchant will not have visibility whether user has received collect request on TPAP or has taken necessary steps. • User has to complete the steps before the expiry of collect request

1.b. UPI Number Flow:

Select UPI Number: First, the customer has to select the UPI Number in her TPAP/UPI App.

UPI Number can be a mobile number or an 8-11 Digit unique number.

- Enter the UPI Number in the specific place given on the checkout page.

NPCI will resolve the UPI Number *(maps to VPA)* and sends a collect request to appropriate TPAP/UPI App

Next Steps will remain the same as those for a VPA based collect request.

Advantages	• Works on all platforms (website, android, iOS, mobile web) • UPI Number *(usually mobile number)* is easier to remember than VPA. • No lock-in with PA or TSP (as there is no SDK)
Disadvantages	• Manual entry - User needs to enter UPI number. • Merchant has to validate UPI Number *(an additional API)* • Broken flow: User enters UPI Number on merchant's website/App and then open TPAP to complete the next steps. • Merchant will not have visibility whether user has received collect request on App or has taken necessary steps

2. Intent Flow:

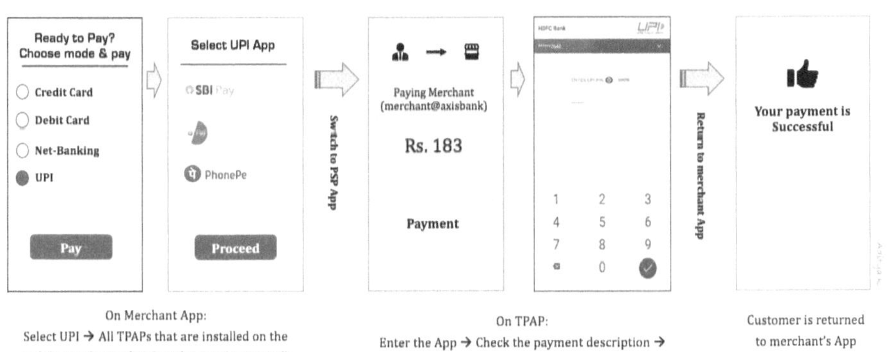

On Merchant App:
Select UPI → All TPAPs that are installed on the mobile are shown → Select the App (& proceed)

On TPAP:
Enter the App → Check the payment description → Enter MPIN → complete the transaction

Customer is returned to merchant's App

Advantages	• No need to enter VPA or UPI Number • Works with SDK (Android, iOS) and without SDK (Android) • Seamless user experience with App-to-App switch • Merchant will know whether user has UPI App/TPAP • Better success rate
Disadvantages	• Works on mobile App and mobile site, and not on website • Not practical to add SDKs of multiple PAs

Selection of Payment Source:

During the transaction, a user can select the bank *(if UPI ID is linked to multiple banks)* or other payment sources *(credit card, PPI wallet)* to make the transaction.

The option of UPI on credit card or PPI wallet is subject the availability of the feature on TPAP/UPI App, and the merchant category *(e.g., UPI on Credit Card is not allowed for NBFCs)*.

Note: UPI Lite is not allowed for P2M transactions; Credit line on UPI is yet to be launched

3. **Other UPI Flows:**

    • **TPAP Specific Flow:** You might have seen PhonePe and Google Pay on merchants' checkout pages of merchants apart from UPI. These are TPAP-specific flows and are not pure UPI flows. Meaning: If you click on PhonePe option then PhonePe App will open, then it will show UPI and/or wallet for transaction.

    • **Google Pay's omni-channel flow**: Users can enter a mobile number, and the UPI ID attached to that mobile number is resolved, and then the UPI transaction flow starts.

Note: After the launch of the UPI Number flow, this flow has lost its relevance

- **TPAP In-App Flow**: Users can complete the transaction on the merchant's App, including entering MPIN. This flow is supported by a few TPAPs *(e.g., Google Pay)*

4. QR Code:

Scan & Pay is nothing but intent or push payment model. There are two types of QRs:

a. Static QR: where user has to enter the amount.

b. Dynamic: User doesn't` need to enter the amount, and QR expires after certain time

Offline merchants use Static QR, whereas online merchants use dynamic QR *(where QR is generated for every order)*, so it is easier to reconcile.

Users can pay on dynamic QR using Bank a/c, credit card, PPI wallet that is linked to UPI Id, and in case of static QR, users can also pay using UPI Lite wallet *(Apart from other sources)*.

5. UPI Plug-in SDK

UPI Plug-in allows a merchant to facilitate UPI transactions within its own App by integrating the bank's SDK. With UPI Plug-in, in a way, a merchant will become 'Partial-TPAP'.

Refer to Chapter 4.E. (UPI) for details.

A merchant who is interested in implementing Plug-in has to fulfill certain requirements related to data transfer, data localization, access to customer data, sharing of data to 3rd parties, and sponsor banks to do complete due diligence of merchants before extending SDK to merchants.

Advantages	• Transaction happens within App *(no redirection, no App-App switching)* so better experience and higher success rate
Disadvantages	• Works on mobile App • Compliance heavy for merchants • Additional commercials • User has to create new VPA *(if already doesn't have VPA with the merchant's sponsor bank)*

F. Alternate Credit Products - BNPL and Cardless EMI

1. BNPL:

- **First time**: Merchant calls eligibility check API (*check whether customer is an existing BNPL user and what is the available credit*). Then, the user needs to complete the authentication leg *(OTP validation)* to complete the transaction.

- **Subsequent flows**: Eligibility check is done, and then customer approves the transaction (*no authentication required as token is stored after first transaction*)

Note: Such seamless payment experience is possible only on direct integration

2. Cardless EMI:

- Merchant calls eligibility check API *(check whether customer is an existing user and what is the available credit line)*.

- The user will select the EMI tenure (3 months, 6 months, etc.)

- The user needs to complete the authentication leg *(OTP validation)* to complete the transaction.

We have covered various transaction flows of the important payment modes.

G. Mini topics related to Transactions.

a. Transaction Status:

Do not assume that a transaction will be either successful or fail in real or near-real time. There is a possibility that the transaction doesn't reach a finite status *(Success or Fail)* and goes into 'pending' status. In such cases, the PA will pull the latest status from the bank, and then push the updated status to the merchant, or merchant can pull the latest status. This is called 'status reconciliation'.

Another way to know the status of pending transactions is through a settlement file - A bank/PSP will settle funds only if the transaction was successful. But this happens only on T+1 working day.

b. Instant Gratification:

A definite transaction status (in real-time or near real-time) is important, as both the merchant and the customer can take appropriate actions based on the status. There are cases where a definite status after the stipulated time is of no use.

Example: The airline has to know that the status is successful (to issue tickets) or failed (to release the seat back to inventory). The Airline cannot wait a long time for the status.

To manage such a scenario, merchants (or PAs) can mark the transaction as 'failed' and ignore status that comes after a stipulated time-period. If the status is 'failed', then good enough *(no action needed)*; if the status is "success", then trigger auto-refund.

Closing Remarks

The transaction is the first and the most important leg of payment flow. Payment flows keep evolving or improvising as the merchants/PAs want to provide a better user experience and achieve higher conversion rate. Also, new flows keep coming to light as NPCI, card networks, and/or banks try to bring new flows and processes.

Even the existing flows are interesting and comprehensive, but it is important for a merchant to implement these flows after considering the utility of these flows, keeping the merchant's own use cases, technical capabilities, and resources in mind.

9.B Transaction Routing

Many merchants integrate with multiple online payment aggregators (PAs), acquiring banks, wallets, and BNPLs to:

- Increase coverage of payment modes and banks
- Avail better commercials or rates
- Avail offers such as cashbacks and discounts.

Most importantly, merchants want to reduce dependency on a single payment provider.

As they say, ***"Do not put all your eggs in ONE basket"***.

It is a good strategy, but integrating with multiple payment service providers brings additional challenges in the areas of:

- Payment Page Design
- Card vault/tokenization strategy
- Transaction routing
- Operations effort

We have covered the ***payment page*** and c***ard tokenization*** in **chapters 8.A and 8.B**. Now, let's talk about '***transaction routing***'.

How do you route the transactions?

Before you set any routing logic, decide on the objective you wish to achieve.

- Backup or failover mechanism
- Higher success rate
- Cost optimization
- Fulfilling volume commitment *(promised to a PA/bank to avail preferential rates)*

Some of the possible transaction routing logics:

A. Business Line Based:

Merchants can configure different PAs for different internal business lines or product lines.

Example: Vehicle insurance is routed through PA <ABC> and Travel insurance through PA <PQR>

B. Channel Based:

Merchants can have channel-wise routing for website, mobile Site, mobile App.

Example: Website transactions routed to PA <ABC> and mobile App transactions to PA <PQR>

C. Primary and Retry:

PA <ABC> acts as primary for all transactions, and backup PA <PQR> is used only when the user of failed transactions retries to make another payment.

D. Performance Based:

Measure the performance or success rate of PAs/acquiring banks that are integrated and route the transaction through PA/bank that is performing better.

Example: Start with 50:50 volume and, based on performance, increase the volume of high-performing PA. Also, keep 'some' volume on low performing PA so you can measure performance of both PAs and adjust the volume based on the performance.

E. Payment Method Based:

Merchants can use different PAs to process different payment methods. It can be done at various levels:

All cards to PA <ABC> and UPI to PA <PQR>

For net-banking: Bank level routing *(e.g., HDFC to PA <ABC> and SBI to PA <PQR>)*

For Cards: Card type *(credit card, debit card)*, card network *(Visa, MasterCard, RuPay)*, card issuer *(e.g., ICICI, HDFC)*, and BIN level.

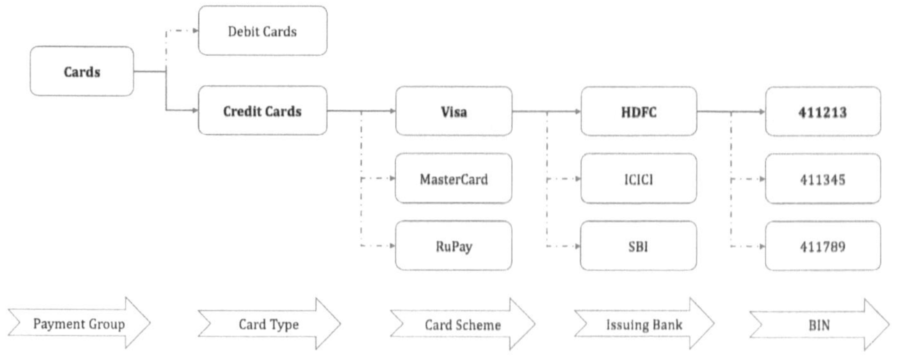

Illustration: Granular Level Routing on Cards

Reason: Different PA + acquiring banks + PG combination tend to provide better success rate for a particular payment mode (E.g., PA <ABC> may be good in RuPay, but other PAs process other cards better). So, set the routing accordingly and keep trying different combinations until the optimal success rate is achieved.

F. Commercials Based:

It is possible that one PA may provide better commercials on few payment methods compared to others.

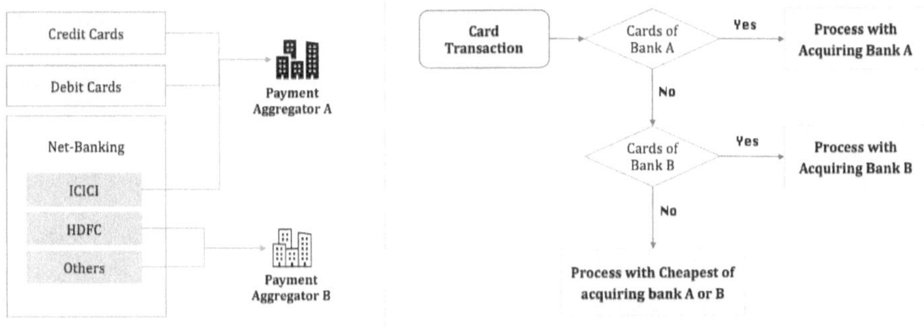

Illustration: Example 1 (explained below)   **Illustration**: Example 2 (explained below)

Example 1: Let us say the merchant has good commercials on credit cards, debit cards and ICICI net-banking from PA <A>. But has good rates from PA <B> for other banks of net-banking. Then the merchant can route the transactions accordingly

Example 2: PA or acquiring banks can provide differential rates for On-US transactions, so route card transactions accordingly. *(On-Us: Acquiring bank is same as card issuing bank)*

Note: *On–Us routing is stopped post CoF tokenization; On–Us works on issuer tokenized cards*

G. Volume Based:

- **Transaction count based**: Volume is split among PAs based on transaction count *(assuming ticket size is same)*. Typically, it works well if there is a 50:50 split between two PAs, but it is not ideal for complicated volume split cases.

  Example: If I need to send 20% volume to PA<A>, 30% to PA<B> and 50% PA<C> then 2 transactions to <A>, next 3 to <B>, and next 5 to <C>, and then start over again. But it requires additional logic to remember the last PA used and its count.

- **Timer based**: Build a timer-based logic that uses the current timestamp to split volumes among PAs. As this model is built on probabilities, it works better *(i.e., split is more accurate)* if transactions are continuous and not sporadic. E.g., Works better for Swiggy but might not for Urban Ladder

  Example: 5% of volume to PA<A>, 25% to PA<B> and 70% to PA<C>. In that case, take the current timestamp and perform mod 100, and if that number is less than 5 then send to <A>, if the number is less than 30 then send to <B>, and the rest will go through <C>

- **Payment method-wise split**: Merchant knows the volume across various payment methods and routes the transactions of the payment modes to fulfill the volume commitment.

Example: Visa Cards and net-banking constitute 50% of volume. So, if volume is to split 50:50 between PAs then route all Visa Cards and net-banking through PA <A> and rest of the payment modes through PA <B>.

H. Amount Based Routing:

Few merchants have amount-based routing as certain 'PA + Acquiring bank + PG' combination works better on high ticket transactions, and few may not, mainly due to higher risk checks.

I. User Level Routing:

Merchants who want to give consistent experience to a user may prefer to route the transactions of a specific user to the same PA.

Example: Merchant is integrated with Cashfree and RazorPay and has enabled Direct OTP flow *(where OTP is captured on PA's page)*. User A is always sent to RazorPay's direct OTP page and User B is routed via Cashfree to provide consistent experience.

Note: This is super advanced level routing but do it if you are up to it.

Important Note: Irrespective of the routing logic that a merchant builds, configure a primary and secondary PA/acquiring bank as a backup or failover mechanism.

Closing Remarks

Performance-based logics are based on the hypothesis that a 'n-1' transaction was successful on a particular PA, so transaction 'n' will be successful.

Think about it!

Routing logic is not a sprint but a marathon; one has to keep fine-tuning and keep playing with various combinations until you achieve the objective, and that too consistently.

Chapter 10

Payment Aggregator – Success Rate

In this chapter, I will cover the most important aspects of the online payments i.e., success rate.

10.A   Understanding Success rate

'Success Rate' is the most important parameter that every merchant is interested in.

During every sales pitch, the merchant asks questions on this, and every salesperson jumps in with the answer, 'we are the best in the industry'!

There are various ways a success rate (SR) is measured. The numerator always remains the same (i.e., successful transactions), but the denominator can be,

- Total transactions initiated by the merchant.
- Total transactions received by Payment Aggregator.

In an ideal world, both these numbers will be the same, but we don't live in an ideal world. Right?

But to keep it simple, we will go ahead with the assumption that both numbers are the same.

A merchant may remove following types of failures from SR calculation,

- User cancellations (e.g., canceled transaction)
- User mistakes (e.g., Entered wrong OTP)

The logic is, why should a PA be held responsible for a user's mistakes or lack of intent to pay?

Fair enough, but things become complicated when you are not sure whether a user dropped out because the user does not want to proceed further with payment *(lack of intent)* or the user is not able to complete the transaction due to technical glitch *(e.g., blank page)*.

Also, more logical merchants remove the failures that a PAs cannot fix *(e.g., If SBI net-banking is down, then it doesn't matter which PA is used for transaction processing)* and scheduled downtimes of PAs that are informed in advance *(if the merchant has back-up PA to manage)*.

Measurement

It is important to set the formula *(aka ground rules)* before you start measuring the success rates, or else you end up comparing apples to oranges (or, worst case, apples to cats).

Success rate can be measured on various levels and combinations:

- Channel (website, mobile site, android, iOS)
- Overall (across all payment modes)
- Payment group (card, UPI, net-banking)
- Card origin (Domestic, International)
- Card type (Credit Card, Debit Card)
- Card scheme (Visa, MasterCard, RuPay etc.),
- Whether the card is tokenized
- Card Flow: CVV less or not, direct OTP or not, 3DS 2.0 or 3DS 1
- Bank Level: Issuing bank (HDFC, ICICI), net-banking banks (SBI, Canara etc.)
- Acquiring bank level (e.g., HDFC)

- Acquiring bank + PG level for cards (e.g., HDFC CyberSource, HDFC FSS)

- BIN level

- International Cards: Currency or country-wise

- For UPI: Collect or Intent, UPI handle level (E.g., Okhdfc, ybl), TPAP level (PhonePe, Cred)

- Amount slabs (e.g., up to Rs.1K, Rs.1K-Rs.10K, Rs.10K-Rs.1 Lakh, >Rs.1 Lakh)

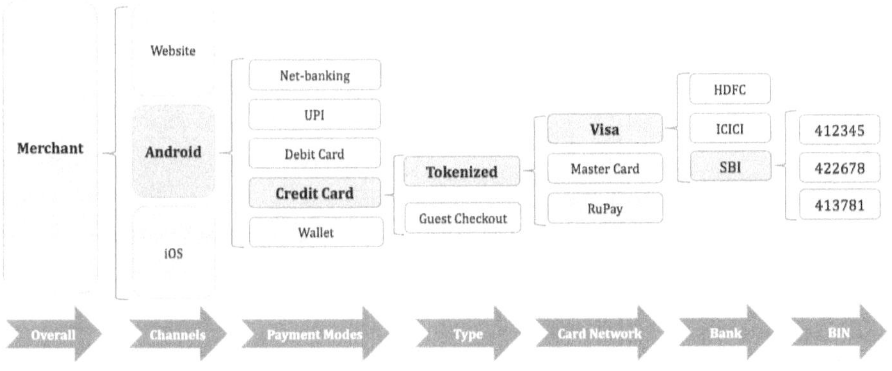

Illustration: Step by step analysis of Success Rate

Typically, a combination of all the above points is used to measure success rate *(e.g., tokenized Visa credit cards of SBI on Android App that is processed by HDFC CyberSource)*

How much does success rate matter?

Example A: 100 users did transactions and 20 transactions failed. So, what is the success rate?

Straight forward, Success rate = 80%... right?

View 1: Airtel customer has to pay the post-paid bill before the due date. Let us say those 20 failed transaction customers paid the bill before the due date. So, what is the success rate now... 80% or 100%?

View 2: On Flipkart, in 10 out of those 20 failed transactions, users did not come back to buy or bought from another site. So, is the success rate 80% or 90%?

Example B: A customer tried to make a payment and failed four times but finally succeeded. So, what is the success rate here?

20% or 100%?

Merchant didn't lose 'sale' as the customer paid anyway. Also, it is possible that the first 4 times the transaction failed as the customer had entered the wrong card expiry date.

Remember two things:

- What does the success rate stand for your business - loss of revenue or just inconvenience?
- Who is responsible for the success rate - PA, customer, or yourself i.e., merchant?

Some cases that will give insights on success rate:

1. High End Fashion Vs. Generic eCommerce:

A high-end fashion apparel merchant might have a better success rate than a generic eCommerce marketplace.

Reason: High end fashion apparel merchants have an urban customer base with better data connectivity, but the eCommerce marketplace's customers are in tier 3-4 towns where data strength may be weak, or user's may not be good at making payments.

Learning: Demography and users' environment counts

2. Food Vs Travel:

A food ordering merchant will have a better success rate than a travel portal. Because the intent of purchase is higher for food order, a user might have opened three travel portals and must be checking discounts and finally buys in one place (drops in other two) or defers purchase.

Learning: Watch out for user canceled cases or intent of purchase.

3. Insurance Vs. eCommerce:

Success rate may not be as important for Insurance merchants as much as for an eCommerce company. An insurance merchant knows that the customer will try again as she wants to renew the policy, but eCommerce merchants fear that customer will defer the purchase.

Learning: Value of success rate varies from business to business

4. Confusion in checkout flow or offers:

A major eCommerce merchant complained about the bad success rate on SBI net-banking. Upon analysis, we realized that the merchant was running an offer on SBI Cards, but users were confused with the offer, and they were clicking SBI net-banking page and then canceling transactions.

Learning: Checkout pages should handle promotions with better flows and messages

5. Do not compare apples to oranges:

Different PAs show success rate differently on their dashboard. Few may remove user cancellations, and others may not. Few may show SR at order level, but few may show it at transaction level (*an order can have multiple transactions if a user retries*).

Learning: Use the same formula for all PAs/PSPs to calculate SR.

6. RuPay Vs. Visa or Canara Bank Vs. ICICI Bank:

RuPay infrastructure is not as robust as Visa/MasterCard infrastructure, so in general, RuPay success rates will be lower.

Similarly, in net-banking the success rate of Canara Bank will be lower than HDFC bank.

Learning: Have right expectations from payment methods/banks

7. Issuing Bank is down:

If the issuing bank is down, then it doesn't matter which acquiring bank we use or the routing logic. If the ICICI card issuer is down, then it doesn't matter whether you use BillDesk or Cashfree.

If SBI net-banking is down, then transactions will fail irrespective of the PA.

UPI transactions will fail if NPCI is down.

Learning: Sometimes waiting is the only option so proactively put a message about bank downtime so user can proceed with different payment instruments

8. Website Vs. Mobile:

The success rate on websites varies from that on mobile. Reasons may include, the website may be for discovery, but payment happens on mobile or vice versa. Website transactions happen on Wi-Fi compared to mobile transactions that may have problems with data connectivity.

Learning: Success rate will vary for different channels

9. Count... Counts:

Out of 2 transactions, if one fails, then the success rate will be 50% (*too bad*). But if you take 100 transactions and 10 fails, then the success rate will be 90%

Learning: More the data, more accurate the calculation

Closing Remarks

I have come across merchants who have asked questions such as 'can you guarantee a 95% success rate?' or 'can you improve the success rate of RuPay cards by another 10%?'

Such questions don't make sense, but below is the answer:

The payment ecosystem involves various entities and actors, just like how a car has various moving parts. Whenever there are multiple moving parts, every part becomes a potential point of failure.

Along with technology, bank and PA integrations, the intent of purchase, ease of payment, user base, user's environment, and checkout flows play vital roles in achieving a better success rate.

The goal is to improve the success rate; PAs and merchants can take a few steps to improve the success rate.

We will talk about those steps in the next two chapters.

10.B   Error Codes and Failure Reasons

Before we dive into ways to improve the success rate, let's understand the failures.

Every transaction will have one of the two possible finite statuses: **Success** or **Fail**

'**Success**' is simple… it simply means everyone involved in payment processing did a 'good job' and the merchant will receive the funds.

'**Failures**' are complicated i.e., because payment systems are complex.

As you know the payment ecosystem involves various entities and actors which perform certain functions and each of these entities can be potential points of failure.

For Example:

- **Cards**: Customer → Merchant → Orchestrator *(if present)* → PA → Acquiring Bank → Payment Gateway (PG) → Card Network → Issuing Bank

- **UPI**: Customer → Merchant → Orchestrator (if present) → PA → Acquiring Bank → UPI PG/TSP → NPCI → TPAP/ UPI App → Issuer PSP → Remitter Bank

Note: I am just listing the main participants. There are many other participants involved.

A transaction fails, if '*something*' goes wrong with one of the entities or actors.

The beauty of the payment system is that there are error codes *(failure reasons)* which every entity conveys to its upstream entity and eventually to PA and to merchants. Those error codes convey what went wrong. There are hundreds of error codes.

And the not-so-beautiful part is that these error codes are not standard across entities *(PAs, acquiring banks, PGs)* and in many cases quite generic. So, it is very difficult to pinpoint the exact problem for all the failed transactions.

Like many things in our lives, we have to live with it and make the most of what is available.

Let's look at different types of errors:

1. **Human Errors:** Errors that are due to manual entry.

   - Instrument details are wrong (e.g., card number, CVV, expiry date, VPA etc.)

   - Wrong authentication (e.g., entering wrong OTP, MPIN, or password)

   - Delays in action (e.g., OTP expired, UPI collect request expired)

2. **Payment Instrument Related**: Failures related to attributes of the payment instrument which can be related to customer or the issuer or bank policies.

   - Insufficient balance or credit

   - Exceeded the usage limit *(set by the bank or user)*

   - Exceeded transaction limit of the payment mode *(set by the RBI/NPCI)*

   - Exceeded number of retries.

   - Card is expired.

   - Card or bank account is blocked.

   - Card or bank account is not enabled for online transactions.

3. **Wrong Configurations:** Failures that are attributed to wrong configurations or poorly designed checkout pages of merchant or PA or bank.

   - Instrument is not allowed for the sector *(E.g., credit card for loan repayment)*

- Instrument is not enabled by the merchant *(E.g., Amex card is not enabled)*

- International card gateway is not enabled for the merchant.

4. **Risk and Fraud Check Related**: Various entities *(acquiring banks, issuing banks)* perform risk checks and decline the transactions that are perceived as *'high risk'*.

   Note: As risk engines are proprietary and confidential so the entities do not disclose the exact logic *(if bad actors know how the risk engine works then they can "fool" it)*

5. **Technical errors**: At times there could be technical issues with APIs and/or the systems *(of network, bank, or PSP)* are down or deteriorate in performance. Such conditions lead to transaction failures.

   Here are few examples:

   - Network or bank or PSP or ACS is down.

   - API timeouts

Pending Cases: Transaction can have only two finite statuses - success or failure. But during transaction processing, it is possible that transactions may go into 'pending' wherein one of the systems is waiting to complete *'the action'*.

But the payment system doesn't wait for 'forever' for 'the action' to be completed. So, such cases will be 'timed out' and marked as 'failed'. Such timed-out cases may not have error code/failure reasons *(for obvious reasons)*. PAs can choose to show them separately.

All transactions are accounted for during settlement reconciliation. So, the final state of the transaction will be available when the issuer/acquirer reconciles the transactions on the next working day. So, pending transactions will become either marked as successful or failed.

User cancellations:

A user who doesn't want to proceed forward with payment can cancel the transaction.

- User can press cancel button - on Checkout page, bank page *(net-banking)* or while entering OTP on ACS page *(for cards)*, common library page *(for UPI)*

  Such actions *(user canceled or pressed back button)* are usually captured, and PA can show these transactions separately.

- In case the user closes the browser or App, then there is no way to identify such actions. So, most likely these transactions go under 'timed out' cases.

In summary, each transaction can be classified into at least 4 buckets:

- Success
- Failed
- User Canceled
- Timed out

Note: PAs/TSPs may use different names and add or reduce the number of buckets, but at the broad level the concept of failures remains same

Transaction Limits:

Many times, the transactions fail due to breach of transaction limits.

Let's talk a bit about limits that are enforced by RBI and NPCI. Apart from product/platform level limits *(enforced by NPCI/RBI)*, banks and users also can set limits.

- Credit card, debit card and net-banking do not have any limits except the one put by the user or available balance or credit line.
- UPI limits vary for different types of use cases *(Note: These are subject to change)*

- Rs.1,00,000 (for P2P, P2PM, P2M) - All categories (with following exceptions)
- Rs.2,00,000 (Capital markets, loan repayment, credit card bill payment, insurance)
- Rs.5,00,000 (IOP, Govt Securities, Education, Healthcare)
- Rs.2,000 (shared intent and shared QR)

Note: I have covered limits of other payment products/platforms in relevant chapters

Closing Remarks:

Few errors/failures can be fixed by implementing special flows, features, or processes, but few errors cannot be fixed.

In the next Chapter, we will learn how to improve the success rate.

10.C   How to Improve Success Rate

Success rate is important as the merchant wants every user to complete the transaction in the first attempt as it not only impacts the sales but also the user experience.

Here are few of the things that a merchant and/or PA can implement to improve success rate:

1.   Infrastructure:

- Uptime: Basic expectation and goal should be 100% *(or near 100%)* system uptime for PAs/PSPs. It is easier said than done. No system in the world guarantees 100% uptime.

  So be practical!

- Scalability: PAs should have the ability to handle transaction spikes *(generally that happens during flash sales)*

- PAs/PSPs should have business continuity and disaster recovery plan in place.

2.   Bank Integration:

As a merchant, make sure the PA provides you a better acquiring bank and/or payment gateway combination as it plays a crucial role in the success rate of cards and UPI.

Note: PA has back-to-back costs with acquiring banks and will be able to enable the best acquiring bank provided the commercials with merchant permits.

3.   Checkout Pages:

- a. **Clean Page:** Keep your checkout page clean and user friendly. Do not clutter the payment modes, offers and discounts.

b. Design Smart Page:

- Show the most frequently used payment instrument on top.

- Pre-fetch payment instrument *(e.g., tokenized card, saved VPA, linked wallet etc.)*

- Show the modes for which either you or bank is running offers.

- Nudge people to select payment mode that has higher success rate.

- Show message if a payment mode is down or not performing well.

4. Performance Based Routing:

A merchant can integrate two or more PAs or Acquiring Banks, and set-up performance-based routing. *(Covered in sub-chapter 9.B)*

Note: At times MDR with merchants won't allow PAs to provide best performing acquiring banks.

5. Smart Routing:

Implement clever routing logics: Issuer or BIN based routing based on historic performance.

Some BIN/Banks/card networks work better on a particular acquiring bank. Identify these patterns and set the routing logic accordingly.

Note: Do not assume such routing works all the time. If ICICI issuer is not performing well then it doesn't matter which acquiring bank or processor is used for the transaction

6. Alerts - Downtimes and Deterioration:

There are two types of downtimes - scheduled and unscheduled.

PAs should have mechanisms to alert/inform merchants about downtimes, so that merchants can show the alert on the checkout page. Such proactive messaging will nudge customers to use different payment methods.

At times, a particular payment mode or bank may not be performing optimally, so identify the low performance and inform the merchant. If the merchant or PA can show it on the payment page, then the customer may opt to pay using a different payment method.

Example: ICICI NB success rate is 70% but if you are observing a success rate of 40% then display the alert on the checkout page - *'ICICI bank is not performing at optimal level, either continue or choose payment method'*

7. Retry Page:

Show the retry page for failed transactions so that customers can change payment instruments to complete the transaction.

Show the failure messages that are easy to understand *(do not show error codes - which users don't understand)* and add relevant recommendations. *(e.g., for UPI transaction failed due to breach of daily limit - show recommendation to use debit card)*

Be Smart - Instead of a standard retry page, show the best alternative payment method to complete the transaction. *E.g., If the net- banking is failed then show the debit card option.*

8. Optimize mobile transactions:

Mobile transactions are tedious especially with respect to cards *(entering OTP)* and net-banking *(pages are not optimized for mobile screens).*

- Integrate features that minimize user inputs/actions such as UPI Intent, Tokenization of cards, skip-CVV transactions.

- Integrate SDKs that auto-read OTP and optimize bank pages to provide seamless payment experience, and better success rate. Such SDKs are provided by PAs and TSPs.

9. **SR improvement for cards**:

- Make sure the correct Merchant Category Code (MCC) is configured.

- Use multiple PAs/acquiring banks to do dynamic routing based on performance.

- If you have relevant business case, **tokenize** the cards with PA or TSP

- Implement **direct OTP/native OTP** (zero-redirection) flow.

- Implement **skip-CVV** (CVV-less) flow for tokenized cards.

- Decoupled Flow: Merchants can build flow where authentication and authorization will be done by different PAs (+Acquiring Banks). This flow will enable merchant to pick the best PA that performance better at granular level *(Note: All PAs do not support such flows)*

- International cards:

  - Perform BIN check whether card is eligible for international transactions.

  - Use the Dynamic Currency Convertor (DCC) so it becomes easier for users to transact in local currency.

  - Capture and pass additional info that is mandated by certain banks (E.g., Zip code)

- Eliminate manual input errors by using SDK to **auto-read** and/or **auto-submit** the OTP on Android Apps.

10. SR improvement for UPI:

a. **General:**

- Use multiple acquiring banks to do dynamic routing based on performance.

- Get merchant specific VPA *(merchantA@bank)* than generic VPA *(PA@bank)*

- Make sure the correct Merchant Category Code (MCC) is configured.

b. **Website:**

- Validate the VPA or UPI number before initiating the payment *(PAs, acquiring banks provide API for this check)*

- Show dynamic UPI QR code; the user doesn't have to type VPA, and just scan UPI QR Code to make the payment; include expiry timer for dynamic QR.

- Save VPA of successful transactions, so customer doesn't have to type it again.

- Reduce typing requirement: Allow customer to select App first then based on App selection and user information *(e.g.: Mobile number and mail id)*, populate the VPA *(e.g., if customer selects PhonePe then populate VPA as 9192939495@ ybl)*

- Set the collect request expiry timer that is reasonable *(e.g., 5 to 7 mins)*

- Show a timer expiry *(how much time is left before the collect request expires)*

- Show the next steps on the wait page *(Example: You will receive notification on your XYZ App, open App, enter MPIN etc.)*

   c. **Mobile App**:

- Implement intent flow for mobile App.

- Show only better performing Apps (hide others) - show top 2–3 Apps, then have a placeholder to enter VPA/UPI Number so that the user can still have provision to initiate 'collect' request.

- Implement TPAP specific intent flows offered by Google Pay and PhonePe

- Implement In-App flow for relevant TPAPs (e.g., G Pay)

- Implement UPI Plug-in *(if it makes sense for your business)*

   d. **Mobile Web**:

- Implement SDK-less UPI intent (for Android)

11. SR improvement for wallets:

- Implement link + pay flow so the customer can see the wallet balance and take decision whether to proceed with wallet or not.

- Most of the wallet users are on Minimum KYC. That means max balance of Rs.10,000. So, if the transaction amount is higher that Rs.10,000, then show a warning message.

12. SR improvement for BNPL and cardless EMI:

- Implement eligibility check API - Where basis the mobile number and/or PAN of users, you will get to know whether the user has approval from BNPL or cardless EMI provider.

13. SR Improvement for Net-Banking:

- For mobile App, implement SDK that optimizes banks' pages *(provided by PA/TSP)*

- For mobile App, implement 1-Click SDK *(available for few banks - ICICI, Axis)* if you have a high number of repeat transactions on net-banking.

14. User Education:

Let's not forget the user education - everyone is not equally competent in using the payment modes, and knowingly or unknowingly they may make mistakes. Also, users may get confused with new payment flows and drop out.

So, a merchant/PA should educate the customers about how to complete the transaction.

- Card not enrolled for online transaction - As per guidelines, cardholder must explicitly enable card for online payments *(in the bank's internet banking portal)*. At present, it is not possible to know whether a card is enrolled for online transactions or not. So, a merchant/PA should put a disclaimer or provide user guide.
- Skip-CVV flow *(for tokenized cards)* is comparatively new payment flow, so users may get confused. So, it is better to show small information, so users feel comfortable.

Remember, payments can be taught to the masses – UPI is the classic example of that.

Closing Remarks:

Sounds simple… Right?

No, it is not.

To implement these success rate improvement measures, one has to consider cost (i.e., MDR), integration efforts, system limitations, and operations efforts.

So, if you know the true value of a higher success rate, then you won't mind putting some extra money and effort to improve it!

Chapter 11

Payment Aggregator – Settlement

The main purpose of online payments is getting 'money' from customers. So, 'settlement' is a crucial part of the payment cycle.

In this chapter, I will cover various aspects of 'settlement'.

11.A Settlement Time

Just because a transaction is successful in real-time that doesn't mean the online PA will receive the funds immediately.

Banks and other PSPs settle funds to PAs at different time durations, and then PA will take time to settle funds to merchants.

So standard settlement time can be T+1 or T+2 working days with exception of certain sectors such as capital markets (Stocks and Mutual Fund investment).

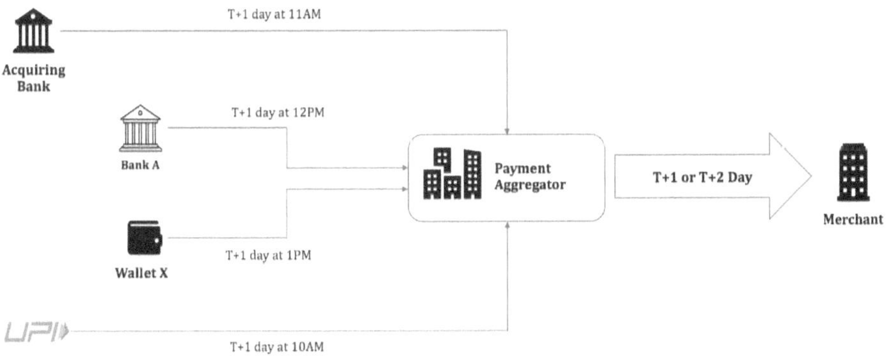

Reconciliation:

Imagine you and your friends go out for dinner. At the end, the bill comes to your table, and one of your friends checks whether the bill amount is correct based on orders you placed. If both matches, then 'reconciliation' is successful, otherwise, you 'call the manager' for corrections.

The exact same process is followed by a PA as well.

A PA reconciles the amount that needs to be received for successful transactions Vs. Total amount received by acquiring banks and other PSP partners. Then, the total successful merchant transactions are checked, and corresponding amounts are settled to respective merchants after adjusting MDR, refunds, and chargebacks *(whichever is applicable)*.

Considering PA work with 80+ banks, wallets, and other PSPs, and lakhs of merchants, reconciliation is a time-consuming process.

Fund Movement:

Card issuing banks *(in the case of cards)* and remitter banks *(in the case of UPI)* will move funds to the acquiring banks that were used for transaction processing. Then, acquiring banks will move money to PA.

For net-banking, wallets, alternate credit products, and containers, respective issuing entities will move money to the PA.

Factors that affect settlement time:

T Count: In the 'payments world', days are always 'working days' as per RBI list. That means there won't be any settlement on the bank holidays.

Transaction time: Different banks have different transaction cut off times. So, any transaction done after the cut-off time will move to the next settlement batch.

E.g.: SBI (20:00), Canara Bank (21:00), Federal Bank (23:30), all other banks (23:59)

a. Regular Working Days

Transaction Time	Tuesday	Wednesday	Thursday
Monday - Before cut-off time	Bank Recon	Settlement	
Monday - After cut-off time	-	Bank Recon	Settlement

b. With a bank holiday in between

Transaction Time	Tuesday	Wednesday	Thursday	Friday
Monday - Before cut-off time	Bank Recon	Holiday	Settlement	
Monday - After cut-off time	-	Holiday	Bank Recon	Settlement

c. With 2nd Saturday (non-working day)

Transaction Time	Saturday	Sunday	Monday	Tuesday	Wednesday
Friday - Before cut off time	Holiday	Holiday	Bank Recon	Settlement	
Friday - After cut off time	Holiday	Holiday	Bank Recon	Settlement	
Saturday - Before cut off time	Holiday	Holiday	Bank Recon	Settlement	
Saturday - After cut off time	Holiday	Holiday	Bank Recon	Settlement	
Sunday - Before cut off time	Holiday	Holiday	Bank Recon	Settlement	
Sunday - After cut off time	Holiday	Holiday	-	Bank Recon	Settlement

Illustration of Settlement Time assuming settlement time is T+2 days

PA/PG Guideline allows online PA to do settlement based on Tp (Payment date), Ts (Shipment date), Td (Delivery date), and Tr (Expiry for refund period). Except Tp based settlement, a PA-O cannot implement other date specific settlement. Why? (Think about it!)

In the next chapter, I will cover how PAs are reducing the settlement time.

11.B Early Settlement

Standard settlement time from PA to merchants can be T+1 or T+2 working days. But what if the merchant wants settlement earlier than that? Or maybe on a bank holiday?

Why a merchant wants an early settlement?

Answer: For fulfilling financial obligations — a hyperlocal merchant wants to make payments to its vendors; a gaming merchant wants to disburse winnings to its users, and an NBFC will use those funds to issue loans to more customers.

Sure, a merchant can use its own funds to fulfill these obligations, but a merchant may not have that kind of liquidity, and there is an opportunity cost for using own funds.

How to address merchant's early settlement requirement?

Merchants want funds earlier, but banks/PSPs won't give it faster - Looks like a deadlock!

Solution: PA can settle the funds to the merchant in advance, and then recover it from the merchant's settlement amount later.

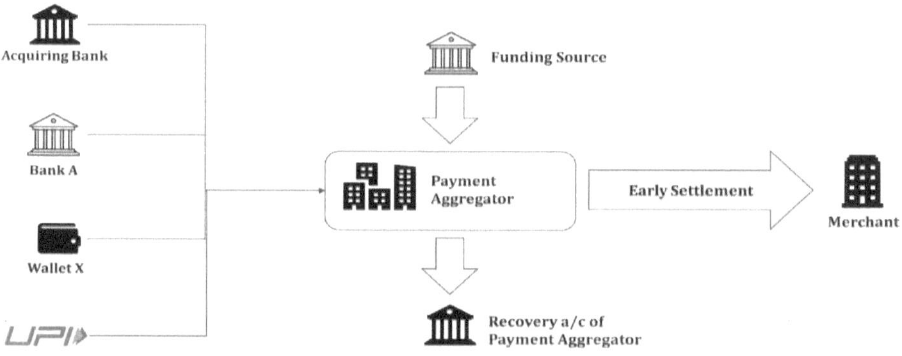

Illustration: Early Settlement Process

Details related to early/instant/faster settlement:

a. **Settlement Type**:

- At regular intervals *(every 1 hour, 3 hour or 6 hour)*

- On-demand *(E.g., only on Sundays)*

b. **Fund Source**:

PA needs to pre-fund these early settlements. PA has two options:

- Use own funds — Technically cannot be done as PA is not a lender. But yes, PA can do it, but such method is neither clean nor scalable.

- Borrow funds from an NBFC or Bank, and repay it back *(clean and scalable model)*

c. **Underwriting**: As you realized, early settlement is nothing but unsecured lending. But who is the borrower in this model? Payment Aggregator or the merchant?

- Usually, the PA will be the borrower on the file — NBFC or Bank will issue the credit to the PA who in turn uses it for pre-funding for early settlement.

- Although a merchant is not the direct borrower, NBFC/Bank may put restrictions in terms of merchant categories *(e.g., gaming not allowed)* or on the amount.

The risk of lending in the early settlement model is low because PA is settling the funds for successful transactions. So anyway, the PA will receive funds from the banks/PSPs on next working day, and amount can be recovered.

d. **Commercial Model**: The NBFC/Bank will have interest charges that may vary from 12–18% per year (or 0.032%-0.049% per day). The PA will recover it from the merchant, and by adding some margin, the PA will make profit.

Step 1	Original Settlement				
	Amount	MDR	Charges (Rs.)	GST (Rs.)	Total Charges (Rs.)
Credit Card	10,000	1.80%	180	32.4	212.4
Debit Card	10,000	0.90%	90	16.2	106.2
Total	20,000		270	48.6	318.6

Net-Settlement Amount	19,681.40	A

Step 2		
Early settlement fees	0.10%	
Early settlement Charges	19.7	B
GST	3.5	
Final Settlement	19,658.18	

Borrowing Rate	0.04%	per day (@15% per year)
Interest Paid	8.09	(A * Borrowing Rate/day)
Profit	11.59	(B - interest paid)

In the above example, let's say there were two transactions of Rs.10,000 each done using credit card and debit card. PG charges for CC is 1.80% and DC is 0.90%. The merchant is availing early settlement at 0.10% charges. PA made a profit of Rs. 11.59.

More the volume, more profit... that is the beauty of the payments game.

Let's make it complex

The above calculation looks quite straightforward, but it is not. Let's assume a merchant is availing early settlement at 0.10% and the PA's borrowing rate is 0.05%. Let's also assume that the transaction is done on Friday and assume Saturday & Sunday are bank holidays.

The merchant receives the settlement on Friday, but the PA can recover that amount only on Monday when banks/PSPs make the settlement.

In the above example, the PA will charge the merchant Rs.10, but NBFC will charge the PA Rs.15 for the same amount. So, the charges for such early settlement cannot be linear, and at the same time, you cannot show complex calculations to the merchant.

A simpler way to avoid any revenue leakage would be having differential pricing on working and non-working days or overall charging higher fees, or charging fees till the time the early settled amount is recovered as part of bank/PSP settlement.

Let's make it efficient.

Why does the merchant want funds faster? It's because the merchant has financial obligations to fulfill *(e.g., paying to vendors or disbursing funds to the winners)*

A merchant can simply connect the settlement to a payout account *(source account for the payout/disbursement solution)* and disburse the funds using payout rails such as IMPS and NEFT.

Please read **Chapter 15.B** for details.

Closing Remarks:

The payment aggregation business is more or less commoditized. PAs operate on thin margins (if at all). Value-added services such as early settlement can improve the 'top line', and there is ample opportunity to make a good margin.

UPI acquiring banks have ability to do settlements in 8 cycles, so it is possible for PA to get UPI settlement amounts within a few hours. *Note: there could be an impact on commercials.*

Early settlement can be viewed as lending. Also, PA/PG guidelines clearly define the permissible credits and debits to PA's escrow account(s). So, a PA has to adhere to digital lending as well as PA/PG guidelines.

11.C Settlement Amount

In the earlier chapters, we covered '**WHEN**' merchant will receive the money, and in this section, let's talk about '**HOW MUCH**'

After 'reconciliation', PA settles funds to merchant's account.

The settlement amount depends on the commercial model *(Upfront deduction, surcharge, invoicing)* the merchant is configured.

*Refer **Chapter 7.B** (Commercial Models)*

Refund and chargeback amounts are recovered from the merchant's settlement amount. Also, PA may hold the amount based on risk or instructions from Law Enforcement Agencies.

Example: Transaction Amount: Rs. 1000, MDR: 1%, GST: 18% on MDR, Refund Adjustment: Rs. 50

1. **Upfront Deduction Model**:

    Settlement Amount = Transaction amount (-) MDR (-) GST Amount (-) Refund adjustment (-) Chargeback Amount Recovered

    Settlement Amount = Rs.1000 - Rs.10 - Rs.1.80 - Rs.50 = Rs.938.2

2. **Surcharge Model**:

    Settlement Amount = Transaction Amount (-) Refund adjustment (-) Chargeback Amount Recovered

    Settlement Amount = Rs.1000 - Rs.50 = Rs.950

    Note: MDR + GST *(Rs.10 + Rs.1.80)* is borne by user so it's not part of settlement

3. **Invoicing Model**:

    Settlement Amount = Transaction amount (-) Refund adjustment (-) Chargeback Amount Recovered

Settlement Amount = Rs.1000 - Rs.50 = Rs.950

Note: MDR + GST (Rs.11.80) is invoiced to merchant so it's not part of settlement

UTR (Unique Transaction Reference) number is generated when settlement amount credited to merchant's account *(via NEFT or RTGS)*. UTR is shared with the merchant for reconciliation.

Settlement Report: PAs share the settlement report that covers settlements *(order id, transaction amount, MDR, GST amount)* and adjustments *(refunds, chargeback recovery amount, hold amount, if any)* for a particular day. The file format will vary for different PAs, and reports can be delivered through mail, dashboard, API, or SFTP.

11.D   Settlement Account

In the earlier chapters, we covered *settlement time* and *settlement amount*, now, let's talk about the settlement account.

Merchants can receive the settlement to the current, nodal, or escrow account with any bank that has IFSC *(Indian Financial System Code)*. PA's use NEFT or RTGS to do merchant payout.

The settlement account is configured during merchant on-boarding or can be changed later.

PAs usually seek a canceled cheque *(for current a/c)* or bank letter *(for escrow/nodal a/c). The a/c should be the* merchant's name. And PA will do a penny drop to the account for confirmation.

1.   Single Account Settlement:

A PA can do settlement to any account that a merchant holds in any bank. The account is mapped to the merchant's Live ID (MID)

2.   Multi-Account Settlement:

What if a merchant wants to settle funds to different accounts?

E.g., Car Company's App allows customers to select the dealer and make payment towards the service provisioned by the dealer. The funds should be directly settled to selected dealer's a/c.

This can be achieved in two ways:

- Assign separate Live Id (MID) for each dealer and pass the appropriate Live Id of the selected dealer. Funds will be settled to the configured bank /ac of that Live ID.

- Create special fields or scheme codes or split codes for each dealer and link that code to the dealer's bank account. During transactions, pass the appropriate code, and settlement will be done to the corresponding bank account.

Note: In both cases, dealers need to be onboarded / KYC-ed.

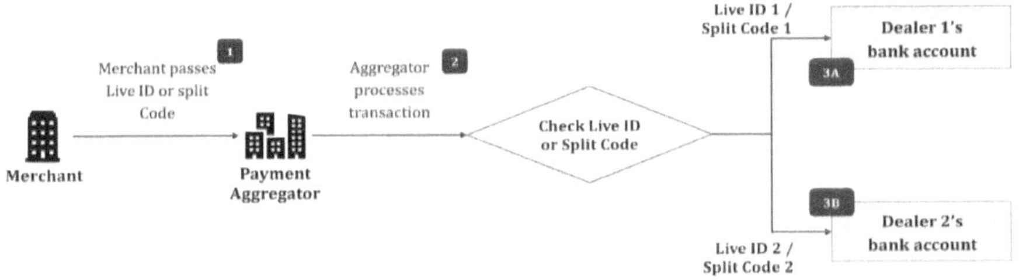

Illustration: Multi-Account Settlement Process

Important point to consider:

If you are enabling multi-account settlement with scheme/special field integration, then make sure refunds are supported for that flow else refunds of one scheme (business unit/dealer) will end up getting adjusted from settlement of different schemes (business unit/dealer).

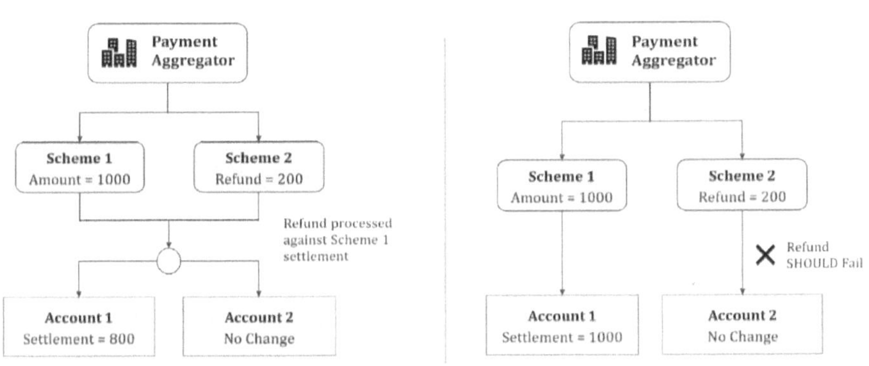

Case A: Mixed up settlement   **Case B:** Clean settlement

3. Split Settlement: In this scenario, the merchant wants to split the transaction amount and then, would want settlement in different bank accounts depending on certain conditions

Example: An education institute is collecting 2 types of fees (Admin Fee and Course Fee) and would like the PA to settle funds into 2 different accounts.

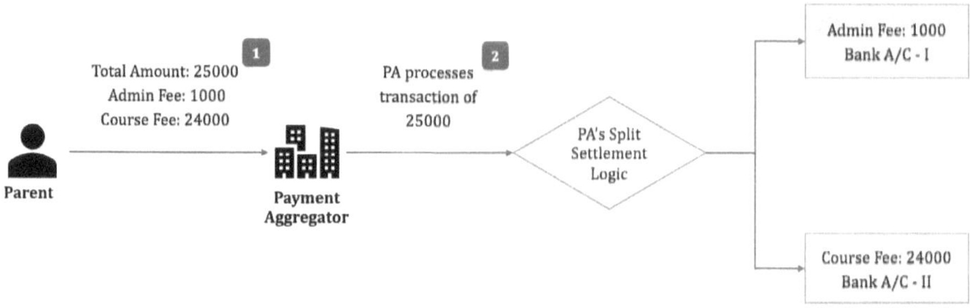

Let the merchant pass various fee headers as part of payload data and then, depending on fee headers, split the amount and do settlement to respective bank accounts.

Split settlement can be done for eCommerce marketplace models *(settling funds to vendors after splitting marketplace's commission)*

Similar to the multi-account settlement model, remember to provision for clean settlement *(factor in refund processing from right vendor)* for split settlement as well.

Chapter 12

Payment Aggregator – Operations

In the next two sub-chapters, we will cover the operational aspects of the payments - refunds, and chargeback.

12.A Refunds

We cancel tickets, cancel hotel bookings, and return products. At times, merchants couldn't fulfil the service or deliver products.

Refunds are an essential part of online business. I think refunds played an important role in the growth of online commerce as they instilled confidence in users.

The customer requests for the refund on merchant's website/App, and then the merchant initiates the refund via:

- Refund API - single refund or bulk refund *(multiple refunds in a single go)*
- PA or TSP's dashboard (single or bulk refunds via file upload)

Refund Process

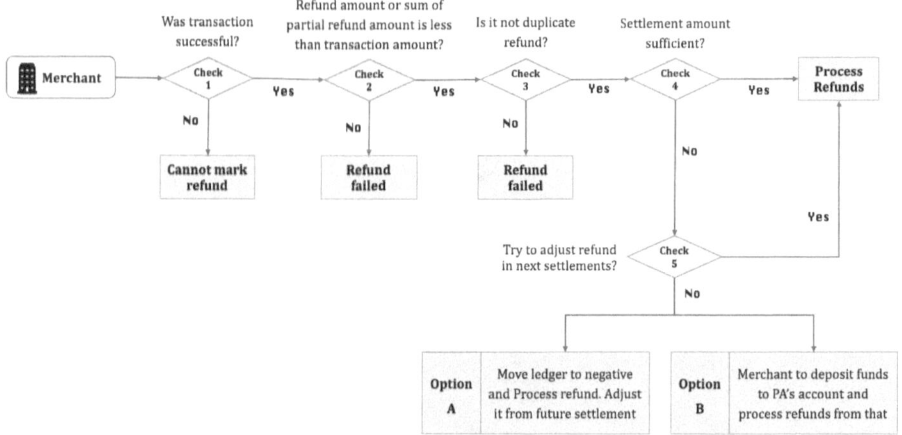

1. Refunds are adjusted from the settlement amount.

2. Only successful transactions can be refunded.

3. A refund can be full or partial *(of transaction amount)*

4. The refund amount or sum of partial refunds cannot be more than transaction amount.

   Example: Transaction Amount = Rs.1000 then 1ˢᵗ partial refund = Rs.500, 2ⁿᵈ Partial Refund = Rs.300 and if merchant marks 3ʳᵈ refund for Rs.300, then 3ʳᵈ refund should fail

5. Duplicate refund should not be processed. To achieve this every refund processed should have a unique id with a status check.

6. In case, the refund fails due to insufficient settlement amount, then PA will retry for couple of days, and then mark it as failed.

7. Alternative methods to process refund in case of insufficient settlement amount.

   – Mark negative entry in ledger and recover the refund amount from future settlements.

   – Merchant to transfer funds to PA's Escrow account to process refunds.

8. Refunds for transactions older than six months cannot be processed through the regular 'refund process'. Such refunds are processed manually by the PA with the help of acquiring banks and PSPs. For certain modes, PA will use alternate channel to process refund *(e.g., do payout to VPA, VDMS payout to credit cards)*

Refunds are cumbersome and costly. Read further to know.

A. **Refunds are cumbersome!**

During refund, the money moves back to the instrument that was used for payment *(card, account, wallet etc.)* through a series of identifiers that were created during the transaction leg.

Once the merchant marks a refund, the PA processes it on the same or next working day.

- **Refund Status**: Once PA processes the refunds, the status will be 'success' or 'failed'. But this status doesn't indicate the money has reached the customer's payment instrument; it simply conveys that the refund process has commenced successfully.

- **TAT (Turn Around Time)**: As the money hops across different accounts *(of PA, acquiring banks, issuing banks)*, it takes time to reach the customer's card or account. Typically, it takes 1-5 days, but it is not guaranteed.

- **Tracking**: ARN/RRN *(for cards and UPI)* and bank reference id *(for Net-Banking)* are generated when the bank processes refunds successfully. These reference numbers can be used by customers to check the status of refund with their respective banks.

The biggest problem with refunds is there is no visibility whether the refund amount is credited to the customer's payment instrument or not.

B. Why Refunds are costly?

PAs do not charge any fee to process refunds *(in the standard model)*, but still the merchant or the customer will lose money.

- **Example 1**: Merchant is in 'upfront deduction' model *(i.e.: MDR is deducted from merchant's settlement amount)*

  Transaction Amount Rs.100, MDR: 1% + GST, so Settlement Amount = Rs. 98.82

  When the above transaction is refunded, the customer needs to get Rs.100, but the merchant has received only Rs.98.82 *(Rs.1.18 was taken away by the PA)*. So, the merchant needs to put Rs.1.18 from its pocket *(not literally)*.

- **Example 2**: Merchant is in invoicing model *(i.e.: MDR is invoiced to the merchant)*.

  This works the same as the upfront model; merchants will lose money.

Example 3: Merchant is in surcharge Model *(i.e.: MDR is passed on to the customer)*.

Order Amount = Rs.100, MDR: 1% + GST so total transaction amount = Rs.101.18

But the merchant can mark only Rs.100 as refund *(any amount higher will be more than transaction amount)*, so the customer receives only Rs.100 and surcharge collected by the PA won't be refunded. Customers lose money in this model.

Auto-Refunds

These are the cases where merchants will ask PA to mark the auto-refund if the transaction status is not definite *(Success or Failed)* within the stipulated time period.

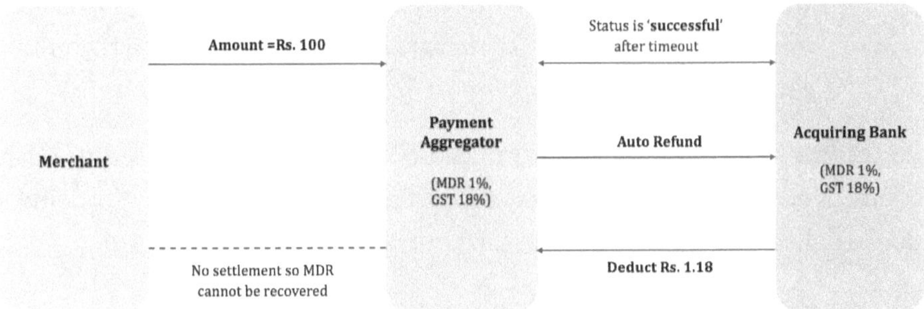

Example: Airline which wants to auto-refund configured post 15mins. Transaction status became successful after 30 mins, and the PA marks it as 'auto-refund'. But from the acquiring bank's point of view, the transaction was successful, and charges will be deducted from PA's settlement.

A PA has two options: (a) deduct from merchant's settlement (b) absorb the charges.

Reversals:

Reversals are special cases where the transaction is either pending/timed out/failed, and the customer's card/account is debited. In such cases, the amount is credited back to the customer.

RBI has imposed a TAT of 5 days and imposes a penalty of Rs.100 per day delay.

Instant Refunds

The time to credit the refund amount to the payment instrument varies for different payment modes and is highly unpredictable. Instead of using the regular refund channel, PAs can push funds to the payment instrument using payout rails.

- Cards: Visa Direct and Master Money Send *(note: Limited to only specific types of cards)*
- UPI: Push to VPA *(note: UPI refunds are already near-real time)*

- IMPS rail to push funds to the virtual card number *(91+mobile number + last 4 digits of credit card)* which is mapped to the credit card *(New solution launched in Q1 of FY '23)*

Note: Prior to CoF tokenization, IMPS and NEFT were used to push funds to credit cards, and it was stopped as CoF tokenization guidelines doesn't allow access to 16-digit card number

Limitations of instant refund solutions:

- All modes and instruments do not support such solutions *(e.g., Visa and MasterCard cards are covered whereas RuPay and Amex are not)*

- To implement these solutions, PA should know the payment instrument details. For a few modes, instrument details are captured during transaction leg *(e.g., cards, UPI)*, but for few, the instrument details are not available *(e.g., customer's a/c number is not captured)*

- These solutions attract additional charges.

- Room for chargeback: The forward journey is different from the refund journey. Such gaps can be exploited. So, the merchant has to make sure both the legs of fund movements are connected so they can show it as proof to defend disputes/chargeback.

Other Refund Strategies:

- Merchant can give the option to the customer to receive the refund in the merchant's closed-loop wallet *(Positive side: customer stickiness, Negative: Build closed-loop wallet)*

- A merchant can prefund the PA's escrow account to process spikes in the refund that may happen after a big sales event.

  Example: After any big sale event, settlement will reduce/normalize, but the refunds will be high. So, there is very high possibility that the settlement amount won't be sufficient to adjust the refunds, so a merchant can pre-fund the account.

Reduce Refunds

As they say, *"prevention is better than cure"* - a merchant can work towards reducing refunds.

- **With business model:** Refunds are beyond the merchant's control. Customers may not like the shirt or cancel the trip, so they would ask for refunds.

  Merchants can put some conditions for refund - few types of apparels cannot be returned *(e.g., undergarments)*, food order cannot be canceled after 5 mins.

- **With Payment Solutions**: Pre-Authorization (Auth and Capture) on cards or One-time mandate on UPI features can be used for reducing refunds.

  Example: Block the user's funds and debit it only if a ticket is allotted.

  Note: These solutions work in specific cases and merchant has to build specific flows or processes. So, if it is worth it, then yes, implement these solutions.

Closing Remarks

Refunds are important for many merchants *(eCommerce, Travel, Insurance etc.)*. Although great improvements have been made on the transaction side, refunds still suffer from many inefficiencies.

Alternative solutions are not completely foolproof, have limited coverage, do not have clear compliance, and come at an additional cost.

RBI has guidelines for harmonization of TAT and compensation for reversals, not just for payment aggregators but all payment platforms.

So, refunds and reversals are not only important for customer delight but also for compliance.

12.B Chargebacks

The interesting thing about chargeback is 'NOTHING'.

Chargebacks are kind of boring, merchants do not like them, PAs despise them, but chargebacks are important as they safeguard the customers.

Chargeback is a dispute raised by a customer with her issuing bank. A user can raise dispute under following circumstances:

Service Related: Merchant fails to provide product/service and refuses to give the refund.

Technical: Amount was debited twice or over debited

Suspected fraudulent cases.

Chargeback Process

Chargeback raised by the customer with her issuing bank reaches merchants through the Acquiring bank and Payment Aggregator

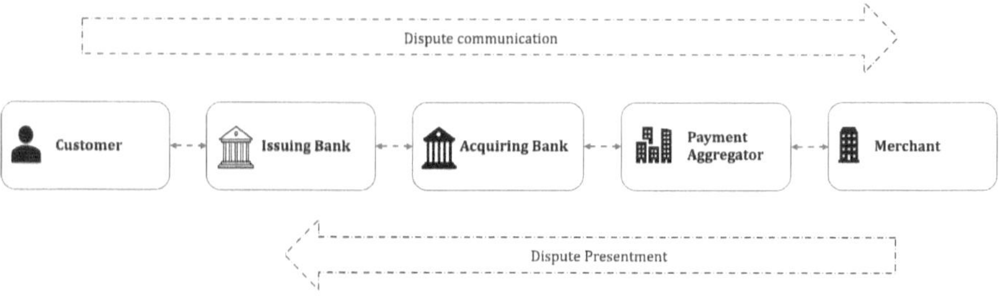

Handling Chargeback

Although the entire chargeback process spans 21 days *(varies for different card networks and UPI)*, after receiving the chargeback intimation, the merchant will have 4–5 days to respond to the chargeback.

There are two possible responses for the chargeback:

- **Accept**: It is a valid chargeback; the acquiring bank recovers funds from the PA, and PA will adjust the amount from the merchant's next settlement.

  In this scenario, customer receives the money.

- **Reject**: Merchant provides proof of product/service delivery as per the terms & conditions or a refund is given to the customer. If issuing bank accepts it as valid proof, then the merchant won't lose money, and the customer won't get money.

Important Points:

- If a merchant doesn't reply to a chargeback case within a stipulated time period, then that chargeback is considered as **valid** chargeback *(meaning, customer gets the money)*

- Merchants should not **'accept'** chargeback when the refund is already initiated.

- The issuing bank won't accept the information provided by the merchant blindly, and if the bank thinks that 'proof' is not sufficient, then the chargeback case will go into a second 'presentment', and the merchant will have to submit more proof to defend the chargeback.

- If the customer is not happy with the result of the chargeback, then the customer can go for pre-arbitration and arbitration levels.

- Chargebacks are not free for customers; banks do charge a fee if the customer loses chargeback and/or the next levels of escalations (pre-arbitration and arbitration)

Importance of Chargeback

a. **For merchants**: The number of chargebacks raised against a merchant shows the health of that merchant's business *(most importantly, chargebacks lost by the merchant).* It is important for merchants to keep chargebacks within specified limits *(typically less than 1%)*. If chargebacks are higher than normal, then acquiring banks and/or the card network may revoke the MID *(Merchant Id)* and may take actions against the PA as well.

A merchant can take a few steps to reduce chargebacks:

- Better product delivery or service provisioning

- Keep logs of transaction and proof of service provisioning (for 180 days)

- Show Terms of usage, refund/cancellation policies on the website/App.

- Consult your PA/acquiring bank whether the processes followed by you and proofs are adequate to defend against chargebacks *(no one will give written commitment, but they can advise)*

b. **For Payment Aggregator**: If the merchant doesn't reply or does not provide satisfactory proof, then the acquiring bank recovers the chargeback amount from the PA. If there are no future settlements to adjust *(e.g., merchant closed business and non-responsive)*, then PA will have no avenue to recover that amount.

This is crucial, as one such chargeback will impact PA's margin.

Example: PG Charge: 2%, back-to-back cost = 1.90%

So, the PA has to process Rs.10,00,000 value to make a profit of Rs.1,000. And one mismanaged chargeback of Rs.1000 will wipe out that entire profit.

Because of this financial risk, it is important for PA to on-board *'good merchant'*:

- Follow good onboarding process *(collect & verify merchant's credentials)*

- Avoid risky merchants *(job search, resume writing, online recharge etc.)*

- Collect security deposit *(to cover the chargeback related financial risks)*

- Hold 'some' amount if merchant terminates the contract *(release it after 120 days)*

Note: As a last resort, PAs can take legal action against the merchant to recover the financial losses incurred due chargebacks.

Hold the chargeback amount:

Considering reputational and financial risks, a PA can 'hold' the chargeback amount as soon as it receives chargeback notification from its acquiring banks.

Eventually, if the chargeback is in the merchant's favor, then release the 'hold' *(merchant receives the amount in the next settlement)*. If the merchant loses the chargeback, PA will return the funds to the customer *(reversal)*.

This is the safest way to manage chargeback related risks, but all merchants *(especially enterprise merchants)* do not agree. So, PA can implement it for small or high-risk merchants.

Challenges in managing chargebacks:

At present, chargeback information is exchanged over email and there is no central system to track chargebacks or map them against refunds. So, it is cumbersome to manage chargebacks.

Special Cases:

- **Chargeback in 'Surcharge Model'**

  Chargeback can be raised on full transaction amount, not partial amount.

  A merchant is configured in a surcharge model (Rs.100 transaction, MDR: 1% + GST, total transaction amount = Rs.101.18). The merchant receives settlement amount of Rs.100

  In this case, the chargeback will be raised for Rs.101.18, and if chargeback is valid, then the entire Rs.101.18 is recovered from the merchant, but the merchant has received only Rs.100. So, the merchant loses Rs.1.18. Hence, merchants who operate in the surcharge model *(such as the education sector)* hate chargeback more than anyone.

- **Partial chargeback in eCommerce:**

  Let's say a merchant fails to deliver one of two products and fails to issue a refund. A customer can raise the chargeback on the full amount. However, as there is clear bifurcation *(at product level)*, a merchant can accept the partial chargeback for the product that is not delivered. In such cases, only the partial amount *(specific to that non-delivered product)* will be reversed to the customer.

Closing Remarks

The chargeback process is in place to protect the customer. No matter how boring and cumbersome it is to handle these chargebacks, they play an important role in the payment ecosystem.

A PA should follow better merchant on-boarding policies, and a merchant should provide better services to make sure the chargebacks are lesser.

Chapter 13

Recurring Payment Solutions

We all make periodic payments.

- Monthly utility, mobile, broadband & DTH bills
- Mutual Fund Investments (SIPs)
- Insurance premiums
- Loan repayments including credit card bill repayment.
- Subscriptions (OTTs, news portals)
- Monthly donations to NGO

We do not want to miss out on our periodic payments because, in some cases, it involves disruption of service *(e.g., electricity bill payment),* and in others, it may involve penalties *(e.g., loan repayment)* or missing opportunities *(e.g., investment in mutual funds).*

So, won't it be nice if such periodic payments are done without user intervention?

That is when recurring payments come into picture, where merchants can pull the money from the customer's payment instrument based on the mandate given by the customer.

Recurring payment solutions provide better control over collections for merchants, and customers will not be worried about late payments or missed payments.

Recurring Payments Use Cases:

Use cases based on periodicity (frequency) of payment and amount type.

	Fixed Amount	**Variable Amount**
Fixed Periodicity	• Subscription, membership • Insurance premium, • MF SIF • Loan Repayment	Postpaid bill payment
Variable Periodicity	Wallet Auto top-up	Ad-hoc purchase (food delivery, cab ride)

- **Fixed Amount & Fixed Cycle**: The amount and periodicity of payment will remain the same. Periodicity can be weekly, monthly, quarterly, half yearly, yearly etc.

  Example: Monthly Mutual Fund SIP or quarterly insurance premium

- **Fixed Amount & Variable Cycle**: The amount is fixed, but periodicity can be random.

  Example: A user wants to auto top-up the wallet by Rs.1000 whenever wallet balance reaches Rs.250. Here, the top-up amount remains the same, but the periodicity is random as the wallet balance may reach the threshold at any time.

- **Variable Amount & Fixed Cycle**: Here the periodicity of payment remains same, but amount may vary for every debit.

  Example: My Airtel postpaid bill amount varies every month depending on usage, but debit happens every month

- **Variable amount & Variable Cycle**: Both periodicity of payment and amount vary.

  Example: I can take Ola rides any time, and my ride charge will vary every time

Requirements from Stakeholders:

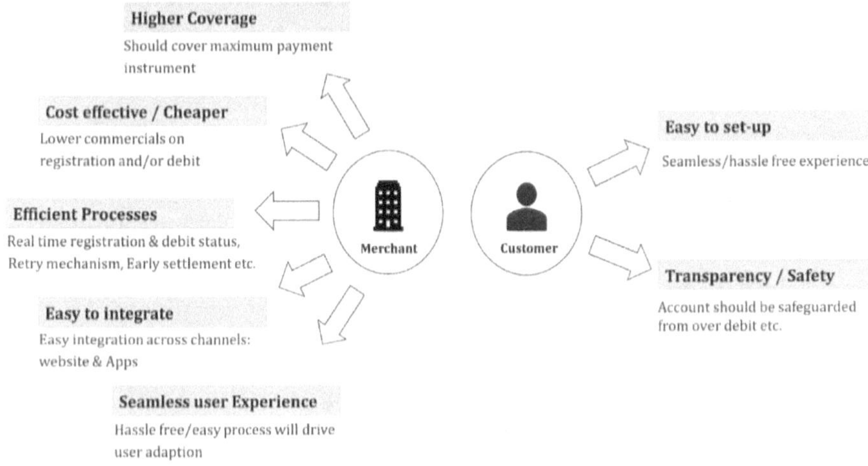

In a nutshell, the perfect recurring solution should address all possible use cases and, at the same time, must have broader payment instrument coverage, low cost, seamless user journey, and be efficient in performance. That sounds simple, isn't it?

Recurring Payment Solutions:

In the offline world, recurring payments started with post-dated cheques and then came RBI's ECS *(Electronic Clearing System)* and then NPCI's NACH *(National Automated Clearing House)*.

In the online world, Standing Instruction on Cards, then came online NACH and UPI AutoPay

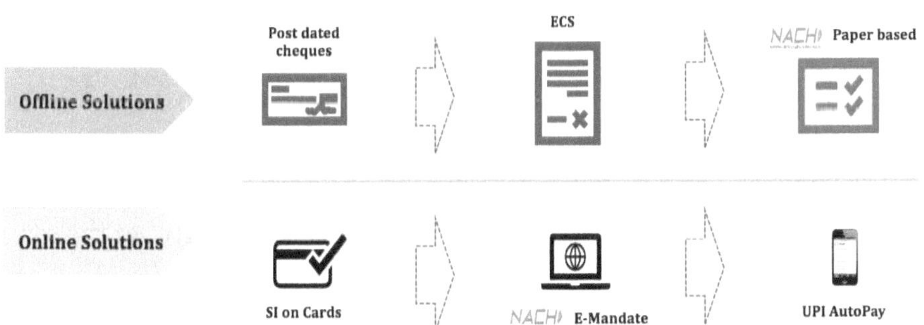

Note: Apart from these mainstream solutions, there are other recurring payment solutions such as Direct Debit and eMandate on bank account *(Offered by few PAs on a handful of banks)*, and on-demand/recurring debit on mobile wallets.

Basics of Recurring Payments:

Irrespective of their format or channel, recurring payment solutions have a similar life cycle:

(1) Mandate Form (Filling) (2) Mandate Registration (3) Mandate Debit (4) Mandate Modification (5) Mandate Pause (6) Mandate Cancellation (7) Mandate Expiry

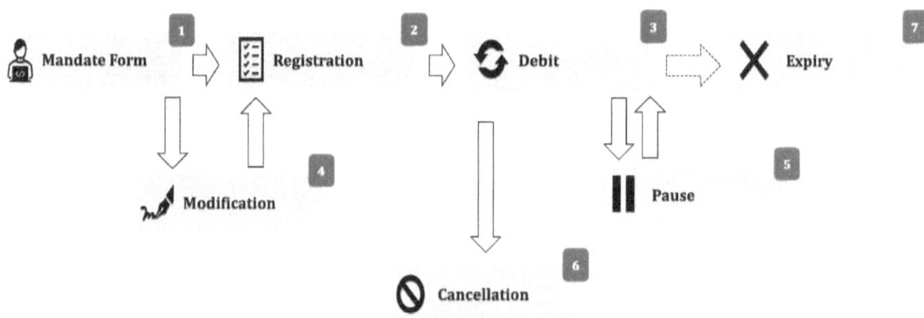

1. Mandate Form: Customers will fill mandate parameters that define boundaries for debit, or merchants can show pre-filled 'mandate form' that can be approved by the customer.

Typical mandate parameters are:

- **Duration**: Start and End date or until canceled. Some mandates are time bound *(E.g., EMI payment towards loan for a duration of 5 years)* and some mandates can run till perpetuity *(E.g., Mutual Fund SIP)* until the user stops them.

- **Maximum Amount per Debit**: Mandate can be debited for the amount that is less than max debit amount. If I have set the max debit amount as Rs.2000, then the debit amount above the limit should fail.

*Note: This amount **cannot** be higher than the maximum debit amount enforced by RBI for various products: for NACH - Rs.1 Cr, for SI on Cards - Rs.15,000)*

- **Fixed or Variable Amount**: There are cases where the debit amount will be variable *(e.g., monthly postpaid bill amount)* and there are cases where debit amount will remain same *(e.g., loan repayment amount)*. So, depending on the amount type, this parameter needs to be chosen. But it is always good to select 'variable amount', so any ad-hoc changes can be accommodated.

- **Cycle/Periodicity/Frequency**: It can be of any periodicity *(weekly, monthly, half yearly, yearly)* or 'as and when presented'. The merchant will stage the debit as per the periodicity.

  Note: The most interesting one is 'as and when presented' - this selection of periodicity allows merchants to debit the mandate any time or for ad-hoc cases.

2. **Mandate Registration**: The mandate needs to be validated *(the customer's credentials needs to be verified)*

- SI on cards: Customer to complete a successful card transaction.

- NACH (Paper): Customer's account status and signature are verified by customer's bank.

- eNACH: Customer to complete successful transaction using net-banking, debit card, or by verifying Aadhar OTP

- UPI Autopay: Customer to approve the mandate on her TPAP/ UPI App

3. **Mandate Debit**: Once the mandate is successfully registered, the merchant can debit the customer's account or card within the boundaries of the mandate parameter. Once the amount is debited, merchant will receive settlement as per standard processes of respective solutions.

- **Pre-debit notification**: In case of SI on Cards and UPI AutoPay, it is mandatory to send the pre-debit notification to the user before debiting the instrument.

  This process gives more confidence to customers about the debit as (a) customers will know about the debit and will not be surprised, (b) customers can stop the debit if needed *(as that control is with the customer)*

4. Mandate Modification: A few solutions allow users to modify certain mandate parameters, and others do not allow changes to existing mandates but need to create a new mandate

5. Mandate Pause: Except for UPI Autopay, other recurring solutions do not provide provision to pause the mandate.

Merchants and PAs can build this feature - if a user pauses the mandate, then the mandate debit request should not be staged until the mandate is 'un-paused' by the user.

6. Mandate Cancellation: UPI AutoPay and SI on Cards allow users to cancel the mandate any time. But such freedom to cancel needs to be handled carefully as there are certain cases *(e.g., loan repayment)* where such cancellation facility may jeopardize merchant's interests.

7. Mandate Expiry: Mandate works in the boundary of time frame except 'until canceled' cases. So, post the expiry of the mandate duration period, the mandate should be made inactive. It is important that users check this parameter while filling the mandate.

Comparison of various recurring payment solutions:

	SI on Cards	NACH (Paper)	eNACH	UPI Auto-Pay
Channel	Online	Paper Based	Online	Online
Governed by	RBI Guidelines	NPCI	NPCI	NPCI
Payment Coverage	All types of cards	1325+ Banks (direct and indirect)	70+ Banks 400+ Banks (on Aadhar eSign)	All banks that support UPI
Max amount / debit	INR 15,000	INR 1,00,00,000	INR 1,00,00,000	INR 1,00,000 (MF, Insurance, Credit Card Bill Payment) INR 15,000 (others)
Commercial Type	Percentage of transaction value	Registration: Flat Fee Debit: Flat Fee	Registration: Flat Fee Debit: Flat Fee	Registration: Flat fee Debit: Flat fee Mandate on file fee: Flat fee
Experience	Mandate can be registered on any amount. Mandate expires on card expiry	Registration is without amount . Mandate Period <=40 years	Registration without amount Mandate Period <=40 years	Registration is done with/without amount User sets mandate on TPAP
Status Update	Near real-time registration & debit	Delayed registration and debit	Near real-time registration; delayed debit status	Near real-time registration & debit
Pre-Debit Notification	Mandatory (24 hours before)	Not Mandatory	Not Mandatory	Mandatory (24 hours before)
Cancellation	Easy (Issuing bank to provisions it)	Merchant or issuing bank can do it	Merchant or issuing bank can do it	User can revoke mandate on TPAP (exception: lending, EMI collection)
Merchants allowed	Restrictions on certain sectors	All types	All types	All types

Note: Limits may change – so refer to latest limits on relevant product websites of NPCI, RBI, or Banks

Closing Remarks:

There is no silver bullet solution for recurring payment problems in India. Each solution has some advantages and some limitations.

In the next chapters, I will cover four popular recurring payment solutions: NACH (paper), eNACH, Standing Instruction on Cards, UPI AutoPay, and a subchapter on One-Time Mandates.

13.A   NACH (Offline or Paper Based)

Offline (paper-based) recurring payment solutions have evolved over a period of time.

A couple of decades ago, post-dated cheques were a popular method for merchants to debit customer's accounts. If I had taken a bike loan for a 6-month tenure, I would give 6 post-dated cheques.

Then came the era of paper-based mandates with **ECS (Electronic Clearing Service)**.

ECS was governed by RBI, wherein RBI and a few Public Sector Banks acted as clearing houses.

ECS fulfilled Credit and Debit requirements of a merchant, but ECS had major problems:

- Wear & Tear: ECS mandate was printed on an A4 size sheet paper.
- Operation Heavy: Collecting and couriering mandates
- Longer TAT: 21+ days for mandate validation *(Few banks processed mandates centrally, whereas many banks sent mandates to customer's branch for validation)*
- Higher failure rates in mandate registration and debit

To overcome these inefficiencies, ECS was discontinued, and NPCI launched NACH (National Automated Clearing House), where NPCI is acting as the clearing house.

NACH (paper based):

Although NACH is a paper-based mandate, the scanned images are used for processing, so the time taken for registration is shorter, providing better conversion and lesser wear & tear.

I. Participants in NACH Process:

- **Customer**: Provides duly signed mandate form to merchant

- **Merchant**: Entity that wishes to debit customers' bank accounts *(E.g.: Utility company, NBFC, Insurance provider etc.)*. Merchants can avail NACH service from a bank or PA.

- **Sponsor Bank**: Banks that are permitted by NPCI to originate transactions in the NACH system (a PA who wishes to be part of NACH would need a sponsor bank)

- **TSP:** A sponsor bank may use TSP to connect with NPCI's OnMAGS

- **Destination Bank**: Customer's bank and the bank needs to be part of the NACH system.

- **Clearing House**: NPCI is the clearing house which provides the central system for processing NACH mandates and fund movement among banks.

- **Payment Aggregator (PA):** It on-boards the merchant and works with Sponsor Bank(s) to manage mandate life cycle.

II. Mandate Lifecycle

a. **Mandate Form**: Typically, a merchant provides a completely pre-filled or partially pre-filled mandate form with basic details such as a Sponsor Bank Code, Utility Code etc.

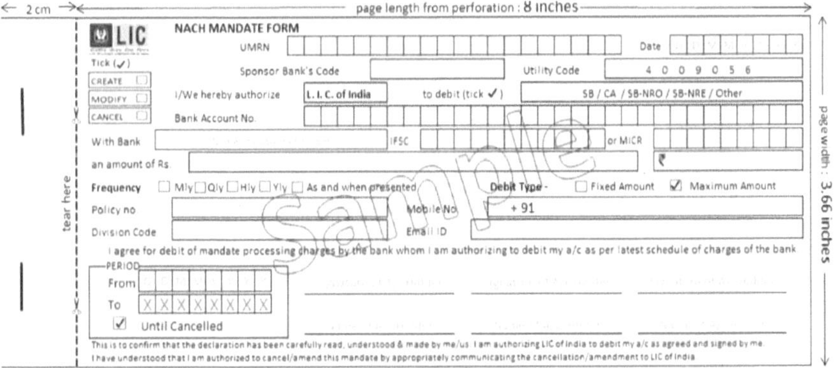

Illustration: Sample NACH Mandate Form (LIC)

For the partially filled form, the customer is to fill remaining information. For a fully pre-filled mandate, the customer will sign the mandate form and share a scanned copy with the merchant.

b. **Mandate Validation (Registration)**:

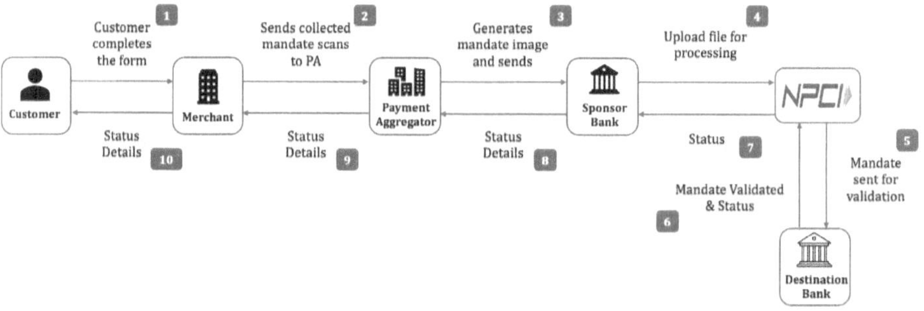

- UMRN (Unique Mandate Reference Number) is created for all mandates that are created in the NPCI system. UMRN is used for debit, modification, and cancellation of mandate.

- Destination banks validate mandate and provide status (Accepted or Rejected) within 5 working days. Banks provide the reason for rejection.

- Mandates that are not validated within 5 working days are Deemed Canceled.

- PA/bank can re-lodge deemed canceled and rejected mandates *(if rejection reasons are not critical – signature mismatch or wrong account details etc.)*

  Note: Sponsor banks connect (own or TSP) with NPCI's OnMAGS to register the mandate.

c. **Mandate Debit**: Once the mandate is validated successfully, merchants can debit the mandate after cooling period of 48 hours.

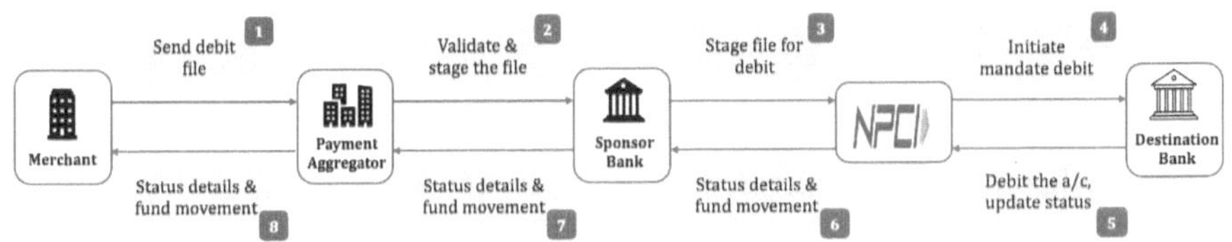

Merchants send the debit file to the PA/Sponsor Bank at least one working day before the 'debit date'. Post successful processing of the debit, PA will receive settlement from sponsor bank, and PA will settle funds to the merchant.

Note: Pre-debit notification to customers is not mandatory, but merchant can send it as best practice

   d. **Mandate Modification**: The mandate cannot be modified because it is paper based. So, merchants make sure that the periodicity of debit, debit amount, and duration of mandate are such that they cover present and future cases. If a user has to modify a critical parameter *(change in bank account)*, then the present mandate will be cancelled and user to provide a new one.

   e. **Mandate Pause**: There is no automated process for pausing the mandate. We know that the debit will happen only if the merchant stages the debit file with the PA/Sponsor Bank. So, if the merchant doesn't stage the mandate for debit, for 3 months, then it is as good as the mandate is on 'pause'.

   f. **Mandate Cancellation**: A customer can request the merchant to cancel the mandate, and the merchant can remove the mandate from its system. Also, customer can request the destination bank to cancel the mandate.

III. Operations:

- **Settlement**: Settlement time is T+1 working day

  Merchant will receive either gross settlement *(if charges are invoiced)* or net-settlement *(if charges are in upfront deduction model)*

- **Refund**: NACH doesn't support refunds. That means, merchant has to find an alternate way to refund the amount *(e.g., Payout to customer's account using NEFT/IMPS)*

- **Migration**: Mandate migration (one PA/sponsor bank to another PA) is possible if the merchant has its own utility code, and is not live on group utility code of a PA.

IV. Commercials:

PAs/Sponsor Banks charge two types of fees:

- Flat fee for registration (one-time) *(Example: Rs. 5 for registration)*
- Flat fee per debit *(Example: Rs.5 for each debit)*

Note: NPCI charges and destination bank charges are baked into this pricing

V. Safeguarding Merchant:

An NBFC merchant has given a loan to a customer, and the customer has set up a NACH mandate for monthly repayment. Let's say the mandate debit fails due to insufficient funds, and the customer is in incognito mode. So, what should the merchant do?

eNACH is covered under Negotiable Instruments Act (1881) that can attract a fine of twice the obligation amount or one year jail term or both *(similar to Cheque Bounce)*

This provision safeguards NBFC/lending merchants where customers have obligation of repayment and need to make sure NACH debits are honored.

VI. Advantages and Disadvantages of NACH (paper):

Advantages	• Flat fee model - economical • Bank coverage: 1325+ banks (direct and indirect) • Higher debit limit (up to Rs.1 Crore) • Scalable solution as digital image of mandate is used for processing. • No restriction on type of merchant that can be on-boarded. • Covered in Negotiable Instruments Act
Disadvantages	• Overhead cost in terms of collection and scanning of mandates. • 5-day delay in mandate registration and delay in debit status • Higher registration failure rate due to signature mismatch • File based debit *(companies are moving to APIs)*

Closing Remarks:

NACH (paper) will continue to thrive because of higher coverage of banks (1325+ banks) and support up to Rs.1 Crore per debit. Also, NACH (paper) is preferred by certain customer demographics and certain merchants that have strong physical touch points with customers.

13.B NACH (Digital) or eNACH

This is the online variant of NACH where mandate form filling and registration is done online.

I. Participants in NACH Process:

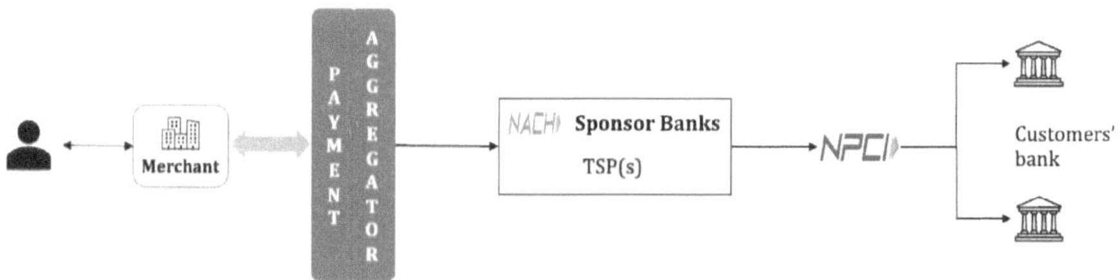

- **Customer**: Provides duly signed mandate form to merchant

- **Merchant**: Entity that wishes to debit customers' bank accounts *(E.g.: Utility company, NBFC, Insurance provider etc.)*. Merchants can avail eNACH service from a bank or PA.

- **Sponsor Bank**: Banks that are permitted by NPCI to originate transactions in the eNACH system *(a PA who wishes to be part of eNACH would need a sponsor bank)*

- **TSP:** A sponsor bank may use TSP to connect with NPCI's OnMAGS for the mandate registration

- **Destination Bank**: Customer's bank and the bank needs to be part of the eNACH system.

- **Clearing House**: NPCI is the clearing house which provides the central system for processing NACH mandates and fund movement among banks.

- **Payment Aggregator (PA):** It on-boards the merchant and works with Sponsor Bank (s) for managing mandate life cycle and charge fees for services.

II. Mandate Lifecycle:

a. Mandate Form:

To capture the mandate parameters such as periodicity, mandate duration, maximum debit amount as well as Account Number and IFSC

Merchant can either pre-fill the mandate parameters for customer's approval or allow customers to enter the details.

b. Mandate Registration:

Different ways a customer can register the mandate:

- Net-Banking: Successfully complete the net-banking transaction using the bank account that is entered in mandate form.

- Debit Card: Complete the regular card transaction using the debit card associated with the bank account that is entered in the mandate form.

- Aadhar OTP: A user can complete registration by validating Aadhar OTP.

  Remember there should be three-way linkage among the bank a/c <> Aadhar <> mobile No

- Aadhar eSign validation based registration.

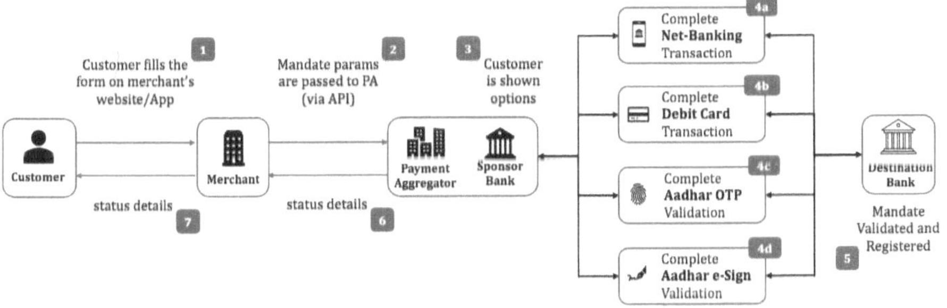

Note: Sponsor banks connect *(directly or use TSP)* with NPCI's OnMAGS to register the mandate.

Note: In July 2023, NPCI rolled out a simplified registration process that is done on the last 4 digits of Aadhar, last 5 digits of PAN, and customer id *(of customer's destination bank)*. Mandate is registered based on the OTP validation.

Rs.15,000 per debit is the limit for mandates registered through this simplified process.

c. **Mandate Debit**:

A merchant to stage the debit on T-2 days (via PA) or T-1 day (via Sponsor Bank) before the actual debit date (T). Customer's bank account will be debited on T-day and debit confirmation is shared on T+1 day *(debit is done in batches by EOD)*

- 1st debit can be done 48 hours after successful registration of mandate.

- Not allowed to debit a mandate multiple times on the same day.

Note: It is not mandatory to send pre-debit notification to users; merchants can send it as a best practice.

d. **Mandate Update**:

There is no provision to update or change any of the mandate parameters. Alternative is to cancel the earlier mandate and register a new mandate.

e. **Mandate Pause**:

There is no specific provision for pausing a mandate. If a merchant wants to provide 'pause' feature to the customer, then the merchant shouldn't stage the mandate for debit during the 'pause duration'.

f. **Mandate Cancellation**:

Customer has to inform the merchant, and the merchant can remove that mandate. Also, the customer can reach out her bank *(destination bank)* to cancel the mandate *(which can be a cumbersome process)*.

g. **Mandate Expiry**:

The mandate expires after the mandate duration is over. If the mandate is registered for 'until canceled', then such mandates will not expire until customer requests the merchant or her bank *(destination bank)* to cancel the mandate.

III. Commercials

PAs/Sponsor Banks charge two types of fees:

- Flat fee for registration (one-time) *(Example: Rs. 5 for registration)*

- Flat fee per debit *(Example: Rs.5 for each debit)*

  Note: NPCI charges and destination bank charges are baked into this pricing

IV. Operations:

- **Settlement**: Usually, T+1 day

  Note: Merchant will receive either gross settlement *(if charges are invoiced)* or Net-Settlement *(if charges are in upfront deduction model)*

- **Refunds**: No APIs for refunds so merchants to manage refunds offline (separately)

- **Migration**: Mandate migration (one PA/sponsor bank to another PA) is possible if the merchant has its own utility code, and is not live on group utility code of a PA.

V. Safeguarding Merchants:

eNACH is covered under Negotiable Instruments Act (1881) that can attract a fine of twice the obligation amount or one year jail term or both (*like Cheque bounce*)

This provision safeguards NBFC/lending merchants where customers have obligation of repayment and need to make sure eNACH debits are honored.

VI. Advantages and Disadvantages of eNACH:

Advantages	• Digital Solution • Flat Fee model *(economical)* • No restriction on merchant category • Debit limit up to Rs.1 Crore
Disadvantages	• Delayed debit status • Not a seamless experience for users • No mandatory pre-debit notification to customer

Closing Remarks:

eNACH is an ideal solution for recurring payment use cases because it is online, works on flat fee model *(economical for large ticket)*, covered under Negotiable Instruments Act, higher debit limit *(Rs. 1 Crore, same as paper NACH)* and wider bank coverage. eNACH will continue to thrive.

13.C   Standing Instruction (SI) on Cards

In this Chapter, we will cover one of the earliest and most efficient recurring payment solutions.

Customers will set 'Standing Instruction' on credit and debit cards *(Visa, MasterCard, RuPay)*, and merchants can debit the card as per given mandate without customer's intervention.

RBI released detailed guidelines for SI on Cards in August 2019, and the guidelines are effective from 1ˢᵗ Oct 2021.

I.   The Past:

Before we cover the latest SI on Cards solution, let's touch upon the earlier variant.

- SI on cards mandate parameters is same as any recurring payment solution.

- It is mandatory that first transaction should go through 2FA.

- Merchant or PA triggers debit instruction on the registered card; the card is debited without 2FA.

- Merchant receives settlement on T+1 or T+2 days (standard)

- No upper limit on debit amount

Problems with past solution:

- The customer doesn't receive pre-debit notification from card issuers.

- No easy process or place to view or delete the mandates.

- Card issuer banks couldn't identify the transaction is for SI on card.

- Upon debit, the issuing bank would send a SMS to the user - 'the card is debited without 2FA' *(which was alarming)*

- At one point, a few banks added SI for Debit Cards and then stopped. So, the solution was not consistent.

To address those problems, RBI revised the guidelines for SI on Cards.

II. RBI Guidelines on SI on Cards (New):

- Coverage: All types of cards *(Credit, Debit, Prepaid)*, as well as Card Networks *(Visa, MasterCard, RuPay, Amex etc.)*

- Card number should be tokenized *(no one should access plain card number)*

- Debit limit: Rs.15,000 *(revised from earlier Rs.5,000 per debit)*

- The first transaction *(during registration)* should follow 2FA.

- Pre-debit Notification: Issuing banks should send pre-debit notification to the cardholder at least 24 hours before debit; Issuing banks should provide an option for the customer to opt out of that debit.

- Debit notification: The issuing bank should send debit notification to the cardholder.

- Cancellation: Issuing Bank to provide an online facility for the cardholder to cancel the mandate *(Customers can either opt only out of a particular debit or can opt entirely out of the mandate)*. Cancellation of mandate should follow 2nd Factor Authentication

- Dispute Management: Set-up separate dispute management process from regular card transaction for recurring payments

III. New SI on Cards Solution

BillDesk is the first one to launch the Standing Instruction (SI) platform called **SI Hub,** and then RazorPay launched its own platform, Mandate HQ.

All other PAs and acquiring banks are mostly using SI Hub.

Note: I am using SI Hub as reference for this article

Architecture: On one hand, card issuing banks will be on-boarded to the SI Hub platform, and on the other hand, the platform will have acquiring banks and PAs who, in turn, on-board merchants.

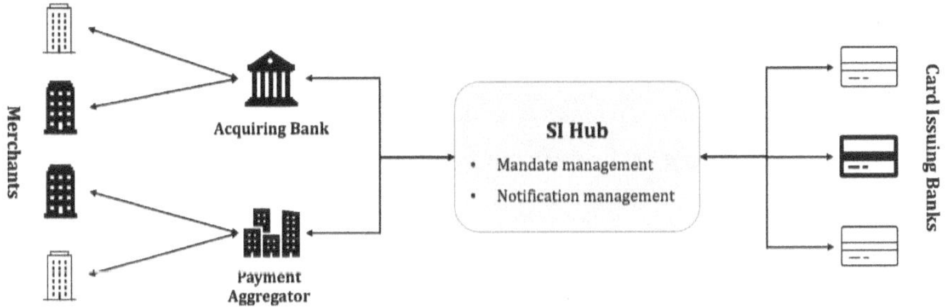

IV. Mandate Life Cycle:

a. Mandate Form:

The mandate form is the place to capture the mandate parameters such as mandate start & end date *(or duration of mandate)* and periodicity *(monthly, quarterly, yearly, 'as and when presented')*. Merchants or PAs can build this page. Customer can fill the form, or merchant can show pre-filled form for the customer's approval.

b. Mandate Registration:

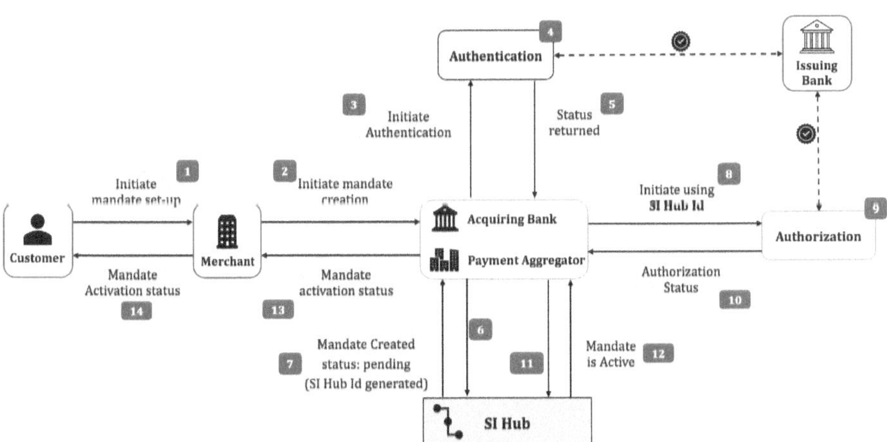

SI Hub generates a unique SI Hub ID (Step 7), and the same ID will be used throughout the mandate life cycle for pre-debit notification, debit, cancellation etc.

The SI Hub ID is used during the authorization stage *(so the issuing bank will know that the transaction is for recurring mandate)*

Note: The card is tokenized during the first transaction. And the tokenized card is used throughout the life cycle of the mandate.

c. **Mandate Debit**:

Mandate debit has two stages - (1) Pre-debit notification, (2) Debit.

1. **Pre-debit Notification**: This leg has to be done 24 hours before the debit. Either the merchant or PA can initiate the pre-debit notification trigger. If the mandate is valid *(based on SI Hub Id)*, SI Hub will inform the card issuing bank to send the pre-debit notification to the cardholder.

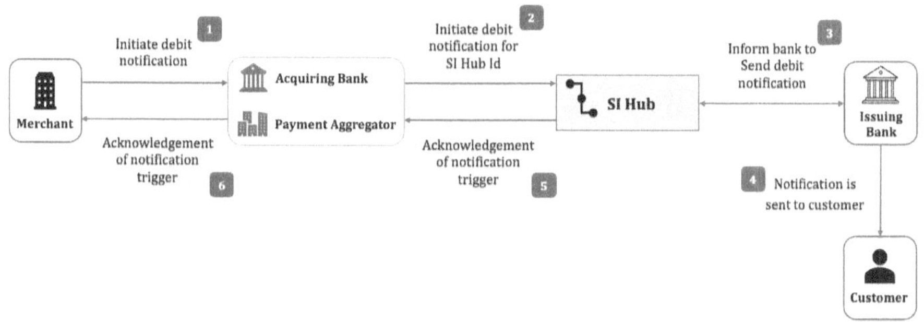

2. **Debit**: Merchant or PA will initiate the debit. Before proceeding with the debit, SI Hub will check whether the mandate is active, and then debit the card without 2FA.

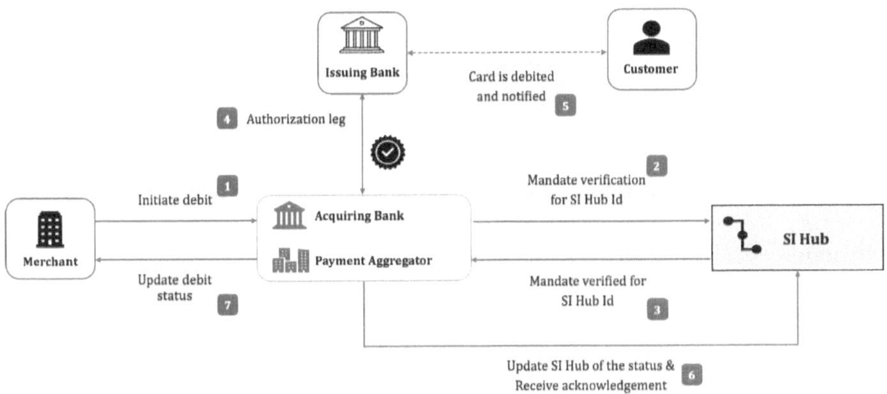

d. **Mandate Modification**:

Any change in mandate *(amount, periodicity, and duration)* requires 2FA *(as good as setting a new mandate)*.

e. **Mandate Pause**:

There is no specific API for pausing the mandate. If the merchant is providing a facility for the user to pause the mandate, then the merchant should not initiate the mandate debit during the 'pause period'.

f. **Mandate Expiry**:

Mandate will be removed post expiry of mandate duration or the card's expiry date. And the card cannot be debited.

g. **Mandate Cancellation**:

Issuing banks to provide a portal for cardholders to manage the card mandates. Cardholders can view the mandates registered for various merchants. Also, cardholders can cancel the mandate by completing 2FA.

V. Operations:

Settlement: Fund settlement will happen like normal card transactions.

Issuing bank → Acquiring bank → Payment Aggregator → Merchant

Settlement time would be T+1 or T+2 working days.

Refund: The standard refund process will be followed

Chargeback: The standard chargeback process will apply, but the only difference would be that the issuer bank has to identify these chargebacks differently from the regular card chargebacks

Commercials: Typically, percentage (%) of transaction value. Commercials/MDR will be dictated by acquiring banks (as PAs will use them to process).

BillDesk will levy charges to PA who is using the SI Hub platform. PA or Acquiring banks can bake those costs into commercials and offer it to the merchant.

Success Rate: Mandate registration leg will have the same success rate as regular transaction, but the mandate debit will be near 100% unless the customer has canceled the mandate, or card balance or credit limit is insufficient, or the card is hot listed.

Lock-in: If you have registered a mandate with 'PA <A>', then subsequent debits will have to be done through 'PA <A>' only.

VI. Limitation of SI on Cards:

- SI Hub and Mandate HQ platforms may not support all banks *(coverage may increase)*

- Amount Limit: Rs.15,000 per debit *(revised from earlier Rs.5,000)*. This limit may not be suitable for large ticket transactions. *(Note: RBI may increase the limit)*

- Because of pre-debit notification step, the solution can be used only for periodic payment cases *(e.g., bill payment)* and won't work for ad-hoc payment cases *(e.g., wallet top-up)*

- Sector Limit: The merchant on-boarding decision would be with the acquiring bank, and the banks won't approve merchants of all sectors.

VII. Advantages and Disadvantages of SI on Cards:

Advantages	• Online Solution - Easy and efficient • Better acceptance - Cardholders are familiar with card transactions. • Near real-time status update for registration and debit
Disadvantages	• Limited coverage: Only cards • Max debit limit of Rs.15,000 • Not economical as MDR is in percentage. • Dependency on SI Hub • Acquiring banks will approve selective sectors, use cases & merchants. • Easy to cancel the mandate

Closing Remarks:

Like any other solution, even *'Standing Instruction on Cards'* has its benefits and limitations.

Card users are savvier, so the solution has a higher success rate and can have great value for OTT, telecom-broadband-DTH, utility, and insurance sector merchants.

13.D UPI AutoPay

The last one to enter the recurring payments landscape… In Aug '20, NPCI launched UPI AutoPay.

I. Entities/Actors Involved in UPI AutoPay:

- **Customer** sets the mandate.
- **Merchant**: Entity which is initiating the mandate *(e.g., Airtel)*
- **Acquiring Bank/PA**: Merchant would need an acquiring bank or PA *(who in turn uses acquiring bank)* to manage the mandate.
- **TPAP/UPI App** on which customer will manage *(approve, pause, revoke)* the mandate.
- **Customer's bank** on which the mandate is registered.
- **NPCI** clearing house and switch.

II. Mandate Lifecycle:

a. Mandate Form:

Like other recurring payment solutions, even AutoPay works within boundaries that are defined by mandate parameters such as:

- Start date: date from which mandate is effective
- End date: end date of the mandate
- Amount type: Maximum Amount *(any amount below this will be debited)* or exact amount *(same amount to be deducted)*
- Frequency: Daily, weekly, monthly, yearly, 'As and when presented'

b. Mandate Registration:

Merchant can initiate the mandate registration and the customer will approve it on her TPAP/UPI App

Note: Users can also initiate a mandate on their TPAP/UPI Apps for either P2M *(e.g., the mandate for Airtel)* or P2P *(e.g., paying monthly salary to the driver)*. The first case is tricky as it will create a reconciliation issue. So, the TPAP/UPI App will only allow merchant initiated P2M registrations. Due to risk factors, acquiring banks will not approve P2P cases *(for now)*.

c. **Mandate Debit**:

Pre-debit Notification: Merchant should send a debit notification to the customer *(on UPI App)* 24 hours before the debit. The debit notification will have the debit time, and the debit '**has to**' happen at that time.

Debit: Merchant to trigger the debit request to PA/Acquiring bank. The customer's bank account will be debited if the mandate is active *(i.e., customer has not revoked mandate)*

Note: Customers will be prompted to enter the MPIN for the merchant's first debit unless the debit happens within 1 minute of mandate registration. Subsequent debits that are within the maximum allowed limit do not require 2FA (MPIN).

d. **Mandate Modification**:

Only the end date and amount can be modified, and for any other changes in the mandate parameters, the entire registration process needs to be repeated.

A mandate is registered for the combination of Acquiring PSP, TPAP/UPI App, and underlying bank account. If you wish to change any of these, then it is as good as registering a new mandate.

Mandate can be modified by the customer *(for customer-initiated mandate)* or merchant *(for merchant-initiated mandate)*.

e. **Mandate Cancellation**:

Mandate can be canceled by a customer at any point in time via the TPAP/UPI App where it is set. If a customer cancels the mandate, then acquiring PSP *(via PA)* will inform the merchant. A merchant can also cancel the mandate by calling API to the PA/acquiring bank.

Exception: Customers will not be allowed to revoke mandates related to loan repayment and EMI collection cases/merchants *(Merchant Category Code, MCC - 7322)*.

f. **Mandate Pause**:

A merchant can pause the mandate, and so can the customer. In case the user pauses the mandate, then the merchant's acquiring PSP will intimate the merchant about this action by the user.

g. **Mandate Expiry**:

Upon expiry, the mandate will be removed, and further debits are not allowed.

III. **Integration:**

- UPI AutoPay is supported in all types of flows: Collect *(customer enters VPA to initiate UPI flow)*, intent *(App-App switch)*, and UPI Plug-in *(In-App flow)*

- Success rate: Registration SR is comparable with UPI transactions. The flexibility given to users to revoke mandates at any time *(except for lending/EMI payment merchants)* leads to lower success rate during debit.

IV. Operations:

- Settlement: T+1 day *(Note: possible to get same day settlement)*
- Refund: Regular refund process or merchant can push refund amount to VPA

V. Commercials:

a. Mandate Registration fee *(slab wise flat fee)*

b. Mandate debit fee *(slab wise flat fee)* (optional)

c. Mandate Management Fee (*Slab wise flat fee per mandate per quarter*)

Note: The above fees model may evolve; NPCI/Banks/PAs may simplify this structure

VI. Safeguarding Merchants:

UPI AutoPay is covered under the Negotiable Instruments Act (1881), which can attract a fine of twice the obligation amount, or one-year jail term, or both (*like Cheque Bounce*). This provision safeguards NBFC/lending merchants where customers have an obligation to repay.

Also, customers cannot revoke mandate on TPAP if the mandate is registered for lending/EMI repayment merchant (MCC: 7322).

VII. TPV Functionality:

Third Party Validation (TPV) functionality enables investment sector merchants (stocks, MFs) to check whether the customer is transacting using the registered bank account.

Merchant will pass a/c number and IFSC as part of payload data.

UPI AutoPay can support TPV for up to 4 bank accounts. *Note: Only the first 4 digits of IFSC are checked.*

VIII. Advantages and Disadvantages of UPI AutoPay:

Advantages	• Supported by all TPAPs/UPI Apps • Covers bank accounts of almost all banks that support UPI. • Real-time registration and debit status • Retry up to 10 times if pre-debit notification stage is successful. • TPV feature for investment merchants • Covered in Negotiable Instruments Act • Cannot revoke mandate for loan repayment and EMI collection cases. • Max debit of Rs.1,00,000 for Mutual Fund, Insurance and Credit Card repayment cases; Rs.15,000 for other use cases
Disadvantages	• Easy to revoke mandate (exception: lending MCC) • Sending pre-debit notification 24 hours before the debit - Solution cannot be used for cases of ad-hoc services. • Complex commercial structure and higher compared to NACH

Closing Remarks

UPI AutoPay took a very long time to mature because the popular TPAPs took months or a year to implement the solution. Although the ecosystem is ready, UPI AutoPay suffers from lower success rate *(especially for mandate debit)*, but merchants are excited about the solution because of UPI's reach and popularity.

UPI AutoPay is constantly evolving - the debit amount limit is increased from Rs.5,000 to Rs.15,000, and then limits are increased to Rs.1,00,000 for Mutual Fund SIP, Insurance premium payment, Credit card bill payment *(and it can be increased further)*.

The solution is made suitable for NBFC sector *(non-revocable mandate and covered under Negotiable Instruments Act)* and is friendly for investment sector *(TPV functionality)*.

At present, customers can set up a mandate on the bank a/c via UPI AutoPay. However, as UPI supports credit cards, UPI AutoPay will also evolve, and users will be able to set-up a mandate on UPI linked credit card. Awesome!

So, AutoPay definitely has a bright future.

13.E   One-Time Mandates

At times, merchants want to block user's funds for a certain duration and deduct the funds based on the service fulfillment. For such cases, One-Time Mandate (*OTM*) solutions fit well.

Working of OTM:

- **Step 1**: User sets one time mandate or fund is blocked on user's payment instrument for specific amount and for certain duration.

- **Step 2**: Merchant can initiate two actions:

    - Capture: Debit the payment instrument

    - Void: Release the block and customer receives funds (instantly)

- **Step 3**: If merchant doesn't take any action, then OTM will expire, and amount is released.

    Debit type *(One-time or multiple)*, debit amount *(full amount or partial amount)*, and block period varies for different payment instruments. We will cover these details in the next section.

OTM solutions:

1. **Pre-Authorization on cards**

    Use cases: Railway ticket booking through OTA, Security deposits towards vehicle rental.

    - Works on Visa, MasterCard, and Amex cards
    - Block can be placed up to 5-7 Days *(special cases: up to 30 days)*
    - Entire blocked amount to be debited or released.
    - No limit on amount *(subject to available credit or balance)*
    - User cannot cancel the pre-auth.

- MDR is applicable only on 'captured' transactions and not on 'void' transactions *(Note: PAs may charge nominal fee for void transaction)*

2. UPI - One time block and One time debit

Use Cases: IPO Subscription

- Works with all major TPAPs for all banks that are on UPI.
- Block period: max. 90 days
- Entire blocked amount to be debited *(no partial debits)*
- Amount limit: Rs.5 Lakh for IPO subscription and Rs. 1 Lakh for other cases
- User can cancel the block through TPAP.
- MDR or fee is applicable only for 'captured' transactions not on 'void' transactions.

(Note: PAs may charge nominal fee for void transaction)

3. UPI - One time block and multiple debit

Use Case:

- Cab rides - User can block an amount and take multiple rides.
- Hyperlocal - User can block amount and keep ordering food or grocery.
- **The most interesting** case is in the Secondary Market. Users can purchase shares from the blocked amount, the customer's a/c is debited, and funds are directly settled to the exchange without moving through the stockbroker's account. The solution will work with the TPV feature.

  Important Note: SEBI is pushing stockbrokers to go-live with the solution.

Features:

- Works with all major TPAPs for all banks that are on UPI.

- Block period: 90 days (max)

- Merchant can do multiple debits as long as sum of partial debits is less than or equal to block amount.

- User can cancel the block through TPAP.

- MDR or fee is applicable only for 'captured' transactions; not on 'void' transactions *(Note: PAs may charge nominal fee for void transaction).*

Closing Remarks:

One-Time Mandates are amazing solutions that solve niche use cases.

There is plenty of scope to stretch the boundaries of OTM solutions in solving problems such as cancellations or refunds of eCommerce or Travel sectors. But such solutions have to work within the boundaries of the OTM solutions *(which are quite restrictive)*, and merchants have to factor in additional work *(of managing new integrations and processes)*.

A word of caution - Just because there is a solution, do not get fixated on using it.

Chapter 14

Virtual Account Number and Virtual VPA

Let's say you have gone out for dinner with your friends. Let's say you paid the bill, and each one owes you Rs.800. If two people do a bank transfer *(without adding any 'remarks')*, how will you know who transferred the amount?

Let's move the same problem to the business world *(not the dinner party but bank transfer)*. Imagine you are collecting funds from multiple parties, and if everyone does bank transfer, then how will you reconcile (who paid and how much)? Of course, they will inform you offline, and then you will have to reconcile the transfers one by one.

To solve this problem, we have a Virtual Account Number (VAN) solution.

A. VAN Solution

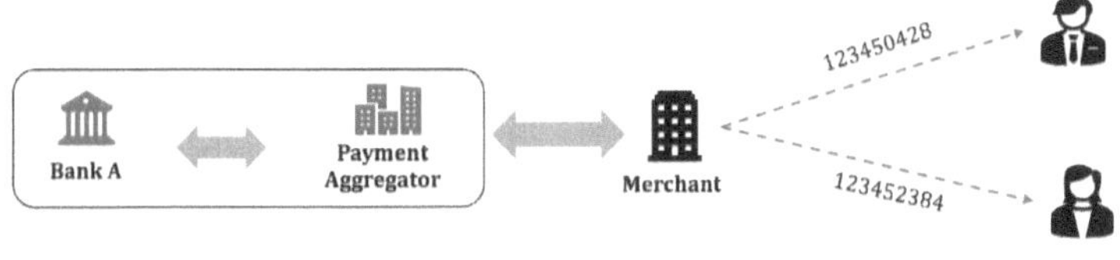

Step 1: Creating & Sharing VAN with Customers

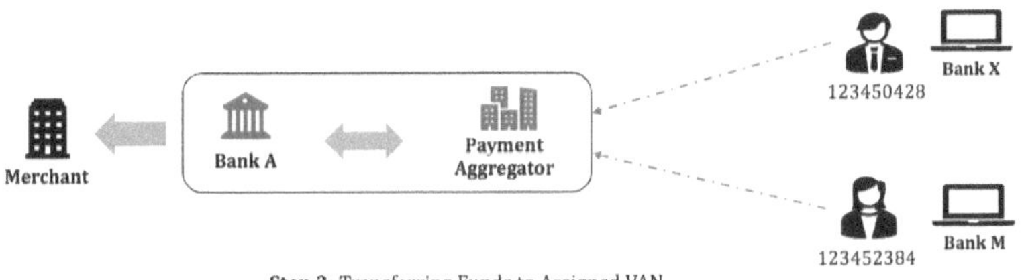

Step 3: Transferring Funds to Assigned VAN

- Step 1: Create Virtual Account numbers for each customer (or businesses) and communicate account number (and IFSC) to customers (through App or mail)

- Step 2: Customer to add this virtual account to her bank account as beneficiary.

- Step 3: Customer will transfer money to the beneficiary account from net-banking either by IMPS or NEFT or RTGS or Fund Transfer

With this solution, the beneficiary (e.g., merchant) can reconcile any number of transfers from a large number of remitters (e.g., customers).

Remitter Lock:

It is possible to enforce a remitter lock. PA/sponsor bank can accept or reject funds from a whitelisted remitter (*payer's name or account number is matched with a whitelisted name or account*) and/or the amount *(received amount is matched with expected to receive amount)*.

With this feature, merchants can emulate the TPV (Third party Validation) feature, which is an important feature for the regulated investment (stocks) sector.

One-Time VAN:

VAN can be configured for one-time usage i.e., once the payee transfers funds, the VAN won't accept further credits *(subject to capabilities of the bank that provides VAN)*

Settlement to Merchant:

Although some of these rails *(IMPS, RTGS, Fund Transfer)* work in real-time or with 30-mins delay *(NEFT)* and 24x7, that doesn't mean the merchant will receive funds immediately.

Usually, PAs or the bank do settlement to the merchants a few times on a working day.

Refund:

There is nothing called 'refunds' for this solution, as these are bank transfers.

In case merchants want to issue a refund, they simply do a payout/transfer to the customer's bank account via IMPS or NEFT rails.

Note: PAs/Bank will charge for these payouts.

Commercials:

Think of it: there are '*no real*' commercials for anyone involved. Customer used her bank account to transfer funds to the beneficiary via banking rails, which are very much free.

"*There are no free lunches*".

So, PAs/banks charge the merchant for the service.

Typically, the commercials will be flat rate (e.g., Rs. 1 per transfer) or a differential flat rate based on the transaction amount (e.g., Rs.2 up to Rs.10,000 and Rs.5 for above Rs.10,000)

Benefits:

- Unlike net-banking which is limited to 50+ banks, VAN solution covers all types of banks *(as long as payer's bank is on IMPS/NEFT/RTGS network)*
- Lower commercials - economical

Limitations:

Consider following limitations before opting for this solution:

- **Adding Beneficiary**:

    Customer has to add the virtual a/c as a beneficiary. Most of the customers will do it if they need to transfer funds regularly (*will you do it if you need to transfer funds one time?*). Also, banks take a few minutes to show newly added beneficiaries, and banks have a limit on transfer amount for the first 24 hours.

- **Broken Flow:**

  PA transactions start and end in a single flow, meaning when the customer clicks 'pay', the merchant knows that 'something' is going to happen. But in the VAN solution, the merchant is clueless about when the transfer will be done and has to rely on webhooks (of bank/PA) to know the transfer.

- **Incomplete info:**

  In the case of PA/PG, a unique order ID ties a payment to an order, but there is no order ID here. In case of VAN, when a customer transfers funds, the merchant gets to know the fund is received and from whom but won't get to know for what purpose. So, the customer will have to add the 'remarks' during the transfer.

Use cases:

There are some really good use cases where the solution works flawlessly:

1. Investment: Customers can transfer funds to the wallet of an investment firm/brokerage and use those funds for investment. This is quite prevalent among stockbrokers, crypto exchanges, and gold harvest investments.

2. B2B Payments: Transferring funds towards pending invoice

3. Loan repayment: Repaying monthly EMI installment.

4. Fee payments: Challan-based payments are quite common in the education sector. A student/parent will get Challan, and they deposit cash/cheque/DD in the bank against that Challan. Instead, VAN can be printed on those challans, and parent/student can transfer to that a/c. Easier to reconcile and convenient for parents.

B. Virtual VPA (UPI ID)

Yes, a similar solution can be built on UPI, where a merchant will create a virtual VPA for each customer, and the customer can make a payment to that VPA.

UPI QR code can be generated for this virtual VPA, and the same can be pasted in stores (E.g., KiranaTech companies or offline QR payments companies use this solution)

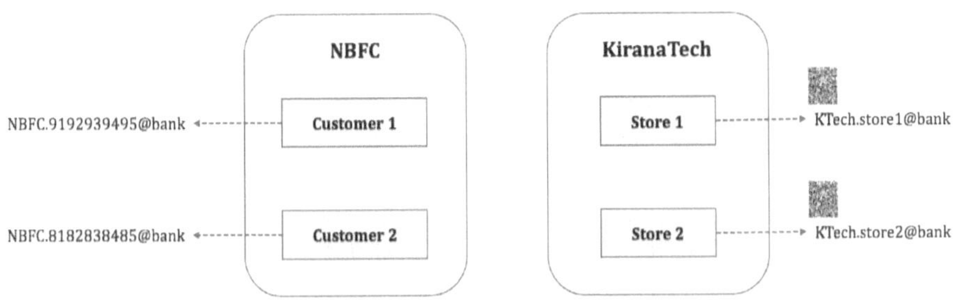

Illustration: Creating Virtual VPA

How it is different than standard VPA:

- Standard VPA: MerchantABC@bank
- Virtual VPA: KiranaTech.merchantABC@bank

Hope you noticed the difference between these two UPI IDs

To create a standard UPI ID/VPA or static QR, merchants would need to have an account and provide KYC *(as needed by the acquiring bank)*. This can be a time-consuming process.

But Virtual VPAs can be created based on a company's (for example: KiranaTech or LendingTech) KYC and account. So, it is easy to create thousands of Virtual VPAs and QRs in no time.

Operations:

- Settlement: Although transfer is real-time, PAs/Banks will do settlement few times on the same day or T+1 working day

- Refunds: No specific API to trigger refunds. If there is a need to do refunds, then merchant has to do payout to remitter's VPA.

Commercials:

Technically, there are no actual commercials for this solution, but banks/PAs may charge nominal fees for VPA creation and transaction fee to cover infrastructure and support costs.

Transaction fees can be flat or percentage, or it is possible to have even an amount-based slab wise flat fee or percentage + flat rate combinations (*Go Creative!*)

Closing Remarks

VAN and Virtual VPA solutions are simple, and economical and have a great value for certain use cases. Although such payer-initiated transactions have certain limitations, with a little bit of customization and innovation, merchants can utilize these solutions effectively and efficiently.

Chapter 15

Payout or Disbursement Solutions

Like two sides of a coin, 'payments' also has two sides — collection and disbursement.

Collections are important for merchants as they are visible to the user and have a direct impact on sales or revenue.

Disbursements or Payouts work behind the scenes and, generally, do not get the attention they deserve. But Payouts are important solutions in the payment ecosystem.

Payout Use Cases

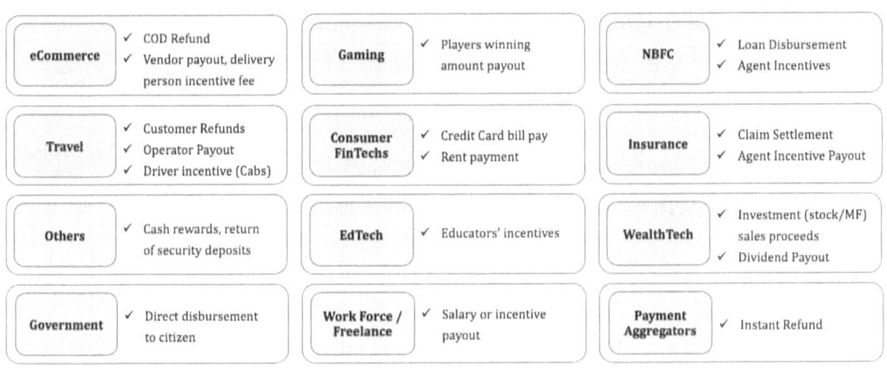

All Payout use cases are not the same as they vary in terms of:

a. **Periodicity/frequency**: Few payouts are periodic *(e.g., weekly incentive payout of delivery persons)*, and few are random *(e.g., winnings of a rummy game)*.

Few payouts are uniform across the time-period *(e.g.: Travel operator's payout)*, and few are random *(e.g., refunds of COD orders of an eCommerce merchant)*

b. **Number of Payouts in a time frame**: Few payouts are of smaller volume *(E.g., incentive payout of insurance agents)*, but few cases have large volumes *(e.g., Winning disbursement of Fantasy game merchants post an IPL match)*

c. **Value of payouts**: Few are small tickets payout *(e.g., doctor appointment fee)* and few are large ticket ones *(e.g., insurance claim settlement)*.

d. **Criticality**: Few payout cases are not time-sensitive *(e.g., refund of an insurance policy cancellation)*, but few cases are time-sensitive *(e.g., partner truck driver's commission)*

e. **Who is disbursing the funds?** In most of the payout use cases, a merchant does the disbursement *(E.g.: Swiggy doing payout to restaurants)*, and in few cases, 3rd parties will do disbursement on behalf of the merchant *(e.g., TPA initiating payout on behalf of an health insurance company)*

f. **Cost**: Few payout modes are cheaper, and few are expensive. With 1-2 exceptions, all types of payout solutions work on a flat rate model. Cost plays an important role in selecting payout solutions.

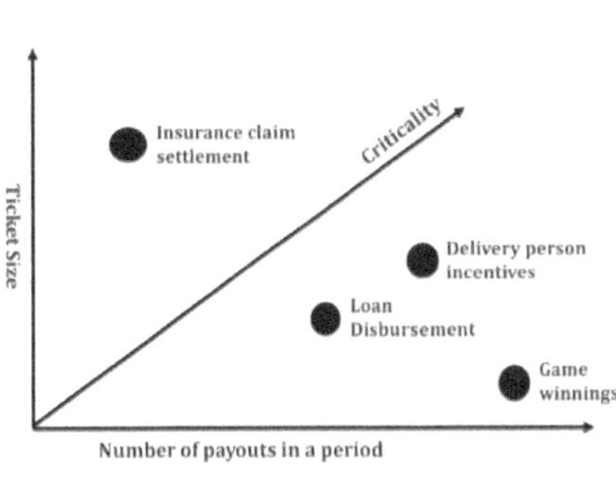

a. Use cases on basis of ticket size and number of disbursements

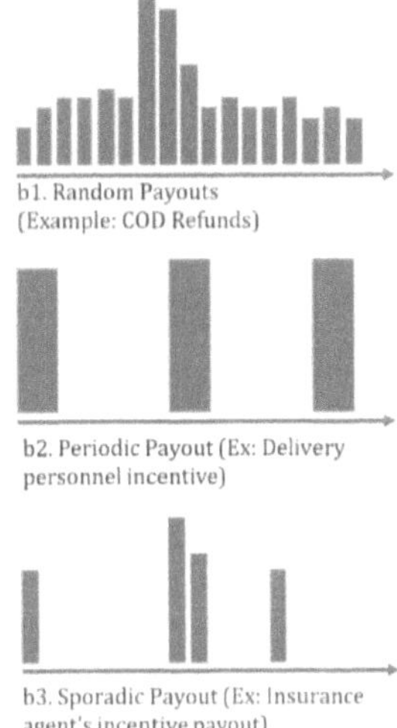

b2. Periodic Payout (Ex: Delivery personnel incentive)

b3. Sporadic Payout (Ex: Insurance agent's incentive payout)

Importance of payout solutions:

Although not directly, payout/disbursement impacts the business.

If your players do not receive the winning amount as promised on time, they will stop playing on your platform.

If your truck partner doesn't receive funds, he won't move the truck, and you will lose that order *(or maybe that customer)*.

In today's super competitive world, these things matter.

In the next three sub-chapters, we will cover details of payout rails, integration models, and operations.

15.A Payout - Rails

To make the disbursement (payout), a merchant would need:

a. **Source account:** Where a merchant will park funds for payout. It can be a merchant's own account with sponsor bank, or payout solution provider's account.

b. **Payment instrument details:** To push funds to the instrument.

c. **Payout Rail:** Depending on the payment instrument, you would need a rail to push the funds (refer below illustration).

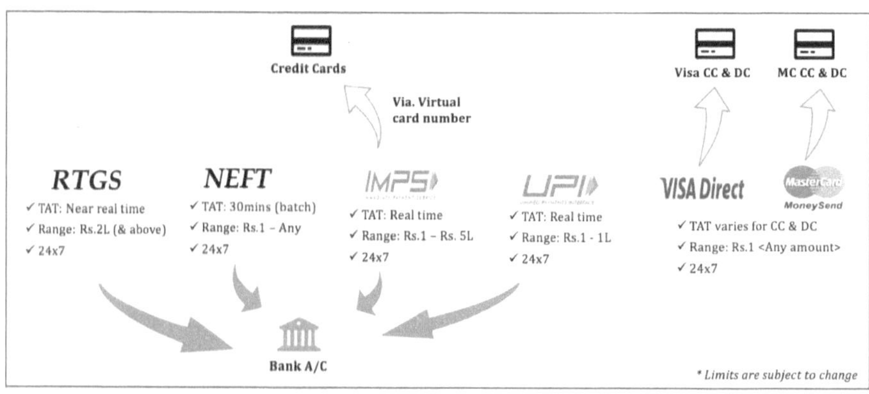

1. RTGS (Real Time Gross Settlement):

Inter-bank transfer platform managed by RBI for facilitating large ticket transfers. RBI acts as a clearing house to square off incoming and outgoing funds.

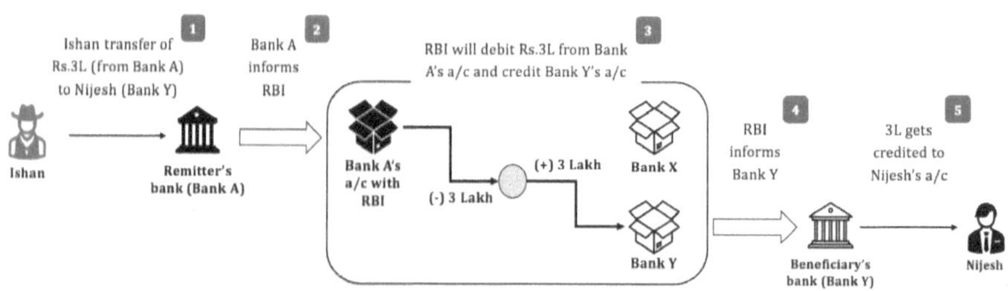

- Transfer amount: Rs.2,00,000 and above (*unless your bank enforces capping*)
- Working hours: 24x7 (*since December 2020*)
- Transfer Type: Real-time
- Beneficiary details needed: Beneficiary Name + Account Number + IFSC.

RTGS works on 'gross settlement' model - each transfer is done separately (*no batch processing during transfer or during inter-bank fund movement*)

2. NEFT (National Electronic Fund Transfer):

Inter-bank transfer platform managed by RBI where RBI acts as clearing house.

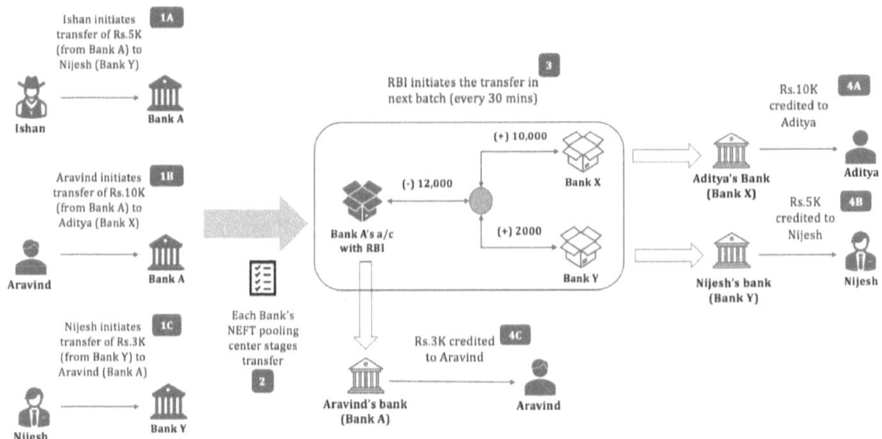

- Transfer Amount: Rs.1 to any amount (*unless your bank enforces capping*)
- Working Hours: 24x7 (*Since Dec'19*)
- Transfer Type: Batch processing of 30mins
- Beneficiary details needed:

    – Beneficiary name + account number + IFSC

    – Credit Card Number + IFSC

NEFT works in 'net' settlement - Bank A has to move a total of Rs.15,000 (Rs.10,000 to Bank X and Rs.5,000 to Bank Y). Bank Y has to transfer Rs.3,000 to Bank A.

During clearing of transfers, Bank A will transfer Rs.10,000 to Bank X but will transfer **only** Rs.2,000 to Bank Y. *(i.e., Rs.3,000 is net-adjusted)*

3. IMPS (Immediate Payment System):

Real-time inter-bank transfer solution by NPCI where NPCI acts as the clearing house.

- Transfer amount: Rs.1 to Rs.5,00,000 *(revised from earlier Rs.2 Lakh)*

- Working hours: 24x7 *(since inception)*

- Transfer Type: Real-time

- Beneficiary details needed:

    – Account Number and IFSC *(Only first 4 digits of IFSC are checked)*

    – Mobile Number + MMID (Mobile Money Identifier)

    – mobile number + bank name

    – Credit card number + IFSC *(before tokenization)*

    – Virtual Card number + IFSC

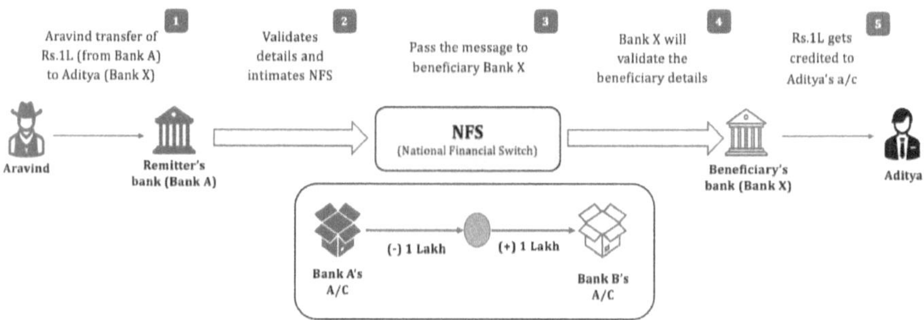

In IMPS, the fund transfer between remitter and beneficiary is done in real-time but the banks do the net-settlement in batches (4 batches per day - As of Apr'23)

4. **UPI:** UPI is a real-time transfer mechanism that works 24x7 and is managed by NPCI.

- Transfer Amount: Rs.1 to Rs.1,00,000 *(Higher limit for few sectors)*
- Working Hours: 24x7
- Transfer Type: Real-time
- Beneficiary details needed: VPA or UPI Number or Account Number + IFSC.

5. **Visa Direct and Master Money Send:** These disbursement solutions are managed by Visa and MasterCard. These solutions allow a merchant to disburse funds directly to a tokenized card.

- Transfer Amount: Rs.1 to any amount (As allowed by the issuing bank)
- Working: Near real time to T+1 Day
- Coverage: Visa and MasterCard debit and credit cards (for selected banks/cards)

6. **Wallets:** Some of the wallet issuers allow payouts to those wallets directly (e.g., PayTM and AmazonPay). These payouts work in real-time and have dependency on KYC compliance and wallet limits. Typically charge percentage (%) of payout/transfer value.

7. **Fund Transfer (FT):** This is an intra-bank transfer *(both beneficiary and remitter are using the same bank)*. In this case, only ledgers are adjusted, so it works in real-time, 24x7, and no upper limit on transfer amount

(theoretically). The bank doesn't route transfers through any of the rails or clearing houses.

Note on 24x7 NEFT and RTGS:

Banks need to keep funds with RBI to square off the transfers. Considering they do not want to lock-in large sums of funds with the clearing house, the banks may enforce limits *(e.g., 24x7 payout is not allowed for business payouts or enforce amount limits for businesses that want 24x7 disbursement)*. Usually, such restrictions are applicable only for business payouts and not enforced on retail users.

Payout Rails - Table:

	RTGS	NEFT	IMPS	UPI	Fund Transfer	Wallets	Visa Direct	MasterCard Money Send
Managed By	RBI	RBI	NPCI	NPCI	Banks	Wallet Issuer	Visa	MasterCard
Minimum Amount	Rs.2,00,000	Rs.1	Rs.1	Rs.1	Rs.1	Rs.1	Rs.1	Rs.1
Maximum Amount	No Limit	No Limit	Rs.5,00,000	Rs.2,00,000	No Limit	Depends on Min or Full KYC	No Limit	No Limit
Working Hours	24x7	24x7	24x7	24x7	24x7	24x7	24x7	24x7
Transfer Type	Real-time	30min batch	Real-time	Real-time	Real-time	Real-time	Up to 30mins	Up to 30mins
Commercials	Zero	Zero	3 slabs	3 slabs	Zero	Percentage	Flat Fee	Flat Fee
Integration Type	Connected banking & PA Recharge	Connected banking & PA Recharge	Connected banking & PA Recharge	Connected banking & PA Recharge	Connected banking & PA Recharge	Recharge / Pre-funding	Recharge / Pre-funding	Recharge / Pre-funding

Special Solutions:

Let's quickly cover slightly unknown but highly used payout rails.

a. **NACH Credit**: In *Chapter 13.A and 13.B* we covered NACH (paper) and eNACH. But we covered only debit capabilities *(as we were discussing about recurring payments)*

   Both eNACH and NACH have credit capabilities, and the merchant can transfer funds to the beneficiary's account by staging a credit request file with the sponsor bank.

This solution is widely used by the regulated investment sector for disbursement of Mutual Fund sale and dividend payout.

b. **AePS Credit**: Aadhar enabled Payments System (AePS) is used for disbursement of Government's direct benefits/subsidy amount to citizens.

15.B Payout - Integration, commercials, operations

These are mainly of two types for transfers:

- P2P (person to person) or B2B (one business to another) transfers

   These transfers are done at the branch or online channels of the bank on NEFT, IMPS, and RTGS rails. UPI transfers can be done from any TPAP/UPI Apps

- Business to customers or businesses (One business to multiple parties)

   A merchant/company will do payout to multiple people and entities. These are more interesting as various factors such as performance, stability, processing capacity, and commercials play a role.

In your bank's portal when you add a new beneficiary, it takes some time *(up to 30 minutes)* for the beneficiary details to get reflected, and there will be limit on the first transfer amount for the first 24 hours.

But in payout solutions, beneficiaries can be added in bulk and in real-time. And there won't be any restriction on number of transfers or amount of transfer to the new beneficiary.

Ways to Integrate a Payout Solution

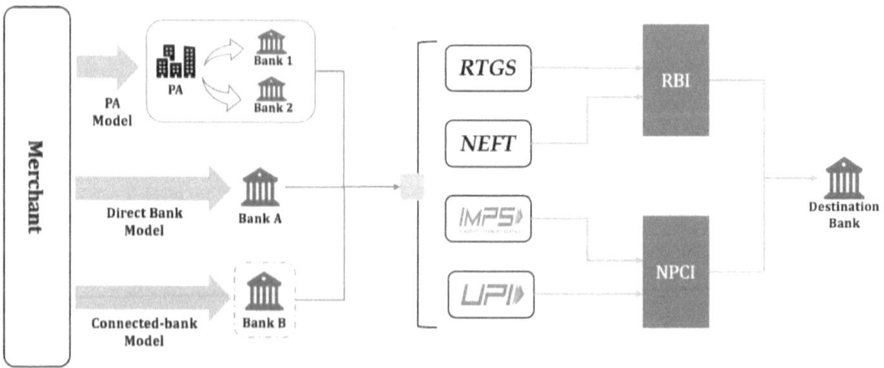

Illustration: Different Types of Payout Integrations

1. **Aggregator Model**: An aggregator will bring multiple banks on a single platform. A merchant will park the funds with the aggregator, and initiate the payout *(either via dashboard, file upload or API)*

   Note: Various Payment Aggregators, API banking FinTechs offer this model

Advantages	• Bank agnostic - No dependency on a single bank • Higher uptime, processing capacity and better success rate
Disadvantages	• Funds are locked-in with FinTech/PA • Merchant has to keep replenishing the funds. • Customer's bank account statement will have FinTech/PA's name and not merchant's (*this can be confusing to the user*)

2. **Connected Bank Model**: A FinTech/PA offers this model where the merchant will park the funds with a designated bank and payouts are initiated from FinTech/PA's APIs or dashboard.

Advantages	• Bank account belongs to the merchant. • No need to move funds to FinTech's account (no fund lock-in) • Customer's statement will have merchant's name. • Better commercials from banks; better service from FinTech • Clean model *(as they say – 'it is kosher')*
Disadvantages	• Paying extra fee to the PA *(TSP charges)* • Dependency on a single bank - if that bank is down then the payout will stop

3. **Bank Model:** A bank can offer its payout solution to the merchant where the merchant can initiate payout via the bank's API/Dashboard. There is no role of any FinTech or PA.

Advantages	• Account belongs to merchant. • No need to move funds to FinTech/PA's account. • Narration will have merchant's name. • Better commercials *(possibly)*
Disadvantages	• Dependency on a single bank - If the bank is down then the payout will stop

4. **TSP Model**: As TSP's are different from FinTechs/PAs so listing it here. Otherwise, this is like the Connecting Bank model *(point 2)*, but instead of a FinTech/PA, a TSP will be integrated with a bank and a merchant will initiate payouts via TSP/Orchestrator.

Important Note: Wallet Payout, Visa Direct, MasterCard Money Send works only on Aggregator model where merchants have to pre-fund Aggregator/FinTech/service provider's account.

Commercials:

A. P2P or B2B transfers: With exception of IMPS, banks don't charge for NEFT, RTGS or UPI

B. Payout Solutions: Yes, there will be some charges.

   • NEFT and RTGS: Flat rate *(e.g., Rs.1 per transfer)* even though most of the banks offer these rails to merchants and service providers/FinTechs at zero cost.

   • IMPS and UPI: Slab wise flat rate based on the transfer amount *(E.g., Rs. 1.5 up to Rs.1K, Rs.4 for Rs.1K to Rs.25K, Rs.7 above Rs.25k)*

   • Visa Direct and MasterCard Money Send: Flat rate *(Rs.3 to Rs.10)* for each transfer *(Note: for credit card repayment, Visa gives plough back (funds) to merchants)*

   • Wallets (PayTM or AmazonPay): Usually percentage of payout amount *(e.g., 2%)*

- Fund Transfer: Usually free, but Banks may charge small flat fee.

Few banks may give the payout solution for free or may charge a one-time fee as banks love 'the float' *(funds that are parked in the bank account)*

Note: FinTechs/Banks can be creative in pricing - flat fee, slab wise fees, hybrid fees (Flat + percentage), slab-based fees on the payout volume, or monthly minimum fee etc.

Commercial model:

Example: A merchant wants to disburse Rs.1,000, the payout charge is Rs.10, GST is 18%

a. **Deduction from beneficiary**:

Working: Charges (+GST amount) are deducted from the beneficiary

Merchant's balance is debited for: Rs.1000

Beneficiary will receive Rs.988.20 *(Rs.1000 - Rs.10 - Rs.1.80)*

b. **Deduction from merchant**:

Working: Charges (+GST amount) are deducted from the merchant

Merchant's balance is debited for: Rs.1011.80 *(Rs.1000+ Rs.10+ Rs.1.80)*

Beneficiary will receive Rs.1000

c. **Invoicing**:

Working: Charges (+GST amount) are invoiced to the merchant

Merchant's balance is debited for Rs.1000

Beneficiary will receive Rs.1000

Merchant is invoiced Rs.11.80

Efficiency of Payout Solutions:

Payout is dependent on multiple entities *(merchant, FinTech/PA, remitter bank, destination bank, clearing houses/switch - RBI or NPCI)* and each entity is a potential failure point.

Points that need to be considered when we talk about the 'efficiency' of a payout system.

1. **Availability**:

   Payouts should work every time and all the time. If payouts are critical, then availability becomes crucial. If any of the entities involved goes offline, then payouts are stalled.

   Solution: Do integration with multiple banks or use a FinTech/ PA who has pre-integrated with multiple banks. Remember, there is no alternative if the clearing house (e.g., NPCI) or destination bank is down. In such cases, just queue the payouts, wait, and then retry!

2. **Load Processing Capacity**:

   Every entity has its own load processing capacity and depends on infrastructure and liquidity with clearing houses. Load handling capacity is crucial as there is a huge difference between processing 10,000 payouts in a day Vs. in an hour.

   Solution: As each bank has limited processing capacity so add multiple banks.

3. **Reconciliation**:

   There will be reversals and pending cases. It is important for the service provider (bank or FinTech) to reconcile those cases so merchants can take appropriate actions.

   Solution: Run multi-level reconciliation (bank, switch) to identify any reversals or drops.

4. **Success Rate**:

The success rate is an important performance indicator.

There are few steps that can be taken to improve the success rate:

- Adding more banks to process payout, so lesser dependency on a single bank.

- Smart routing: Experiment to identify which sponsor bank works better on which destination bank on which rail (IMPS, NEFT) at which time of the day then route the payouts accordingly - Hard work but worth it.

- Retrying and queuing of payout instructions

- Validating beneficiary's instrument details *(e.g., validating bank account, beneficiary name, VPA, UPI Number)* before initiating payout to those instruments

15.C Payout - Special Solutions

Payout or disbursement solutions are tweaked and customized to address special use cases. Here are a few important solutions.

A. Beneficiary Validation:

To reduce the failure rates, merchants should validate whether the beneficiary's payment instrument is valid, whether it is active, and whether it belongs to the customer.

1. For Bank Account:

There are different ways to validate the bank account *(apart from legacy method of asking user to share canceled cheque or bank statement)*

- **Penny Drop**: Merchant can transfer Rs.1 to the account by passing account number and IFSC. Beneficiary's name is returned in response.

  Two things happened with this: (1) Confirmed that account number is correct, and account is live (2) Got the account holder's name *(which merchant can validate)*

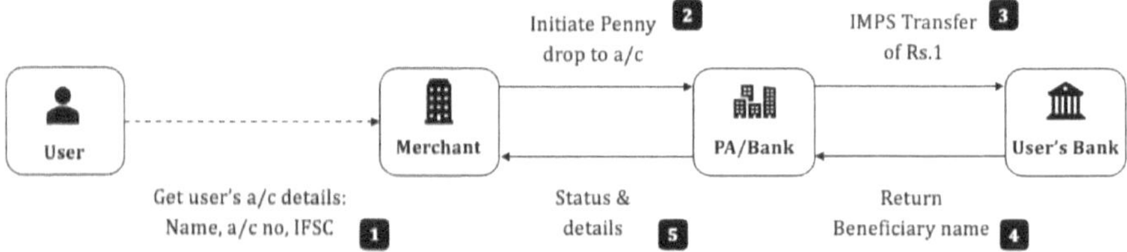

  As a merchant wants the response in real-time, so IMPS is used for penny drop. Do remember that IMPS checks only first 4 digits of IFSC.

  Note: Merchant cannot validate the beneficiary's name as is because many banks won't send complete name *(truncate the name)* or add prefix Shri or Mr. to beneficiary name or expand the initials as per KYC *(e.g., Tony Stark will become Tony Howard Stark)* or change the order of name and surname *(Aditya Kulkarni will be shown as Kulkarni Aditya).*

A merchant has to write fuzzy logic to match the names but still cannot achieve 100% result, so manual review is inevitable.

Variable Penny Drop: Merchant can drop variable amounts *(any value between Rs.1 and Rs.2)* instead of standard Rs.1. Merchants can ask users to confirm the amount they received – a kind of additional authentication.

- **Fund Transfer (FT)**: Penny drop can be done using Fund Transfer *(remitter's bank is the same as beneficiary's bank')*. For FT, the penny drop amount can be less than Rs.1, and as it just ledger adjustment for the bank, so the transfer fees are less or zero.

- **Reverse Penny Drop**: As the name suggests, instead of the merchant, the customer will transfer Rs.1 to the merchant's account. The merchant uses webhooks to get the *customer's* name, account number, and IFSC.

  The merchant will return Rs.1 back to the customer. Merchant can use NEFT to return the Rs.1 as NEFT is cheaper *(technically Rs.0)* compared to IMPS.

  Note: Solution provider may charge nominal fee for this service. Merchant will save Rs.1 needed for penny drop.

- **Name Enquiry API**: NPCI has built a *'Name Enquiry'* feature in which the remitter bank will validate the beneficiary's name based on the account number + IFSC (for merchants) and MMID *(for P2P).* This feature is live with a couple of banks.

  Note: Technically it is a free solution but there will be some API charges

2. For UPI validation:

Merchants can call the *'validate VPA'* API. No need to transfer the funds *(penny drop)*.

'Validate VPA' API validates with NPCI whether the VPA is active and returns VPA holders name as registered with the TPAP.

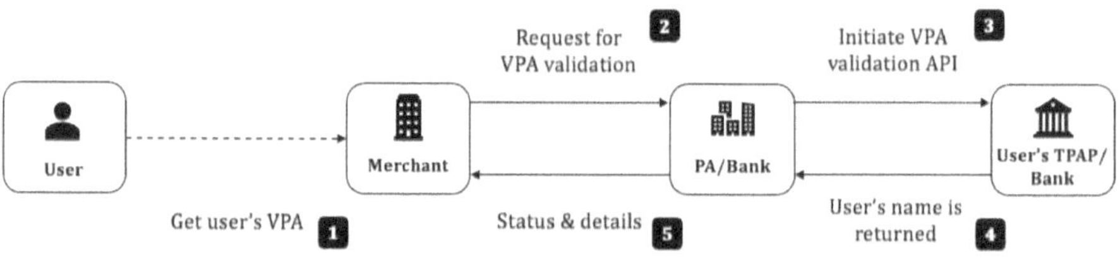

'Validate VPA' API can be used to check beneficiary name of bank account without penny drop by sending API request in following format: ***<Account-Number> @ <IFSC>*ifsc.npci**

Note: It may not work for all banks

Note: Validation is a one-time activity *(mostly) but* do perform this activity once in six months or a year to make sure if a customer's account/ VPA has become inactive *(it is a possibility)*.

Merchants don't need any certification/license to store customers' account number or VPA/UPI Number. Considering these are PII (Personal Identifiable Information), take necessary steps to store such data safely and securely.

B. Connecting Collection and Payout:

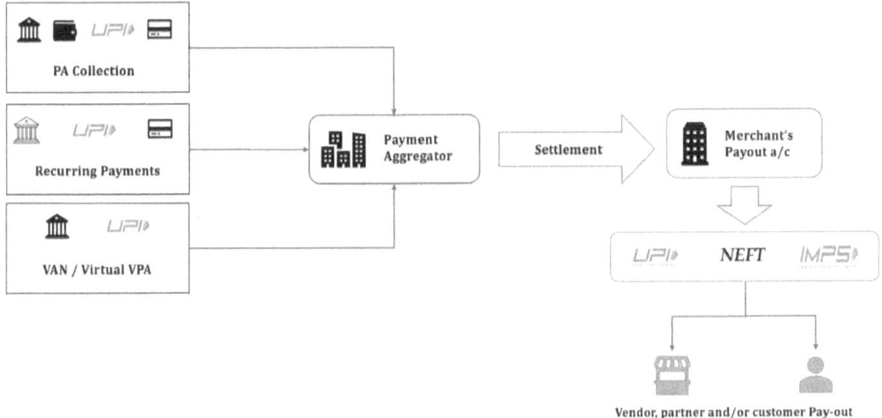

Many merchants will have use cases for both collections and disbursements. Funds are collected from Payment Aggregation, Recurring payment, or Virtual account solutions. And later disbursed using IMPS, NEFT, or UPI rails. So, a merchant can connect both collection and disbursement legs and manage the financial supply chain more efficiently.

C. IMPS to Credit Card

16-digit credit card number is similar to a bank account number, and each credit card issuing bank has single IFSC for credit cards *(e.g., HDFC CC — HDFC000128, ICICI CC: ICIC0000103)*

That means, a merchant *(via remitter bank)* can use IMPS, NEFT (and even UPI) rails to push money to a credit card.

This mechanism was used for credit card bill payment and instant refunds to credit cards.

But card tokenization guidelines changed it!

Except for the card issuer and card network, no other entity is allowed to access the card number. Pushing funds *(doing payout)* to tokenized cards is not possible, so merchants are using Visa Direct and MasterCard Money Send rails.

And then,

NPCI came up with an easier and efficient way of doing **credit card bill payment using IMPS rails.**

Let's see the working:

Virtual Card Number is simple and interesting concept.

16-digit virtual card number will be created that is in line with tokenization guidelines *(actual card number will not be shown or used)*

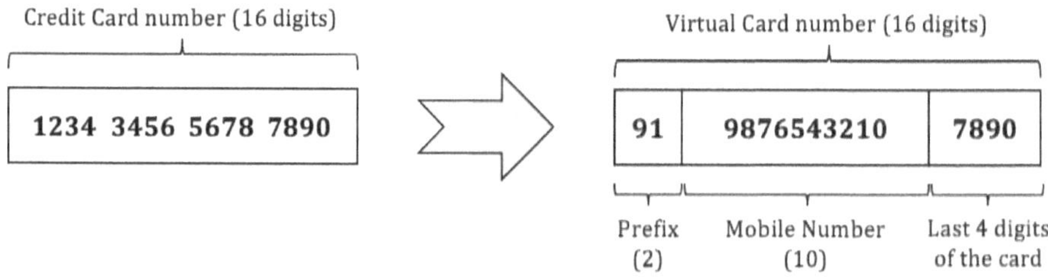

Card issuing bank has to do bunch of things:

Educate and inform customer about virtual card number.

Mapping of virtual card number and credit card number

Do a bunch of validations during CC bill payment, crediting to the card in real-time, and communicating the status in real-time *(as shown below)*

Note: Nothing changes for remitter bank or NPCI (as it is standard IMPS transfer)

Transfer:

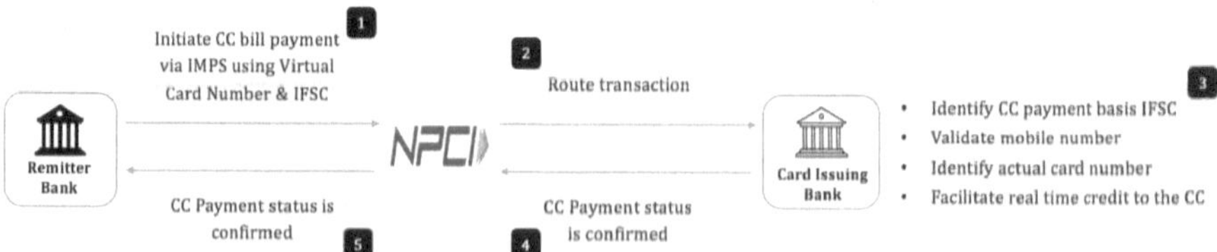

Credit to the card is done in real-time, and the issuing bank will give the status in real-time.

Fund settlement between the remitter bank and beneficiary bank will happen as per the standard IMPS inter-bank fund settlement process i.e., in batches — 4 per day via RTGS.

Ideally, the above solution should cover all issuing banks and card networks, and as per guidelines, the issuing banks were supposed to be ready to support this flow by 31st May 2023. But most of the banks are not ready!

Note: Although this solution exists, RBI is mandating Credit Card bill payment via BBPS

Instant Refund Use Cases:

The *Virtual Card Number* solution can be used for instant refund to credit cards.

Merchants can build seamless process - During the credit card transaction leg, if the PA/merchant can capture the customer's mobile number and identify the issuing bank, then during the refund, create the virtual card number *(based on the issuer bank, you will have IFSC)*, and then initiate IMPS transfer and thus achieve an instant refund to the credit card.

Challenges in this solution:

- User may not be using own number but spouse/family member's credit card.
- Limited card issuer coverage - this is new solution so banks will take time to implement.

Closing Remarks:

Payout solutions where merchants pre-fund FinTech/Solution Provider's accounts are opaque. It is difficult to trace the fund movement when merchants and the FinTech move funds across different accounts to do payouts. And there is a growing concern about such opaque fund movement models, especially in the 'gaming' sector.

RBI's digital lending guidelines enforce that loan disbursement should happen directly from NBFCs' account to customer's account, irrespective whether customer is onboarded by NBFC or the Digital lending App *(who has partnered with NBFC)*.

Such guidelines and compliance related concerns will shift the payout models to the *'**connected banking**'* model or direct bank integrations. This may impact the revenue and margins of Solution Providers *(FinTechs, PAs, TSPs)*.

At present, payout solution doesn't come under any regulations and RBI will regulate the payout models in the near future.

With more & more payout use cases coming up and merchants wanting to achieve higher efficiency & scalability, 'Payout Solutions' have become as important as 'collection solutions '.

So, we can easily assume that **payouts** will continue to grow!

Chapter 16

International Payments

Those who have read Dan Brown's 'Da Vinci Code' or watched the movie with the same name starring Tom Hanks, would be familiar with 'Knights Templar'— a holy warrior order with the purpose of protecting Jerusalem during Crusades.

Here is a little-known fact about Knights Templars — they founded the first cross-border payment/banking system. There was always risk *(theft, loss)* in carrying cash/gold on a pilgrimage. A pilgrim could deposit the funds in one of the Templar Churches in London and get a receipt, which can be shown in a Templar Church in Jerusalem, and collect the funds.

Today, the world is very different from the one in medieval ages, as the cross-border trade and travel increased, the cross-border payments also evolved.

And in this Chapter, we will cover cross-border payments with India as the focal point.

Jargons:

- **Nostro Account**: A foreign currency account maintained in a bank in a foreign country. When Party A (in the US) remits to Party B (in India), the funds flow through a Nostro a/c, or an intermediary account, or a correspondent bank.

   E.g., ICICI Bank holding an account with JP Morgan in the USA is called a Nostro Account.

- **Vostro Account**: When a bank maintains a local or home currency account of a foreign bank or branch in its own country it is called a Vostro account.

  E.g., JP Morgan holding an account with ICICI in India would be a Vostro A/C

- **SWIFT** *(Society for Worldwide Interbank Financial Telecommunication)* is an organization founded in 1973 with the purpose of standardizing messaging and processing of cross-border transactions. The SWIFT network doesn't transfer funds; instead, it sends payment orders between institutions' accounts using SWIFT codes. SWIFT standardized IBAN *(International Bank Account Numbers)* and BIC *(Bank Identifier Codes)*

- **FIRC** *(Foreign Inward Remittance Certificate)* is issued by an entity's bank for every inward remittance that is received. Apart from working as a legal proof for international payments, FIRC is required to claim export incentives and GST waiver on products sold overseas.

  Note: FIRC is also called as FIRA (Foreign Inward Remittance Advice)

- **Forex** *(Foreign Exchange Rate)* means how much of a currency of another country *(E.g., US $)* a user can buy using a different currency *(E.g., INR)*. For various macroeconomic reasons, this rate varies unless a country has pegged its currency to another country's currency.

- **FATF** *(Financial Action Task Force)* is the global money laundering & terrorist financing watchdog that sets the international standards to avoid any illegal activities.

- **Sanctioned list**: Sanctioned countries, people, or businesses that are subject to restrictions on certain types of financial activities.

E.g., Iran has a restriction on imports, exports, or financial transactions.

- **OFAC** *(The Office of Foreign Assets Control)* is a part of the US Treasury that regulates trade sanctions on countries or individuals.

Authorized Money Changers (AMCs): In cross-border payments, one currency gets converted to another. In India, only RBI authorized entities, such as Authorized Money Changers (AMCs), are allowed to conduct exchange or conversion.

Different categories for AMCs:

- Full Fledged Money Changer (FFMC) is a money changer authorized to purchase foreign exchange from non-residents visiting India and residents and to sell foreign exchange for private and business travel purposes only *(E.g., Department of Post)*

- Authorized Dealer (AD) Category-II Banks are entities that deal in foreign exchange for specified purposes *E.g., Upgraded FFMCs, select Regional Rural Banks (RRBs), select Urban Cooperative Banks (UCBs)*

- Authorized Dealer (AD) Category-I Banks are authorized dealers of foreign exchange & securities *(E.g., Scheduled Commercials Banks)*

Use Cases and Solutions:

1. **Outward Remittance**: Funds move outside India.

   Use cases: (a) Payout to a seller from Singapore who sold product in India, (b) User investing in Tesla shares in USA, (c) parents transferring money to their kid in USA.

2. **Inward Remittance**: Funds move to India from other countries.

Use cases: (a) A migrant worker in Dubai sending money to India, (b) a Freelancer getting fees from a UK client, (c) a craftsman from Channapatna receiving money for products sold on Amzon.US.

3. **International Payment Gateway (IPG)**: The customer is outside India and paying on Indian merchant's website/app using her non-INR credit card.

Use case: An NRI ordering furniture for her parents in India on Pepperfry.com

Note: IPG is nothing but inward remittance but let's keep it separate as it is one of the most common payment options used by the merchants

16.A   Outward & Inward Remittance

As the name suggests, outward remittance is about moving money from India to abroad, and inward remittance is about bringing money from abroad to India.

Inward and outward remittances are done under various models that operate under different regulations, transfer limits, processes, and commercial models.

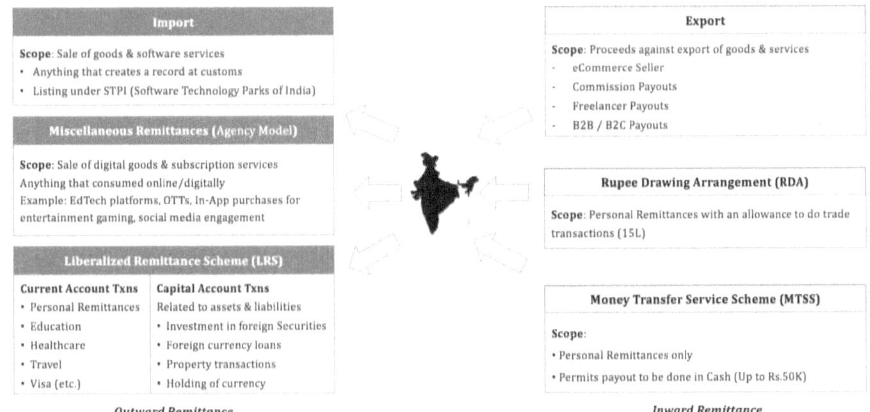

Outward Remittance   *Inward Remittance*

RBI has defined 16 main categories and then multiple subcategories for remittance.

Capital Account	Exports (Goods)	Royalties & License Fees
Transportation	Financial Services	Computer and Information Services
Transfers	Insurance Service	Personal, cultural & Recreational Services
Income	Construction Service	Government, not included elsewhere (G.n.i.e)
Travel	Communication Service	Other business Services & Others

Complete list here: https://www.rbi.org.in/upload/ notification/pdfs/52220.pdf

When funds are being moved cross border, it is essential to establish an end-to-end transaction trail by capturing following details:

- Remitter details — Name, Email, Mobile No
- Beneficiary details — Name, Address, Bank Account Details
- Invoice Details — Invoice Number, Date, Amount, Description
- AWB (Airway Bill) — where physical goods are moved.
- Remittance Scheme Declarations e.g., LRS declaration
- Purpose Code *(Covered in above table)*

I will divide inward-outward remittances into two: (1) import-export (2) other models.

I. Import-Export Model

Import and export are cornerstones of the economy. The import and export could be products and services (e.g., Software).

Import: Product/service is imported, and funds are moved outside India (INR → non-INR)

Export: Product/service is exported, and funds are moved into India (Non-INR → INR)

A. License

1. Past model and guidelines:

Earlier, the remittances of small value import and/or export were operated under **OPGSP** *(Online Payment Gateway Service Providers)* guidelines.

To operate the OPGSP model, an entity has to partner with **AD-I bank** and seek authorization from RBI.

2. PA-CB License:

In Dec '2023, RBI announced **PA-CB** (Payment Aggregator - Cross Border) guidelines to regulate the entities who want to operate small-value import and/or export remittances.

We have covered the details of the PA-CB guidelines in *Chapter 4 (Guidelines)*

Summary:

- PA-CB guidelines define three distinct licenses for entities:

  - **PA-CB-E (Export)** - To move funds inside India against export of goods/services.

  - **PA-CB-I (Import)** - To move funds outside India against import of goods/services.

  - **PA-CB-E&I (Export and Import)**: To do both activities.

- PA/PG guidelines are applicable to PA-CB as well, so everything that is expected of online PA in terms of process, security, compliance, etc., are applicable.

- Registration with FIU-IND *(Financial Intelligence Unit - India)* and expected to monitor the transactions, beneficiaries, and remitters and report suspicious cases.

- Accounts: PA-CBs are to have accounts with **Authorized Dealer - I** scheduled banks.

  - PA-CB-I will have an Import Collection Account (ICA)

  - PA-CB-E will have an Export Collection Account (ECA) and non-INR a/c. Separate ECA accounts for each of non-INR currencies.

- Domestic PAs to have separate escrow account to be separate from ECA and ICA

- Transaction Limits: Rs. 25,00,000 per unit of goods or service. For import transactions, if the amount exceeds Rs.2,50,000 per unit, then PA-CB-I to do due diligence on the buyer.

- Online PAs who have existing cross-border business (under OPGSP) to inform RBI by 31st Dec 2023 to seek approval *(E.g., RazorPay, Cashfree, BillDesk)*

- Entities that operate Cross-border payments *(under OPGSP)* apply for approval and continue to operate till the license process is concluded. *(E.g., Skydo, EximPe)*

- New PA-CB to take approval before commencing business.

- Authorized PA-CB wants to change activity (import or export) then seek approval from RBI before starting new business.

PA-CB-Import and PA-CB-Export are similar in many ways, yet they are different; I will start with the model-specific details, and then we will cover the common aspects.

A. PA-CB-Import

Product/Service is imported, and INR is moved outside India and remitted to the beneficiary in home currency *(e.g., USD, SG Dollar, etc.).*

PA-CB-I supports both B2B and B2C cases.

Use cases: Software subscriptions, Software download, eCommerce purchases, and B2B imports.

Account Set-up: PA-CB-I to open an Import Collection Account (ICA) with AD-I banks.

Working:

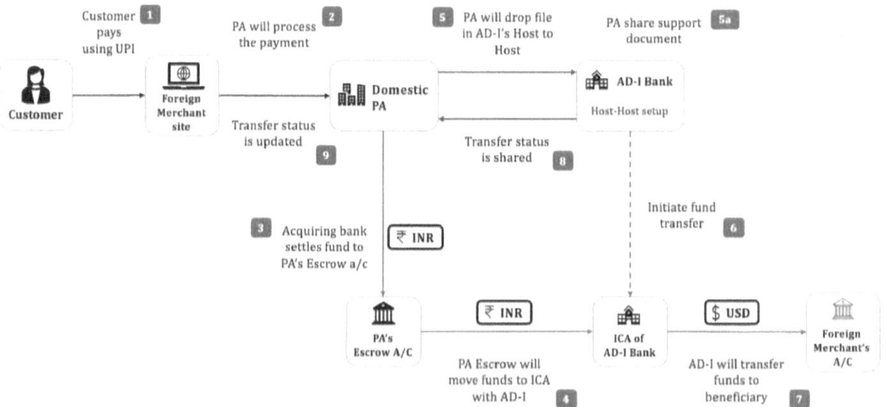

Stage 1: Domestic Payment Leg:

- PA-CB-I can enable online PA services, and the remitter can pay using UPI or net-banking *(Note: Only few UPI Acquiring Banks give MID for such cases)*

  Note: The remitter can deposit funds via NEFT/RTGS to PA-CB-I's ICA.

Stage 2: Domestic Fund Movement:

- Domestic online PA will pool the funds in PA Escrow Account
- Move the funds to PA-CB-I's ICA account.

Stage 3: Transfer:

- PA-CB-I will stage the transfer instruction to AD-I bank *(upload transfer details file and/or supported documents to AD-I bank's host-to-host set up)*
- AD-I bank will perform a sanity and compliance check *(Sanction, FATF check, etc.)* and then initiate the transfer to merchant's account.

KYC:

PA-CB-I will do merchant due diligence as per Master KYC guidelines. Considering the merchant is outside India, the PA-CB-I has to collect country-specific KYC.

Taxation:

- B2B: Remitter to submit 15CA and 15CB *(For > Rs.50,000 per transfer and yearly remittance of Rs.5,00,000)*
- B2C: 15CA and 15CB are not applicable; Import merchants are expected to pay the GST in India. Import merchants (who do not India entity) can appoint tax agent.

Typically, PA-CB-Is are not responsible for merchant's tax compliance.

Many AD-I banks do not ask for 15CA & CB to stage the outward remittance. But it is a good practice to collect these docs *(they may come handy during bank audits and investigations)*

Challenges:

PA-CB-Import looks very lucrative.

Indians and Indian businesses purchase products and software from foreign companies.

PA-CB-Import is not a simple; it has higher compliance, as money is moving outside India.

KYC of Import merchant (foreign entity), 15 CA & CB, taxation for the merchant, and alignment with UPI acquiring banks are few of the challenges.

And most of the foreign merchants do not want to take these additional challenges as

- Indian users constitute a small fraction of overall customer base.
- Indian users can pay using their credit or debit cards *(Foreign merchants use international PayFacs, such as Stripe, Adyen, etc. to process cards)*

B. PA-CB-Export

Product/service is exported, and non-INR currency is moved to India and Indian beneficiary will receive the amount in INR.

PA-CB-E supports both B2B and B2C cases.

Typical use cases: B2B product exports, freelancing, software export

Account Set-up: PA-CB-E to open an Export Collection Account (ECA) with AD-I banks.

KYC: PA-CB-E to do merchant due diligence as per Master KYC guidelines. In this case, the merchant is in India, so it is easy to do KYC.

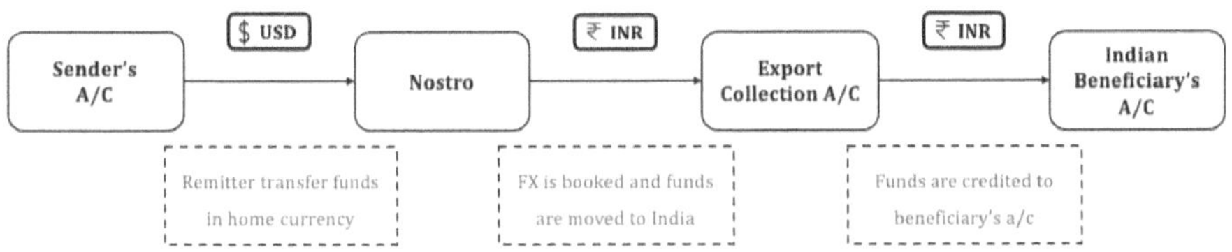

In export flow, the remitters (foreign entities) transfer funds to a designated account (e.g., account with JP Morgan, USA). Collecting all funds in one account is a reconciliation nightmare.

Virtual Account Solution is a good solution *(read the basics in Chapter 14)*

PA-CB-Export can partner with foreign banks or service providers *(e.g., currency cloud)* to create virtual accounts.

Let's assume PA-CB-Export's **merchant ABC** wants to collect funds from 2 entities in the USA.

Step 1: PA-CB-E will create two virtual accounts and share them with the merchant ABC.

Step 2: The merchant will share those virtual account details with entities in USA.

Step 3: The foreign entities will transfer funds (in USD) to the respective virtual accounts.

Step 4: The funds are repatriated to India, and credited to ECA account of PA-CB-E

Step 5: AD-1 bank will transfer funds to PA-CB-E's merchant's account (in INR)

Challenges:

PA-CB-Export is a huge opportunity.

The compliance is simpler *(as money moves to India)*, and the solution is much simpler.

However, the challenge is a fragmented market; large exporters avail the services directly from the AD-I banks. Onboarding smaller merchants and individuals (e.g., freelancers) is cumbersome and expensive *(resources, tools, and compliance cost)*.

C. Common to PA-CB-Import and PA-CB-Export

- ### Commercials

   Commercial models *(fee breakup)* remain same for both inward and outward remittance:

   - GST on Currency Conversion
   - SWIFT Cost (borne by sender)
   - Correspondent Bank Charges (can be borne either by sender or receiver)
   - FX Margin: Calculations will vary as funds are converted from INR to USD in case of outward remittance and USD to INR in case of inward remittance.

Outward Remittance			
A	Amount to be converted (Rs.)	10,00,000	
B	Market Rate	75	1 USD = Rs. 75
C	Bank Margin	0.1	10 Paisa / dollar
D=B+C	Bank FX Rate	75.1	
E=A/B	Conversion at Market Rate	13333.33	
F=A/D	Conversion at Bank Rate	13315.58	USD
G=E-F	Bank Margins	17.75	

Inward Remittance			
A	Amount Sent (in USD)	1,00,000	
B	Market Rate	75.1	1 USD = Rs. 75
C	Bank Margin	0.1	10 Paisa / dollar
D=B-C	Bank FX Rate	75	
E=A*B	Conversion at Market Rate	75,10,000	
F=A*D	Conversion at Bank Rate	75,00,000	INR
G=E-F	Bank Margins	10,000	

Other Fees and Costs:

- Domestic PA fees/MDR on UPI and Net-banking *(PA-CB-Import)*

- Virtual account set-up fee *(PA-CB-Export, charged by banks or service provider)*

- AD-I banks may charge a one-time fee, periodic maintenance fee, or other miscellaneous fees.

- **Sanction Checks:**

  It is mandatory to do sanction checks on beneficiaries, remitters, authorized signatories, directors, and ultimate beneficiary owners to ensure that they do not belong to non-FATF compliant geographies/sanctioned countries. OFAC rules prohibit transactions with certain foreign countries or their nationals and, hence, are to be complied with.

  India abides by the OFAC regulations because:

  - The US dollar is the most traded currency globally.

  - Most correspondent banks are based out of the US or associated with the US.

  - Cross-border payments could directly or indirectly involve US banks.

- **Monitoring:**

  All transactions pertaining to merchants, remitters, and beneficiaries have to be monitored as per the Red Flag Indicators of FIU-IND *(Financial Intelligence Unit - India)*. Any suspicious transaction or entity is to be analyzed, and reported to FIU-IND.

Note: Sanction check and monitoring *(transaction, beneficiary, remitter)* are the responsibilities of PA-CB or any other FX service providers, as well as Authorized Dealer banks. Based on the checks, these entities can initiate appropriate actions *(holding of remittance, reporting to FIU-IND)*

II. Other Cases

A. Outward Remittance:

- **Liberalized Remittance Schemes (LRS)**

  There are two main models: (1) current account (2) capital account.

  - **Current Account** transactions include personal remittances *(parents sending money to their kids in the USA)*, education fees *(student paying to foreign University)*, travel expenses, including Forex cards.

  - **Capital Account** transactions cover the transactions done by users to invest in foreign exchanges *(e.g., buying Tesla shares in NYSE)*, purchase of property, or holding foreign currencies.

  Note: LRS has the limit of US $2,50,000 annually per person; TCS *(Tax Collection at Source)* is applicable on LRS transfers. Deducted taxes can be claimed during Income Tax Returns.

B. Inward Remittance:

- **For MTSS (Money Transfer Service Scheme)**, money transfer companies abroad *(operating as Overseas Principals)* should be licensed in India and should get the necessary approvals from the DPSS *(Department of Payment and Settlement Systems)* of RBI. Funds are sent to an Indian Agent *(licensed FFMC - Full Fledged Money Changer) (E.g., Western Union)*

C. Special Accounts:

- ### SNRR (Special Non-Resident Rupee Account)

  As the name suggests, it is a special account that can be opened with an Authorized Dealer (AD) - I banks in India by the person/businesses based outside India. The account can be used for specific transactions of inward and outward remittances.

  SNRR accounts can be used by foreign entities to collect funds related to sales in India. The account can be used to pay Indian vendors/service providers, and the amount can be used to remit funds to the entity's home country.

- ### For RDA (Rupee Drawing Arrangement), the entity should be licensed as an exchange house in India. These non-Indian entities enter into a partnership with AD- I Banks for a Vostro A/C (or INR A/C) from which payouts are made to the receivers in India. The funds should be received from licensed and regulated entities in the sending country for sourcing the funds from the remitters (established exchange houses) *(E.g., Wise)*

- ### EEFC (Exchange Earner's Foreign Currency) Account

  This account is maintained in foreign currency by the Authorized Dealer (AD) - I bank. The account allows entities that earn in foreign currency to hold the earnings in that currency (e.g., USD) without converting to INR *(Do not incur FX conversion charges)*.

  - The funds in EEFC can be used for
  - Payments to foreign entities *(e.g., vendors)* in foreign currency
  - Payments of taxes in Indian Rupee

- Payments towards loan repayment or vendor payments in Indian Rupee

- EEFC balance can be withdrawn in INR, but cannot be credited back to EEFC

- Receive the settlement of international credit card payments *(Processed by Indian online PA or Acquiring bank)*

Closing Remarks:

With strong Indian diaspora, increased travel, growing MSME exports, and growth of software services, both inward and outward remittances will continue to grow.

Because of higher margins, banks, PAs, and FinTechs are super keen in this space.

Overall cross-border numbers are quite high *(runs in 100s of billions of dollars per year)*, but large importers and exporters use Authorized Dealer banks, whereas market size of small MSME importer or exporter or individuals looks big, but it is highly fragmented.

Cross-border payments have higher compliance requirements - KYC checks, sanction checks, and transaction monitoring. That means the 'compliance costs' will be high.

Cross-border payments were operated by few FinTechs and handful of PAs, but new PA-CB guidelines will allow all licensed PAs to operate Cross-border remittance, so this space will become crowded or competitive, and that will bring down the margins *(just like how it happened in domestic PA business)*.

Irrespective, there is a lot of scope of innovation in cross-border remittances. To unlock those innovations, RBI's 2nd cohort under the regulatory sandbox was focused on 'cross-border' payments.

'Cross-border' is one of the most exciting areas of the payments landscape. Keep an eye on this!

16.B International Payment Gateway

An eCommerce merchant based in India wants customers based outside India to make payment on its website.

This is a very common requirement for eCommerce *(daughter living in Singapore orders furniture for her parents in India)*, travel *(NRI who is coming to India wants to book a flight for her domestic journey)*, education *(parents who are in Dubai want to pay their kid's college fees)*.

Solution: Indian merchant enables international PG from online PAs or acquiring banks

Solution Coverage: (a) Non-INR Visa and MasterCard credit and debit cards (b) Amex

Working Models:

1. Standard

    *   Merchant shows the amount in INR.
    *   Customer will make the payment in merchant's currency (i.e., INR)
    *   Customer's card statement will show the amount in local currency (i.e., US $) - customer sees final converted value (amount + Forex + markup fee)
    *   Settlement will be done to merchant in India in INR

2. Dynamic Currency Convertor (DCC)

    *   Merchant shows the amount in user's currency (e.g., US $ or SG $)
    *   Customer will make the payment in base currency of the card (e.g., US $)
    *   Customer's card statement will have the amount that is shown (Forex charges + Fees will be embedded in the checkout amount)
    *   Merchant will get the settlement in India in INR

Note: DCC is customer friendly as the amount is shown in the user's home currency.

Commercials & Settlement

- International PG is more expensive than domestic PG. Typically in the range of 2.50%-3% (+GST). No sector specific pricing *(i.e., No MCC specific differential pricing)*

- Typically, the settlement time is T+2 days; PAs can offer early settlement as well.

- Settlement amount is in Indian Rupees; merchants can get settlement in foreign currency in the **EEFC** *(Exchange Earners' Foreign Currency)* account.

- For every transaction, the merchant has to get FIRA (Foreign Inward Remittance Advice) from its acquiring bank.

Problems with International PG:

- 2nd Factor Authentication is not mandatory outside India except for high-risk transactions *(sort of step-up authentication leg)*. So, when the customer is posed with 2FA (OTP), then they may simply drop off, and thus, the success rate will tank.

- Additional Charges: As the base currency and transaction currency are different, a cross-currency mark-up fee *(in the range of 3-3.50%)* will be applied. As customers may not be aware of this, they will assume that the merchant has over-deducted the card and raise a dispute or chargeback.

- Refunds: The exchange rate may change from the time of transaction, and when the refund is marked. So, it is possible that the refund amount *(in foreign currency)* may be different than the original transaction amount.

  Note: If a PA wants to refund the same amount in home currency, then PA has to absorb the losses due to exchange rate change.

Interesting Points:

- Worldwide, Visa and MasterCard have migrated to 3DS 2.0. Since Dec '22, Indian acquiring banks/PAs started supporting 3DS 2.0 for international cards.

- Few PAs offer 'zero chargeback' features where merchant doesn't get any chargeback and all chargeback related losses are borne by the PA. To enable this feature, PAs charge an additional MDR of 2-3%. *(Clever model - this is simple mathematical model)*

Enabling International PG:

The acquiring banks consider International PG as high risk. So, the approval is not simple, and bank(s) may enforce limitations & conditions for enabling international PG:

- Sector restrictions (*easy to get approval for eCommerce but not for gaming or NGOs*)

- Merchant restriction based on vintage and reputation (*a good brand eCommerce can get approval, but a new unknown eCommerce merchant may not*)

- Additional documents such as audited financial reports

- Security deposit to cover chargeback risk.

- Capping on the value of transactions that can be processed in a day or a month.

Closing Remarks

For Indian merchants, international PG is the simplest and economical way for processing international card payments. International PG volumes are low, but the margins are high. So, international PG is an important mode for PAs/Acquiring banks to earn high margins.

16.C   Internationalization

In this chapter, we will cover payment products that are 'going international' and catering international users.

a.   **Trade Settlement in INR**

USD is the main currency *(apart from Euro, Pound, Yuan, SGG)* used for cross-border payments especially for international trade settlements.

India is also pushing for using INR for international trade settlements.

To facilitate INR-denominated cross-border payments, RBI has allowed banks from foreign countries to open '***Special Vostro Rupee Account (SVRA)***' with Indian banks.

As of April-2023, 18 banks from 18 countries have opened SVRA with 13 Indian banks.

Countries: Botswana, Fiji, Germany, Guyana, Israel, Kenya, Malaysia, Mauritius, Myanmar, New Zealand, Oman, Russia, Seychelles, Singapore, Sri Lanka, Tanzania, Uganda, and the UK.

Supporting Banks: UCO, IndusInd, UBI, Canara, HDFC, Yes Bank, SBI, IDBI, Indian Bank, PNB, BOB, Axis and ICICI.

b.   **UPI Outside India**

Indian travelers can pay using UPI in 20 countries: Bhutan, Cambodia, Hong Kong, Japan, Malaysia, Nepal, Philippines, Singapore, South Korea, Taiwan, Thailand, Vietnam, Oman, UAE, Belgium, France, Luxemburg, Netherlands, Switzerland, UK

Drawback: Outside India, when you make payment using INR *(via UPI),* the user will have to bear the forex charges, which may fluctuate. That is the reason people use forex cards on foreign trips.

c. **RuPay Outside India**

Just like UPI, even RuPay have ventured outside India. RuPay is accepted in 200+ countries *(for online, POS and ATM transactions)*.

This coverage is achieved by partnering with international card networks, such as Discover, Diners, JCB, Pulse, UnionPay.

Note: The partner card network logo will be printed on the back of the card

To be on par with features and performance offered by global card networks, NPCI is implementing MOTO, DCC *(Dynamic Currency Convertor)*, Contact Less payment, Pre-Authorization (Auth and Capture), and step-up 3DS features for RuPay cards.

To know the details about these features, refer **Chapter 4.A** and **Chapter 9.A**

d. **PayNow and UPI connectivity**

In Sep '21, India and Singapore signed a Memorandum *of Understanding* to link UPI and **PayNow** *(Real-time Payment rail of Singapore… in simple words, Singapore's UPI)*.

In Feb '23, the linking of **UPI and PayNow** was 'officially launched', and in Jan'24, users of PayNow (Singapore) can remit funds to UPI (India). And of course, vice versa.

Road Ahead: NPCI is in discussion with Thailand, UAE, Sri Lanka, and other countries to connect their Real Time Payment rails with UPI. Soon, we will see these cross-border remittance corridors with various countries.

e. **BBPS for NRIs:**

Everyone pays bills — even the Indians who are living abroad pay bills in India. It could be for them or for their families back home.

Now, the users based out of India can make bill payment via BBPS. As of April-2023, the service is live with selected 'exchanges' in UAE, Kuwait, and Oman.

For details, please refer to **Chapter 17. B** (BBPS)

Above solutions for users who are outside India.

Let's talk about solutions that are specifically designed for NRIs and Tourists who visit India.

a. **UPI for NRIs:**

NRIs (Non-Resident Indians) of 10 countries *(Singapore, Australia, Canada, Hong Kong, Oman, Qatar, USA, Saudi Arabia, UAE, UK)* can link their international mobile numbers to their NRE/NRO accounts and enjoy UPI payments.

Member banks should follow FEMA guidelines and are responsible for AML *(Anti-Money Laundering)* and CFT *(Combating the Financing of Terrorism)* checks.

b. **UPI One World**

UPI is made available to tourists visiting India, so they do not have to carry India Rupees *(after converting their home currencies)* or have to use their credit/debit cards of their home countries *(and incur forex charges)*.

UPI One World was launched in partnership between FFMC *(Full Fledged Money Changers)*, PPI *(Prepaid Payment Instrument)*, and *(of course)* UPI infrastructure.

For details, please refer to **Chapter 4.E (UPI)**

Closing Remarks:

'Internationalization' is not new to us… Basmati Rice, Mangoes, Butter Chicken, IT services, movies, many CEOs of Fortune 500 companies…. and the list goes on and on…

This time… India is on the path of internationalization of India's payment platforms and establishing INR as the dominant currency on the world map.

Onwards, upwards, and Outwards!

Chapter 17

BBPS – Bharat Bill Payment System

We all pay different types of bills regularly: electricity, mobile, DTH, insurance premiums, credit card bills etc. To give flexibility *(choice of channel and payment mode)* to customers, a biller enables multiple channels for bill payment.

Example: BESCOM (electricity) has various channels to collect bill payments:

- BESCOM website
- BESCOM collection counters
- Bangalore-One counters.
- Third party Apps/website: PhonePe, Google Pay etc.
- Your net-banking account

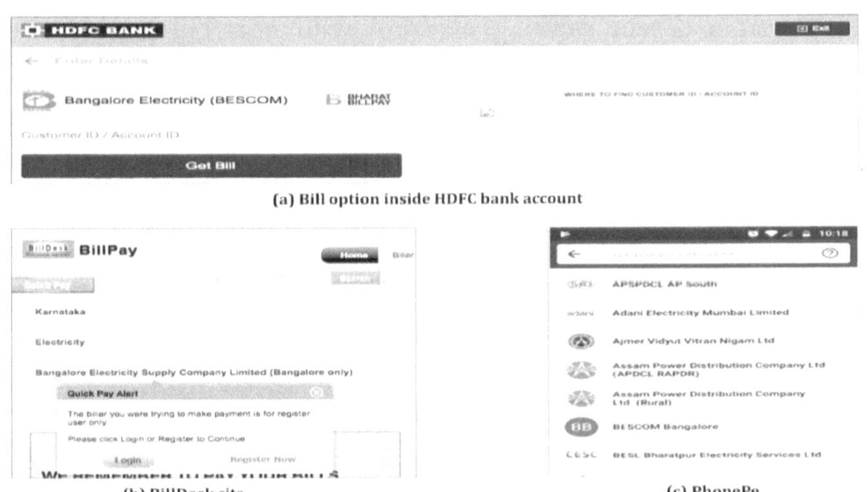

(a) Bill option inside HDFC bank account

(b) BillDesk site

(c) PhonePe

Of the mentioned channels, the last three are of our interest as it is interesting to know how a user can pay a utility bill on a 3rd Party Apps/ agents or through a bank account.

This is where BBPS (Bharat Bill Payment System) comes into picture.

Journey from EBPP to BBPS:

Before we jump into details of BBPS, let us understand its evolution.

In the early 2000s, BillDesk and TechProcess *(which was acquired by Ingenico and then acquired by worldline)* developed a bill payment platform called ***EBPP (Electronic Bill Presentment and Payment)*** platform.

On one side, billers *(utility companies, Telco, insurance, MF, card issuers etc.)* are integrated into the platform, and on the other side, agents *(third party Apps, banks etc.)* are on-boarded.

By integrating with the EBPP platform, agents could extend bill payment services to their customers.

EBPP platform providers charge a fee from the biller for every bill payment and share part of that fee with the agent. Agents bear the customer acquisition and payment processing costs.

EBPP was a decent working platform with neat bill payment and settlement flows, a commercial model, and revenue-sharing arrangements with agents. In fact, EBPP played an important role in making BillDesk India's leading online Payment Aggregator.

EBPP had few problems,

- A biller on-boarded with BillDesk will be available only for agents of BillDesk. If a biller is exclusively available with TechProcess then the agent has to do integration with TechProcess' EBPP platform as well.

- Only BillDesk and TechProcess dominated this space; other PAs couldn't enter the space

- No uniform frameworks for integration, refunds, and disputes
- Non-standard commercial models

Considering bill payments are the important payments and needs to be managed by uniform framework, NPCI launched the **BBPS** platform in 2016.

In 2020, NPCI floated a new subsidiary, NPCI Bharat BillPay Limited (NBBL) to promote BBPS.

In the next two sub-chapters, we will learn about BBPS, its participants, and commercial models.

17.A   BBPS - Participants and Operations

BBPS platform that brings billers and agents on a single platform. The platform allows customers to make various types of bill payments on 3rd party service providers' apps/websites/branches.

I. Participants of BBPS Platform:

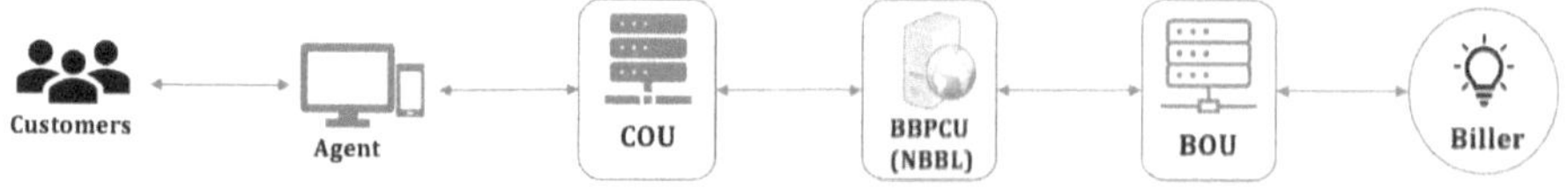

- **Billers**: Entities that generate bills such as utility companies, Telecom, DTH, Insurance companies, education institutes etc.

- **BBPCU (Bharat Bill Payment Control Unit)**: NPCI's subsidiary NBBL which manages BBPS platform, facilitates off-us transactions, and acts as clearing house *(along with RBI)*.

- **BBPOU (Bharat Bill Payment Operating Unit)**: RBI licensed entities *(banks, PAs, PSPs)* who can participate in the BBPS ecosystem.

  There are two types of Operating Units (OUs)

  – BOU (Biller Operating Unit): Entities that are licensed to onboard billers.

  – COU (Customer Operating Unit): Entities that are licensed to onboard agents.

- **Agent Institutes**: Entities that work with COUs to access the BBPS platform. Agents bring the customers to the platform through their App, website, or collection counters (e.g., Google Pay, HDFC Bank's net-banking portal, Bangalore One centers)

- **Customers**: Users *(retail and corporate)* who make the bill payment

- **Biller Aggregators**: Entities that aggregate billers to connect to BOU.

- **TSPs (Technology Service Providers):** Entities that are certified by NBBL to provide tech solutions to Agent Institutes, COUs and BOUs to integrate with BBPS platform.

II. Licensing:

Any entity that wishes to operate as BBPOU (BOU or COU or Both) needs to be licensed by RBI. In the beginning, it was expensive to be a BBPOU as net-worth requirement was Rs.100 Crore, and in May '2022, the net-worth requirement was reduced to Rs.25 crore.

As per Feb '2024, Master Directions of RBI, a licensed online PA can operate as BBPOU without need for a separate license but required to get acknowledgement from RBI before commencing business.

So, in summary, banks *(all scheduled commercial banks)*, licensed online PAs, and existing licensed COU/BOUs can operate as Operating Units (COU or BOU or both).

Escrow Account:

A COU and BOU can have separate Escrow A/C for the fund movements related to BBPS transactions.

- **COU Escrow a/c**: Opened by COUs to credit funds collected from the agents and debit toward biller related settlements. Any reversals related to disputed transactions or refund, and recovery of fees will be managed through this account.

- **BOU Escrow a/c**: Opened by BOUs to credit towards settlement of bill payments and debit to billers. Any reversals related to disputed transactions or refund, and recovery of fees will be managed through this account.

Note: Online PAs can have separate COU and/or BOU escrow accounts, apart from 2 escrow accounts of online PA business

III.   BBPS Working Details:

A.   Types of bill payments:

1. **Bill payment**: The bill is fetched from the biller and presented to the user to make the payment. User has to make full payment and before the due date.

   (Full payment = if bill amount is Rs.1000 then user has to pay Rs.1000, and not allowed to pay more or less)

2. **Quick Pay**: Bill fetch is not done. Users can make the payment *(any amount)* either before or after the due date.

Note: Whether bill payment is allowed post due date, late bill payment fees, whether partial bill payment is allowed - these are part of biller configuration and are agreed between BOU and the biller during biller onboarding stage.

B.   Types of transaction flows:

- **On-Us transaction**: Cases where the biller and agent belong to the same BBPOU. Here BBPOU confirms the payment status and moves the funds from agent to biller without involvement of BBPCU i.e., NBBL.

- **Off-Us transaction**: Cases where biller and agent are with different BBPOUs. Here BBPCU facilitates the bill payment and acts as clearing house to move money from the agent to the relevant BBPOU who in turn will settle funds with the biller.

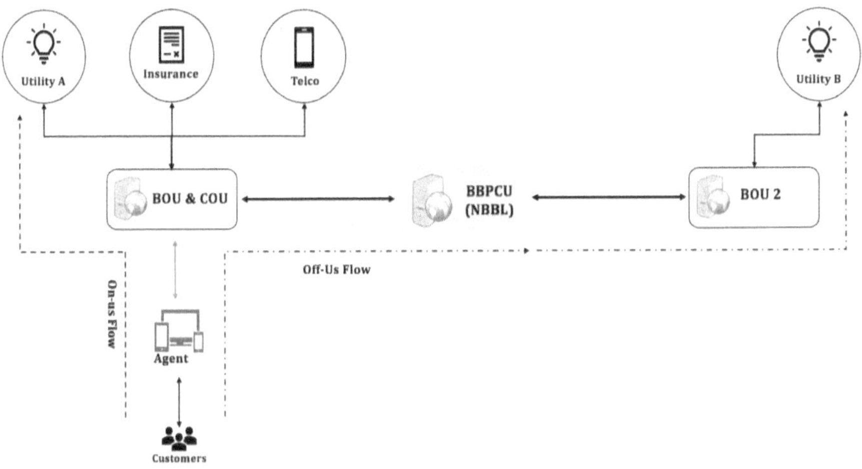

C. **Bill Payment Process:**

Let's consider an Off-Us flow and biller works on 'bill payment model'.

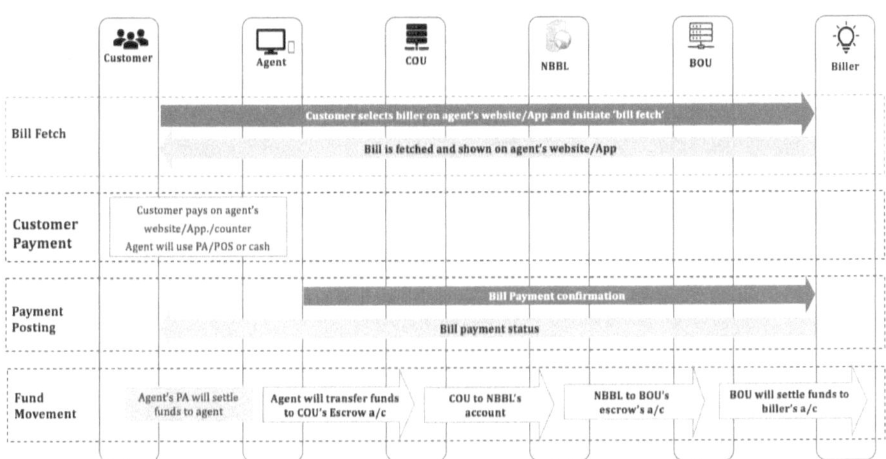

1. **Bill Fetching and payment:**

   - Customer visits agent's website/app/physical counter

     Note: Customer registration on agent site is not part of BBPS process

   - Customer selects the biller and initiates 'bill fetch'.
   - Customer will be presented the bill and due amount.
   - Customers will make the payment using cards, UPI, or cash at the counter.

     Note: Agents has to partner with PA/acquiring bank to facilitate online payment

2. **Payment Posting:**

   - Once the payment is successful, the agent will communicate it to COU.
   - COU informs status to NBBL → BOU → the biller.
   - Biller marks the bill as 'Paid'.
   - 'Bill Paid' status is communicated to user via BOU → NBBL → COU → Agent.

3. **Fund Movement:**

   - COU receives the bill posting report from NBBL, and COU shares it with the agent.
   - Agent's account → COU's Escrow account → NBBL (RBI) → BOU's Escrow a/c → Biller's a/c. *(This fund movement happens few times in a day).*

     Note: Agent receives funds from its PA/Banks partners (This is not part of BBPS flow)

D. **Commercial Model:**

- **BBPCU** earns a flat fee on all off-us bill payment. Fee varies for different sectors (e.g., Rs.0.20 per bill of utility)

- **COU** receives a fixed fee or percentage fee for every bill paid *(e.g., Rs.2.50 for online and Rs.5 to Rs.25 per bill for offline i.e., cash)*

- **BOU** earns a flat fee or percentage fee from the biller for every bill paid *(finalized during the biller on-boarding)*

- *Note: Simple math suggests that BOU should charge the biller a fee above COU fee + NBBL fee to make profit (but generally this won't happen)*

- **Agents**: COU will have a revenue sharing arrangement with agents (50:50, 60:40 etc.).

  Note: Agent bears all the costs *(customer acquisition, PA's MDR, or cash management fees)* and they earn a small fee. And also, RBI explicitly doesn't allow agents to charge convenience fees to customers *(for most of the bill categories)*. So, you can conclude that agents operate on thin margins *(if at all)*.

Closing Remarks

The grand idea of BBPS is to bring all types of billers such as utilities, insurance, mutual fund, FASTag, credit card, loan repayment, education fees, subscription fees, mobile recharge etc.

Although mobile prepaid recharges category is available on BBPS, agents do direct partnership with Telcos *(better commissions)*. And RBI may curb such bilateral partnerships.

RBI is pushing for all types of bill payments under BBPS umbrella. B2B payments *(corporate card to vendor payout)*, rent payment, and credit card bill payments are/will be moved under BBPS.

17.B BBPS - Special Solutions

Let's talk about two more interesting things about BBPS platform.

I. UPMS

By virtue of BBPS, I can pay bills via third-party Apps. Let's assume that I paid the bill using Google Pay, and then next month I used PhonePe. Then every month, both these Apps will send me an alert that a new bill is available for payment.

This is one of the drawbacks of BBPS.

- Each Agent *(PhonePe and Google Pay)* fetches the bill and sends a notification to the user.

- An Agent *(Google Pay)* will not get to know if the user has paid the bill via another COU's Agent *(PhonePe)*

So, the existing BBPS' presentment model burdens the billers' system as every agent will call API to fetch bills. Also, leads to bad user experience as multiple agents will send notifications to users.

Remedy for this problem is **UPMS (Unified Presentment Management System)**

The UPMS provides the centralized presentment platform where UPMS fetches the bill (one-time), and then agents (of COUs) can fetch it from UPMS.

Once the bill is paid through an agent, it is marked as paid, and other agents will know *(via status check API)* that the bill is paid, and they can avoid sending notifications.

UPMS will also allow users to set-up the mandate (e.g., UPI AutoPay) for recurring bill payments.

II. BBPS for NRIs:

Everyone pays bills — even the Indians who are living abroad pay bills in India. It could be for them or for their families back home.

Now the users based outside India can make bill payment via BBPS.

At present, this facility is available with selected 'exchanges' in three countries: **UAE** (*Lulu Exchange in partnership with Federal Bank*), **Kuwait** (*Al-Muzaini Exchange*), **Oman** (*Musandam Exchange in partnership with Canara Bank*)

Note: 'Exchanges' are the licensed entities *(by their operating country)* that provide cross-border remittance service. These exchanges operate via physical branches as well as website/Apps. The migrant population is quite familiar with 'exchanges', and logically, it makes sense for an exchange to offer bill payment service.

Working: Bill-fetch and bill payment APIs will remain same as regular BBPS flow except the amount is shown in foreign currency

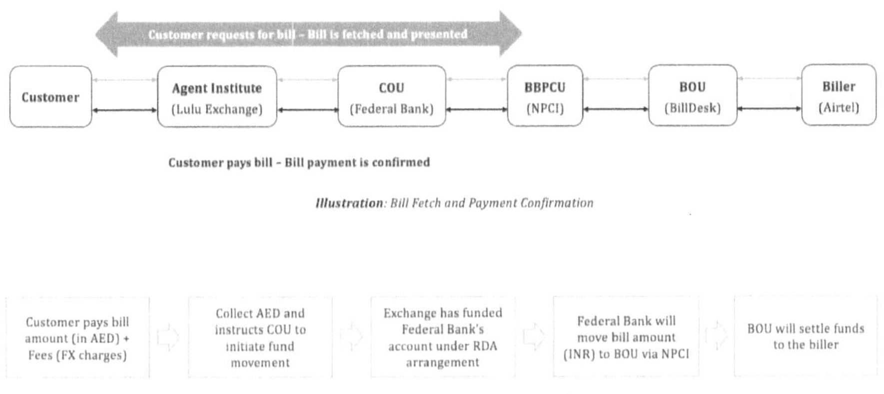

Illustration: Bill Fetch and Payment Confirmation

Illustration: Fund Movement

The exchange will have ***RDA (Rupee Drawing Arrangement)*** with the bank *(acts as COU)*.

The customer will make the payment in AED (local currency), and based on the exchange's instruction, the COU bank will move funds from RDA to Biller *(via NBBL and BOU)*

Bill payment facility for NRIs is a good use case, but 'fees' can be a road blocker.

Closing Remarks

BBPS provided an interoperable platform that created level playing fields to participants by providing easier access to billers and agents. Even in this so-called level playing field, BillDesk continues to dominate just like it did since the EBPP days. Introductions of TSPs and online PAs to participate in the BBPS ecosystem may change the status quo. Will it?

BBPS is one of the grand success stories. The platform has not only grown in India but is also available in other countries.

As we continue to pay bills, BBPS will continue to grow!

Chapter 18

TSP (Wrapper /Orchestrator)

Russian Nesting Dolls - one of my favorite toys.

Why?

Because they are a perfect analogy for India's payment ecosystem, one payment service provider using another provider, who, in turn, uses another one, and so on.

I have used this analogy multiple times throughout this book.

I am mentioning it here again because we will be talking about the outermost doll of payments nesting doll – i.e., Technology Service Provider (TSP) or wrapper or Orchestrator (*if you want to use a fancy word*).

TSPs (Wrapper/Orchestrator) have mushroomed across various areas of the payment ecosystem, such as online payments, payout, BBPS, and API Banking *(Banking as a Service)*.

Let's start the 'unwrapping'.

Basic Principle:

TSPs aggregate service providers and extend it to the merchants *(corporates, online commerce, neo-banks, LendingTech, consumer FinTech etc.)*.

A typical TSP is not involved in money movement (e.g., settlement)

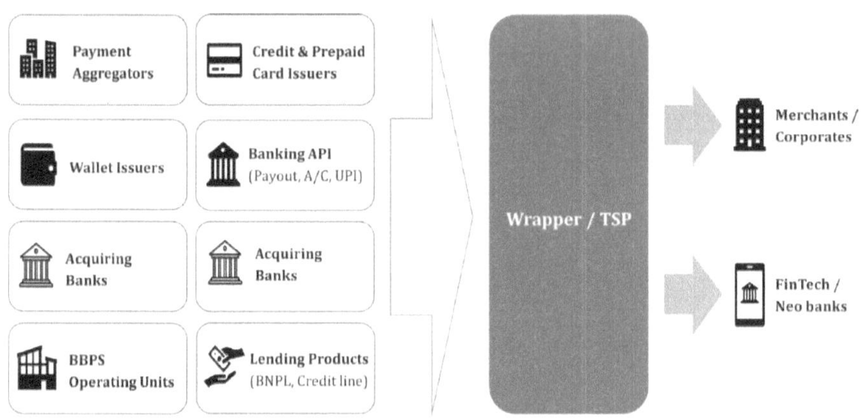

There are various types of TSPs that are specialized in a particular area.

Example: Online Payment - Juspay, BBPS - setu.co, Credit Card issuance - Hyperface.co

Benefits of TSPs:

- *For consumption side entities* (merchants, corporates, neo banks):

  Access multiple payment service providers on a single platform - Lesser integration effort

- *For provider side entities* (Banks, issuers etc.):

  Another low-cost distribution channel to promote their products and services

Drawbacks & Limitation of TSPs:

- All eggs in one basket: A TSP may become a single point of failure.

- Operations: A TSP unifies the integration (APIs) but if a merchant adds more payment service providers, then it will increase their operation efforts and related costs.

- Extra cost: Along with payment service providers charges, merchant has to bear additional charges of the TSP.

Commercial Model:

These companies can be creative in terms of pricing *(similar to SaaS companies)*:

- Percentage (%) of the transaction value (e.g.,0.10% of successful payments)
- Fixed fee per transaction *(e.g., Rs.1 per pay-out)*
- Hybrid mode *(percentage + fixed fee)*
- Slab wise fees
- Monthly fixed fee
- Feature wise charges *(e.g., Additional charges of card tokenization etc.)*

  Note: TSP works in invoicing model as they are not involved in money movement.

TSP Models:

A. **Payments**:

As you know, big or enterprise merchants integrate with multiple PAs, acquiring banks and other PSPs to reduce dependency on a single PA, increase payment coverage, command better pricing etc.

But this strategy will bring in additional challenges such as additional integration effort, effort related to transaction routing, reconciliation & operations, and unifying card token vault.

A TSP provides platform to solve these challenges (almost):

- PA/Acquiring Bank neutral card token vault (*no lock-in with any PAs*)

- Ease of managing PAs, Banks, and PSPs *(adding and removing)*

- Routing engine to manage route transactions to different PAs, banks, and PSPs based on merchant's preference to optimize success rate, availability, and commercials.

- Unified dashboard to manage multiple PAs/banks/PSPs.

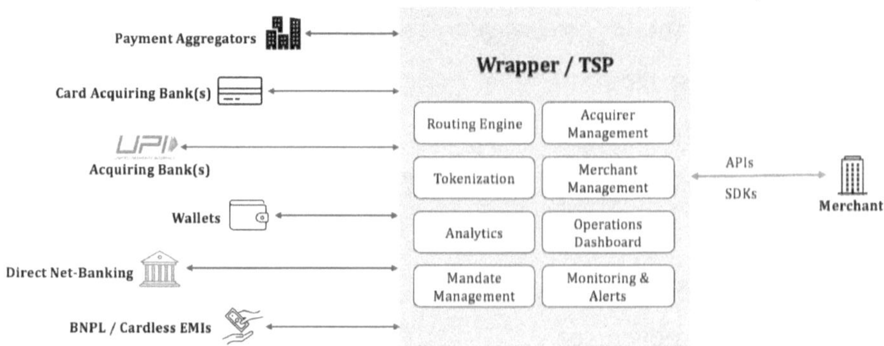

Players:

- Juspay is the market leader in this space.
- Other players - Nimbbl, DreamPay, Inai
- Online PAs such as RazorPay, Cashfree, and PayTM

B. **Others - BBPS, Banking API, Card as a Service**:

There are TSPs in different areas of the payments' ecosystem. A few notable ones:

- The open banking concept is based on TSPs, which allow an entity to offer banking products and services without being banks.

- Neo-banks, FinTechs, Lending Tech companies are either will build things or use TSPs.

- **Payouts**: As covered in *Chapter 15.B* - Payouts, a **Connected-Banking** payout is nothing but a TSP model.

- Merchant parks funds in their bank account but use APIs of PA/TSP to initiate a payout.

- Many PAs *(Cashfree, RazorPay etc.)* offer this solution.

- **BBPS (Bharat Bill Payment System)**: For decades, BillDesk has been acting as a TSP for banks to enable EBPP and then later BBPS.

- BBPS Master Directions of RBI (Mar-2024) officially allowed NBBL certified TSPs to build solutions for agent institutes and BBPOUs.

- **UPI**: Google Pay is a TPAP that operates in TSP model. Google Pay has partnered with multiple banks, and those banks process transactions and do settlement. Unlike PhonePe, Google Pay is not involved in the money movement.

  Now, with an online PA license, Google Pay may change its business model.

- **Credit Card as a Service (CCaaS)**: Many companies/ brands/merchants partner with banks to launch co-branded credit cards *(e.g., Citi-India Oil, ICICI-Amazon)*. Companies can directly work with banks or, alternatively, use TSPs that provide the CCaaS platform (e.g., Hyperface). A TSP can add tremendous value in such large-scale programs.

Considerations:

All said and done, a merchant *(corporate, neo bank, FinTech etc.)* must think whether it needs a TSP. So, as a merchant, I would consider the following points:

- **Need**: Do I really need to integrate with every service provider because I have options? Maybe not. If you don't need many service providers, then you may not need TSP.

- **Build Vs Buy**: If I really need to add many service providers/products and have shorter GTM plan then I will buy (go for TSP) and may be build it later.

- **Cost Optimization**: I will factor the additional cost of TSP on top of costs of payment service providers. But if I really need to take service from a TSP, then I will limit the scope to optimize the cost.

  Example: A payment orchestrator has great value for cards, but what is the value for net-banking? So why incur extra cost for routing net-banking?

- **All Eggs in one basket**: A TSP may become a single point of failure. So, I would still need a back-up *(hope for the best and plan for the worst)*

Closing Points:

TSPs are playing important role in the payment ecosystem. However, many types of TSPs do not come under any regulation or framework. An online PA has to adhere to hundreds of compliances and guidelines, whereas a payment orchestrator doesn't have to follow any specific rules *(except of PCI-DSS and tokenization)*.

If the country wants to build robust and secure payment ecosystem, all entities including TSPs/Orchestrators should come under 'some' oversight.

Recently, RBI/BBPS introduced certification of TSPs *(that can work with agents and BBPOUs)*. This is a good start. I presume, RBI will think about other significant TSPs or Orchestrators.

There is no silver bullet for solving a merchant's payment requirements. And as long as there are gaps, one or the other company will try to come up with a solution. Thus, keep adding more layers/dolls to our Payments Nesting Dolls

Chapter 19

Offers, Platform and Pay with Rewards

We all are familiar with offers such as discounts, cashback, and reward points.

Reward points are a little bit related to payments *(we will talk about it later in this chapter)* whereas cashback and discounts have nothing to do with payments, just that these things are closer to *'payments'*, so it is good to understand the modus operandi of these.

A. Basics of Offers

Firstly, why run offers?

Drive growth/sales/revenue, acquire new users, and create customer stickiness.

Who funds the offers?

"No free lunches" - there is a real or notional cost associated with these goodies and someone has to bear that cost. Broadly there are 3 models:

- Payment network funded: Card issuing bank, card network, wallets, and TPAPs.

- Merchant Ecosystem funded: Marketplace, seller, OEMs, or merchant's partners.

- Hybrid or co-funded: Where merchant/marketplace, vendor/seller/OEM and/or payment network players foot the bill *(E.g., Amazon-HDFC-Samsung)*

Types of offers:

- Cashback: User receives 'some money' back on qualified purchases
- Discount: User will pay 'less' while paying for qualified purchases
- Rewards: Token points for every qualified purchase

a. Cashback:

Assumption: 5% cashback up to Rs.100, transaction Amount: Rs.5,000

	Merchant Sponsored	**Bank/PSP Sponsored**
Transaction Working	User Pays: Rs. 5,000 User Receives Rs.100 later	User Pays: Rs. 5,000 User receives Rs.100 later
Cashback Working	Rs.100 is credited to 'closed loop' wallet (usually)	Rs.100 is credited to user's payment instrument
Financial Impact	From merchant's books (merchant will absorb the cost)	Rs.100 is borne by bank/PSP

In instant gratification cases where a purchase is done in real time and no refund (e.g., paying credit card bill on CRED), cashback is given in real-time.

But in the case of e-commerce purchases where the user can avail refunds, cashback is given only after the refund date is over.

b.   Discount:

Assumption: 5% discount, Max: Rs.100, Transaction Amount: Rs.5,000

	Merchant Sponsored	**Bank/PSP Sponsored**
Transaction Working	User Pays: Rs. 4,900	User Pays: Rs. 4,900
Discount Working	User pays Rs.100 less	User pays Rs.100 less Bank/PSP will pay Rs.100 to the merchant
Financial Impact	Merchant will absorb the cost	Rs.100 is borne by bank/PSP

Discounts get applied in real-time, so make sure the conditions are validated correctly.

c. Reward Points

Assumption: 2 points on Rs.100 spend, transaction Amount: Rs.5,000

Additional point: sponsor assigns monetary value to each point (E.g., 2 points = Rs.1)

	Merchant Sponsored	**Bank/PSP Sponsored**
Transaction Working	User Pays: Rs. 5,000	User Pays: Rs. 5,000
Rewards Working	100 points added to the user	100 points added to the user
Financial Impact	Rupees equivalent of reward points when redeemed (Rs.50 in this cases)	Rupees equivalent of reward points when redeemed (Rs.50 in this cases)

Let's assume the user accumulates 2000 points which is equal to Rs.1000

These points can be redeemed in following ways:

1. Use the points directly to purchase items *(usually done by merchants or few cards)*

2. Convert those points of gift cards/vouchers and use it on partner merchant's site *(usually by credit card issuers)*

3. Reward points can be used to pay outstanding credit card bill *(Amex allows it)*

Note: Reward points are removed if the purchase is refunded.

Conditions Applied*:

Offers come with conditions such as:

- **Purchase**: Minimum amount, maximum cap on offer amount, number of transactions in a particular duration, amount spent in a particular duration

- **Period**: Only for a certain duration, certain days, certain time of the day, etc.

- **Channel**: in-store, only on mobile App etc.

- **Product Specific**: Applicable only on select products (or SKU) or services.

- **Payment Mode**: Only on specific payment mode *(e.g., Not applicable on COD, only on HDFC credit cards, only on RuPay cards, etc.)*

Irrespective of the reason for running offers, sponsors *(merchant, bank, PSP, etc.)* have to factor in the financial impact of running these programs. Hence, there is a limit on how much a sponsor can spend, and these goodies dry out over a period.

That is the reason payment network sponsors *(banks, card networks, wallets, etc.)* run offers for large brands/merchants so that the impact is higher.

If you are big enough, then you really don't have to spend your money. Rather, make your partners spend for you. PhonePe started by burning its cash to run offers, but later moved to a model where other merchants spend money. In fact, PhonePe might be earning revenue by promoting other merchants' offers on the App.

Special mentions: Referrals and Gamification

- **Referrals:** If you refer a new user and once the new user completes 'qualification stage' *(e.g., complete 1st transaction, spend Rs.1000, etc.)*, you will get Rs. X or some goodies.

  This is one of the most popular ways to acquire new users, and almost every company does it, ranging from eCommerce and gaming to FinTechs.

- **Gamification:** People get bored of anything 'plain vanilla' *(without any disrespect to Vanilla ice cream)* — thus 'gamification', and there are many ways to do it.

- Milestone-based: Give some 'bump up or additional goodie' for reaching a milestone *(e.g., additional 5K reward points for spending Rs.50K in a month)*

- Scratch card: Without giving away a fixed amount every time, give a scratch card with a variable amount. Apparently, it triggers something in the brain when you win a 'small amount' once in a while rather than winning a 'super small' amount every time.

Gamification is designed to 'hook' users to spend more.

B. Offers Engine or platform:

Running offers is a complex work as the offers are dynamic and have a financial impact. To manage such complex and fluid conditions, merchants would need an Offer Engine that can (1) manage offers *(create, edit, delete)*, (2) validate conditions, (3) make sure people do not exploit them. It will be awesome if it could add a little bit of gamification.

Enterprise merchants build their own 'Offers Platforms', whereas others may not have the capabilities, time, or resources to invest in such platforms.

So, PAs/TSPs can provide such a platform to merchants as a value-added service.

A cherry on top would be if a PA/TSP can extend offers to merchants by partnering with banks or PSPs *(as many merchants may not have capabilities to get offers from banks)*.

The Offer Engine is a SaaS product. So, the platform provider can have creative pricing.

Typical commercials: (1) Integration fee (2) Fixed fee per month (3) usage based (4) commission from funding partners such as banks/wallets.

C.   Pay with Rewards:

Every large merchant has rewards (points) program where users earn rewards for their purchases.

As of today, I have 150 reward points from Bata, and I can use those reward points on my next purchase *(pay the rest using card, UPI etc.)*

What if I do not have plans to buy another pair of shoes from Bata? Then, eventually, those reward points will expire.

So, what if I could use those reward points to order ice cream on Swiggy?

Hmm… that's a nice (in fact, tasty) idea!

Similarly, credit cards and debit card issuers provide reward points. I can redeem those credit card reward points and buy a voucher of partner brands and then make a purchase. Banks use companies like Rewards360 to manage such reward programs.

But what if I want to redeem those points to pay the Airtel bill? *(outside the partner network)*

Thus, the concept, Pay with Reward points, wherein,

- A brand will allow a user to spend the reward points within the App and even on a partner network (E.g., Cred)
- A third-party FinTech can combine the reward points of various card issuers, and the user can redeem on the partner merchant network (E.g., Twid Pay)

Working:

- Every reward point has a monetary value. For example: 2 Reward points = Rs.1
- Reward issuer needs to be integrated with PA or TSP who can enable it on merchants.

Pay with rewards work like a wallet flow.

- On the checkout page, the user selects the pay with rewards option.

- The user authenticates (enter OTP) and can see the rewards and INR value.

- The user can pay using those reward points.

- Merchant/PA can provide a split payment option where the user can use reward points and another payment mode to pay the full amount.

Operations:

- MDR: % (percentage) of transaction value *(decided by reward issuer and PA/TSP)*

- Settlement: The merchant will receive the settlement amount on T+1 or T+2 days

- Refund: Reward points are credited back to user in case of refunds

Closing Remarks:

In a highly competitive market, customer stickiness or loyalty is extremely important. Offers such as reward points play an important role in creating customer stickiness.

Many large consumer brands or merchants wish to externalize the reward program where the reward points can be used on any merchant.

So, it would be interesting to see how the 'offers ecosystem' will evolve in the coming days!

Chapter 20

Value Added Service (VAS) Products

The payment business is quite strange - Although it is super big and ever-growing, the core payment solutions are getting commoditized, so PAs are struggling to make decent margins.

Also, switching cost for merchants is low, so PAs are always in a battle to defend their merchants.

So, how do PAs improve their margins or earn additional revenue while creating stickiness or raising exit barriers for merchants?

There is no one answer, and there is definitely no easy answer!

However, one of the ways is PAs/PSPs offer Value Added Services (VAS) that work in conjunction with core payments.

In the earlier chapters, we covered two such VAS products - **TSP or Orchestrator** *(Chapter 18)* and **Offers Engine** *(Chapter 19)*.

In this chapter, we will cover other VAS products.

A.   Smart Payment page:

PAs have been offering payment pages since the dawn of the PA business model. Non-Seamless or PA hosted pages are quite the norm among smaller merchants. Usually, large merchants build their own payment pages.

Payment pages have evolved - earlier, it was just a place to show available payment modes, but now, merchants can show saved cards, saved VPAs, preferred payment instruments, the instrument that was used for the last transaction, linked wallet etc.

The next stage of the payment page is making them smarter - where, based on the customer's spend pattern and available instruments, merchants will show relevant recommendations and retry options.

For example, if a customer's debit card transaction fails, then show the UPI as an alternative, or if the ticket size is more than Rs.2 Lakh, then do not show the UPI option. If a customer has 'saved' HDFC credit card, then show that there is a zero cost EMI facility on that card.

PAs/TSPs can leverage their platform-level data and merchant-specific data about the customer to derive highly personalized recommendations.

B.   Reconciliation Module

Reconciliation of funds is the process of matching of funds that a merchant expects to receive against the actual credit that a merchant receives from payment intermediaries (PA/PSP/banks).

A merchant who is using one PA will get one settlement file and one credit to its account. This is a simple use case and simple reconciliation process.

But the reconciliation becomes quite complex in case of enterprise merchants. Such merchants collect money in various ways:

- Through multiple PAs/banks/PSPs from various payment modes *(CC, NB, UPI etc.)*
- Through different solutions - PG, NACH, AutoPay, BBPS

And the commercial for each solution, payment mode, and payment partner varies.

Also, a merchant may have multiple sales channels - own website/app, cash on delivery, franchises, and resellers or partners.

Not done yet… we have to include other cases of fund movements.

- Disbursement cases such as payout to vendors, partners, and customers.
- Adjustments such as Refunds, chargebacks, fraud cases,
- Special cases such as self or partner-funded offers *(Cashback, discounts)*

Let's add some more complexity - Merchants may use multiple bank accounts to receive settlements of different business lines, channels, and solutions.

Now… think about reconciling such cases… It is complex. Isn't it?

That means, merchants put considerable effort in this activity; A reconciliation tool/module can be useful for merchants to save cost, achieve efficiency, and stop fund leakages.

A recon module should take inputs from various sources *(merchant's order management system, settlement files of PAs/PSPs, bank account statements)*, cover all possible scenarios, different file formats, different way of sharing files *(mail, SFTP)*, and then produce **the result** - how much money received, adjusted, disbursed and what is the balance in different bank accounts.

There are companies who provide reconciliation tool *(Fancy word - Reconciliation as a Service - RaaS)*. Examples: Recko (Acquired by Stripe), Cointab, Recon Art etc.

Considering reconciliation is closer to the payments, even PAs/TSPs can provide reconciliation modules to the merchants.

Everyone does reconciliation - banks, marketplaces, D2C brand, NBFC, omni-channel brands, WealthTech, FinTechs, Insurance companies, utility companies. So, the scope is big!

But remember, people pay for a solution when they think the problem **is important** and **not just big.** That is why most of the entities think that reconciliation is a people problem… meaning, it can be solved by adding more people to the job. That is one of the reasons the '***Reconciliation as A Service***' module may not fetch big money.

C.   Fraud and Risk Engine

Frauds are common in the online payments space - if not all, a few of these frauds can be stopped by doing risk checks.

Risk checks are already done at various levels by different entities such as issuing banks, acquiring banks, and Payment Aggregators.

Even a merchant can add a layer on top of it and perform risk checks at its end.

Risk engines are built on rules such as user location, users instrument, spending pattern, average ticket size, hot listed BINs, etc. And those rules keep refining, so the risk engine becomes robust.

Enterprise merchants' usually build these engines in-house, but definitely they may be interested in using the platform, which is built by a PA or FinTechs, if it reduces fraud cases.

FRM solution is ideal for eCommerce, Travel, and Gaming sectors.

D.   Chargeback Module

In ***Chapter 12.B*** (Chargebacks), we covered that chargebacks are quite cumbersome mainly because communication and information exchange happen over mails.

PAs have ticketing systems to manage these chargebacks efficiently.

What about the merchants?

Managing chargeback is equally cumbersome for merchants, especially those who use multiple PAs and Acquiring banks.

A good chargeback module should

- Log all chargebacks that received via mail; link them to respective sales orders.

- Manage proofs (complete, incomplete, send follow-up mails to internal teams)

- Send responses to appropriate PAs/Acquiring Banks

- Track the status (open, closed-in favor, closed-lost, pending, Arbitration etc.)

- Analytics and insights

Chargebacks directly impact the business numbers, so merchants may value chargeback platform.

E. RTO (Return to Origin) Protection

D2C brands sell products directly to consumers without using distributors or marketplaces.

Returns are quite high in the eCommerce (and, by extension, even in the D2C) sector. Returns can be due to customer cancellations, incorrect addresses, customer unavailability, or decline.

When a product is returned, a merchant not only loses the revenue but also incurs the cost. And the returns become more cumbersome for COD orders *(we covered this in **Chapter 4.F**)*

Many FinTechs, including PAs, have developed RTO protection solutions to reduce RTOs.

Smart logics are built to correct the address (based on past delivery status and geographical data). Also, COD options are not shown based on the user's cancellation history.

An RTO Protection service takes complete liability for financial losses due to returns. To provide the service, the RTO service provider charges a premium fee (3-4%).

So, the service provider's business runs on simple math: Fees earned on orders should be greater than losses due to returns. Tough!

To build a better RTO protection product, the service provider has to create a database of users and addresses, which is a time-consuming process, and the service provider may have to 'incentivize' merchants to share their customer's address details. Alternatively, the company can partner with third parties *(e.g., delivery companies or eCommerce marketplaces)* to get the data.

Note: There will be privacy concerns in sharing PII (Personal Identifiable Information) data

---

F.   SDKs - Bank page optimization and OTP Reading

Doing transactions on mobile app is a bit cumbersome

- Net-banking: Bank pages are not optimized *(meaning - page layout won't be mobile form factor compatible)*. So, the user has to expand pages and type the details.
- Cards: Memorizing 6-digit OTP and typing in

PAs and TSPs provide SDKs to solve these problems,

- Net-banking: Form factor compatible pages *(bank pages are rendered in a custom SDK browser)* so the pages become easily navigable.
- Cards: Auto-reading and auto-submitting of OTP

G. Merchant's Closed Loop Wallet:

Many eCommerce, Travel, and Gaming merchants have a closed loop wallet *(funds can be used only to purchase on that merchant's site).*

Mainly, the closed loop wallet is used to push the refund amount *(it is better than refunding to the source).* Also, merchants allow the user to load the wallet and use the balance to purchase *(a more seamless payment experience during transaction)*

Wallet may look like a simple product, but it is not, as a wallet function involves complex processes such as user life cycle management, ledger *(to manage balance)*, and fund movement.

A PA/FinTech can provide a platform to merchants to manage these complexities.

H. BaaS Products:

We will cover BaaS (Banking as A Service) in detail in *Chapter 23.*

A PA can offer Banking Products *(current account, corporate credit card, credit)* to its merchants by partnering with banks.

Payment Solutions *(PG, Recurring payment, payout)* combined with BaaS can be a great value proposition for small and medium size merchants.

By providing such products, PA will earn revenue from banks *(referral fee)* and also create stickiness for the merchant.

I. Onboarding Solutions:

Merchant onboards customers before providing services. In some cases, it is a simple process of validating mobile and/or mail id *(e.g., eCommerce or travel site),* but in some cases, the customer's KYC details as well as bank details are verified *(e.g., investment, insurance, lending, gaming).*

A Payment Aggregator can offer **'customer onboarding'** solutions to merchants,

- Bank a/c validation solution *(covered in **Chapter 15.C)***

- Customer KYC (PAN and Aadhar Validation) - PA can partner with registered KYC service providers to offer these services.

Many merchants *(e.g., marketplaces)* onboard vendors from whom they avail services. The above-mentioned onboarding solutions can be extended to such cases as well.

Closing Remarks:

I have covered a few big VAS products, but there can be many more products that a PA can build *(e.g., payroll management, ERP for Institutes, receivable platform for B2B companies).*

This sounds good on paper, but very few PAs are able to build successful VAS products *(created substantial revenue stream).* Nonetheless, in this highly competitive payment business where margins are super thin, such VAS products can definitely add some revenue and create some stickiness.

Chapter 21

Offline Payment Solutions

India's payments story is incomplete without offline / in-store payments.

In this chapter, I will touch upon POS (Point of Sales), ePOS/Soft POS and QR Codes

21.A   POS (Point of Sales)

These are the machines provided by acquiring banks *(E.g., HDFC, SBI, etc.)* or offline payment aggregators *(e.g., Pine Labs, PayTM, mSwipe, World Line)* for processing of cards at stores.

Different types of POS devices *(Source: Internet)*

a. **Acceptance**: POS predominantly works on cards - Credit cards, debit cards and open loop prepaid cards of Visa, MasterCard, RuPay. POS machines need to have additional capabilities to process Amex or Sodexo cards.

Entities Involved:

- Offline Payment Aggregators: Entities that configure different acquiring banks and install POS machines at stores; Offline PAs do settlement to merchants.

- Example: Worldline, Pine Labs, Innoviti, etc.

- Acquiring Bank: Bank that process card transactions.

- POS OEM: Companies that manufacture the POS machines (Worldline, Verifone)

- Issuing Bank: The bank that has issued the card (E.g., ICICI, HDFC)

- Card scheme: Card network (Visa, MasterCard, RuPay)

- Merchant: Entity that is collecting the funds (e.g., stores)

- Cardholder: Person who is using the card

UPI Acceptance: UPI QR (dynamic) can be shown on a POS device, and users can scan & pay using their TPAPs/UPI Apps. To facilitate UPI payments, offline PAs will partner with UPI acquiring banks.

b. **Transaction**: Transaction processing works almost the same as online payments, with a major exception. Even POS transactions need to adhere to 2FA/AFA, but instead of OTP, cardholder to enter the PIN *(Personal Identification Number – Usually 4-digits)*.

In a nutshell, POS transactions have three steps:

- Authentication: PIN is verified post machine reads the card successfully

- Authorization: Transaction is approved by the issuer bank after post risk checks

- Capture: The funds start moving (Issuer → network → Acquiring bank → offline payment aggregator → merchant)

In online payments, capture is done automatically *(Except in case of Pre-Authorization flow)* but in case of POS the storekeeper will have to press a button on the machine to capture the transactions.

c. **Transaction Types**: There are three different ways POS machine reads the card:

- **Swipe**: Card's magnetic stripe is swiped in the machine

- **Insert**: Card's EMV chip is inserted in the slot of the machine

- **NFC** *(Near Field Communication)* based: Card is tapped on the machine. An amount less than Rs.5,000 doesn't require 2FA (PIN).

  NFC works in close range (5mm) and NFC forum intends to increase it to 30mm.

Note: A cardholder can set-up limit on maximum debit amount and can have separate limit for NFC based ones (<=Rs.5000)

d. **Commercials**: POS transactions are called CP - Card Present *(user is present at payment point)*, whereas online transactions are called CNP - Card Not present *(user is remote)*.

CP transactions are less risky *(as the user is present at point of sales)*, so POS transactions have lower commercials compared to CNP (online) transactions.

For example: MDR for eCommerce merchants is 1.80%, whereas the MDR for in-store POS will be 1.20% *(Remember, MDR is risk adjusted)*.

Merchants not only bear the MDR but also may be charged one-time installment fees and monthly maintenance fees.

e. **UPI QR on POS**: POS are predominantly designed for card acceptance. Today, POS also supports UPI as merchants can show dynamic QR on the POS screen that can be scanned by any TPAP/UPI App.

Different types of POS:

- **mPOS**: These are lightweight POS machines that can be carried in the pocket. Although the working of mPOS is the same as regular POS because of cost and convenience *(of carrying)*, these are popular among eCommerce delivery and smaller stores.

- **Wear & Pay**: This is the new payment channel. The card is tokenized in a device *(key chain, wristwatch, or mobile App or even a ring)*. Customers can simply tap it on the POS to make an NFC-based contactless payment of up to Rs.5000.

- A few of the entities that have already launched such programs: Axis bank, SBI + Titan Watch, Transcorp, Samsung

21.B   Soft POS (ePOS)

As the name suggests, these are hardware-less POS solutions *(or at least they can be claimed as that)*. Instead of the hardware, a mobile SDK is used, and this SDK can be integrated into a mobile app *(for delivery person or store owner/manager)* to accept payments. ePOS is a good solution for converting Cash on Delivery (COD) to 'Payment on Delivery'.

Let's say, you have ordered something on COD. The delivery person will reach home, and then you can make payment in Cash.

But what if the delivery person gives you the option to make payment using a card or UPI?

A typical ePOS product does few things:

1. Sending payment link: A delivery person can send a link to the customer. Once a customer clicks on the link, a payment page will open where the customer can select cards, net-banking, UPI, or wallet to do a regular online transaction.

2. Dynamic UPI QR: Generate dynamic UPI QR *(the amount is embedded in QR),* and customer can scan & pay using her TPAP/UPI App (e.g., Google Pay or PhonePe)

3. Tap and Pay: The new development in this area is embedding ePOS SDK with NFC capabilities so the user can simply tap the card on the delivery person's app.

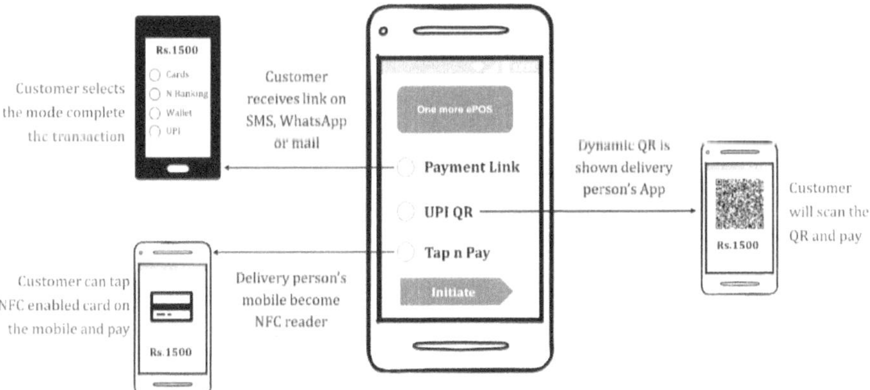

21.C UPI QR Code

How to convert COD to online payment? Solution: QR Code!

How to facilitate agent collection? Solution: QR Code!

Are people scared to touch ATM buttons? Solution: QR Code!

QR Code is like the 'Yoga' of the payment world; for any problem, it is "the solution".

If you are in India, then you wouldn't have missed these QR codes, which are pasted in almost every store by companies like PayTM, PhonePe, AmazonPay, BharatPe, and a few banks.

There are three types of QRs:

- Proprietary: Works only through QR issuer's App *(e.g., PayTM 'wallet' QR)*

- UPI QR: Supports only UPI through any TPAP/UPI App (e.g., PhonePe, PayTM)

- Bharat QR: Supports Visa, MasterCard and RuPay along with UPI.

  Note: UPI QR/Bharat QR also supports eRupee (CBDC) payments

Furthermore, QR can be static and dynamic.

- **Static:** User has to enter the amount; no expiry timer; suitable for stores

- **Dynamic:** Amount is pre-populated; dynamic QR will have expiry time; easy to reconcile as linked to order; suitable for online payment cases

*Note: UPI QR payment is a push / intent flow. We have covered it in **Chapter 4.E (UPI)**.*

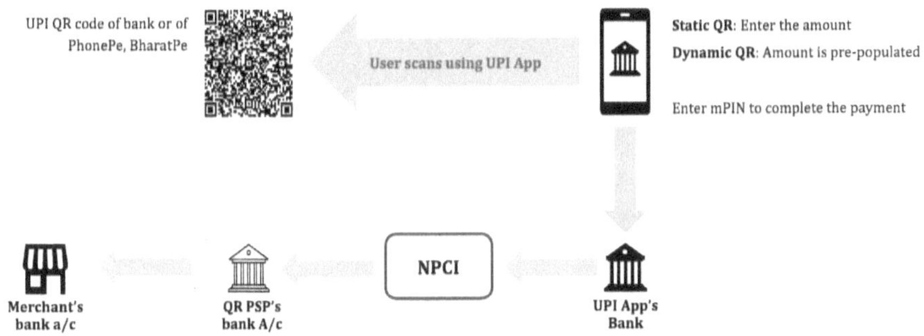

Sound of Payment: PayTM is the first company to provide a sound box that announces the amount paid *(small but yet huge creative innovation!)*. This is quite useful for shopkeepers. PayTM also made handsome revenue on these soundboxes. Now, every other QR provider has sound box solution that does announcement multiple languages and in celebrity voices!

Closing Remarks

As expected, after online Payment Aggregators, offline payments will be regulated. Non-bank entities that want to operate offline payment aggregation (PA-P) are expected to get authorization from the RBI. *Refer to Chapter 5.A*

Offline transactions outweigh their counterparts in online space. The majority of offline transactions are still in cash. India will be a truly digital economy if we convert a substantial part of cash transactions to digital. That's why offline/in-store payment solutions are important.

Lack of low cost and efficient infrastructure was always a problem in increasing the coverage of digital payments in offline space, but QR changed the scenario dramatically. Today, we have ~270 million QRs (UPI QR and Bharat QR) compared to ~8 POS. Isn't that something?

Thanks to UPI, we have nailed the formula for building a strong, economical, and efficient offline payment system. We are not done yet; we have a long road ahead!

Chapter 22

Sectors – Industries

Every sector has different working models, and so are the payments in those sectors. Even merchants in the same sector work differently.

It is important to understand how each sector works and requirements w.r.t. payments.

Here are a few of the top sectors and sub-sectors.

Sector	Sub-sectors
eCommerce	Marketplace, Apparels, Cosmetics, Furniture, Jewelry, Electronics
Travel	Operators, OTAs, Package tours, Taxis, ERPs
Healthcare	Hospitals, ePharma, Diagnostics, Telemedicine, Appointments, Omni-Pharma
Gaming	Fantasy Sports, Rummy, Poker, Others
Entertainment	Movie tickets, Multiplex, event ticketing
Digital Content	OTT, Music, Audio Books, Magazines, News Papers
Hyperlocal	Grocery, Q-Commerce, Daily Needs
Logistics	Long haul, local, eCommerce Delivery
Rentals	Vehicle, Furniture
Education	Institutes, EdTech, ERPs, Examinations, Trainings
Insurance	Insurer, Web Aggregator, Broker, TPA
Investment	Stockbrokers, MF/Bond Distributor, AMCs, Chit Funds, Nidhi Banks, Advisories
Hospitality	Aggregators, Hotels, Resorts
Utilities	Telco, DTH, Broadband, Recharge

Lending	NBFC, Digital Lending Apps, Invoice Discounting Platform, LMS
Government	Utilities, Institutes, Urban Local Bodies, services
FinTech	Consumer Tech, Neo-Banks, Kirana Tech
Food & Beverage	Delivery aggregator, Restaurant food delivery, Food Processors
Miscellaneous	DMT, SaaS, Rent Payment, Apartment Fees, credit card bill payment

Before we dive into a few of the prominent sectors and workings of payments in those sectors, let's do a quick recap of what we learnt about merchant payments.

Summary: Payment Strategy for Merchants

A. Payment Page / Checkout Page:

We covered different types of payment pages *(Chapter 8.A)*.

Depending on the use case, merchants should decide whether to use PA's payment page or build their own payment page. Think of an overall checkout experience.

Few suggestions:

- Show preferred payment mode on the top.
- Show saved cards, save UPI and other payment methods.
- Show wallet balance *(if wallet linking is available)*
- Perform eligibility check for EMI and BNPL products.

B. Payment Coverage:

Do not add a payment method just because it is available in the market. Also, think about how many PAs, acquiring banks, wallets, or alternate credit products do you need to have optimal coverage of payment methods.

Example: If you are a food delivery merchant, then you won't need EMIs, but if you are selling airline tickets then EMIs will be a good sales booster

Merchant has to develop capabilities to handle API calls uniformly. APIs of different PAs and PSPs have different parameters; some are mandatory, and some are optional *(e.g., the mobile number of the customer)*. Similarly, response codes and error codes also vary from PA to PA.

Yes, a TSP/Orchestrator can solve many of these problems, but do you need one?

*Please refer **Chapter 18** for details*

C. Flavors of Payment Flows:

In **Chapter 9.A** *(Transactions)*, we touched upon various flavors of card, UPI, and wallet transactions. So, decide on payment flows needed.

- For Cards: Standard card flow or direct OTP flow, skip-CVV flow, or take it to next level with de-coupled flow.
- In case of wallets, standard re-direction flow or Link & Pay flow.
- For UPI: Intent flow if you have more transactions on mobile App.

Note: Multiple flow means you should be ready to do different integrations

D. Mobile Strategy:

If mobile is the dominant channel, then enable mobile-friendly features that can provide better user experience and performance.

Few suggestions:

- Save payment instrument details *(e.g., card tokenization or VPA)*
- Intent and/or in-app flow for UPI

- Auto-Reading and auto-submitting of OTP
- Optimize Net-banking pages.
- UPI Plug-in *(if you are up to it)*

PAs/TSPs provide SDKs for such features. Plan carefully about your mobile strategy, as adding different SDKs will increase the size of your app, you may get stuck with the PA/TSP who gave the SDK, and your users may have to update the App *(whenever you make significant updates)*.

E. Card Vault Strategy:

Do you want your users to tokenize (save) cards?

Think about whether you have a genuine use case to save customers' cards. If not, then avoid it as you may get locked-in with one PA.

If you are vaulting cards, then with whom?

In **Chapter 8.B** *(Save Card or Card tokenization)*, we covered various entities *(merchant, PAs, TSP)* that can tokenize cards. Understand pros and cons of each model and then proceed forward.

F. Success Rate:

Success Rate 'holds' different value for different businesses/merchants. We have covered these details in **Chapter 10.A** *(Understanding Success Rate)*.

Firstly, decide on the way you want to measure the success rate. Do you want to include user drop-out cases? Do you include issuer bank downtimes or not?

Use a uniform formula to measure SR across all PAs/TSPs.

Merchants can work with PAs/TSPs to improve the SR. Those details are covered in **Chapter 10.C**.

Push for higher Success Rate but be practical!

G. Routing Logic:

Define your objective *(Success Rate, cost, volume commitment, etc.)* and build the routing logic accordingly.

We have touched upon various routing logics in ***Chapter 9.B (Transaction Routing)***

Remember, routing logic is not a sprint but a marathon, so keep fine-tuning the routing logic till you consistently achieve the results.

H. Commercials & Settlement:

Your settlement model depends on your commercial model - whether you are on an upfront deduction, invoicing, or surcharge model.

Few PAs offer early or instant or priority settlement features, but this solution comes at an additional fee. If there is a need for liquidity, then you should opt for the same.

Settlement Reconciliation: Every new PA/PSP will give you a new settlement file. So, more the PAs/PSPs, then more settlement files. Your finance team will not be happy handling so many files. Think of automating settlement reconciliation

I. Refund Management:

As it is, the refund is complex and expensive, but it is extremely crucial. Build a decent refund management system to track refunds.

If you are ready to spend a few additional bucks, then use 'instant refund' solutions.

J. Chargeback Management:

With more payment providers, your chargeback management will become cumbersome. As chargebacks are managed over mail, you need system to manage chargebacks of multiple parties efficiently.

Make sure the proofs (product/service delivery and refunds processed) are available to defend against chargebacks.

K. Dashboards:

Every PA/PSP will give a dashboard. So, if you have five payment service providers, then you will end up looking at five dashboards.

You may want to think of unifying the dashboard.

L. Recurring Payment Solutions:

If you have recurring payments use cases, then select the solution that fits your business model, as every solution has certain advantages and few limitations.

Example: If the average debit amount is more than Rs.15,000, then NACH is the option. If you want real-time debit status, then SI on Cards and UPI AutoPay are better.

*Read **Chapter 13** (Recurring Payment Solutions) for details.*

M. Other Payment Solutions/Features:

There are various other payment solutions such as Virtual Account solutions, Payout, Payment links, or QR codes. Implement those based on your business cases.

Example: Payment links - for sending insurance renewal payment reminder

----

Points to consider while changing your existing Payment Aggregator:

1. **Integration Efforts:**

    Integrating a new PA is an effort. And things may get a bit complicated if you have to replace one SDK with another.

Switching from one PA to another not only involves tech/engineering but also impacts your operations and finance.

Different PAs may follow different processes *(E.g., different settlement file format)*, so you have to realign your operations as per new PAs product, process, and people.

2. **Card/Token Vault**:

If you have tokenized your customers' cards with PA <ABC>, then while switching to PA <PQR>, you need to migrate the vaulted cards as well because your customers will panic if they do not see their vaulted cards.

However, the problem is that, at present, tokenization guidelines do not allow migration of tokens.

Here are some options:

- Start afresh *(check the total number of saved cards, active users, and expired cards and decide whether you want to start afresh)*
- Use PA <ABC> to process already saved cards and save new cards with PA <PQR>
- Use your own vault *(become token requestor)* or TSP/wrapper's vault.

3. **Refund Management**:

Let's say the transaction was processed using PA <ABC>, and you removed it later. You cannot mark 'refund' for that particular transaction *(as integration doesn't exist)*, and even if you can mark refunds through the dashboard, then the PA <ABC> cannot process the refund as there are no settlements to adjust.

Alternatives: Merchant can transfer funds to PA's account for manual processing or PA can hold 'some' funds for certain duration to adjust any future refunds *(and later release the funds)*

4. **Chargeback Management:**

If a chargeback is raised, then the merchant needs to respond within a specific period to defend it. Just because a merchant has plugged off a PA doesn't mean the merchant's obligations are over. If PA loses money because of chargebacks, then they can recover from the merchant, and if the merchant doesn't oblige then PAs can very well initiate a legal process against the merchant.

Alternatives: Defend chargeback with proper proof or deposit funds to PA's account for valid chargeback cases.

PA can hold 'some' funds up to 180 days to cover any chargebacks of 'high-risk' merchants *(and later release the funds)*.

Closing Remarks

Every design and every flow contribute towards a seamless user journey, better performance, and a higher success rate.

The best payment pages, payment flows, and routing logics are not implemented in a week or a month but took years to reach where they are today. So, you can start working on it right now!

That was the recap... Let's talk about few important sectors

22.A   eCommerce

eCommerce — one of the most visible sectors with small, medium, big, and gigantic merchants with different types, flavors, and business models.

Today, without stepping outside the house, I can buy things that I need, things that I don't need, and things that no one needs - all thanks to eCommerce!

There are various types of eCommerce companies:

- Own Inventory Vs. Marketplace *(merchant sells inventory of other vendors)*

- Horizontal *(sell all types of products e.g., Flipkart)* Vs. Vertical (sell specialized product e.g., pepperfry.com that sells furniture)

- Sell to customers i.e., B2C *(e.g., Amazon),* or sell to businesses i.e., B2B *(e.g., Udaan)*

Each of these models is complex and fascinating when it comes to their inventory management, sellers, logistics, returns, etc. We are not here to talk about those things or their profitability model *(if they have one!!!)* but to talk about our area of interest - how the money is moved.

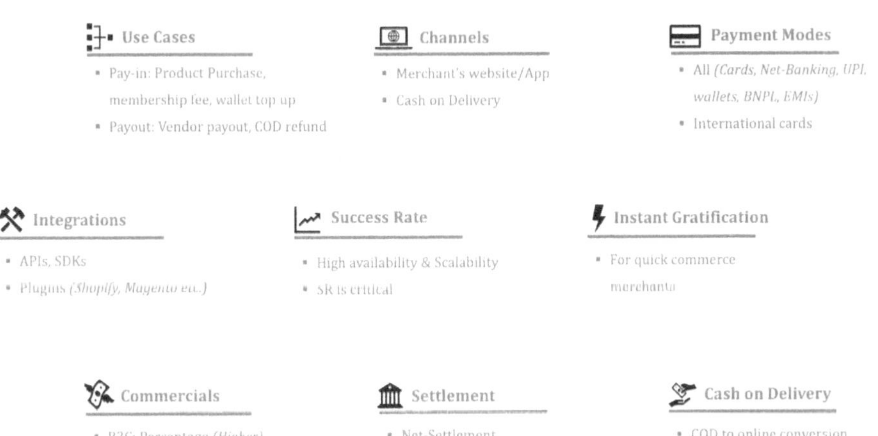

1. **Use Cases**:

   - Pay-in: To purchase products or wallet top up or membership fees.

     Solutions: Standard PA, recurring payments (*extreme low relevance*)

   - Payout: Vendor payout, delivery personnel payout, COD refunds

     Solutions: Payout solutions

2. **Channels**:

   - eCommerce merchants sell on all channels - website, m-site, and mobile Apps.

   - Payments happen both online (website/App) and in cash (Cash on Delivery cases).

     Note: If mobile is the most dominant channel, then the merchants should have mobile-centric solutions such as SDK for auto-reading OTP, UPI intent, card tokenization, etc.

3. **Payment Modes**:

   - All modes - CC, DC, NB, UPI, wallets, alternate credit products *(More the merrier)*

   - International card acceptance *(if applicable)*

     Note: Practicality *(order value, fitment, commercials & operation effort)* dictates whether payment mode is enabled.

4. **Payment flow & Integration**:

Customer acquisition cost is high, and once the customer decides to purchase, the payment flow should not create any hindrance/hassle for the user to complete the transaction. So, the checkout page, position of payment modes, save card option, placeholder for coupons, etc. - all these things matter.

- Merchant expects the PAs to support flows as per their requirement.
- eCommerce platform plugins (e.g., Shopify, WooCommerce)
- Considering mobile is an important channel so they would require mobile SDKs.

5. Performance & Success Rate:

- Availability: Payment systems should work every time and all the time
- Scalability: Payment systems should handle the transaction spikes *(transactions tend to spike when merchants run promotional sales campaigns)*
- Success Rate: Super crucial as a failed transaction can be considered as loss of revenue since the user may defer the purchase or might purchase from another merchant *(unless you are selling something exclusive)*

Note: Before jumping into analyzing the success rate, merchants need to factor in their customer demography as well as intent of purchase.

*Refer **Chapter 10.C** for more details on Success Rate.*

6. Instant Gratification:

There is a possibility that some transactions go into a pending state. So, the merchant would want to know the status *(Success or fail)* to take appropriate action. *(If success - shop, if failed - No shipment).*

A merchant who has the liberty to ship later can wait, but in case of quick commerce, where delivery is done within hours, it is important to know the final status near real-time.

7. **Commercials**:

- B2C: Percentage of transaction value *(higher than insurance, utility sector)*

- B2B: Enjoys flat fees on net-banking from majority of banks.

- Commercial model: Generally, for B2C merchants, upfront deduction where MDR is deducted from the settlement amount. B2B merchants may pass the MDR to the payer.

Note: Refer **Chapter 7.A (PA/PG Charges or MDR)** for more details

8. **Settlement**:

- In case of 'upfront deduction' model, merchant receives net-settlement.

- Typically, a standard settlement cycle of T+1/T+2 days. PAs do offer 'early-settlement or on-demand settlement' for additional charges.

- Marketplaces receive settlement in their nodal account, then payout to vendors and keep commission amount. Smaller marketplaces may opt for 'split settlement' solution where vendor's share is directly settled to vendor's account and commission to marketplace's account.

9. **Refund Management**:

Refunds are an important reason for the growth of eCommerce. A user can confidently buy if she knows that product can be returned easily. However, refunds are a big hassle and expensive for merchants.

- Expensive: E.g., @1.80% MDR, merchant would bear Rs.21.24 PA charges for products worth Rs.1000. When the refund is done, then merchant not only loses Rs.1000 worth sale but will also lose Rs. 21.24 extra as customer would want the entire Rs.1000 back.

(Plus, delivery and reverse logistic costs)

- Hassle: Refunds do not have a clear TAT as it may vary from 1 day to 5 days or more, and it is not possible to know the status of refund credit. Such uncertainties burden merchant's customer support teams.

An alternative to standard refund is Instant refunds, which can be done by processing refunds via Visa Direct, MasterCard Money Send, UPI, IMPS and NEFT rails.

Another way is having a closed-loop wallet - A refund amount is added to the wallet. It is much faster, and customers can use that amount to purchase from the same merchant.

10. Cash on Delivery (COD) & Refund:

All said and done about online payments. Still, cash (on delivery) is the king.

COD helped eCommerce companies grow in India. Consumers prefer cash for various reasons *(lack of knowledge, comfort, lack of trust, security concern, etc.)*. That is the reason nearly or more than half of eCommerce transactions go through COD. Handling cash is difficult, and refunding is more complex.

Merchants try to convert COD (Cash on Delivery) transactions to POD (Payment on Delivery) by sending payment links, ePOS, mPOS, or static QR or dynamic QR solutions.

Refunding COD transactions is problematic as merchants can't send a person to return the money to the customer. The merchant will have to collect the customer's a/c details or UPI Id/UPI number and then transfer the money using NEFT, IMPS, or UPI rails.

11. Payouts:

There are 2-3 different types of payouts. (1) COD Refunds, (2) Seller Vendor payout, (3) Delivery person incentive payout.

A merchant uses payout solutions from banks or FinTechs or PAs to do these disbursements.

Closing Remarks

Indian eCommerce is an amazing story. It all started with Indiaplaza in 1999 (Yes, 1999), and today, we have e-commerce companies of all types and sizes and with complex models that involve inventory & fund movement within and across borders.

We witnessed a consolidation in this sector, with 2-3 industry leaders and others creating their own niche space. Nevertheless, eCommerce market share is in the single digit of overall commerce. So, there is a growth opportunity for all types of players, provided they bring some value to the table.

Today, eCommerce has evolved in various business models, such as D2C (Direct to Consumer) and Quick Commerce. I will touch upon these sub-sectors in ***Chapter 22.I***.

22.B   Travel

Mankind invented the wheel in 3500 BCE and since then that wheel has been revolving. Today we have various modes of travel and when they say, 'the world has become smaller', they are quite right.

Once. my family traveled from Walldorf (Germany) to Venice (Italy) in a cab, bus, train, flight, and boat in a single day, yes, in a single day. Thanks to multiple transportation modes and online booking facilities.

Types of travel merchants:

- Operators: Companies that run the vehicles *(e.g., VRL, SpiceJet, IRCTC etc.)*

- OTAs (Online Travel Agents/Aggregators): Companies that sell tickets of travel operators *(e.g., RedBus, MakeMyTrip, Ixigo etc.)*

- ERPs: Platform companies who provide booking software to operators *(e.g., BitlaSoft)*

Let's start with the Payments:

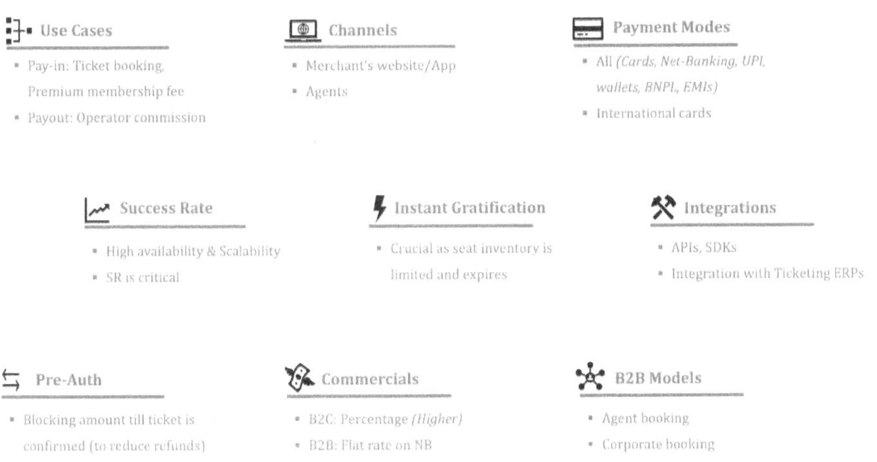

1. Use Cases:

- Pay-in: Ticket purchase, membership purchase.
- Payout: Operator commissions

2. Channels

- Website/mobile App of operators or OTAs. This is B2C model.
- Agents - buy inventory from operators/OTAs and then sell to clients *(individuals or Companies)*. This is B2B model.

3. Payment Modes

- All modes - CC, DC, NB, UPI, Wallets, EMIs
- International card acceptance
- No cash/COD (except for physical agents)

4. Payment Flow and Integrations

- Customers look for a clean and superior payment experience. Integrate SDK to optimize the payment journeys on mobile Apps.
- PA can directly integrate with merchants or need to integrate with ERP platforms *(e.g., Amadeus for Airline, Bitla Soft for bus operator)*

5. Performance and Success Rate:

Success rate is critical for both merchant *(travel inventory has expiry date)* as well as customers *(Need to block the seat which may be sold through various channels)*

6. Commercials and Settlement

- B2C: Percentage MDR (all modes)

- B2B: Flat rate on net-banking and percentage MDR on other modes

- Commercial model: Upfront dedication for B2C. It is possible that B2B models may work on surcharge model where payer bears the MDR.

- Settlement: Standard T+1/T+2 days; PAs may offer early/on-demand settlement

7. Instant Gratification

The bus is scheduled to travel from Bangalore to Mumbai on 15th August, and it has 20 seats.

Here are the things that need to be considered:

- Inventory is limited *(as there are only 20 seats)*

- Inventory has an expiry date *(bus is leaving on 15the August)*

- Can't sell the same seat to two customers *(The fight it may trigger on the bus over the seat will be entertaining at some level, but let's not do it!)*

- To maximize the sales of seats, the seats are distributed to and sold by various entities such as the bus operator's own site/app, OTAs, and agents. So, one entity cannot block the seat for longer without receiving the payment for it.

Let's say you are booking a seat on this bus. If the transaction is successful, then the merchant issues the ticket, and if the transaction fails, then the seat is released back to inventory.

What will the merchant do if the transaction goes into 'pending' state?

The transaction can't be in limbo. So, the merchant will have to act.

One of the ways is to wait for 15–20 mins and try to fetch latest transaction state *(if the transaction is successful, then issue the ticket)*, but if transaction is still in a pending state, then release the inventory and mark the transaction for auto-refund *(if the transaction becomes successful eventually, then it is refunded)*.

8. Refunds:

Refunds are common in travel sectors - we usually cancel our tickets for various reasons. Unlike eCommerce, a travel merchant won't give full refunds and may deduct certain fees for cancellation and last-minute cancellations may not get the refund.

Merchants can use standard or even instant refund solutions to manage refunds.

9. Auth and Capture (Pre-Authorization)

Let's say the booking system needs to interact with an operator (E.g., IRCTC) to issue the ticket, and the operator's system fails to respond. Then what will the merchant do?

The merchant either waits indefinitely *(not ideal)* or initiates a refund to the customer. But as you know, refunds are cumbersome and expensive.

In such cases, Pre-Authorization can be a useful feature.

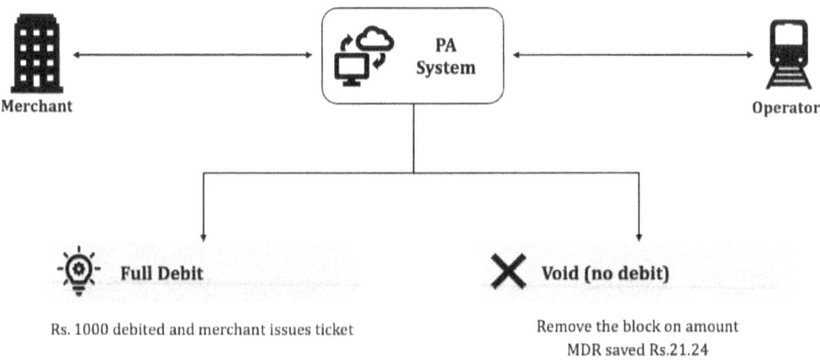

Illustration: Pre-Authorization Scenarios

Example: Rs.1000 is the ticket amount. MDR: 1.8% and GST: 18%

The amount is blocked temporarily and debited or voided depending on the status of the ticket issuance. With this feature, merchants can avoid refund related hassles, save on MDR *(no charges for void transaction),* and give a better customer experience.

- Coverage: Credit and debit cards of Visa, MasterCard, Amex, and UPI

- All issuers do not respond to void or capture call consistently.

- Pre-Auth can be set for 7 days (for cards) and 90 days (for UPI)

10. B2B /Agent Model:

Operators (e.g., Airlines) and OTAs appoints agents who serve corporate and walk-in clients. Such agents have to buy inventory from operators or OTAs by

- Agent to load the operator's/OTA's wallet and use the wallet funds to buy the inventory.

- Operators/OTAs tie-up with banks to provide corporate credit cards to their agents. The agent will use that corporate credit card to buy inventory and repay the outstanding amount as per credit card rules.

  These transactions are processed in the On-Us model *(where the card issuer and acquirer are the same bank).*

  Such closed user group (CUG) models enable banks to make good money *(card interchange),* merchants also benefit from lower MDR *(As On-US transaction),* and agents get credit line/ period to buy more inventory.

11. Corporate Booking:

There are entities that cater to companies by booking tickets for the company's employees. Such agents raise invoice to the Company, and the company will make the payment by bank transfer or corporate credit card.

Before tokenization, agents used to keep corporate credit card details on file and deduct the same in MOTO flow that doesn't require 2FA (OTP).

Post tokenization, MOTO flows are allowed, but only few acquiring banks are supporting it.

Closing Remarks

Travel was one of the most affected sectors during the pandemic. Now, the travel sector is growing rapidly and continues to grow.

Travel is an essential part of our lives - it is not the way people travel should be comfortable but also the way they make the ticket booking.

22.C Gaming

Let's start with - Aren't online rummy or fantasy sports equivalent to gambling?

No - Online rummy and fantasy sports are 'skill-based games' as per Supreme Court and other Courts' rulings. These games are exempted from Public Gambling Act of 1867.

'Gambling is betting and wagering on 'games of chance' but in 'game of skill', success depends on superior knowledge, training, attention, experience of the player but not just chance'.

As per the Supreme Court, 'game of skills' is legal, but few States *(Telangana, Andhra, Sikkim, Assam, Nagaland, Orissa)* have banned such games.

- **Online Rummy:** Most of us have played rummy during summer vacation or in hostel rooms. The same rummy game is online, where you play without money for fun or play with money to win some more money.

- **Fantasy Sports:** In fantasy sports, a user will select players and get rewarded based on their performance in the actual game. As a 'sports watching nation', Fantasy Sports has seen great growth in India with large companies.

- **Poker** is another card-based game that falls under skill-based gaming.

Games such as Ludo gained popularity during the pandemic. There is no consensus whether Ludo falls under skill-based games. Few PAs support such merchants on a case-to-case basis.

Requirements for Gaming Merchants:

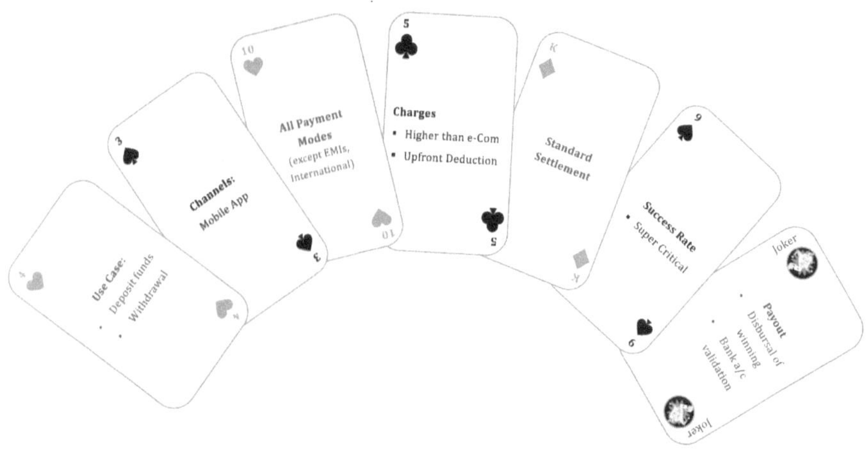

1. **Use Cases**:

    •   Pay-in: User deposits funds to merchant's wallet.

        Solution: PA solution

    •   Pay-out: User will withdraw the winnings

        Solutions: Payout (IMPS, NEFT, UPI) and bank account validation solution

2. **Channels**:

Mobile Apps are the de facto channels. However, companies have websites that mostly display Terms & Conditions or contact details. Actual payment and games happen on the App.

Due to high commission *(around 30%)* and enforcement to use default billing systems, gaming merchants avoided Play Store or App Store, and distributed their Apps through their website.

In 2022, Google Play Store did a pilot that allowed gaming merchants on Play Store without high commission and also gave flexibility to use their own payment partners.

3. Payment Modes:

Merchants accept all payment modes except EMIs and international cards. UPI is the dominant mode (more than 80-85% of traffic)

Note: Few banks (e.g., HDFC) do not support gaming merchants due to their internal risk or compliance policies.

4. Commercials:

Percentage of transaction value *(on the similar lines of eCommerce rates. Refer **Chapter 7.A**).*

PAs may charge a bit higher MDR due to higher risk.

Charges work in an upfront deduction where merchants bear the charges and receive a net-settlement. To avoid reconciliation efforts and bridging of funds, merchants may push for gross settlement, i.e., invoicing model.

5. Settlement:

Standard settlement time of T+2 or T+1 days with net-settlement to merchants. It is possible to get early or on-demand settlement from PAs.

6. Performance & Success Rate:

Super crucial, and gaming merchants are super demanding.

- Rummy: The user wants to play at that moment *(has a gut feeling that he will win)*. So, the transaction has to be successful.

- Fantasy Sports: Users make a payment to participate in the tournament before the game starts. As it is a time-bound activity, success rate becomes crucial.

Users typically start paying closer to the deadline *(as the human tendency is to do things at the last moment),* so merchants need a robust PA/PSP/Bank that can deliver better success rates and handle the spikes in transaction volume.

7. **Refunds**:

Typically, it is not required as the user is loading the wallet, and merchants expect users to play, so they do not allow refunds.

There is a possibility of auto-refunds in fantasy sports. If the transaction is 'pending' before the game deadline, then merchants would prefer auto refunding that transaction.

8. **Chargeback**:

As service is consumed online, the gaming industry is prone to frauds and chargeback. So, merchants need to put in more stringent processes and clearer Terms & Conditions to defend chargebacks.

9. **Withdrawal of Winnings**:

- The winning amount can be withdrawn to a bank account or VPA or PPI wallet.

- Merchants may enforce minimum and maximum limits on the withdrawals.

- The user is required to provide PAN for withdrawal *(without PAN, TDS will be higher - Merchant gives TDS certificate that user can use for Income Tax Returns filing)*

A merchant can do an integration with banks or PAs or FinTechs to facilitate payout using IMPS, NEFT, UPI, or wallet rails.

Shift in model: In recent times, merchants are moving from the recharge model *(merchants pre-fund FinTech's/PA's account and initiate payout)* to connected-bank model *(where payout is done directly from merchant's bank account)* by integrating with bank or PA or TSP.

Adhering to State level Bans:

As mentioned earlier, few of the States have banned online gaming *(including skill based)*. Merchants follow many processes to adhere to this.

- Play Store doesn't allow users to download App in the banned States.
- Block the user if KYC or bank account details belong to banned state.
- Block the user from playing basis the geo-location.
- Do not allow withdrawal if the IFSC of the bank account belongs to a banned State.
- Do not allow withdrawal to Payments Bank *(e.g., Indian Post)* account as all accounts of a Payments Bank will have the same IFSC.
- Do not allow payout to UPI or wallet *(not possible to identify IFSC and thus the State)*

Bank Approval:

To get approval from banks *(for MID)*, gaming merchants have to prove that they are compliant and follow fair practices. Merchants usually submit legal opinions from law firms and also may provide undertaking letters *(meaning, the merchant is ready to bear financial liabilities and penalties if they fail to follow compliance)*.

Schematic of deposits and withdrawals

- Account Set-up: Merchant maintains a nodal account to hold the users' funds - both deposits and winnings *(but show the balances separately)*

- Deposit: A user deposits Rs.1000, the PA will deposit Rs.976.40 to the merchant's a/c after deducting MDR (assuming 2%) and GST amount

- Bridge the fund gap: The user deposited Rs.1000 and expects to see Rs.1000 in the wallet balance. But considering PA has deducted its fees, the merchant has to bridge the gap of Rs.23.60 by transferring funds from its current a/c to the nodal a/c.

- Playing: When a user participates in the game, the wallet will be deducted, and the amount will be moved to the merchant's current a/c

- Winnings: If a user wins the game, then the prize money is credited to 'winning wallet'. And users can withdraw funds from this account.

You can see the complexity in the money movement and reconciliation for one transaction. Now imagine millions of users depositing, playing, winning, and withdrawing money.

Closing Remarks:

Skill based gaming has huge potential. During the 2023 IPL, Fantasy Sports merchants earned gross revenue of Rs.2300 Crore, and 61 million users participated.

However, the gaming industry has seen many ups and downs *(more downs and ups)*.

Firstly, many states have banned this sector. Although the industry could win court cases to overturn the ban in a few states *(e.g., Karnataka)*, still 7-8 states do not allow gaming.

In 2022, Google Play Store relaxed its policies around using its proprietary billing system for Fantasy Sports merchants. That means, Fantasy games can distribute their Apps on Play Store.

Skill-based gaming is largely self-regulated. Consortiums such as FIFS *(Federation of Indian Fantasy Sports)* and AIGF *(All India Gaming Federation)* define examples for fair play practices and also engage with policy makers.

Niti Aayog also voiced that Fantasy Sports should be regulated to achieve growth while safeguarding the users. At the beginning of 2023, MeitY *(Ministry of Electronics and Information Technology)* issued draft policies for regulating the gaming sector.

In July 2023, the Government of India announced 28% GST on online gaming sectors, which has impacted the sector adversely.

Even with all these ups and downs, gaming is one of the most exciting and interesting sectors.

22.D Utilities

Because of common requirements and solutions, I am clubbing both Utilities (e.g., electricity, water board) with Telecom and DTH sectors.

- Utility: Electricity, Water, Gas connection e.g., BESCOM

- Telecom: Post-paid bills E.g., Airtel

- DTH Service e.g., Tata Sky

- Broadband e.g., Hathaway

Payments in this sector are versatile as users use various channels and payment solutions.

Below are some of the requirements:

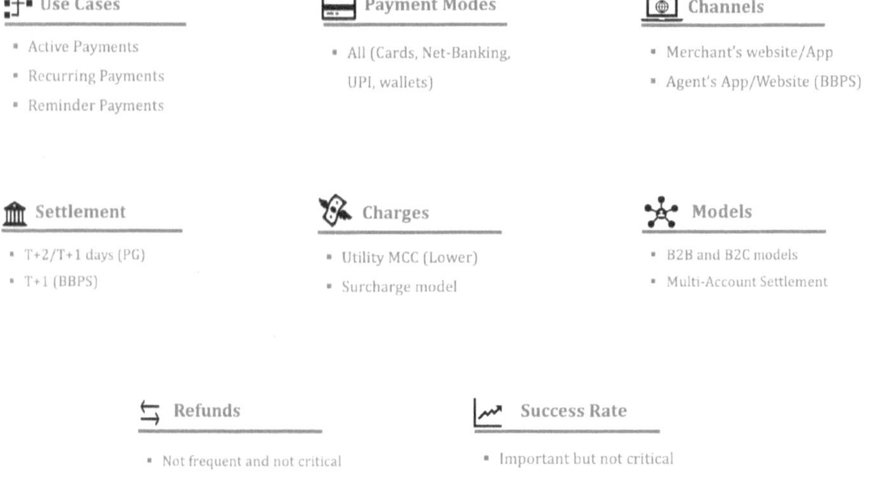

1. **Types of Payments**:

- Active payments: Users will make payment on the merchant's website or App.

- Recurring Payments: Users may set-up a mandate for recurring bill payments on bank accounts (NACH, UPI AutoPay) or cards (SI on Cards)

- **Reminder Payments:** Merchants can send reminders for payments via SMS, WhatsApp, email, or in-App notification to users.

2. Channels:

- **Biller's website or App:** By integrating with Payment Aggregators or banks.
- **3rd Parties:** Apps (PhonePe, Google Pay), physical counters (Bangalore One, Suvidha) by integrating the BBPS platform.

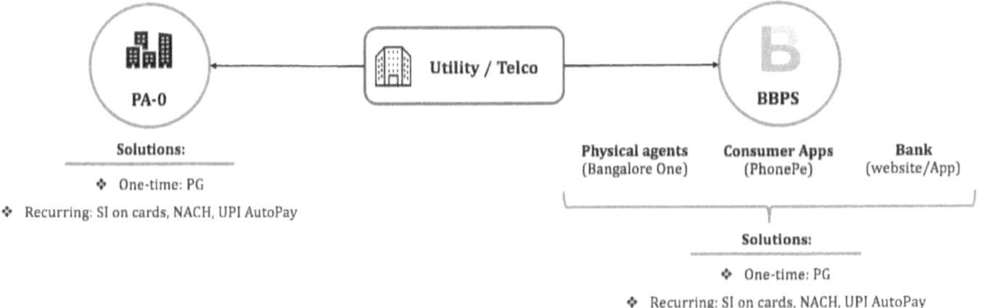

Here are some examples:

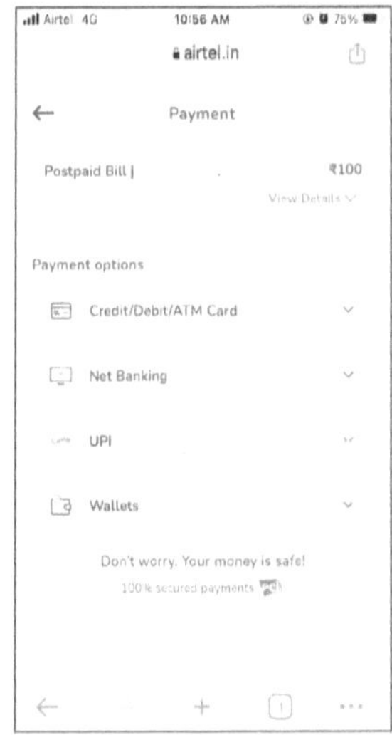

Direct Integration – User Pays bill on biller's website

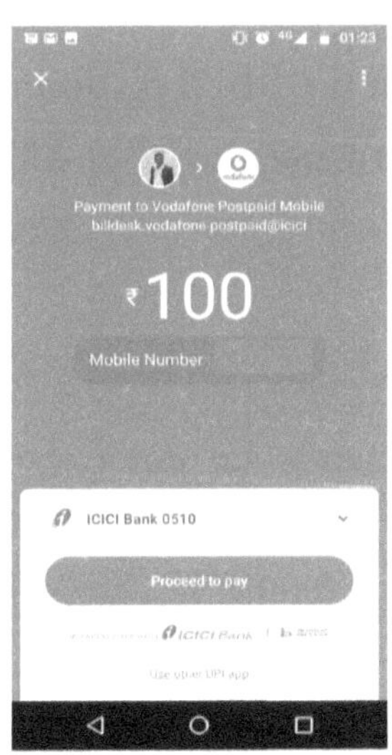

BBPS Integration – User Pays bill through 3rd party App

3. **Payment Modes**:

- All payment modes: CC, DC, NB, UPI, containers, wallets, BNPL, etc.

- Practicality dictates which payment mode is to be enabled. *E.g., Considering small ticket size, EMI on cards may not be useful.*

4. **Charges:**

- The utility sector has lower charges (Refer to **Chapter 7.A**)

- Telecom, DTH, and Broadband merchants technically do not fall under the Utility category, but usually they get Utility MCCs. *(this practice is slowly changing)*

- Government Utility merchants work on Surcharge model where MDR is passed on to the customer, but MDR is absorbed by Telco, DTH, and Broadband merchants.

5. **Settlement:**

- Standard settlement of T+2/T+1 days *(possible to get early settlement)*

- For the BBPS platform, settlement will be done on T+1 day.

- Settlement amount will be gross *(in case of surcharge)* or net *(in case of upfront deduction)*

6. **Refunds:**

- Refunds are not frequent. Any additional amount paid to a utility merchant can be adjusted in the next billing cycle.

- If a refund is necessary, then standard refund cycle will be followed.

- Utility sector works in a surcharge model. So, when the refund is marked, then the customer will not get a surcharge (+GST) amount back.

7. B2B Payments:

Just like individuals, even companies subscribe to utility, telecom, and broadband services *(Example: Your company pays the BESCOM bill every month)*. So B2B payments constitute a big chunk of transactions *(in value)*.

Apart from the online payments, NACH (paper based and digital), and Bank Transfer (via BBPS) solutions play an important role in facilitating these payments.

8. Multi-Account Settlement:

Telecom companies operate in circles *(E.g., Karnataka Circle, Mumbai Circle, etc.)*. If such a model is followed, then each circle may have different settlement accounts.

To enable such a model, a separate Live ID can be configured for each circle or enable multi-account or split settlement solution.

9. Success Rate:

How critical is the success rate for these types of merchants? Have you ever heard of someone switching from Vodafone to Airtel because a transaction failed?

Utility bill payments are mandatory, so the intent of payment is very high, and even if a transaction fails, the customer will attempt to pay again. Considering a failed transaction affects the customer's experience and may attract late payment penalties, a better success rate is 'good to have' but not critical.

10. BBPS (Bharat Bill Payment System):

BBPS is one of the important platforms for bill payment (Refer to **Chapter 17**). Thanks to BBPS, customers can pay BESCOM, Airtel, or Tata Sky bills on third party Apps and websites or physical counters (e.g., PayTM, PhonePe, Google Pay, or internet banking)

11.   Prepaid Recharges:

Most of the mobile users are on 'prepaid model' - a user needs to recharge and then utilize the allotted airtime, data, and tenure. Recharges can be done directly on Telecom company's website, nearby stores, as well as on 3rd party Apps (PhonePe, Google Pay, etc.).

Only in 2022, the mobile prepaid recharge category was added to the BBPS.

Closing Remarks

Utility (including Telco, DTH) is one of the biggest and evergreen industry verticals.

Utility merchants have multiple channels for collections — The merchant's website/App, the agent's website/app, and collection centers. For these merchants, collection is not a big problem as these are mandatory services, but a bigger challenge will be reconciliation of payments collected through various channels!

22.E   Education

Education is a diverse sector with various types of entities, different types of payment use cases and multiple payment channels.

Entities that collect fees

- Institutes: Schools, colleges, Universities
- Coaching Centers
- Competitive/entrance exam boards *(e.g., NEET exam, UPSC Exam)*
- EdTech Companies that deliver online courses.
- Private Coaching classes *(Unorganized and fragmented segment)*

Basic payment requirements for the Education sector

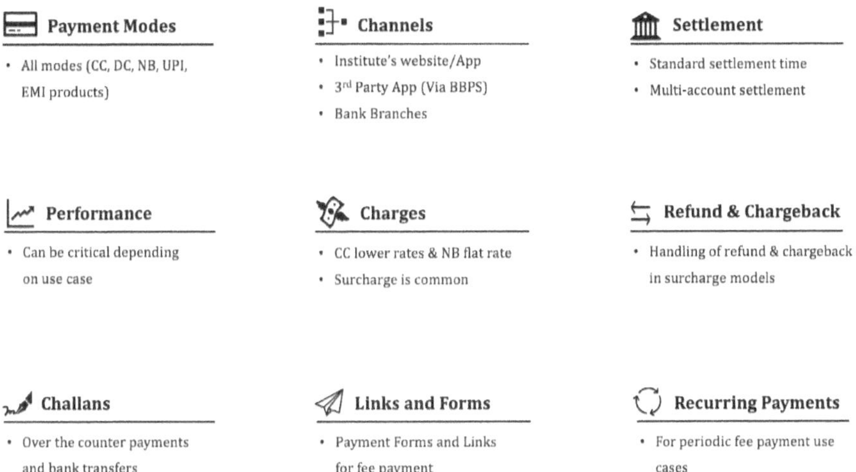

Payment Modes
- All modes (CC, DC, NB, UPI, EMI products)

Channels
- Institute's website/App
- 3rd Party App (Via BBPS)
- Bank Branches

Settlement
- Standard settlement time
- Multi-account settlement

Performance
- Can be critical depending on use case

Charges
- CC lower rates & NB flat rate
- Surcharge is common

Refund & Chargeback
- Handling of refund & chargeback in surcharge models

Challans
- Over the counter payments and bank transfers

Links and Forms
- Payment Forms and Links for fee payment

Recurring Payments
- For periodic fee payment use cases

1.   Payment Use Cases:

- Pay-in: Various types of fees.
- Pay-out: Teaching partner incentive payout *(in case of EdTech)*

2. **Payment Modes**:

- All modes (CC, DC, NB, UPI, wallets, BNPL, EMIs) - all are welcome!

- Be practical while enabling payment modes *(for small ticket size, EMI products are of no use but EMIs can be useful for large fee amount)*

3. **Payment Channels**:

- Online: Parent/student pay online on website or App

- Offline: Bank branches located in Institute's premises accept cash, Cheque, and DD (Demand Draft) over the counter

  Note: These can be moved to online with Virtual Account Solution *(Refer **Chapter 14**)*

4. **Charges**:

- Education sector has a lower MDR - Flat fee on Net-banking and Cards on lower MDR than eCommerce (Refer **Chapter 7.A**)

- Usually, the MDR is passed on to the parent/student (surcharge model). EdTech companies absorb charges (upfront deduction model)

5. **Settlement**:

- Standard: T+1/T+2 days *(early settlement doesn't have much value)*

- Settlement amount will be gross *(for surcharge model)* and Net-Settlement *(for upfront deduction model)*.

6. Split Settlement:

An institute may collect different types of fees (Admission fee, hostel fee, etc.) and would want different types of fees to go to different settlement accounts.

In such a case, split settlement solution is ideal.

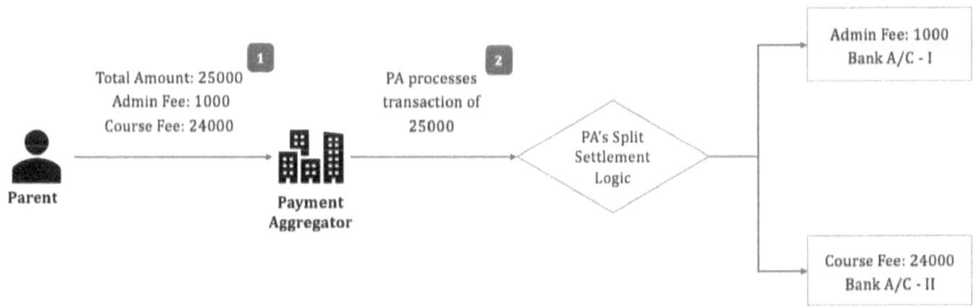

Also, it is possible that an educational institute may have multiple locations (e.g., VIT - Chennai, VIT - Delhi, etc.). Either institute can get a separate MID for each institute or use a multi-account settlement solution.

7. Performance & Success Rate:

The importance of these two metrics depends on the fee type.

Let's say you are paying a semester fee, and the transaction fails; then you will retry, and even if there is a delay, the college won't send you home.

But let's say you are paying a competitive examination fee on the last day, and the first transaction fails. You will definitely do a second transaction but think of your mental status when that first transaction failed. Right??

So, the importance of success rate will vary from moderate to super critical.

8. Challans:

Payment over the bank counter using cash and DD is quite prominent. For easier reconciliation, the Institute gives a challan *(has a unique number, student details, amount, etc.)*, and Cash & DD are paid at the bank counter against that challan.

A few PAs and ERPs provide features to generate challans, which can be used during payment across the counter.

Also, the Virtual Account solution (***Chapter 14***) can be a good replacement for challan payments.

9. Recurring Payment:

Although some of the fees *(e.g., semester fees)* are periodic, very rarely a parent will set up mandates for these recurring payments.

Even institutes are not that keen on pulling money from parent's accounts on time because education is not a business *(even if it is not true, let's not say it loudly)*.

10. Refund & Chargeback Problem:

Surcharge model is quite common in the education sector, i.e., the parent bears MDR + GST amount.

Reiterating issues of the surcharge model during refunds and chargeback.

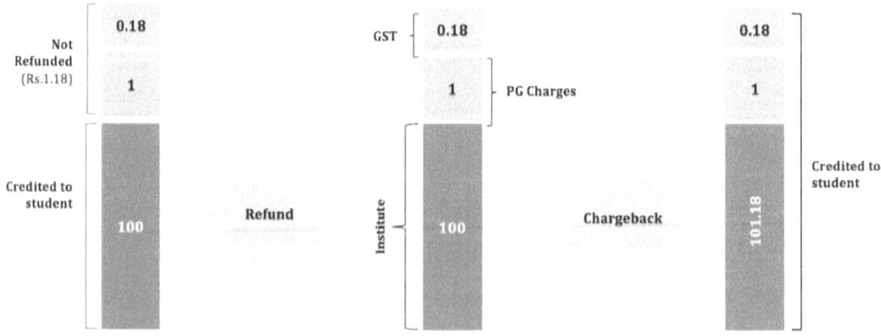

Refunds can be marked for transaction amounts, not for the entire amount. So, when a parent asks for a refund, they won't get the entire amount as the surcharge amount is not returned.

On the other hand, a chargeback can be raised for the entire amount *(including surcharge fees)*. So, if a chargeback is valid, then the entire amount is debited/adjusted from the institute, so the institute will end up losing.

More Problems with Refunds:

Most payment cases in the education sector are seasonal. Example: Admission fee is paid in May-July, but then there are no transactions till next year. If a refund is marked post the fee cycle, then the merchant doesn't have ongoing settlements to adjust the refunds. So, these merchants should define a clear refund process *(whether refunds are allowed or not)*. Anyway, for such outlier cases, PAs provide the provision of transferring funds to PA's a/c and then mark the refund.

On the positive side, there are very less refunds for education institutes, and even chargebacks are less. That is why this sector is considered 'less risky'.

11. Payout:

Not a major use case except for EdTech companies where the EdTech company needs to disburse incentives to tutors.

Important Payment Solutions in Education Sector

A. Education Institute

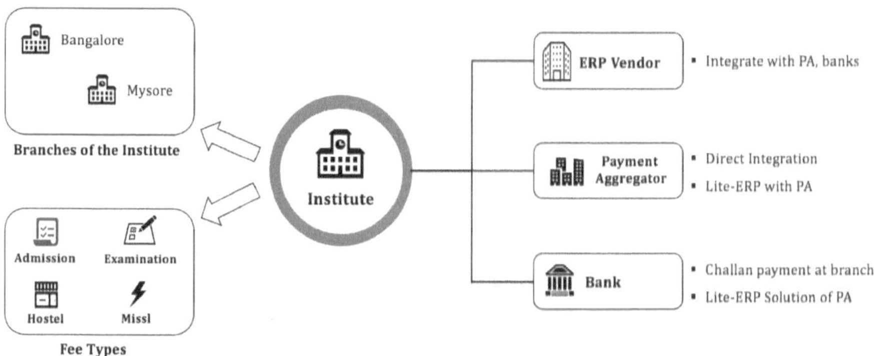

Integration: An Institute might be running multiple institutions (branches) and can have various types of fees.

Below are the ways for integration with different service providers:

- ERP vendor: Provides an integrated payment solution as well.

- Payment Aggregator: Integrate directly or use lite-ERP provided by PA.

- Banks: Provide lite-ERP solution, direct integration, and cash/ DD collection at branches

Integration Options:

- Institute can have one MID to collect all types of fees.

- Procure multiple MIDs for different use cases.

- Implement split settlement and multi-account settlement solutions to manage fee collection for multiple branches and bifurcation of different types of fees.

3rd Party Apps and BBPS:

Users can make fee payment through 3rd Party consumer Apps (e.g., PayTM, PhonePe).

There are two possible ways.

- 3rd Party Apps should directly on-board institutes to platform (*inefficient model*)

- BBPS: Education institutes will be on-boarded as billers by BOUs *(Biller Operating Unit)* and 3rd Party Apps *(Agent Institutes)* can access those institutes by integrating with COUs *(Customer Operating Unit)* (*Efficient and faster model*)

Note: As of Mar '22, there are 19,770+ education institutes on the BBPS platform.

B. ERP Vendors:

ERP vendors play an important role in the Education sector as these entities provide solutions to institutes to manage student data, student activities, fee types, fee cycles, etc. Such ERP vendors integrate with PAs, Banks, or PSPs to enable online fee payments.

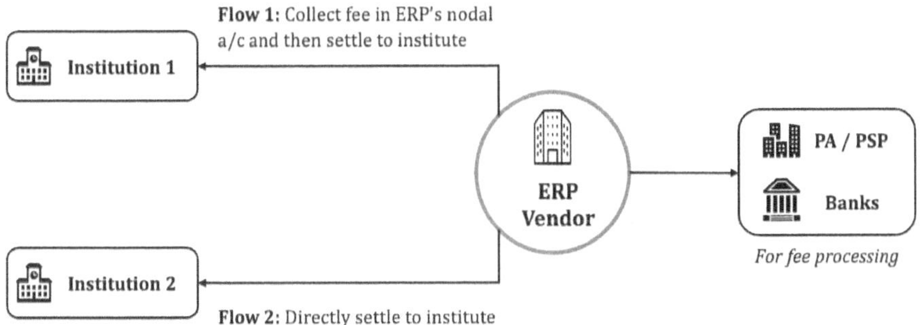

PA Charges: ERP vendors are not educational institutes but software companies, so they do not qualify for the MDR that is given to the education sector.

To avail such lower rates, an ERP vendor needs to prove that PA is used on-behalf of the institution by submitting an undertaking letter from the institution or let institutions procure MID from PA and configure that in their ERP system.

Integration Type: The ERP vendor needs to support different types of payment flows depending on the institution's requirements.

Example: Single MID, multi-account settlement, split settlement. etc.

Settlement:

- Direct: Settlement is done directly to the Institute's account *(most popular)*

- Nodal A/C: ERP vendor gets the settlement into its nodal a/c and then disburses it to institute after deducting its commission.

Revenue Model: ERP vendor makes revenue from online payment services *(over and above core ERP revenue)*. There are different revenue models:

- Add a mark-up fee above MDR, and mark-up amount is credited to ERP vendor.

- Instead of adding mark-up, ERP vendor will raise invoice to institute.

- ERP vendor can strike revenue-sharing arrangement with PAs or banks.

C. EdTech Companies:

New-Gen companies that are delivering content/courses to students over the internet or offline. They offer tutorials for students on regular syllabus, competitive exams, and also, certificates in professional courses.

Integration: Standard online payments through PAs and direct bank(s) on website and App.

All types of payment instruments are allowed.

If there are periodic transactions, EdTech merchant may use recurring payment solutions.

MDR: Although these are not education institutes, they may get MDR of the education sector. It is not a straightforward case, but considering their volume, PAs and banks may relax their rules. Typically, EdTech merchants works in upfront deduction (where merchant bears MDR)

D. Examination Boards:

Competitive exams are conducted by Education Boards. Example: NEET, Nursing Board

Integration:

- Directly integrate with PAs or banks. A few PAs give a simple form that can be used to capture applicant's details along with various payment options.

- Examination platforms: These companies provide solutions to conduct examinations along with integrated payment solutions *(E.g., Merittrac, Manipal Technologies).* Such companies conduct various examinations on their platforms, so they either use a single MID with specific scheme code per examination or procure individual MID for each examination, depending on time and effort.

E. Private Tutorials: Local private tutorials typically use cash or UPI to collect fees. This is a highly fragmented and unorganized segment, but quite large.

Closing Remarks

With 250 million school-going students and 36 million students enrolled in higher education, the education sector is worth $100 Billion. Apart from the institutes, professional certification, EdTech, coaching, test preparation, etc. are on the rise.

Education fee payment is evergreen, cyclic, and versatile. Isn't it?

One thing is for sure… the online fee payments in this sector will continue to grow.

22.F Insurance

Two Scottish men, Robert Wallace, and Alexander Webster came up with the idea of *'insurance'* in the 18ᵗʰ Century. The idea was simple: Build a fund by periodically collecting small amounts ('premiums') from policyholders and give a one-time settlement to the policy holder's widow. Invest collected funds for 'good returns' so that claim amount is settled from returns on the investment while keeping fund corpus intact. Over the centuries, the assessment of risk, investment methods, and things that can be insured have evolved, but the concept remains the same.

I pay Rs.25,000 per year for health insurance for Rs.5,00,000 coverage. I may pay this premium for decades but may never claim any amount, and it is also possible that I may claim the cover amount within four years of premium payment.

To be in business, insurance companies need to make sure the outflow is lower than the inflow. To reduce the risk of outflow, insurance companies decide on whom to give insurance *(e.g., do not give health insurance to octogenarian)* or qualify the person *(e.g., medical check-up to issue term policy)* or add conditions to the policy *(e.g., pre-existing diseases are not covered)* or increase the premium amount to compensate for risk *(E.g., a smoker pays more premium than a non-smoker or 45 year person pays more premium than a 25-year-old)*

The insurance premium is similar to the MDR of payments ecosystem - higher risk, higher premium or MDR.

Insurance Landscape:

The insurance sector is governed by the Insurance Regulatory and Development Authority of India (IRDAI). Only IRDA of India approved insurers can issue the insurances.

There are two main types of insurances:

1. Life - Term policy

2. Non-Life - General Insurance can be for health, vehicle, property, travel, etc.

Users can purchase insurance from three IDRAI licensed entities:

- Insurers: The companies that give you insurance (E.g., LIC, HDFC Life, Acko)

- Web Aggregators: The entities that sell policies of Insurers online (E.g., Coverfox)

- Brokers: Specialist in insurance who sell insurance both online and offline (branches) (e.g., Mahindra Insurance Brokers)

Below are the requirements related to Payments:

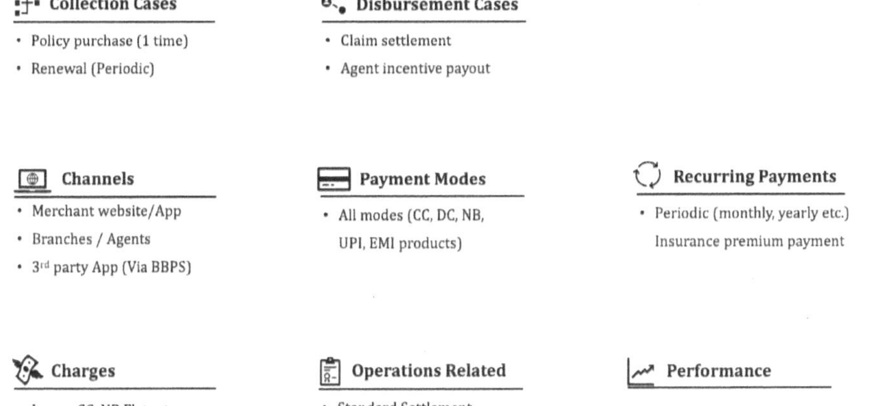

1. **Payment Use Cases**:

- Pay-in: (i) Policy purchase, (ii) Policy renewals.

- Pay-out: Disbursement of claim amount and incentive payout to agents

Insurance is an ideal sector for,

- Active Payment: User actively pays (Solution: online PA)

- Recurring Payment: Customer sets a recurring mandate for periodic policy renewal (Solutions: UPI AutoPay, Paper NACH, eNACH, SI on Cards)

- Reminder Payment: The merchant can send a payment link to user via SMS, mail and/or WhatsApp for policy premium payment.

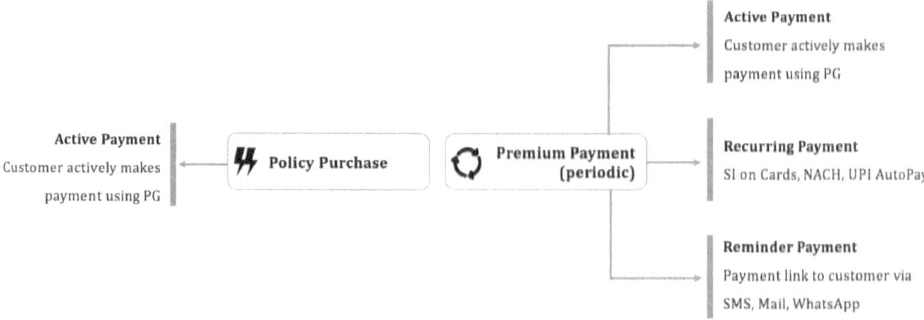

Consider few things:

Insurance has repeat payment use cases, but the periodicity is quite long (half-yearly, yearly). So, few products/features won't add much value.

- Card Tokenization: If I have to make payment once a year then will I save/tokenize the card? Mostly not!

- Recurring Payments Solutions: If the periodicity is once a year, then will the customer set a recurring mandate?

  Also, factor in the limitations on the debit amount for various solutions *(e.g., SI on cards have limitations of Rs.15,000)*. So, in such cases, UPI AutoPay and NACH will work.

2. Channels:

Insurance companies deploy multiple channels for policy purchase and renewal: Own website/App, agents, Web Aggregators, Insurance Brokers, and 3rd Party Apps (e.g., PhonePe).

Even Web Aggregators and Insurance Brokers have their own App, websites, or agents.

Payment solutions should cover these channels:

- Both online and offline payment solutions are deployed for these channels to cover purchase as well as policy renewal use cases

- Agents collect Cheques or may have App to facilitate payments on-premises.

Think of it, mobile Apps are not an important channel, considering the customer needs to fill in a lot of details during policy purchase, so a desktop/laptop is a better channel.

Also, you pay a premium either once or twice a year, so why will you install an App that has very less utility?

3rd Party Apps: Insurance premiums can be paid through PhonePe, PayTM etc.

Insurers are on-boarded on the BBPS platform by BOU, and customers can make premium payment on these 3rd Party Apps (which are agents of COU).

3. **Payment Modes**:

- All modes (CC, DC, UPI, NB, wallets, alternate credit products)

- Few merchants may enable international card acceptance.

    Note: Decision to enable a payment mode is dictated by practicality. Example: If ticket size is big then wallets are useless but EMI on cards will be useful.

4. **Charges**:

- Lower rates on credit cards and flat fee on net-banking (refer *Chapter 7. A*)

- PG charges are mostly absorbed by the merchants *(there could be few exceptions where MDR is surcharged to the customer)*.

5. Settlement:

- Standard settlement time of T+1 or T+2 days

- Insurance companies may want product-wise settlement. Example: Vehicle policy should go to a different bank account than health policy.

  Solution: Multi-account settlement or by configuring a different Live ID for each type of insurance.

- Insurance companies may allow a user to buy or renew multiple insurances in one go, but settlements should go to different accounts.

  Solution: Multi-account or split settlement solutions.

- Web Aggregators or Insurance Brokers will not be part of settlement; in such cases either they procure MID in the name of the insurer or use a split settlement solution where 100% settlement is done to the insurer.

6. Refunds:

Insurers allow cancellation of the policy by customer within a specified period, or the insurer may trigger a refund if it decides not to issue the policy to customer *(if pre-conditions are not met e.g., health check-up for term policy)*.

Also, considering the ticket size is large, refunds need to be efficient.

Instant/faster refunds solutions can be an efficient solution.

7. Performance & Success Rate:

Overall, success rate is important but not critical.

- Policy purchase is a long process, so the checkout (final leg) should be seamless, else you have an angry customer who may defer to buy.

  Note: Insurance is purchased based on various criteria *(insurance company, coverage, claim settlement ratio, etc.)*, so even if a transaction fails, a customer will not switch immediately to a different insurer as intent of purchase is high.

- A large number of policyholders do not renew policies, so if any user intends to renew her policy, then payment shouldn't fail.

8. **Payout Use Cases**:

   - Agent incentive: Agents are important sales channels for insurers and brokers. These agents receive sales incentives. Payout solutions offered by banks/PA/TSPs can be used to disburse such incentives efficiently.

   - Claim Settlement: Policyholders may receive interim bonuses, a coverage amount, or a maturity amount is given to the customer. These disbursements can be done using payout solutions of banks/PAs/TSPs. Many times, claim settlement is done by the insurer's TPA and not by the insurer directly.

Closing Remarks:

India is one of the under-insured countries in the world, and it has a huge scope of growth. The sector suffers issues such as high customer acquisition costs and lower policy renewals.

Certain insurances are mandatory *(travel insurance for foreign trips and vehicle insurance)* due to Government policies. The pandemic triggered panic, and also created a lot of awareness for health insurance.

The Government of India has rolled out various insurance schemes for its citizens *(e.g., Pradhan Mantri Suraksha Bima Yojana)* and for agricultural produce. But still, we have a long way to go!

IRADI has taken the initiative of BIMA Sugam - a platform for buying, selling, and claiming settlement of insurances. A few say that it is the UPI moment of the insurance sector - Let's see!

As the sector is moving towards 'digital' with paperless on-boarding till claim settlement, online payments will continue to play a crucial role in this sector.

22.G Lending

Lending/Credit is one of the oldest financial instruments since the Mesopotamian civilization. Over time, lending products have become more complex and come in different shapes and forms.

For simplicity, let's consider only two types of loans.

- Secured - that is backed by collateral (e.g., gold loans)
- Unsecured - without collateral (e.g., personal loans)

Lending entities:

A. **Regulated Entities:**

In India, only banks *(excluding Payment Banks)*, NBFCs *(Non-Banking Financial Company)*, MFIs *(Microfinance Institutions)* are licensed entities and regulated by the RBI that give different types of loans to consumers and companies.

B. **Digital Lending Apps**:

FinTechs also play a part in lending without being regulated entities. Basically, they ride on their partner NBFCs' license. Such FinTechs are called 'Digital Lending Apps'.

In 2022, RBI issued *'Digital Lending Guidelines'* (DLG) to regulate the role of FinTechs in the lending ecosystem to safeguard consumers.

Guidelines are quite detailed and explain the roles and responsibilities of various parties (NBFC, DLA or LSPs).

Here, we will focus on the payment cycle.

- Loan disbursement should be done from DLA's partner NBFC's account to customer's account.
- Loan repayment amount should be settled to DLA's partner NBFC's account.

This means:

1. The loan amount *(disbursed or repaid)* should not touch DLA or LSP's account.

2. For Payout (loan disbursement) - Prefunding of FinTech's account is not allowed, so only **connecting banking** model is allowed *(NBFC's account → Customer's account)*

3. PAs can play a role in the repayment cycle as long PA is not LSP; else DLG guidelines will apply on PA

Two things happen when you take a loan - you will bear interest charges, and you need to repay the original loan amount either in installments or one-time. So NBFCs need effective mechanisms to collect these installments.

Requirements for Lending Sector:

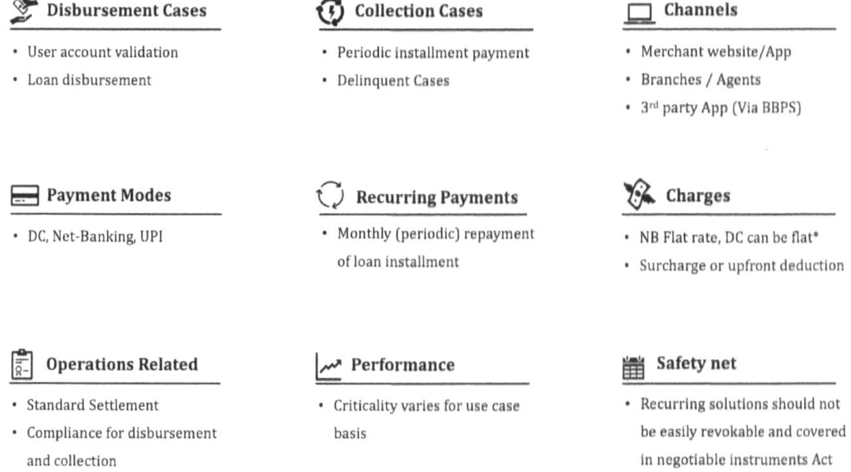

1. Disbursement:

The first leg is customer on-boarding, where the customer is approved for a loan by checking certain criteria *(e.g., CIBIL score)* and KYC documents. Once the loan is approved, disbursement is made to the customer's bank account.

There are two solutions:

a. **Beneficiary name validation:** Check whether customer's name as per bank records is same as per KYC document:

- Do penny drop - credit Rs.1 to customer's bank account using IMPS.

- Reverse Penny Drop - where customer will transfer Rs.1 to NBFC's account and NBFC will get remitter's bank details (Rs.1 is refunded)

- NPCI's APIs that allows penny-less solution (*live on few banks*)

b. **Loan Disbursement**: Use IMPS or NEFT to disburse the loan amount to the customer.

Solutions: Payout solution (IMPS/NEFT based) solutions are used. As the funds should be disbursed directly from NBFC's account so the recharge/pre-funding model won't work. So, DLA/NBFC have to use Connected-Banking model *(from FinTechs/PAs/Banks)*.

2. **Collection**:

Collection is done through all variants of payments (active, recurring and reminder).

a. **Active Payments** - Where customer makes payment on NBFC or DLA's App

- PG solution: Standard PA (only DC, Net-banking, and UPI on bank a/c)

  Note: Few merchants want to implement TPV flow (to make sure the repayment is coming from the same account to which loan amount is disbursed

- Virtual Account Number/Virtual VPA solution: where customer transfers funds to assigned VAN/Virtual VPA

b. **Recurring Payments** - Customer registers mandate and NBFC/DLA can debit funds without customer's intervention on periodic basis.

   - NACH (paper): In case there is physical touch point with the customer.

   - NACH (Online): Customer can set mandate on bank account.

   - UPI AutoPay: A customer can set a mandate on her bank a/c through TPAPs (PhonePe, Cred, etc.). Customer cannot revoke the mandate for loan repayment and EMI collection MCC (7322)

   Note: Loan Repayment is an obligation, so all these recurring payment solutions are covered under the Negotiable Instruments Act (1881). This means a debit failure due to insufficient funds or closure of bank account will be treated same as Cheque bounce, which is a punishable offense.

   Note: SI on Debit Cards can be used, but the solution is not economical due to percentage fees.

c. **Reminder Payments** - The merchant will send payment reminders to borrowers via mail, SMS, or WhatsApp, along with a payment/UPI deep link. The backbone of such solutions is PA or UPI.

3. **Channels**:

    a. **Physical**: It can be an NBFC's office or agents. Considering the customer touch point is strong as the customer needs to submit other details *(fill form, submit KYC documents)*, NBFC can sign up for a paper NACH mandate. It is a diminishing channel but still relevant.

    b. **Online**:

        •   NBFC's website/App - where customers can get onboarded and also, make repayments and register mandate for recurring payment solutions.

        •   DLA's website/App - where customers will initiate the onboarding and repayment journeys. Remember, funds will be disbursed directly from DLA's partner NBFC's account, and repayment amount will be settled to the partner NBFC's account.

    c. **3rd Party Apps (via. BBPS):** Borrowers can make loan repayment through 3rd Party Apps (e.g., PayTM, PhonePe) if the NBFC is available as biller on the BBPS platform.

4. **Payment Modes for Collection**:

    •   Only debit cards, net-banking, and UPI (linked to bank a/c) are allowed for repayment.

    •   NACH (paper), eNACH, UPI AutoPay are used from recurring solution.

Note: Credit Cards and BNPL products are not allowed, as you can't pay one loan with another loan. Wallets are not allowed as a source of wallet top-up can be credit cards.

5. **Charges**:

- PG Charges: DC - RBI standard or flat fee (by few banks), Net-banking - flat rate and UPI & RuPay DC are free (or nominal fee) (Refer *Chapter 7.A*)

  - Recurring Payments: Flat rate on NACH, eNACH and UPI AutoPay. SI on DC will be on percentage (%), so not economical.

  - Payout Solutions: Flat rate (NEFT) or slab-wise flat rate (IMPS)

Note: Charges are either absorbed by the merchant (upfront deduction) or passed on to the customer (surcharge). Few merchants also have hybrid models where the merchant absorbs fees for net-banking and passes the debit card charges to the user.

6. **Settlement**:

- Gross-settlement *(for surcharge model)* or net-settlement *(for upfront deduction model)*

- Settlement time is standard T+2/T+1 days. Few PAs may offer early or instant settlement.

Note: Early settlement can be useful for NBFCs/Lending companies as they can disburse more loans from the collected amount

7. **Refunds**:

Not much of a use as extra payment done *(by any chance)* by a customer will be adjusted either in principal amount or in the next installment unless it is the last installment. If needed, the merchant can use the standard refund process.

8. Success Rate:

Performance and success rate can be crucial as failed cases may impact a customer's credit score or attract additional interest or penalty. The customer's intent of payment is high.

In the case of recurring payment solutions, the merchant has control to re-run the mandate. And in the case of online payments, customers will retry if the transaction fails.

Closing Remarks

India is an underserved country when it comes to credit. Banks still remain the main entities for lending *(that is why banks are always referred to as 'lenders')*. NBFCs are playing a big role in increasing credit penetration, and DLAs are driving the growth in their own way.

Lending is a profitable business *(that is why loans are called 'assets')*. Giving money is easy *(as people need it)*, but collecting it is not. So, banks/NBFCs use different strategies to lend 'the right amount' to 'the right customer'.

Lending space has become super interesting - Digital Lending Guidelines are aimed at cleaning up the lending space and make it safer for the consumers; the Account Aggregator (AA) framework will allow lenders to access consumer's financial data and assess the credit worthiness, digital KYC solutions will make the customer on-boarding easier, and various payment solutions makes the fund movement efficient.

Opportunities in the lending sector are quite evident, and we are witnessing different types of lending models *(secure, unsecure, P2P, Invoice discounting, etc.)* for different types of users *(consumer, MSME, businesses, etc.)*. As the sector grows, so do the payments.

But remember - "Credit is fun…. and suddenly stops being".

22.H   Investment

Here, we will talk about how payments work in the regulated investments sector and use cases such as those for stock/equity and Mutual Funds.

Note: I will not get into details of how these investment instruments work and am definitely not going to give you advice on where and how to invest.

Regulated investments *(MFs, Stocks, Commodities, Bonds)* are governed by SEBI *(The Securities and Exchanges Board of India).*

I will limit this chapter only to:

a.   **Stocks/Equity:** A registered (KYCed) user of a stockbroker (e.g., Zerodha or Groww) can buy or sell common shares of companies that are listed on BSE *(Bombay Stock Exchange)* or NSE *(National Stock Exchange)*

b.   **Mutual Funds**: A user can invest in Mutual Funds through Mutual Fund Distributors *(e.g., Zerodha, Groww)* or AMC *(Asset Management Companies) (e.g., Parag Parekh, HDFC AMC)*

I will segregate the requirements/solutions in two parts:

(1) Generic - applies for all types of investment

(2) Investment instrument specific basis the April 2022 SEBI guidelines

Generic:

 **Use Cases**	**Payment Modes**	**Recurring Payments**
• SIP and ad-hoc purchases	• Only Net-Banking, UPI	• For Systematic Investment Plans –
• IPO	• Debit Cards (exceptional cases)	NACH (Paper, Digital), AutoPay

Charges	**TPV**	**Settlement**
• Charges are flat rate	• Investment need to be done by	• To AMC, Exchange or Broker
• Surcharge or invoicing model	registered bank account only	• T or T+1 settlement depending on cases

Disbursement Cases	**Performance**	**Other Requirements**
• Dividend Payment	• Can be critical as pricing or NAV	• Registration and advisory Services
• MF withdrawals or share sales	will change	• User validation (penny drop)

1. Use Cases:

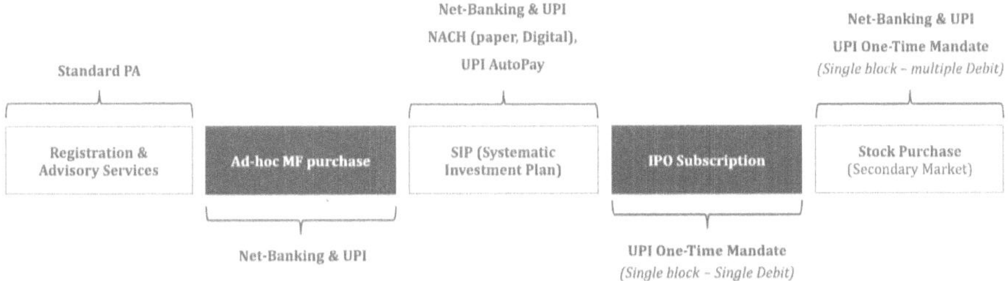

- **Registration fee or advisory fee**: Standard PA solutions *(all Payment Modes)* - This is tertiary use case, so we will skip the details.

- **Ad-hoc purchases:** Solutions: PA with only net-banking and UPI, Bank Transfer, Virtual Account Number solution

- **SIPs (Systematic Investment Plans):** User will invest on period basis.

  Solutions: NACH (paper and digital), UPI AutoPay, PA - NB & UPI

- **IPO Subscription**: User will participate in IPO *(Initial Public Offerings)*, and user will be allotted a block of shares if selected.

  Solution: One-time mandate on UPI with limit of Rs.5 Lakh

- **Bank account validation**: To check whether the bank account belongs to the customer.

  Solutions: Penny drop, reverse penny drop

- **Disbursement** - When user sells the shares/MFs/Bonds [Solution: Payout]

2. Third Party Validation:

During user on-boarding, the user has to register bank account(s) and the investment should happen through the same account(s).

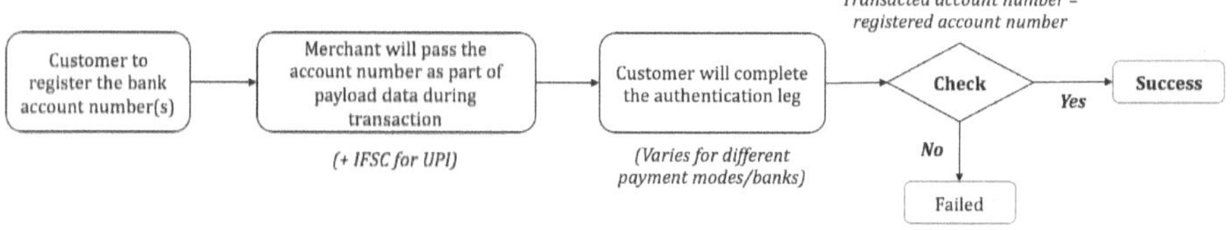

- **Net-banking TPV**: The merchant will pass the account number as part of the payload data. Once a customer completes the necessary authentication steps, the bank will check whether a transaction is done through a registered bank account number. If yes, then the transaction will be successful, else the transaction will fail.

  Note: TPV feature is supported for net-banking (40+ banks)

- **UPI TPV**: The flow of UPI TPV is the same as regular UPI transactions *(collect or intent)*. Merchants are to pass the account number and IFSC in payload data *(up to 4 bank a/cs)*. If the registered account is different from the transacted account, then the amount is credited back.

  UPI TPV functionality is available for standard UPI, AutoPay, and One Time Mandate

- **NACH & e-NACH**: The account validation is done during mandate registration.

- **Virtual Account Number Solution**: This one works a bit differently. When a user transfers the funds to the virtual account, the sponsor bank will do the remitter check, and funds are accepted only if the remitter account is the same as the registered account, else the amount is returned to the remitter.

- **Debit Cards**: Debit cards do not have TPV flow, so most investment merchants do not allow debit cards. Also, debit card commercials will be higher.

Merchants who allow Debit Cards expect investors to comply with guidelines *(use the debit card of the registered bank account)* and pass the liability to customers.

Note: Only 2 banks have built TPV on debit cards. There is not much upside for card issuing banks to build this feature.

3. Commercials:

As per the guidelines, the entire amount should go towards investment. So, merchants have two options:

- Merchant will bear the charges, but charges are invoiced to the merchant.
- Surcharge the customer wherein the customer will bear the charges.

Note: For the investment sector the charges will be Flat Fee (Refer *Chapter 7.A*)

4. Settlement:

Gross settlement *(charges are either invoiced to the merchant or passed on to the user)*. Settlement model will vary based on the investment instrument *(Covered in next sections)*.

5. Performance & Success Rate:

The user's intent of payment is high. Success rate is important as proceeds go towards investment and a delay can change the value of investment.

Investment Instrument specific:

A. Stocks/Shares:

a. **IPO Subscription**: IPO (Initial Public Offerings) are important events for investors. Investors will apply for an IPO and pay the required amount. If shares are allotted, then it is fine; otherwise, the paid amount is refunded.

UPI One-Time Mandate allows brokers to block the amount *(up to Rs.5,00,000)* and release if shares are not allotted and deduct the amount if shares are allotted.

b. **Purchase / Secondary market**: Typically, the user loads the broker's wallet and purchases shares from the wallet balance.

Solutions for wallet top-up:

- PA - Only UPI and Net-banking
- Virtual Account Number solution
- NACH, eNACH, and UPI AutoPay: To top-up the wallet with fixed amount periodically
- A user can set-up a One-Time Mandate on UPI that allows single block and multiple debits. So, whenever the user wants to purchase shares, the broker will debit the blocked amount. [Read the details in *Chapter 13.E*]

c. **Settlement:**

- Gross-settlement is done to broker's nodal account.
- Brokers expect real-time settlement as user may want to buy funds as soon as they top-up the wallet *(especially during trading hours)*
- In case of UPI One Time Mandate (Single debit and multiple debits), the funds are directly settled to exchange *(and not to the broker)*

Note: Similar to the Mutual Fund settlement model, even here we can expect the settlement model will change in future where funds will not touch the broker's account

d. **Selling**: Once the user sells the shares, the proceeds will go to the broker's wallet. Users can invest the funds in another share or can withdraw funds to the registered bank account.

Solution: Payout solution or NACH credit solution of banks

B. Mutual Fund (MF):

A user can purchase/sell MFs through registered MFDs (Mutual Fund Distributors) or directly through Asset Management Companies (AMCs)

a. **Integration**: Most of the MFDs use the BSE Star platform that manages buying and selling of mutual funds. Any PA who wishes to cater to MFDs would integrate with the BSE Star platform.

b. **Purchase**:

- One time purchase: PA solution - UPI and Net Banking with TPV feature
- SIPs: NACH (paper, digital) and UPI AutoPay with TPV

c. **Settlement**:

- As per SEBI guidelines of April 2022, funds will be settled directly to ICCL's *(Indian Clearing Corporation Ltd.)* account *(which works with BSE Star)*.

  Note: MFDs should not be involved in the fund movement.

- From time-to-time SEBI defines cut-off times, ideally the AMCs/MFDs expect settlement accordingly. Settlement time may vary from the same day *(cut off time of 12PM for Liquid and 2PM for non-liquid funds)* to T+1 day.

Note: To achieve this, PAs forge direct settlement arrangements with UPI acquiring banks and net-banking banks (6-7 top banks).

d. **Selling**: The user will initiate the selling of Mutual Funds through MFD's or AMC's platform, and the proceeds are settled to the customer's registered bank account by the AMCs *(Asset Management Company)*.

Solution: Payout solution or NACH-Credit solution of banks

Closing Remarks:

As on Mar '24, there are 151 million Demat account holders. That is an impressive number… just do not go into figuring out how many of them actually made 'money'.!

The investment sector may be exciting but not for PAs due to low margins *(if at all)* as mostly driven by payment modes such as Net-banking, UPI, NACH, and UPI AutoPay.

This is one of the ever-green sectors with interesting companies *(that are diversifying into other financial services)*, so PAs are interested in capturing the volumes and potential opportunities!

22.I Other Sectors

In this chapter, I will touch upon a few sub-sectors and interesting use cases.

1. D2C brands:

D2C brands sell their products directly to consumers on their website/ App.

Also, D2Cs sell their products on marketplaces *(Amazon, Flipkart)*. (Hybrid model)

Requirements of a D2C brand (direct model) are similar to an eCommerce company. We have covered the details in ***Chapter 22.A***.

A standard PA solution can cover those requirements. There is some uniqueness to this sector:

- RTO Protection - Applicable for any eCommerce merchants where the merchant wants to reduce the losses due to returns.

- The majority of D2C companies use eCommerce plug-ins *(Shopify, WooCommerce etc.)*, so a PA should have integrations with these platforms.

- WhatsApp is the most important communication channel for shopping and payments. Conversational commerce can be quite helpful for such merchants.

----

2. Healthcare

Healthcare space has various types of companies that have various different use cases:

- Hospitals - *Use case: Appointment booking*
- Diagnostic Centers - *Use case: Appointment booking*
- ePharma (online pharma) - *Use case: Medicine purchase*

- Omni-channel pharma (both online and stores) - *Use case: Medicine purchase*
- Telemedicine - *Use case: Consulting fees*
- Doctor appointment - *Use case: Typically, free or consulting fees*
- B2B - equipment and medicines - *Use case: Product purchases*

Typically, these merchants use standard PA solutions and enable all payment modes.

Commercials and settlement are similar to the eCommerce sector.

Note: Many card acquiring banks do not support this ePharma merchants.

----

3. Apartment Related

There are few use cases related to apartments or housing societies where both collection and payout solutions are used in an integrated/coupled manner.

- Apartment maintenance fee payment - PA or virtual account solution for collection of fee, and payout solution to disburse collected fees to apartment/society

- Rent payment - PA or virtual account solution for the collection of rent and payout solution to payout funds to the owner.

  - Credit cards are quite popular for rent payment *(for obvious reasons)*

  - Merchants will prefer early settlement solutions.

Many acquiring banks classify these cases under a merchant category code (MCC: 6513) which has lower MDR on credit cards.

Typically, both cases work in surcharge mode, where MDR is passed on to the user. Few issuing banks may levy additional charges on cardholders for rent payment.

Rent is one of the biggest expenses, so many consumer FinTechs and Real-estate tech companies have added rent payment use cases.

Problems in Rent payment Model: Rent payment is an easy and economical way to convert credit card to cash - so merchants (FinTech) enforce conditions and checks to make sure only genuine users are paying and receiving money.

That's not it. The FinTech allows customers to pay using credit card and collects the money it's in account, and then disburses it to merchants. A FinTech is acting as a payment intermediary and without following rules and having license to operate as an intermediary.

RBI is closing watching this space and may enforce some conditions or stop it. And eventually, such cases will be moved under BBPS (Read *Chapter 17*)

----

4.   Credit Card to Vendor payment

Also known as the BPSP *(Business Payments Solution Provider)* model, in which a company can use a corporate credit card to pay its vendors.

Visa operates BPSP, and MasterCard also has a similar model.

Let's say a company pays its vendors after 30 days after receiving an invoice. Although the company has money they wait for this period (let's assume 30 days) - the money in account earns interest or can be invested for a short term.

Corporate credit cards give up to a 45-day credit period, which means a Company doesn't have to pay back the utilized period *(just like our credit card)*. So, when a Company pays its vendor using a credit card, it effectively gets a 45-day to 75-day time window. So, the company can use its own money for other purposes or investment.

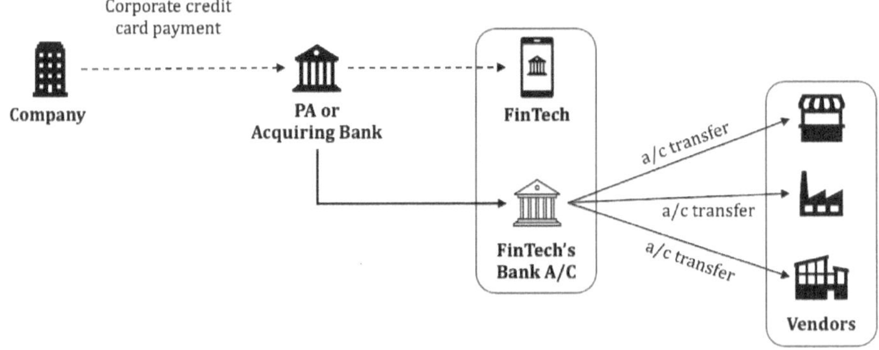

- FinTech who are offering BPSP service will get card MID from an Acquiring Bank(s) or PA to process corporate credit cards.

- Fintech will receive the settlement in its account *(Nodal account)*

- Transfer funds to vendor's bank account via NEFT/RTGS

The problem: FinTech collects money in its account and disburses it to vendors without being a payment aggregator. And thus, the RBI has stopped this model.

Considering that business payments are important and are quite large volumes, RBI may come up with a framework for the BPSP or simply move this model under the BBPS.

---

5. Grocery and Quick Commerce

Grocery is the 'holy grail' of eCommerce as it is extremely complex when it comes to operations compared to other sub-categories *(say, selling mobile phones)*.

- **Quick Commerce**: Online Grocery stores took a drastic turn in 2020, and now we have Quick Commerce, where groceries or anything is delivered in 10-30 mins.

  This model requires 'instant gratification' - As the product is delivered within a few minutes, the transaction should reach finite status *(success or failure)* within a short period so merchants can take appropriate action.

- **Daily Needs**: Sub-category of grocery merchants who deliver daily needs such as milk, eggs, etc. *(the online version of 'milkman Papanna', who delivers milk everyday morning).* These merchants have created subscription services where users will get a fixed daily quantity of milk, egg, etc.

  Such merchants can use recurring payments solutions: (1) Deduct the payment instrument on periodic basis, (2) Auto top-up the closed loop wallet (if the wallet balance reaches the threshold) and debit the wallet.

  Also, the latest version of One-time Mandate on UPI *(single block and multiple debits)* can be an appropriate solution to meet the requirements.

Commercials: The grocery sector operates on MCC - 5411 that has lower MDR on credit cards compared to the eCommerce sector

----

6. Radio Cabs / Bike Taxis

At one point, radio cabs and bike taxis have made our commutes easy. I will not get into what went wrong with these companies as it may take up a few pages.

These merchants use few payment solutions.

- Wallet - Standard PA solution with various payment modes is used to top-up the wallet and ride fee is debited from the wallet.

- Post journey payment: User can make payment post completion of journey. If the user doesn't pay, then the cab App will not allow the user to book the cab next time unless the due amount is paid. For such cases, a standard PA or UPI solution is used.

These companies intend to provide a seamless payment experience when the ride is over. The wallet is an amazing solution that works well, as other solutions create some friction.

The latest version of One-time Mandate on UPI (single block and multiple debits) can be an alternative solution to provide seamless user experience.

The radio cabs model is evolving where the driver partners have to be pay a small subscription fee to use the booking platform. The customer will pay to the driver directly (cash or UPI).

A UPI AutoPay solution can enable radio cabs to collect the driver subscription fees.

---

7.   Rentals - Furniture, Vehicle

There are different types of rental companies such as furniture, home electronics, and vehicles.

Customers do three different types of payments:

- Security deposit or Initial amount
- Periodic payment (for monthly rental products)
- Difference amount *(if the initial amount was not sufficient to cover the usage or damages)*

Also, there are payout use cases where the merchant will return the security deposit.

Solutions: Merchants use standard PA for collecting security deposits or additional payments. Merchants also utilize recurring payment solutions for monthly rental payments or use payment links to collect monthly installments.

Merchants can refund the security deposit through standard PA refund or payout solution.

---

8. Digital Content including OTT

During the pandemic, we got hooked on OTTs, and we still continue to *(at least, I am)*. There are 40+ OTTs in India, and the landscape is dominated by 4-5 OTTs.

Let's not forget the music streaming Apps. Even these merchants have subscriptions where users can buy memberships so they can listen to songs without advertisements.

Another sub-category is digital books, audiobooks, magazines, and newspapers - customers can pay for membership (one-time and/or periodically) and consume the 'full' content.

Solutions:

- eNACH, SI on Cards, and UPI AutoPay to collect periodic subscription fees.

- Standard PA to collect one-time fees, membership fees, or ad-hoc purchases.

- International PG to collect fees from customers across the world.

----

9. Software Companies

Here, we are not referring to large IT or SaaS companies. We are talking about thousands of small companies who cater to both domestic and international clientele.

For international clients, merchants use International PG and PA-CB-Export (earlier, OPGSP Export) to collect the payments from international clients.

For domestic clients, merchants use standard PA or recurring payment solutions (SI on cards or eNACH). Note: Recurring payments are not popular among these merchants.

Freelancers: A large community of individuals who work for clients across the globe. Usually, they use standard PA or UPI or bank transfer for collecting fees from their domestic clients.

For international clients, they use PA-CB-Export service provided by PayPal, Payoneer, etc.

----

10. NGO

NGOs rely on donations from both domestic and international donors.

NGOs enable all types of solutions to maximize the donations.

A PA for one-time donation *(on website)*, payment links *(through SMS, WhatsApp)*, and recurring payment solutions *(NACH, SI on Cards, UPI AutoPay)* for periodic donations.

Also, NGOs enable international card acceptance for foreign donors. Banks perform additional due diligence before providing MIDs for such use cases. Banks seek FCRA certificate, financial statements, and 80G registration certificate.

Banks are a bit cautious about NGOs – all acquiring banks may not support all NGOs.

Also, there are crowdfunding sites *(e.g., Milaap, Ketto)* that collect funds for various cases/causes, and then transfer collected donations to the beneficiary.

Typically, use standard PA and payout. Although crowdfunding sites check/validate whether the cases are genuine, it is impossible to get them right all the time. So, banks/PAs are cautious in supporting such crowdfunding sites.

----

11. Classifieds

We have various types of classifieds - Job search, matrimony, and real-estate. Such companies charge a fee to provide premium services.

Typically, a standard PA would be sufficient to address the payment requirements.

At times, merchants will implement recurring payment solutions (SI on cards, UPI AutoPay) for membership subscription renewals.

----

12. Hospitality

The hospitality sector can be segregated into different types of merchants - Resorts or luxury hotels and aggregators *(e.g., Oyo)*. The hospitality industry uses booking platform providers *(e.g., Simplotel)*

There are mainly two types of online fees:

- Booking Fee *(solution: Standard PA for both domestic and international)*
- Membership Fee *(Solutions: Standard PA or recurring payment – eNACH, Cards, AutoPay)*

The hotel industry *(especially the luxury ones)* use MOTO flow, where a customer's card is taken on file during booking, and charged only when the customer checks-out, or the hotel may deduct some fee for cancellation or no-show.

MOTO flow doesn't require 2FA *(exempted from RBI)*. Considering the risk *(as there is no 2FA)*, acquiring banks are super picky about enabling this flow. Also, merchants have to own 100% chargeback liabilities.

Offline payments (QR/POS) are more prominent as the customer is on the premises.

----

13. Government

There are different types of government entities to which citizens make payments:

- Education institutes and Universities (Use case: fee payment)

- Tourism (Use case: Entry fee to national parks)

- Transport (Use case: Ticket booking)

- Utility companies - Power distributors, water boards (Use case: Bill Payment)

- Urban Local Bodies (ULBs) - (Use case: Municipal tax payments)

- Others - Tax collection, commercial/residential taxes, e-Tender, Treasury

Payment solutions:

- Typical solutions: Standard PA, NACH (Paper) for recurring bill payment cases.

- Government Sector enjoys lower MDR on all payment modes.

- Usually works on surcharge model *(MDR is passed on to users)*

- PA is selected through RFP/Tender process *(Many PAs won't even qualify to participate)*

- Prefers working with banks; banks partner with PAs to provide payment solutions *(one more reason for PAs to maintain good relationship with banks)*

- One of the biggest categories on the BBPS platform. Users can make bill payment through any of 3rd party agents *(e.g., PhonePe, PayTM)* who are on the BBPS platform.

Closing Remarks:

Each sector is unique, and merchants within those sectors also may have subtle differences. I have tried to cover as much as possible. I am sure you have got a good understanding of these important sectors, so you can easily understand any nitty-gritty that I may have missed.

Just like the payments landscape, even the merchant landscape is dynamic and prone to various internal *(funding, acquisitions)* and external *(regulations, market conditions, competition, substitutes, etc.)* factors.

As merchants' business models keep evolving, so will the payments.

Chapter 23

BaaS (Banking as a Service)

Do you know that the price of a Big Mac burger can be used to calculate the Purchasing Power Parity (PPP) and, thus, determine whether a currency is undervalued or overvalued when compared to the USD?

It is called 'Big Mac Index', an interesting concept, not accurate, but still an interesting concept.

Talking of burgers, I am craving for a McSpicy Chicken Burger, and I have three options: (1) Go to the nearest McD outlet (2) Order on the McD App (3) order on a food delivery App.

Each of these models have their own pros and cons (Refer below):

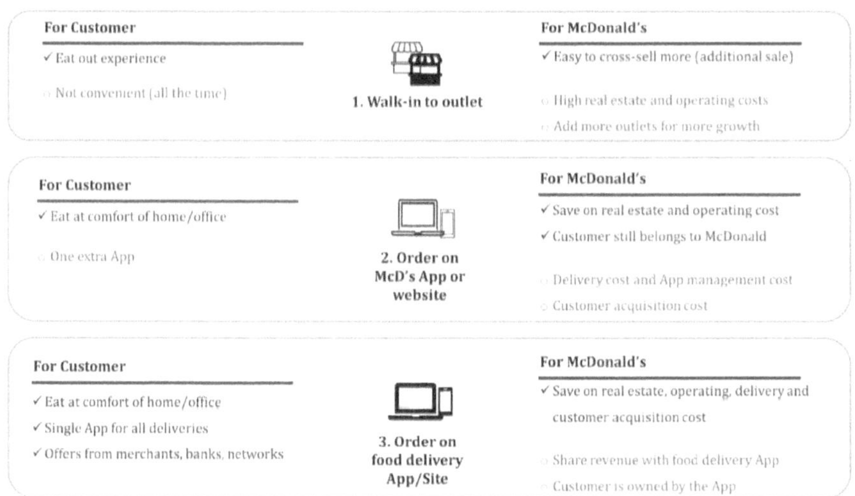

The model that we are more interested in is the third one. The burger is from McD (quality, quantity is controlled by McD) but the distribution and customer acquisition belong to the food delivery App (remember this point!)

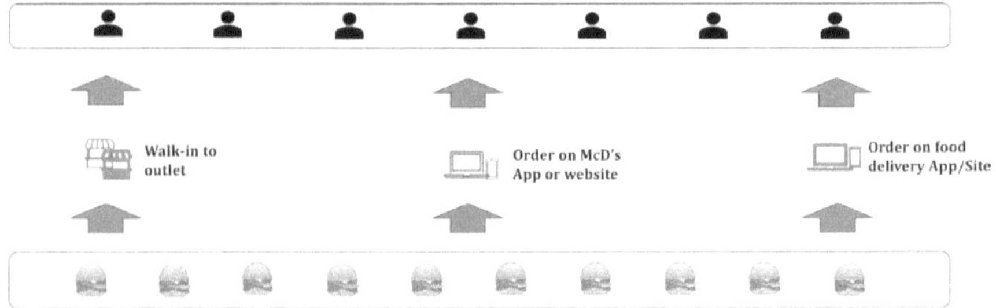

That is the summary of BaaS (i.e., Burger as a Service) ... ha... ha.

Let's start with the BaaS that we are interested in — 'Banking as a Service'.

The fundamentals of BaaS are the same as those of the burger model — there are products that need to reach customers via distribution channels. We will eventually get to BaaS, but before that, let's touch upon a few basics.

Banking Products and Services:

Below are some of the standard banking products and services that we are familiar with.

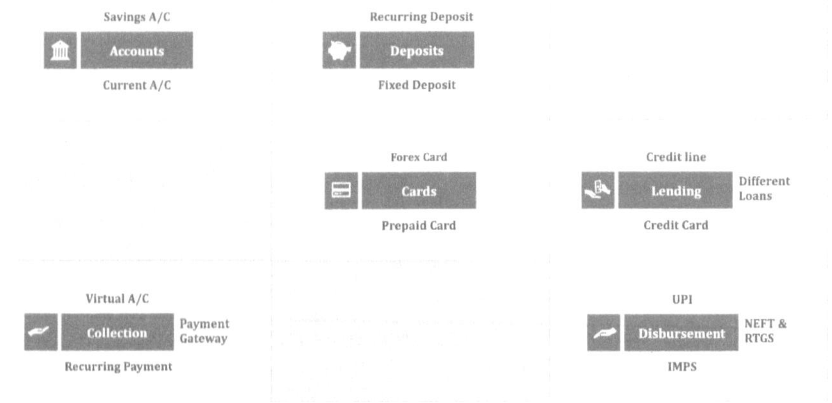

Bank's Distribution Channels:

- **Branches**: For a long time, branches have been the main touch points for sales, customer engagement, cross-selling, and everything related to customers.

  Branches drive linear growth. So, to grow, a bank needs to add more branches.

  That means additional costs related to real estate, operations, and resources. *(Same as the McDonald's outlets)*

- **Digital Channels (Website/App)**: With the penetration of the internet, banks have adopted a 'Digital Strategy' wherein Banks' websites/App allow consumers to engage with the banks. *(Same as McDonald's App)*

The above two models are straightforward, but is it possible to replicate a third model where third parties can sell banking products?

Yes, that is what BaaS is about, where banking products are sold to customers via third parties who can manage customer acquisition and distribution, but the bank controls the product, compliance, and governance.

Who are these Third Parties?

Any entity that is interested in extending a bank's products or services to its customers *(SMBs, corporate or retail)*, partners *(delivery personnel)*, or vendors *(e.g., seller or restaurants)*.

Some of the usual suspects are,

- Payment Aggregators (PAs)
- Neo banks
- FinTechs

- Corporates / merchants
- API platforms / Technology Service Providers (TSPs)

I will talk about each of these entities in detail in a while. For now, let's move on to the next point.

How do they achieve this?

APIs - API (Application Programming Interface) allows two systems to communicate, exchange data. APIs are simple to understand, implement and manage.

BaaS works in two steps:

- **Step 1**: Banks develop APIs for their product or services and externalize them to third-party partners. Through the APIs, banks govern the product. *(E.g., Bank's UPI APIs to a PA won't have the check account balance API, but banks offer it to TPAPs)*

- **Step 2**: Third parties can consume the APIs and launch banking products. As usual, there are multiple ways one can go about it.

  A merchant can integrate with the bank API directly, but efforts will increase if the merchant wants to add multiple banks.

  Alternatively, a merchant can use a PA or TSP's API, which, in turn, would have integrated with multiple banks. *(As I always say... think of Russian Nesting Dolls whenever you think of FinTech or Payments).*

A bunch of APIs and processes should work together to launch a single product.

Let's take the example of a savings account:

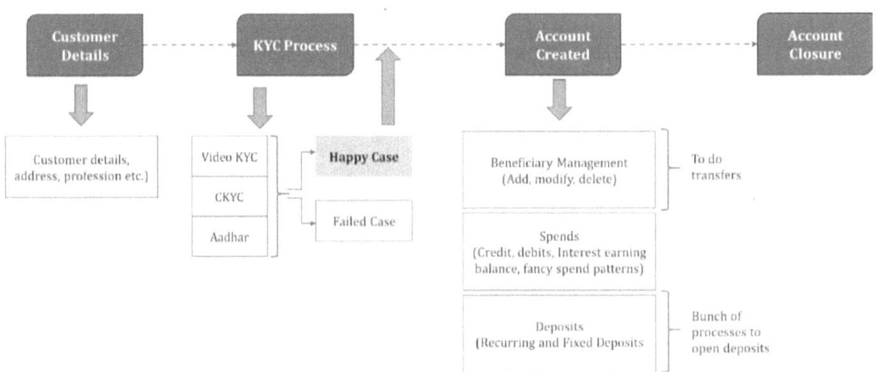

The idea is to give you an understanding that banking products are not simple. For years, we have been using our bank accounts and do not think about how things work in the background. When you start thinking of lending products, the process becomes more complex as more financial aspects *(cost of capital, underwriting)* and collection aspects kick in apart from customer qualification *(credit check)*.

Governance and Compliance: Banking products follow high governance and guidelines. Every bank has its own risk & compliance frameworks; banks make sure the APIs are exposed as per the compliance framework and third parties follow the processes to the letter.

Third Parties

As mentioned in the earlier section, these entities are interested in extending banking products to their customers, partners, and vendors. The usual suspects are:

A. Payment Aggregator (PA)

PAs have built their businesses on the bank's collection *(Payment gateway, recurring payment, UPI, etc.)* and disbursement services. PA is a more than two-decade-old story and pay-out has been out there for the last few years. So, BaaS is not new to them. However, PAs definitely want to use BaaS to extend their portfolio of services and offer banking products to their merchants.

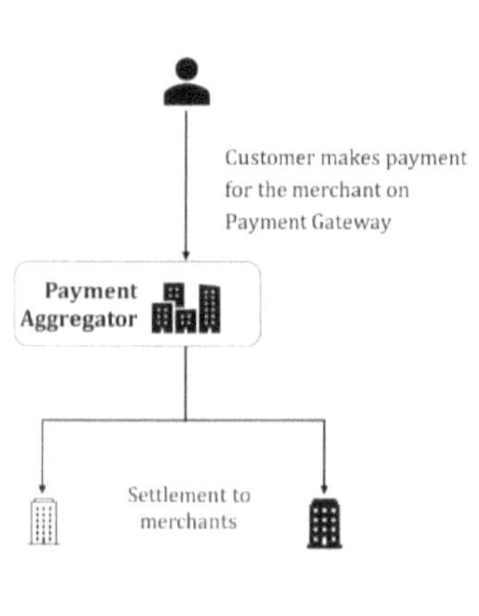

a. Regular Payment Aggregator Model

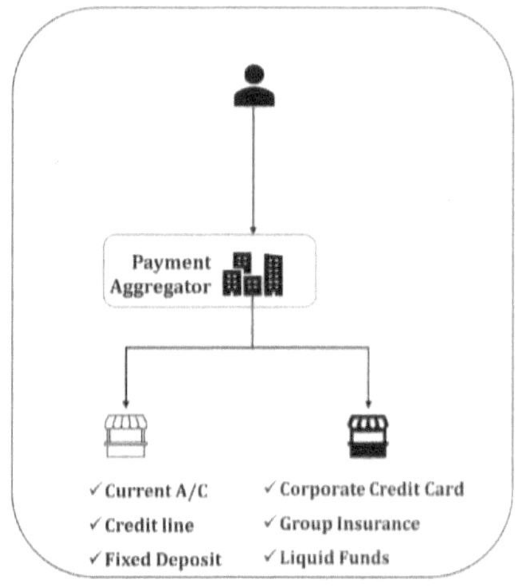

b. BaaS opportunity in Payment Aggregator model

In a regular PA model, a PA will facilitate collections from customers and do settlements to merchants. However, in the BaaS model, a PA can provide additional banking products to merchants *(refer to the above illustration)*.

These offerings can be explicit or implicit.

Explicit Offering: A PA will provide stand-alone products to merchants.

- Opening a current account for the merchant during sign up for payments solution.
- Issue corporate credit card to the merchants.

Implicit Offering: A PA can bake these banking products in their core offering.

- Early Settlement offered by PAs is a credit to the merchant and recovered from the next settlement.

As a PA knows its merchants better *(vintage of the business, business types, risks, chargebacks, settlement cycles, settlement amount, etc.)*, they can position the products as per the merchant's business & requirements.

B. Neo Banks

These FinTechs offer banking products/services without being banks or having branches like traditional banks. As we know, there is no silver bullet for all the problems and for everyone. So, the neo banks target specific demographics or cohorts such as couples, families, teens, women, freelancers, blue collared workers, SMBs, etc.

Neo banks take standard products from the bank(s) and then stitch features that address the problems of their customer base and add value to their customers. I recommend you to check their websites to understand how they are different.

Few of the visible ones: open.money, Jupiter.money, Fi.money, FamPay etc.

Note: These are not real banks, and they can't **call** themselves 'banks' as restricted by Section 7 of the RBI's Banking Regulation Act of 1949

C. Merchants/Corporates

Anyone who has a captive user base or vendors, or service partners can offer banking services to them. These entities can be Lending Techs, WealthTech, FoodTech, KiranaTech, Travel OTAs, eCommerce marketplaces, Auto makers, or even Corporates.

Let's take an example of an eCommerce marketplace.

In the standard model, the marketplace collects money from customers and then pays to vendors and delivery persons.

But in the BaaS model, an eCommerce marketplace can extend various banking products (e.g., co-branded credit cards to customers, lending products to vendors, insurance to delivery people, etc.) (Refer below illustration)

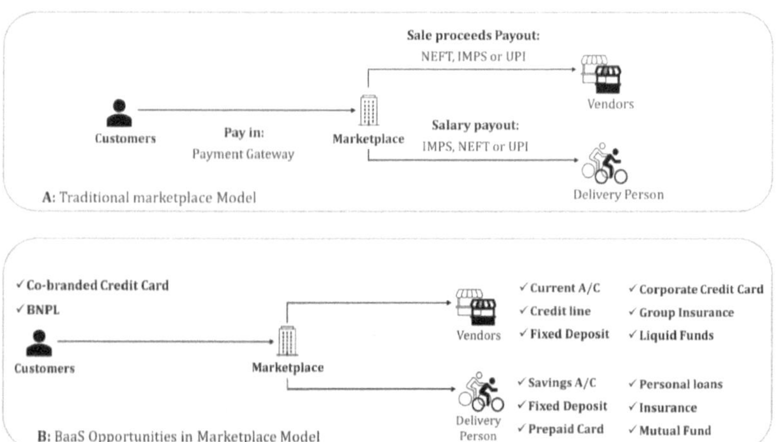

A merchant/corporate knows *(have data pointers)* its customers, vendors, and partners better than anyone. So, they can do a better job at selling banking products to them.

In a nutshell - any company can become FinTech, but the road to achieving this may vary.

Here is a simple chart to show it.

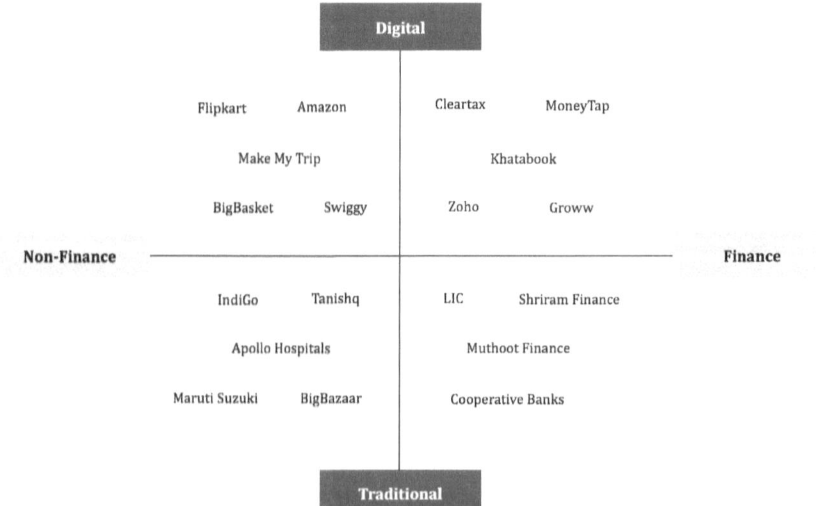

The transition is simpler for 'digital heavy' companies, but it may take a longer time for traditional & non-finance companies. It is very much possible if they have the intent to head in that direction.

This trend has already started with examples such as:

- Flipkart launched its own Buy Now Pay Later (BNPL) product.

- Groww (Investment platform) venturing into Payment Aggregation business

- Swiggy, Amazon, Flipkart, and Ixigo have co-branded credit cards.

- Zoho (SaaS company) became RBI licensed Payment Aggregator

A merchant or company can directly work with the banks, use PA's services to offer banks' products, or use API provider/TSP to enable the services.

D. API Providers/TSP

These entities unify the APIs of bank(s) and then offer to third parties (PAs, FinTechs, or merchants). They help the third parties with faster GTM *(basically, 'build Vs. buy')*.

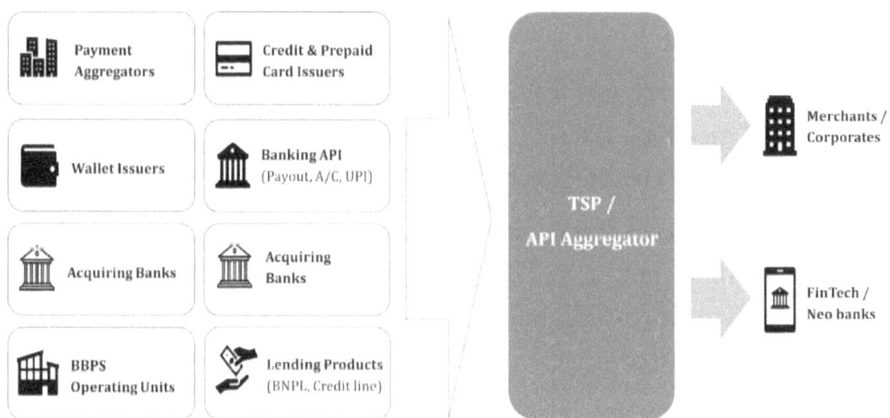

The illustration above shows that a TSP can offer all types of services *(in theory, yes)*, but that is not the case. TSPs are not one stop shops — Some TSPs offer an array of products from multiple banks, but few TSPs are super specialized in what they offer.

*Note: Refer to **Chapter 18** to know more about different types of TSPs.*

What do these third parties know or do which a bank cannot?

That is a very good question - pat on your back.

Banks have been around for centuries. I am sure they know how to sell their products, and, over decades, they would have learned a thing or two about their customers. Let us not make the mistake of assuming that banks are monoliths and slow entities. Remember, banks are the ones who are building APIs, which are the backbone of BaaS.

Before we answer above question, let me list strengths of these third parties:

1. Technology: These companies will invest in technology that may deliver better user journeys, custom features, dashboards, and analytics

2. Accessibility: Some of these entities *(Merchants and PAs)* have existing users, so distribution is simple *(i.e., customer acquisition cost is lower)*

3. Data: Merchants/PAs are sitting on a lot of customer, vendor, and merchant data. This data can be leveraged to make decisions related to customization or lending.

4. Brave: These third parties have an appetite to take risks that a bank may not have. These entities are ready to challenge norms, ready to invest big bucks *(thanks to VC money) and* capture the market faster.

Now, the answer to the above question is that banks want to leverage the capabilities of third parties to fuel their own growth, just like how McDonald's doesn't mind using food delivery Apps to sell 'more' burgers.

Plus, banks also keep doing what they do best, and they won't shut down their own distribution network *(branches and App)*.

Great... but why do it?

- There is a market which is underserved *(in terms of distribution, product, experience, pricing, etc.)* — so there is definite growth opportunities

- Someone has more data/info than the other — so work together to increase the size of the pie. For example, a bank has money to lend, but a marketplace knows its sellers better. Thus, this data can help banks to underwrite better.

I have saved the best one for the last – **Money!**

These third parties can create a substantial revenue stream as banks may work with them in referral fee or revenue sharing model. For some entities, this is the main revenue *(e.g., Neo banks)*, but for a few, it can be an additional revenue channel *(e.g., eCommerce merchants)*.

Interesting... How much money?

This is where it becomes tricky. Revenue share depends on various factors:

- Responsibilities of parties *(distribution, customer on-boarding, support)*

- Liabilities *(who is underwriting — in case of lending)*

- Bargaining power of the parties

Payments, banking, or FinTech is a game of 'scale'; the more the active customers, the more the volume, if more the volume, then more revenue.

And companies can bring down costs to increase the profit.

Embedded Finance

In simple words, embedded finance is about offering (or embedding) financial products *(e.g., UPI, insurance, credit line)* in the user journey.

Few Examples:

- While booking international tickets, enable users to buy travel insurance.

- On-board user on BNPL *(Buy Now Pay Later)* product while doing the purchase.

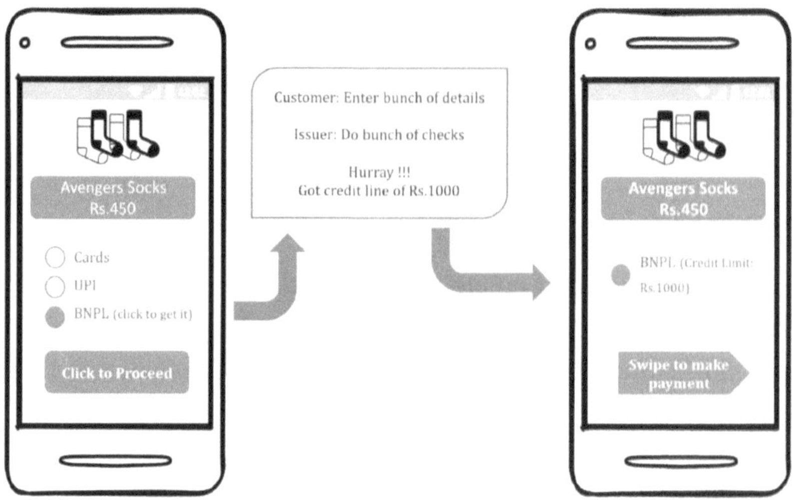

Illustration: Embedded BNPL Journey

What is new about it?

Mostly, nothing.

This has been done for years as a part of cross-selling. But in embedded finance, you offer them as part of the integrated user flow. So, 'the new' part is reimagining the product, process, and user journeys while taking care of compliance and risk.

It is more complicated than I made it look like, as there are a set of processes that need to be embedded without distorting the user's journey. Otherwise, users will neither book a ticket nor buy your insurance.

Closing Remarks

We have come to realize that while banks are a bit boring, **they make money**.

So, everyone wants to look like a bank and sell banks' products/services to make money. But still, they have a mammoth task of bringing customers and retaining them.

Still, a word of caution: There is one thing banks fear; compliance and risk.

So, it is the responsibility of these third parties *(FinTechs, merchants, TSPs)* not to deviate *(cut corners)* for the sake of growth, as one's mistake may cost others or the entire ecosystem.

BaaS, neo banks, embedded finance, and invisible finance - All these names sound fancy and interesting. But will they succeed in this uber-competitive and highly regulated environment and, on top of that, satisfy customers with unpredictable user behavior/requirements who are extremely price sensitive?

So, instead of getting impressed by funding stories, we should wait and watch whether these companies really make a difference in the user's banking experience or just end up creating a lot of confusing banking products.

I feel this space is exciting, exhausting, boring and interesting - all at the same time!

Chapter 24

Dark Side of the Payments

Digital payments bring many benefits to the ecosystem and to the country. But there is a dark side to digital payments. The platforms which are built for betterment can also be used by bad actors to cheat others. *(When I say bad actors… don't think about movie actors who are bad at acting — Just bad people and companies)*

I am sure many of you or your friends/family have received messages and calls about expired KYC, some bonus from the insurance company, or some parcel which is stuck in the customs department. People end up giving their OTP or access to their accounts and getting cheated.

In this chapter, we will talk about the bad actors and what can be done to stop them.

Who are these bad actors?

Individuals and companies who cheat people or launder money.

Why do they do it?

Greed, easy money, and other laundry list of things.

Why do people fall prey to them?

Greed, ignorance / lack of understanding, fear.

How to stop bad people?

Here is a 6 Ps model:

Policies
- License: PA/PG, PPI etc.
- Transaction limits

Process
- KYC of merchants, users
- Due diligence

Platform/Product
- Tokenization, SI Hub
- Risk Engine

Participants
- Follow guidelines, Processes
- Educate Users

Protect
- Support numbers / DigiSaathi
- Cyber Crime police, ED, Courts

People
- Awareness
- Never share OTP/PIN

A. People

RBI and banks do run campaigns to **create awareness** about digital payments, what to do (when defrauded), and what not to do, but somehow, people forget to follow.

So, I am reiterating a few points:

- Do not share OTP or PIN with others *(no matter what)*
- Do not write your ATM PIN on ATM card cover.
- Nigerian Prince who wants to be saved is as fake as the '$1Million lottery' that you won.
- Do not click on links that says, 'free iPhone' or 'download KGF2 movie'.
- SBI doesn't block your debit card randomly and then call you.
- LIC or IRDA will not call you to give dividends or bonus.
- No one can double your money in 30 days.
- Do not share OTP or PIN **(Very important: revise this point)**

Here are some do's:

- Understand the basics of payments - how refunds work, how to raise disputes, etc.

- Keep customer support numbers handy *(do not believe what you see in Google Search results — visit the bank/PSP website/App).*

When conned, 'do not panic' — take a deep breath and (1) reach out to the bank/payment service provider (2) file a complaint with the police, and (3) Raise dispute or chargeback.

Most importantly, do not keep quiet… get help from your friends/ family or your bank.

B. Policies

RBI is the regulator that governs the payments in India. One of the key goals of RBI is to protect the customers. From time to time, RBI issues guidelines related to products and processes to achieve this goal.

Few of these are,

- Licensing: PA/PG, PA-Cross Border, PPI, Account Aggregator (+)
- Guidelines: Master KYC, Data localization, Tokenization, geo-tagging (+)

The Regulated Entities (REs), entities that are licensed by RBI to operate payment systems, are responsible for onboarding the right merchants and protecting customers. If these REs do not follow these guidelines, then RBI imposes penalties, enforces embargoes, and even revokes licenses.

C. Product/Platform

NPCI, card networks, and banks develop products and features as per RBI guidelines or, in general, keeping the best interest of users or even merchants.

Here are few such products/features:

- Mandatory 2nd Factor Authentication (2FA)
- Mandate on cards that gives control to the user to manage the mandates.
- NPCI recommends merchants to implement 'UPI intent'.

D. Processes

Under various guidelines *(e.g., PA/PG, PPI, etc.)*, RBI mandates that payment companies follow proper KYC and due diligence processes. This is to ensure that 'right' entities are availing payment services.

Few guidelines: Master KYC guidelines, AML *(Anti-Money Laundering)* and CFT *(Countering the Financing of Terrorism)*.

Which payment companies?

- **Issuers (PPI and banks):** Conduct the KYC process as prescribed by RBI. PPI issuer has to complete minimum or full KYC depending on PPI type. Banks have to collect KYC for the user and complete due diligence of companies including directors.

- **Payment Aggregators**: These are required to follow Master KYC guidelines and conduct due diligence of the merchant before enabling PA services for collection.

- **Acquiring banks**: Make sure the PAs are onboarding merchants after following the correct process and not onboarding shady merchants.

- **Merchants**: If they are in financial services *(e.g., Brokerage services or NBFC)*, then follow proper KYC and also validate the payment instruments *(using UPI validation, penny drop, Third Party Validation — TPV)*.

Following the right process involves effort, cost, and time and may slow down growth. Unlike a few years back when everything was paper based, now we have tools/solutions that bring efficiency to the process *e.g., PAN and Aadhar Validation, Video KYC, CKYC, Credit Score and Account Aggregator model.*

But still, you will see there will be gaps… why? We will talk about it in a separate section.

E. Participants

Payment Ecosystem participants — banks, PAs, PSPs, TPAPs are obliged to follow the guidelines and processes *(above two points)*. Also, these entities are responsible for providing secure APIs and card vaults that cannot be tampered or hacked.

Apart from that, these entities have risk checks and velocity checks to flag and/or block the suspicious transactions. Mostly, the risk engines analyze the pattern such as user, location, payment pattern, vintage of merchant, etc. and flag those transfers and hold the amount until they get assurance that the transaction is genuine.

There are other entities that are not directly part of the payment ecosystem but still shape and safeguard the sector, such as **IRDA** *(Insurance Regulatory and Development Authority)* and **SEBI** *(Securities and Exchange Board of India)* who, from time to time, send SMS/mails warning about bad actors.

TRAI *(Telecom Regulatory Authority of India)* is planning to come up with a framework where users will see the caller's *name as per KYC (easy to know who is calling you).*

F. Protect and Prosecute

Every bank, PSP, and FinTech is mandated to have a support number/ mail that users can contact.

RBI and NPCI have implemented platform level customer grievance redressal frameworks.

Here are few examples: **DigiSaathi, UPI Dispute redressal, RBI Ombudsman**

Cybercrime police help finding the culprits and recover the money. But again, it is not always possible.

The Regulated Entities *(banks, NBFCs, PPIs, PAs)* are required to monitor the suspicious transactions and merchants, and file reports with FIU-IND *(Financial Intelligence Unit - India)*. The FIU-IND will analyze the cases and involve the appropriate LEA *(Law Enforcement Agencies)* to investigate the cases.

Summary:

In summary, payment systems are designed to provide a secure, efficient, and economical way of transactions/payment processing, and it is done in various stages (shown below)

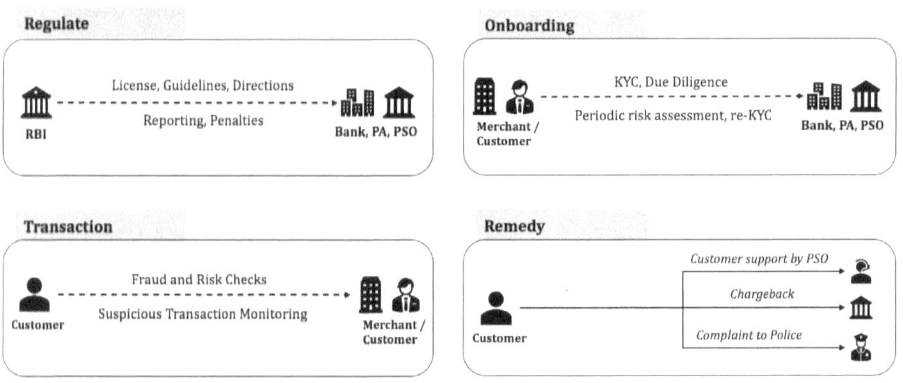

You should be happy that Rs.10 that you paid using UPI in that roadside tea shop has so many safeguarding measures.

But still… Yeah… but still, there is no guarantee that bad actors won't get access to payment systems. If humans stop being greedy, then frauds won't happen, and we all know that it is never going to happen.

So, a simple and practical solution is… ***Knowledge.***

Make users understand the payment system, how to safeguard themselves, and what to do when conned. This is not just the responsibility of RBI or banks or Payments companies.

We should teach our parents, uncles, aunties, cousins, and friends about how cards or UPI work, and what to do when they get a call about their account being blocked or when they receive OTP from an unknown party — Do not scare them, instead prepare them.

As RBI says — "Jaankar Baniye, Satark Rahiye" *(Be Aware, Be Alert)!*

Chapter 25

One World – Many Payments

"You can't be a real country unless you have a beer and an airline – it helps if you have some kind of football team, or some nuclear weapons, but at the very least you need a beer." – Frank Zappa (American Music Composer)

A payment professional would have quoted – *"You can't be a real country unless you have Real Time Payment (RTP) rail and domestic card network – it helps if you have some kind of CBDC or mobile wallet, but at the very least you need an RTP rail"*.

Today, we see trends of RTP, CBDC, and domestic card networks across the globe. Countries are building digital payment infrastructure for domestic usage and also for cross-border transactions.

One may have to write a book(s) to cover payment ecosystems of 190+ countries.

So, I will keep it simple & crisp and touch upon a few popular payment modes across the globe - Card networks, Real-Time Payment Rails, Cash payments *(at stores)*, wallets, and BNPLs. We will also touch upon a few payment processing entities.

25.A Payment Modes

A. Card Networks

Throughout the world, cards (credit, debit) are the prominent payment instruments.

As you know, cards are issued by card issuing entities *(e.g., Banks)*, and the card networks provide infrastructure, processes, platforms, and frameworks for issuance, acceptance, fund movement, and dispute management.

Visa and MasterCard are the largest card networks with presence in almost all countries *(just like Coca Cola and McDonald's)*.

Other global card networks are American Express, Diners, and Discover.

The common thing among all these 5 networks is that they are based out of the USA. *(we will visit this point later)*

Then there are non-US card networks - which started to cater to the domestic market and, eventually, expanded to other territories.

JCB (Japan Credit Bureau) is one of the first card networks that originated outside the USA. As the name suggests, it started in Japan and spread to many countries.

Then came the dragon (China) with its **UnionPay** card network, which is now present in 150+ countries.

In the last couple of decades, many countries have launched their own domestic card networks.

As of today, there are more than 30 countries that have thriving domestic card networks.

Reasons for launching domestic card networks:

- Reduce dependency on global networks *(Visa, MasterCard)*; in geo-political terms, reduce dependency on the USA.

- Global Card Networks are expensive, and usually the fees are in US Dollar *(e.g., Indian card issuing banks pay Visa/MasterCard in USD and incur forex charges)*

- Provide cheaper issuance and acceptance card network.

- Drive innovations for the domestic use cases / requirements which global card networks may not entertain (or even understand)

Domestic Card Networks

Nigeria	Verve		**Serbia**	Dina Card		**Israel**	Isracard
China	Union Pay		**Belgium**	Bancontact		**South Korea**	BC Card, Shinhan, T Money
India	RuPay		**Norway**	Bank Axept		**France**	Cartes Bancaires, Carte Bleue, Aurore
Japan	Pasmo, JCB		**Switzerland**	MyOne		**UAE**	Mercury, Nol
Singapore	NETS, Ez-Link		**Turkey**	Tory		**Argentina**	Argen, Cabal, Naranja, Cordobesa
Canada	Interac Debit		**Germany**	Gircard		**Brazil**	Aura, Elo, HiperCard
Russia	MIR		**Bahrain**	Benefit		**Chile**	Cencosud, BCI Lider, RedCompra, Ripley

Geo-Expansion: Just like JCB and Union Pay, a well-established domestic card network will expand to other territories.

There are two types of expansion models:

- **Acceptance**: The card will be accepted in multiple geographies *(both at POS and Online)*

- **Issuance**: The card network will issue the cards in other countries

The card network can do this expansion on their own *(how Visa or MasterCard did)* or partner with other country's domestic card networks or global card networks.

Direct expansion examples:

- **Cencosud** is from Chile and present in Argentina, Colombia, Brazil, Peru, USA

- **Verve** is Nigerian card network with presence in Kenya, Tanzania, Burundi, South Sudan, Rwanda, Uganda
- **RuPay** is accepted in 20+ countries *(in SEA, Middle East)*

Partnership based expansion:

- Giro Card (Germany) has partnership with Visa and MasterCard
- JCB has partnered with Amex, Union Pay, RuPay, Discover and Diners
- RuPay has partnered with JCB, Discover, Diners, UnionPay, and Pulse

Partner card network's logo(s) will be on the back of the card.

Example: RuPay <> JCB partnership cards, RuPay logo is on the front and JCB logo on the back.

A country can completely rely on its domestic card network if the card network is accepted both domestically as well as internationally.

Still, a country cannot cut off global card networks *(unless the country is forced due to an embargo by the USA)*. Global card networks still play an important role in cross-border commerce.

Prepaid cards:

Prepaid card networks are much simpler - there are thousands of stored value or prepaid cards that are popular in their domestic markets.

Example: Octopus (Hong Kong), Ez-link (Singapore), Sodexo (Global)

B. Real-Time Payment (RTP) Rails

No matter which part of the world you live in, the users/merchants expect the small ticket transactions *(what you pay at a nearby shop)* and fund transfers *(P2P and P2M)* to happen in *(near)* **real-time,** and such payment modes should be **economical** *(acceptance infra and processing cost).*

Real-Time Payment (RTP) rails meet these requirements and beyond. Many countries want to achieve various objectives with the RTP rails.

- Financial inclusion
- Reduce cash usage *(As cash printing, distribution is expensive)*
- Reduce dependency on cards *(Due to expensive infra)*
- Holistic payment solution *(P2P and P2M)*
- Cheaper merchant acceptance *(QR code based)*
- Mobile friendly *(most common device)*

List of countries that have Real-Time Payment Rails:

Asia Pacific	
Australia	New Payments Platform (NPP) (2018)
Cambodia	Real-Time Fund Transfer (2019)
China	Internet Banking Payment System (IBPS) (2010)
Hong Kong	Faster Payment System (2018)
India	IMPS (2010), UPI (2016)
Indonesia	BI-Fast (2021)
Japan	Zengin System (1973)
Malaysia	IBFT (2006), DuitNow (2018)
Pakistan	Raast (2021)
Philippines	InstaPay (2018)
Singapore	FAST (2014), PayNow (2017)
South Korea	CD/ATM (1999), Electronic Banking System (2019)
Sri Lanka	CEFTS / LankPay (2015)
Taiwan	Interbank ATM Fund Transfer (1987), Financial XML (2003)
Thailand	PromptPay (2016)
Vietnam	NAPAS Quick Money Transfer (2016)

Americas	
Canada	Interac e-Transfer (2002)
USA	RTP (2017), FedNow (2023)
Argentina	PEI (2016), DEBIN (2017), Transfer 3.0 (2020)
Brazil	SITRAF (2002), PIX (2020)
Chile	Transferencias en Líea (TEF) (2008)
Colombia	Transferencias YA (2019)
Honduras	SIP (2008)
Mexico	Sistema de Pagos Electrónicos Interbancarios (SPEIS) (2004)
Peru	Immediate Interbank Transfers (2016)
Uruguay	ACH Transferencias Inmediatas (2021)

Eurasia	
Azerbaijan	Instant Payment System (IPS) (2020)
Kazakhstan	Interbank System of Money Transfer (ISMT) (2025)
Russia	Faster Payment System (FPS) (2019)
Serbia	Instant Payments Serbia (IPS) (2018)

Middle East	
Bahrain	Fawri++ (2015)
Kuwait	NBK QuickPay (2018)
Lebanon	Zaky (2020)
Oman	MPCSS (2017)
Qatar	QMP (2020)
Saudi Arabia	Sarie (2021)
UAE	Immediate Payment Instructions (IPI) (2019)

Africa	
Egypt	Instant Payment Network (IPN) (2022)
Ethiopia	Ethiopia Automated Transfer System (EATS) (2011)
Ghana	GhIPSS InstantPay (2007)
Kenya	Pesalink (2017)
Nigeria	NIBSS Instant Payment (NIP) (2011)
South Africa	Real Time Clearing (RTC) (2006)
Tanzania	Tanzania Instant Payments System (TIPS) (2019)

Europe	
Bulgaria	Borica Instant Payments (2021)
Croatia	NKS Inst (2020)
Czech Republic	Instant Payment (2018)
Denmark	Straksclearing (2014)
Finland	Siirto (2017), SEPA Instant Credit Transfer (2018)
Greece	IRIS (2017)
Hungary	Azonnali Fizetesi Rendszer (AFR) (2020)
Iceland	CBI (2020)
Latvia	EKS Zibmaksajums (2017)
Lithuania	CENTOlink (2017)

Europe	
Luxembourg	BILnet (2020)
Norway	Straksbetalinger (2011), Vipps (2015)
Poland	Express Elixir (2012), BlueCash (2012)
Romania	Plati Instant (2018)
Slovenia	Flik (2020)
Spain	Bizum (2016), SEPA Instant Credit Transfer (2017)
Sweden	BIR (2012)
Switzerland	TWINT (2016)
Turkey	Retail Payment System (RPS) (2012), FAST (2021)
UK	Faster Payments (2008)

SEPA Instant Credit Transfer (2017)	Portugal, Spain, France, Belgium, Netherlands, Germany, Austria, Slovenia, Italy, Greece, Slovakia, Lithuania, Latvia, Estonia, Finland.

RTPs are mostly operated by the banks and restrict participation of non-bank FinTechs, but few countries allow participation of FinTechs (e.g., UPI of India, PayNow of Singapore).

Internationalization:

Just like domestic card networks, even RTP rails are expanding their horizon - first in the domestic market and then expansion to other countries.

Taking the next step, RTPs of different countries are partnering to create cross-border remittance highways which can make remittance easier, faster, and cheaper.

Example: PayNow (Singapore) <> PromptPay (Thailand), UPI (India) <> PayNow (Singapore).

Growth and Success:

The success of RTP rail depends on simplicity, wider acceptance, cost efficiency (cheap), meeting different requirements (P2P, P2M), and customer *(mass)* education.

Many countries have built an amazing success story. And these countries are actively partnering and collaborating with other countries to share this knowledge.

The trend of RTPs will continue to grow, which may cannibalize card networks (and other dominant payment modes) and also add more participants (merchants, users, banks) to the digital payment ecosystem.

C. Cash to Online Payments:

Cash is common across the world - the currency may vary, but cash works the same everywhere!

Here, we are talking about a unique *(at least for Indians)* payment method where cash is used for online payments… not directly, but indirectly.

Convenience stores are quite common in many countries. These are small outlets/stores that are operated by an entity (7 Eleven, Lawsons etc.).

I frequented these stores when I lived in Japan and Singapore. Many times, I used to have my breakfast or midnight supper in these stores.

These convenience stores act as a channel of cash to online payments.

Generic Working Model:

Step 1: Select the convenient store name among the payment mode *(on checkout page)*

Step 2: Create the reference ID.

Step 3: Visit the convenience store and pay in cash.

Step 4: Convenience store will update the merchant, and customer receives confirmation.

Note: Depending on the amount, convenience stores may check the customer's ID document

Countries where convenience store payments are popular:

Country	Stores
Morocco	Binga
Bolivia	Pagosnet
Canada	Open Bucks
Portugal	Payshop
Singapore	7 Eleven
Taiwan	Konbini Payments
Vietnam	pay@store
Kazakhstan	QIWI
Russia	QIWI
Czech Republic	SuperCash

Country	Stores
Germany	Barzahlen
UK	Paypoint
Spain	Teleingreso
France	Cashway, Waricash
Romania	SelfPay, Paypoint
UAE	7 Eleven, MBME
USA	7 Eleven, Open Bucks,
Hong Kong	7 Eleven, Open Bucks
Lithuania	Maxima, Paypost, Perlas

Country	Stores
Argentina	Pago Facil, Rapipago, Cobro Express, RIPSA, Provincia NET
Brazil	Boleto Bancario, Boleto Flash
Chile	Efectivo Multicaja, Sencillito, Servipag
Colombia	Efecty, Via Baloto, Almacenes Exito, Carulla, Davivienda, Surtimax, Banco De Occidente
Mexico	Oxxo, BBVA Bancomer, Santander
Peru	Pago Efectivo, Kasnet, BCP
Indonesia	Alfamart, Indomaret, Alfamidi
Malaysia	7 Eleven, Speed Point, Paystore
Philippines	7 Eleven, PesoPay, PI. ePay
Thailand	7 Eleven, Tesco, CenPay, Big C
Japan	7 Eleven, Pay Easy, Paidy, Konbini Payments

7-Eleven was one of my favorite stores *(when I lived in Singapore and Japan)*. Today, 7-Eleven has built a great payment business from these stores in 20+ countries.

Convenience store-based payments are popular across the globe in both developed as well developing countries, particularly popular in Southeast Asia and South America.

These convenience stores play an important role as they allow users to be part of the digital commerce even if they do not have the required device *(do not have smartphones)*, payment instruments *(do not have bank account)*, or merchant restrictions *(do not allow Cash on Delivery)*.

D. CBDCs

Central Bank Digital Currency is the digital money issued by the central bank of a country. We have covered the basics of CBDC in *Chapter 4.H.*

100+ countries are researching, piloting, and launching CBDCs.

Different countries have different reasons/motives to launch CBDC.

- Reduce usage of paper cash; reduce cost of printing, distribution, and cash management.
- Provide 'something similar' to 'cash' but in the digital form.
- Make cross-border transfers faster and cheaper.
- Counter private virtual currencies (aka cryptocurrencies) by providing something similar to cryptocurrencies without the risks that come with those.

Countries are investing in different types of CBDC project.

- Retail (R): for businesses and retail consumers
- Wholesale (W): for financial institutes

Countries that are in different stages of CBDC:

Launched			
Nigeria *(e-Naira)*	St Kitts and Navis *(DCash)*	Montserrat *(DCash)*	Grenada *(DCash)*
Jamaica *(JAM DEX)*	Bahamas *(Sand Dollar)*	St Vincent & Grenadines	St Lucia *(DCash)*
Anguilla *(DCash)*	Antigua and Barbuda	Dominica *(DCash)*	

Pilot Phase			
Australia *(eAUD – R & W)*	Thailand *(R & W)*	Ukraine *(E-Hryvnia)*	Saudi Arabia *(W - Cross border)*
China *(E-CNY - R & W)*	Singapore *(W – Cross border)*	Sweden *(E-Krona – R)*	UAE *(Digital Dirham - R & W)*
Hong Kong *(e-HKD – R &W)*	South Korea *(R)*	Turkey *(Digital Turkish Lira – R)*	Ghana *(E-cedi - R)*
Japan *(Digital Yen – R & W)*	Russia *(Digital Ruble – R & W)*	Iran *(Crypto Rial - R)*	South Africa *(Khokha - W)*
Malaysia *(W – Cross border)*	Kazakhstan *(Digital Tenge – R)*	Israel *(Digital Shekel - R)*	Tunisia *(W)*
India *(eRupee - R & W)*			

Development					
Bhutan	Palau	Estonia	Italy	Spain	Brazil
Cambodia	Philippines	Finland	Lithuania	Switzerland	Colombia
Indonesia	Taiwan	France	Montenegro	United Kingdom	Haiti
Laos	Bahrain	Germany	Netherland	Canada	Mexico
Macau	Belarus	Ireland	Norway	USA	

Research					
Alegria	Gabon	Zambia	Honduras	Sri Lanka	Andorra
Botswana	Kenya	Zimbabwe	Paraguay	Vietnam	Azerbaijan
Cameroon	Madagascar	Trinidad & Tobago	Peru	Fiji	Czech Republic
Chad	Morocco	Argentina	Bangladesh	New Zealand	Georgia
Egypt	Namibia	Chile	Myanmar	Solomon Islands	Hungary
Equatorial Guinea	Rwanda	Qatar	Nepal	Tonga	Jordan
Eswatini	Uganda	Guatemala	Pakistan	Vanuatu	Oman

Reference: atlanticcouncil.org

Impressive list… isn't it?

However, not all countries are equally enthusiastic about CBDC.

Few countries are interested in either retail or wholesale CBDCs, whereas few are interested in both types of CBDCs.

A country may not be interested in domestic CBDC but is participating in cross-border CBDC.

There are few countries which have shutdown/canceled or inactive CBDC programs for various reasons *(lack of adoption, no real need, political crisis, economic conditions, wait & watch, etc.)*

CBDC for cross-border payments:

Yes… CBDC will have a big value in cross-border payments *(for now, a theory)*.

But how will cross-border payments among 100+ CBDCs *(of 100+ countries)* that are built on different technologies work?

SWIFT plays a key role in regular cross-border payments. And looks like SWIFT is planning to play that role for CBDCs as well.

Countries have formed groups and are working on cross-border payments among the group.

It is better to solve for the smaller group and then make it big... right?

Few such cross-border Project:

Project Name	Type of CBDC	Countries
Aber	Wholesale	Saudi Arabia, UAE
Aurum	Retail & Wholesale	Hong Kong, BIS
Dunbar	Wholesale	Australia, Singapore, Malaysia, South Africa
Helvetia	Wholesale	Switzerland, BIS
Ice Breaker	Retail	Israel, Norway, Sweden, BIS
Jasper	Wholesale	Canada, UK, Singapore

Project Name	Type of CBDC	Countries
Mariana	Wholesale	France, Switzerland, Singapore, BIS
mBridge	Wholesale	Thailand, China, Hong Kong, UAE
Polaris	Retail	Denmark, Finland, Iceland, Norway, Sweden,
Jura	Wholesale	France, Switzerland
Rosaland	Retail	United Kingdom, BIS
Sela	Retail	Israel, Hong Kong, BIS

BIS: *Bank for International Settlement*

I would say the world is in the early stages of CBDC as nations are figuring out many things, such as utility, risks, operationalization, adoption, resources, etc.

This is a '**new money**' and it is expected to redefine how we use the money. So definitely there are challenges, but it will also be equally exciting!

E.   Wallets:

Wallets are prepaid payment instruments where users will load the funds and utilize the funds for payments at shops or online merchants.

Wallets have certain guidelines, such as license to operate a wallet, limit on balance amount, loading channels, acceptance network, withdrawal limits, etc.

Wallet is a simple payment instrument - that involves a wallet-issuing entity that has to bring customers and build acceptance networks.

Few of advantages of wallets:

- Ideal for small ticket purchases and transfers
- Faster checkout experience
- Secure payment *(as not exposing card or bank details)*
- Financial inclusion *(where users do not have bank account)*

Wallets are popular in many countries, and different countries have governing rules and licensing processes for operating them.

The majority of wallet operators work in their domestic market, but there are few wallets which operate in multiple countries.

Countries and Popular Wallets.

Chad	Tigo Cash
Egypt	Fawry
Ethiopia	HelloCash, M-BIRR
Ghana	SlydePay
Nigeria	Kongapay, Paga Wallet, Pocketmoni
S. Africa	FNB Cell Paypoint, PayD, Snapscan
Tanzania	EzyPesa, Tigo Pesa
Argentina	Tarjeta Shopping, VALEpei
Brazil	iUPay, KOIN, PicPay
Mexico	BBVA Wallet, Todito Cash
Armenia	Mobidram
Russia	Moneta.ru, MTS Money, QIWI
Austria	Paybox, Bluecode
Bulgaria	EasyPay, epay.bg
Croatia	Aircash
Finland	Aktia Wallet

USA	PayQwick, Venmo, Zelle
Afghanistan	M-Paisa
Bangladesh	Gpay, MYCash
Bhutan	Chharo
Cambodia	Pi Pay, Smartluy, Wing
China	AliPay, WeChat, Baidu Wallet, QQ Wallet
Indonesia	Dana, Doku, GoPay, OVO, Jenius Pay
Hong Kong	Octopus, Payme, TNG Wallet
Japan	AuPay / KDDI, Line Pay, MerPay, Pasmo, Pay Pay, Rakuten Pay
Malaysia	Boost, Fave Pay, Kiple Pay, Speed Point
France	Paylib
Germany	Bluecode
Italy	BANCOMAT Pay, MySi di CartaSi, Nexi Pay
Luxembourg	Satispay
Poland	Yeti Pay
Portugal	MB Way, MEO Wallet

Nepal	iPay, Khalti
Pakistan	EasyPaisa, Jazz Cash
Sri Lanka	eZ Cash
Taiwan	JKOPay
Singapore	GrabPay, NETSPay, SAM
S. Korea	Kakao Pay, Naver Pay, Toss Pay
Philippines	Coins.ph, GCash, Pay Maya
Vietnam	Bao Kim, Moca, MoMo, NAPAS, Ngan Luong
Thailand	mPay, Rabbit Line Pay, Tot Quick Pay, True Money
Myanmar	KBZ Pay, MPietsan, OK$, Wave Money
Spain	Bizum
Sweden	Swish
Turkey	BKM Express, Bonus Pay, Garanti BBVA
Switzerland	Twint
Bahrain	Benefit Pay
UAE	eWallet, Klip

Wallets that operate in multiple countries:

Line Pay	Japan, Indonesia, Taiwan, Thailand
Twisto	Czech, Poland, Romania
Yoo Money	Asia, Eastern Europe
MTN Mobile	Middle East, Africa
Tigo Money	South America
Razer Gold	Global

Satispay	Luxembourg, Belgium, France, Germany, Italy
Orange Money	Europe, Africa, Middle East
Cashu	Middle East, Africa
Boloro	South America
Neteller	Global
Skrill	Global

Shopee Pay	Indonesia, Malaysia, Philippines, Singapore
M-Pesa	African Countries
Moov	Middle East, Africa
Mercado Pago	South America
Paysera	Global

Wallets are typically operated by FinTechs *(after procuring relevant licenses)*, but there is a growing trend of merchants getting into this business as well. Check out the names Grab, Shopee from the above list.

Many types of mobile based payment entities are clubbed under wallets.

In India, PhonePe is put under wallets, but it is a payment container. Similarly, you will see Apple Pay, MasterPass, Google Pay, and PayPal under wallets, but remember, these are not wallets but payment containers where a user can pay using their linked cards.

Wallets solve many of the payments-related challenges of a user and/or merchant. And they are successful to a large extent.

Wallets may be struggling in a few countries due to the rise of RTPs *(e.g., India, Singapore, or Brazil)*, but in the global context, wallets are thriving and continue to do so.

F. BNPLs:

BNPLs are quite new to the payments landscape.

The basics of BNPL remains same,

- Give small credit to user.
- Provide acceptance infrastructure to spend that credit.
- Customer will repay the utilized credit amount.

This sounds simple… the challenges of customer acquisition, building a large acceptance network, cost of capital, and non-performing assets is the same across the globe.

The basics of BNPL are covered in *Chapter 4.D*.

Here is the list of popular BNPLs:

Argentina	Pago MisCuentas
Australia	Bpay, Post Billpay, Sezzle
Bahrain	Fawateer
Canada	Pay Bright

France	Oney
Netherlands	Billink
Poland	eRaty, P24 Now, PayPo
Saudi Arabia	Sadad

South Africa	Mobicred
Sweden	Paylevo
Switzerland	Power Pay
USA	Affirm, PayNearMe, QuadPay

Few BNPLs have expanded to multiple countries:

BNPL Name	Origin	Other Countries
Klarna	Sweden	Europe, US and APAC
Walley	Sweden	Finland, Norway
After Pay / Clear Pay	Australia	UK, Canada, USA, New Zealand

BNPL Name	Origin	Other Countries
Zip	Australia	USA, New Zealand
Splitit	USA	Europe, APAC
Atome	Singapore	SEA

You can see a convergence of wallet operators providing BNPL services.

In India, PayTM is the classic example - leading wallet provider and also, has a BNPL product.

Similar trend can be observed across the globe: Apple Pay Later, PayPal Credit, and Grab Pay

BNPL companies started in the online commerce space but have created a presence in offline models as well. Many BNPLs (e.g., Klarna) are accepted in physical stores as well.

Last couple years, many global BNPL companies have lost their 'shine' *(in other words: Valuation)*.

So, has the BNPL model hit the dead end of the road? Or will the models shift from a FinTech-led model to a consumer brand-led model? Or the BNPLs will move to 'instalment' models?

G.   Cash

Cash is universal - our world has 180+ currencies that can be used for purchases or exchange.

The quantity of products/services that you can purchase from that currency may vary because of macro-economic conditions such as supply-demand, inflation, etc.

Cash is still the most widely used and popular payment instrument because it is simple, easy to understand, and widely accepted.

Cash usage depends not only on the maturity level of a country's payment infrastructure but also on the way money is perceived in that country.

Example: Germany is a developed country with easier access to credit cards, but the majority of Germans prefer cash, followed by debit cards, as 'credit' is frowned upon in German culture.

A country's currency is accepted in that country. However, the same currency can also be accepted in multiple countries.

Example: Indian rupees are accepted in Nepal and Bhutan.

Euro is a zone-specific currency and accepted in all countries of the Eurozone.

The US Dollar, the most dominant currency in the world, is accepted in many countries either as primary currency *(e.g., Panama, El Salvador, Ecuador)* or additional currency *(e.g., The Bahamas, Canada, Cayman Islands).*

I cannot use Indian Rupee in Singapore. So, I have to convert the INR to SG Dollars at the licensed money changers and vice versa. In both cases, INR → SGD and SGD → INR are done as per foreign exchange rate (FX Rate), and the customer will bear the forex charges.

The foreign exchange is the conversion ratio between two currencies and is determined by supply-demand. The difference between buy rate (INR → SGD) and sell rate (SGD → INR) is called 'FX Spread', and it is a good revenue stream for changers and authorized dealer banks.

Since the end of World War II, the US Dollar ($) has been the dominant currency, and thus, many commodities *(e.g., crude oil)* are traded in US dollars. Many countries keep US dollar reserves.

Many countries are pushing their own currencies as global currencies, e.g., Russian Ruble, the Chinese Yuan, and the Euro.

Recently, India has also been trying to push the Indian Rupee for global remittance.

H. Other Payment Modes

I am listing few other popular payment modes:

- **Payment Containers**: User can add their cards, wallets, and BNPL accounts, and pay using any of those payment modes.

  Examples: Apple Pay, Google Pay, PayPal, MasterPass

- **Carrier Billing**: In this payment mode, the user can use a prepaid amount balance to purchase the product, or the product purchase amount will be added to postpaid bill. Carrier billing is an ideal solution for low ticket transactions.

  Major players: Mobiamo, Softbank, Dao Pay, Siru Mobile

- **Bank Transfer**: Similar to our net-banking; usually referred to as EFT *(Electronic Fund Transfer)*

- **Virtual Account Solutions**: Similar to virtual account-based solution that we covered in Chapter 14

25.B   Payment Processing

Such diverse payment modes are processed by different types of entities.

- Banks - Used for cards, RTP, or bank transfers.

- Wallet and BNPL issuers - where merchant can integrate directly.

- FinTechs such as Apple Pay, Google Pay, PayPal etc.

- Payment Gateways: To process the cards - CyberSource, MPGS

- PayFac (Payment Facilitators): Payment processors who enable merchants to process payments. In many ways, PayFacs are similar to our online Payment Aggregators

PayFacs can be further classified based their operational territories.

A. **Country Specific:** PayFacs that work in particular country.

   Example: Zepto (Australia)

   Note: In fact, most of the Indian PAs to this list as they operate only in India

B. **Regional:** PayFacs that operate in multiple countries of a specific region (e.g., SEA, Euro)

   Example: Xfers (Singapore, Indonesia), Peach Payments (Africa)

   It takes a lot of effort and resources for a PayFac to get operating licenses and implement the *process or rules of the land*' of multiple countries, so a company may build their capabilities in a few countries of a specific region.

C. **Global:** These PayFacs have presence in multiple countries across various continents. They either have their license or partner with domestic PayFacs.

   Example: Stripe, Adyen, Nuvei, Rapyd, Dlocal

To operate in multiple countries, the PayFacs deploy various strategies:

- **Local Licensing**: Procure local regulatory licenses in multiple countries or at least procure the license where regulations are extremely stringent.

  Example: Adyen, Nium are in process of procuring PA license in India

- **Global Processing Model:** Cards of global card networks *(Visa, MasterCard etc.)* can be processed globally without the need of local license or partnership. Commercials will be high, and settlement will be done after 7-10 days, but the merchants are fine with it.

- **Local Partnership model**: The global PayFacs partner with local PayFacs/PAs/PSPs to process the local payment methods. In such models, the global PayFac will act as **Merchant on Record (MoR)** for the merchant who wants to collect payments in that local market.

  Note: MoR models are not the cleanest business models (banks/ the regulators view those suspiciously) and also, funds are moving outside the country (so more alarming).

Regulations related to payment systems across the globe are evolving. The regulators and Governments are emphasizing data privacy, data protection, and data localization while heightening AML and KYC compliance. These trends will definitely impact the business and operating models of global PayFacs.

Closing Remarks:

World is diverse… our cultures, languages, traditions, and stories are different.

Different countries and cultures have different views and values regarding money. The maturity levels of payments infrastructure and regulatory landscape varies for different countries. All of these factors impact the way citizens of different countries make payments.

The world payments landscape is extremely diverse, interesting, and evolving. We are witnessing the rise of Real-Time Payment (RTP) rails, domestic card networks, and the world is excited about the potential of CBDCs.

In this connected world where trade, commerce, and travel are happening at a global level, countries want to provide free movement and seamless cross-border payments for their citizens and businesses.

At the same time, the country wants to safeguard its citizens' data and protect its sovereign interests. Also, the country wants other countries to use its payment infrastructure or currency.

It would be interesting to see how a country will balance between localization and globalization at the same time.

Irrespective of how each country is tackling or building their payment infrastructure, the goal is clear - Digital Economy and Financial Inclusion.

One World... Many Payments... One Goal!

And the Journey Continues...

Here we are ... the last chapter of this book. Hope you enjoyed the payment journey!

So... What next?

The book is only a primer, and you can explore/learn many things.

Think of it as driving school lessons where you understand the basics of driving. And now, it is up to how fast you can drive and how far you can go. *(I assume you have a car :))*

Payments Domain is vast, complex, and dynamic, but at the same time, interesting.

So, keep learning, and there is ample information around you to read.

- Set up google alerts on keywords such as 'NPCI', 'RBI' 'payments' to receive related news.
- Regularly visit RBI and NPCI websites; read new circulars and reports.
- Read 'Developer Guides' of various Payment Aggregators
- Read PA or FinTech company's blogs *(warning: most of these are product marketing contents praising the company's own products)*

Most importantly, be curious and be observant... observe how payments are happening while you order food, while tapping your card in a store, or while subscribing to an OTT.

Digital Payments are integral to our lives - it doesn't matter if you are a Product Manager in a payments company or a tea shop owner, or a regular user of UPI.

You are part of the Payment Ecosystem.

Everyone should understand the basics of payments, if not the product, process, or policies, but at least how to safeguard themselves and should know the remedies, if defrauded.

Here... I am ending the book.

I will continue to write the blog, so keep reading!

Link: https://medium.com/authncapture or scan the QR on the back of the book.

References

- RBI website: https://www.rbi.org.in/home.aspx
- RBI Notifications, Master Directions, Circulars, Draft notifications/guidelines: https://rbi.org.in/Scripts/NotificationUser.aspx
- NPCI website: https://www.npci.org.in/
- CBDC: https://www.atlanticcouncil.org/cbdctracker/ (for CBDC)
- Generic Reference: https://www.investopedia.com/
- EMV Co: https://www.emvco.com/
- Authorized PSOs: https://www.rbi.org.in/Scripts/PublicationsView.aspx?id=12043